SOCIAL DIFFERENCE AND CONSTITUTIONALISM IN PAN-ASIA

In many countries, social differences, such as religion or race and ethnicity, threaten the stability of the social and legal order. This book addresses the role of constitutions and constitutionalism in dealing with the challenge of difference. The book brings together lawyers, political scientists, historians, religious studies scholars, and area studies experts to consider how constitutions address issues of difference across "Pan-Asia," a wide swath of the world that runs from the Middle East, through Asia, and into Oceania. The book's multidisciplinary and comparative approach makes it unique. The book is organized into five parts, each devoted to constitutional approaches to a particular type of difference – religion, ethnicity/race, urban/rural divisions, language, and gender and sexual orientation – in two or more countries in Pan-Asia. The introduction offers a framework for thinking comprehensively about the many ways constitutionalism interacts with difference.

Susan H. Williams is the Walter W. Foskett Professor of Law and the Director of the Center for Constitutional Democracy at the Indiana University Maurer School of Law. She is the author of *Truth, Autonomy, and Speech: Feminist Theory and the First Amendment* (2004), which won the Outstanding Academic Title Award from *Choice* magazine, as well as many articles and book chapters. She is the editor of *Constituting Equality: Gender Equality and Comparative Constitutional Law* (2011). Her scholarship focuses on issues related to gender equality, constitutional design, and feminist theory.

COMPARATIVE CONSTITUTIONAL LAW AND POLICY

Series Editors:

Tom Ginsburg
University of Chicago

Zachary Elkins
University of Texas at Austin

Ran Hirschl
University of Toronto

Comparative constitutional law is an intellectually vibrant field that encompasses an increasingly broad array of approaches and methodologies. This series collects analytically innovative and empirically grounded work from scholars of comparative constitutionalism across academic disciplines. Books in the series include theoretically informed studies of single constitutional jurisdictions, comparative studies of constitutional law and institutions, and edited collections of original essays that respond to challenging theoretical and empirical questions in the field.

Volumes in the Series:

Comparative Constitutional Design edited by Tom Ginsburg (2012)

Consequential Courts: Judicial Roles in Global Perspective edited by Diana Kapiszewski, Gordon Silverstein, and Robert A. Kagan (2013)

Social and Political Foundations of Constitutions edited by Denis Galligan and Mila Versteeg (2013)

Constitutions in Authoritarian Regimes edited by Tom Ginsburg and Alberto Simpser (2014)

Presidential Legislation in India: The Law and Practice of Ordinances by Shubhankar Dam (2014)

Social Difference and Constitutionalism in Pan-Asia edited by Susan H. Williams (2014)

Social Difference and Constitutionalism in Pan-Asia

Edited by

Susan H. Williams

Indiana University, Maurer School of Law

CAMBRIDGE
UNIVERSITY PRESS

32 Avenue of the Americas, New York, NY 10013-2473, USA

Cambridge University Press is part of the University of Cambridge.

It furthers the University's mission by disseminating knowledge in the pursuit of education, learning, and research at the highest international levels of excellence.

www.cambridge.org
Information on this title: www.cambridge.org/9781107036277

© Cambridge University Press 2014

First published 2014

Printed in the United States of America

A catalog record for this publication is available from the British Library.

Library of Congress Cataloging in Publication Data
Social difference and constitutionalism in Pan-Asia / Susan H. Williams, Indiana University, School of Law.
  pages cm. – (Comparative constitutional law and policy)
Includes bibliographical references and index.
ISBN 978-1-107-03627-7 (hardback)
1. Constitutional law – Social aspects – Asia – Congresses.   I. Williams, Susan Hoffman, 1960– editor of compilation.
KNC524.S65   2014
342.5–dc23   2013028339

ISBN 978-1-107-03627-7 Hardback

Contents

List of Contributors

Asma Afsaruddin is professor of Islamic studies and chair of the Department of Near Eastern Languages and Cultures at Indiana University, Bloomington. She is the author and/or editor of six books and has published numerous articles on many aspects of premodern and modern Islamic thought and intellectual history. Her publications include *Striving in the Path of God: Jihad and Martyrdom in Islamic Thought* (2013); *The First Muslims: History and Memory* (2008); and the edited volume *Hermeneutics and Honor: Negotiating Female "Public" Space in Islamic/ate Societies* (2000). She was named a Carnegie Scholar in 2005 and has also won research grants from the Harry Frank Guggenheim Foundation and the American Research Institute in Turkey, among others.

Gardner Bovingdon is an associate professor of central Eurasian studies and international studies at Indiana University. He has conducted research in China, Taiwan, and Central Asia on the topics of nationalism, autonomy regimes, and historiography. His book *The Uyghurs: Strangers in Their Own Land* was published in 2010. He is now conducting research comparing nation building in Central Asia and China.

Benjamin B. Cohen is an associate professor of history at the University of Utah. He received his PhD in history from the University of Wisconsin, Madison. His first book, *Kingship and Colonialism in India's Deccan* (2007), won wide acclaim. Cohen has also published several peer-reviewed articles on such topics as environmental history, institutional history, and gender history.

Sean Dickson is a Washington, DC–based associate with Sidley Austin LLP, practicing in health care and government strategies. He received his JD from the University of Michigan Law School, cum laude, where he also received his MPH in health management and policy. Prior to graduate study, Sean worked extensively in international public health, focusing on HIV prevention, maternal health, and sexual minority rights and organizing. Sean received his BA with honors in public policy from the University of Chicago, where his undergraduate thesis was presented to Bill Gates as a gift from the university on a 2010 visit.

William Fierman is a political scientist with a specialization in Soviet and Post-Soviet Central Asia. His interests focus on policies relevant to creation of identities in Central Asia, including such areas as demography, land, and Islam. Fierman has written many articles and book chapters on language policy, particularly in Uzbekistan and Kazakhstan. Professor Fierman served for eleven years as director of the Inner Asian and Uralic National Resource Center, and was the founding director when it was established in 2002. He is a professor of Central Eurasian Studies and adjunct professor of Political Science at Indiana University, Bloomington.

Ran Hirschl is a professor of political science and law and holds a Canada Research Chair in Constitutionalism, Democracy and Development at the University of Toronto. He is the author of three books: *Towards Juristocracy: The Origins and Consequences of the New Constitutionalism* (2004 and 2007); *Constitutional Theocracy* (2010), winner of the 2011 Mahoney Prize in Legal Theory; and *Comparative Matters* (2014), as well as more than seventy articles and book chapters on comparative constitutionalism, the judicialization of politics, constitutional law and religion, and the intellectual history of public law. He holds a PhD from Yale University.

Paul D. Hutchcroft is the founding director of the School of International, Political and Strategic Studies (IPS) and professor of political and social change in the Australian National University's College of Asia and the Pacific. He is a scholar of comparative and Southeast Asian politics with particular research interests in state formation and territorial politics, the politics of patronage, political reform and democratic quality, state-society relations, structures of governance, political economy, and corruption. In addition to *Booty Capitalism: The Politics of Banking in the Philippines* (1998), his work includes articles published in *Governance, Government and Opposition, Journal of Asian Studies, Journal of Democracy, Journal of East Asian Studies, Philippine Review of Economics, Political Studies, TRaNS,* and *World Politics* as well as chapters in edited volumes published by Cambridge, Cornell, Georgetown, Harvard, Oxford, Wisconsin, the Asia Society, and Freedom House. He is currently completing a manuscript entitled *The Power of Patronage: Capital and Countryside in the Philippines from 1900 to 2010,* and he has undertaken a major new collaborative project on money politics in four Southeast Asian countries (Indonesia, Malaysia, the Philippines, and Thailand).

Feisal Amin Rasoul al-Istrabadi is the founding director of the Center for the Study of the Middle East at Indiana University (IU) – Bloomington, where he is also professor of the practice of international law and diplomacy at the Maurer School of Law and the School of Global and International Studies. He holds a visiting professorship by courtesy at the IU School of Public and Environmental Affairs. From 2004 to 2010 he served as Iraq's ambassador and deputy permanent representative to the United Nations in New York. He was the principal legal drafter of Iraq's interim constitution, the Transitional Administrative Law, in 2003–2004.

Huong Thi Nguyen is currently a PhD student in law and democracy and a research Fellow at the Center for Constitutional Democracy, Indiana University Maurer School of Law. Her research focus includes Vietnamese constitutionalism, constitutional design from a multidisciplinary perspective, and judicial review in new democracies. Huong was educated in Vietnam and France before coming to Bloomington. She received a bachelor of law degree from the University of Rennes I, a master I degree in French public law, and a master II degree in the common law from the University of Paris II, France. Huong is a co-founder of Viet Youth for Democracy and of The 88 Project, an interview project for freedom of expression in Vietnam. She also served on the constitutional study team of the Democratic Party of Vietnam.

Christabel Richards-Neville is a law student at the University of New South Wales in Australia and has been working with Professor Kim Rubenstein on her research in gender and constitutional law.

Kim Rubenstein is director of the Centre for International and Public Law at the Australian National University (ANU). In 2011–2012 she was the inaugural convenor of the ANU Gender Institute. She is the coeditor, with Professor Thomas Pogge, of the Cambridge University Press series *Connecting Public Law and International Law*. Her publications are in the areas of citizenship, nationality and gender, and constitutional law.

Steve Sanders is associate professor of law at the Maurer School of Law at Indiana University, Bloomington, where he is also an affiliated faculty member in the Department of Gender Studies and with the Kinsey Institute for Research in Sex, Gender, and Reproduction. He previously practiced for four years with the Supreme Court and appellate litigation practice group of Mayer Brown LLP, based in Chicago. He received his

JD, magna cum laude, from the University of Michigan Law School, where he also received the Bates Scholarship, the highest award to graduating seniors. Before law school he held various positions in university administration.

David C. Williams is the John S. Hastings Professor of Law and the executive director of the Center for Constitutional Democracy (CCD) at the Indiana University Maurer School of Law. He graduated magna cum laude from Harvard Law School after earning the Sarah Sears Prize for being first in his class. Williams then clerked for Ruth Bader Ginsburg on the U.S. Court of Appeals for the DC Circuit and taught at Cornell Law School before relocating to Indiana University in 1991, where he was named the Distinguished Faculty Research Lecturer in 2003. He has taught at the University of Paris and lectured around the world. He was a member of the faculty of law at the University of Cambridge and a Fellow at that university's Wolfson College, as well as the European University Institute. Williams has written widely on constitutional design, the constitutional treatment of difference, and the relationship between constitutionalism and political violence. He is the author of *The Mythic Meanings of the Second Amendment: Taming Political Violence in a Constitutional Republic* (2003). He is also coeditor and primary author of *Designing Federalism in Burma* (2005). In his work with the CCD, Williams consults with a number of reform movements abroad. He advises many elements of the Burma democracy movement, the government of Liberia, the Democratic Party of Vietnam, and, most recently, the world's newest democracy, South Sudan.

Susan H. Williams is the Walter W. Foskett Professor of Law and the director of the Center for Constitutional Democracy (CCD) at the Indiana University Maurer School of Law. She has also been a visiting faculty member at the University of Paris II and a visiting Fellow at Wolfson College, Cambridge University, and at the European University Institute in Fiesole, Italy. She is the author of many articles and book chapters and has published two books: *Truth, Autonomy, and Speech: Feminist Theory and the First Amendment* (2004) and *Constituting Equality: Gender Equality and Comparative Constitutional Law* (editor, 2009). In her work with the CCD, she has acted as a constitutional advisor to the governments of Liberia and South Sudan and to democratic activists and women's organizations in Burma, Libya, Liberia, Vietnam, and Cuba. Her scholarship focuses on issues related to gender equality, constitutional design, and feminist theory.

Introduction:
Constitutions and Difference:
Ideology and Institutions

Susan H. Williams

One of the most vexing problems in the theory and practice of politics is the issue of difference. How do we build a just and stable polity in the face of identity differences that have historically been the basis for inequality, injustice, and violence? Such differences can take a variety of forms, including religious difference, race and ethnicity, language difference, urban/rural tensions, and gender. In many countries, divisions such as these are the fault lines that threaten the stability of the social and legal order. This book addresses the role of constitutions and constitutionalism in dealing with the challenge of difference.

In the spring of 2011, a conference held at Indiana University (IU) brought together a distinguished group of lawyers, political scientists, historians, religious studies scholars, and area studies experts to consider how constitutions and constitutionalism address issues of difference across a wide swath of the world we called Pan-Asia.[1] Pan-Asia runs from the Middle East through Central Asia, South Asia, Southeast Asia, East Asia, and into Oceania. This is a meta-region across which ideas and influences have traveled for centuries. It is also an area of the world that includes every type of difference in abundant supply. Pan-Asia, therefore, provides a wonderful laboratory for examining the role of constitutions in addressing difference.

The existing literatures, while rich in other ways, do not speak directly to this issue of constitutions as a mechanism for addressing difference. There is a vast political theory literature on the relationship between

---

[1] The conference was supported by the Australian National University (ANU), the Pan-Asia Institute at IU, the Maurer School of Law, and several Centers at IU, including the Center for Constitutional Democracy, the Center for the Study of Global Change, and the Center for the Study of the Middle East.

democracy and difference. There is also a substantial political science literature on the connection between specific governmental structures – particularly electoral systems and federalism – and the management of difference. This book differs from these existing literatures in three ways.

First, unlike the political theory literature addressing difference as an issue in democratic politics, this book focuses on the role of constitutions and constitutionalism as a tool for the management of difference. Not all democracies are constitutional and not all constitutions are democratic. Indeed, the countries discussed in this book include authoritarian regimes along with both stable and struggling democracies. Although the connections and tensions between democracy and difference have been deeply examined by political theorists, the role of constitutions in particular is much less studied. Thus, the political theory literature addresses issues such as whether difference is best understood as a matter of interests or of identities,[2] or whether pluralist liberal democracies are required to respect and accommodate illiberal communities within them.[3] This book, alternately, asks about the roles that constitutions play in defining, mediating, or exacerbating difference. This inquiry raises questions about the institutional and the ideological implications of the basic legal order in managing difference.

Second, the book is interdisciplinary and speaks across the discipline-based boundaries that often divide this conversation. The broad range of approaches and the explicit effort to be accessible to a cross-disciplinary audience differentiate it from the political science literature concerned

---

[2] *See generally, e.g.,* Seyla Benhabib, *Democracy and Difference: Contesting the Boundaries of the Political* (Princeton: Princeton University Press, 1996); Nancy Fraser and Axel Honneth, *Redistribution or Recognition? A Political-Philosophical Exchange* (London: Verso, 2003).

[3] Much of the political theory literature is cast in terms of multiculturalism, which focuses on a particular subset of issues relating to the handling of difference in Western liberal democracies. For a sampling, *see* Seyla Benhabib, *Democracy and Difference, supra* n. 2; Monique Deveaux, *Cultural Pluralism and Dilemmas of Justice* (Ithaca: Cornell University Press, 2000); Bonnie Honig, *Political Theory and the Displacement of Politics* (Ithaca: Cornell University Press, 1993); Will Kymlicka, *Multicultural Citizenship: A Liberal Theory of Minority Rights* (New York: Oxford University Press, 1995); Anne Phillips, *Multiculturalism without Culture* (Princeton: Princeton University Press, 2007); Ayelet Schachar, *Multicultural Jurisdictions: Cultural Differences and Women's Rights* (Cambridge: Cambridge University Press, 2001); Sarah Song, *Justice, Gender and the Politics of Multiculturalism* (New York: Cambridge University Press, 2007); Iris Marion Young, *Inclusion and Democracy* (New York: Oxford University Press, 2000); Will Kymlicka, ed., *The Rights of Minority Cultures* (New York: Oxford University Press, 1995); Avigail Eisenberg and Jeff Spinner-Halevy, eds., *Minorities within Minorities: Equality, Rights and Diversity* (New York: Cambridge University Press, 2005).

with specific political and legal institutions in the management of difference.[4] The contributors to this book are a distinguished collection of law professors, historians, political scientists, area studies specialists, religious studies scholars, and activists. They bring an extremely broad range of educational backgrounds and practical experiences to the project. The interaction of different sets of disciplinary assumptions and goals, different theoretical lenses, different practical agendas, and different experiences generates a synergy impossible within any single discipline.

Third, the book has a wide geographical focus that allows for important comparative perspectives.[5] The Pan-Asia region covers approximately two-thirds of Earth's land mass and an even higher percentage of its population. It also represents a meta-region across which ideas, goods, and peoples have moved for millennia. Pan-Asia includes all the major world religions, countless ethnic and linguistic groups, and a wide range of constitutional systems. It offers an incredibly rich set of cases through which to examine the complex interplay of constitutions and difference.

THE CONTENTS AND ORGANIZATION OF THE BOOK

The book is organized conceptually – around the types of differences that have created challenges in countries around the world – rather than

---

[4] *See generally, e.g.,* Donald Horowitz, *Ethnic Groups in Conflict* (Berkeley: University of California Press, 1985); Andrew Reynolds, *Designing Democracy in a Dangerous World* (Oxford; New York: Oxford University Press, 2011); Arend Lijphart, *Patterns of Democracy: Government Forms and Performance in Thirty-Six Countries* (New Haven: Yale University Press, 1999); Donald S. Lutz, *Principles of Constitutional Design* (Cambridge: Cambridge University Press, 2006). Andrew Reynolds, ed., *The Architecture of Democracy: Constitutional Design, Conflict Management, and Democracy* (New York: Oxford University Press, 2002) is an usually interdisciplinary exception. The essays in that extremely useful book include a few written by people in disciplines other than political science. The book is, however, focused on specific institutional mechanisms for managing conflict, rather than on the broader implications of constitutions, which include ideological impacts as well.

[5] This geographical breadth distinguishes this book from one of the few other books addressing constitutions and difference in general: Michel Rosenfeld, ed., *Constitutionalism, Identity, Difference and Legitimacy: Theoretical Perspectives* (Durham: Duke University Press, 1994). The contributions in Rosenfeld's excellent volume are overwhelmingly focused on North American and European examples and literatures, whereas this book will focus on a wide swath of the rest of the world. In addition, of course, much has happened in the world in relation to both constitutionalism and difference over the past twenty years.

geographically. There are five sections, each devoted to a particular type of difference: religion, ethnicity/race, urban/rural divisions, language, and gender and sexual orientation. In each section, the chapters examine the constitutional significance of the particular difference at issue in two or more countries in Pan-Asia.

Part I of the book addresses language. In Chapter 1, Benjamin Cohen looks at the development of the successful constitutional approach to language policy in India. He traces the history of the politicization of language difference and describes how the drafters of India's constitution managed to defuse this issue. By taking a fundamentally pragmatic approach – recognizing and accommodating language diversity while building on existing foundations for a common language – the Constitution transformed a line of division that was fraught with violence at the start of the nation into a source of strength and stability.

In Chapter 2, William Fierman looks at the issue of language in Kazakhstan and compares it to the Baltic and Caucasus republics on the one hand and the other Central Asian republics on the other hand. He finds that although all of these countries shared a political focus on shifting from Russian to the language of the titular group in each republic, the outcome varied because of two important factors. First, in some countries the status of the language of the titular group facilitated this shift, whereas in others that status inhibited it. Where the titular group's language was not strong – in terms of usage, particularly by elites, and usability in a range of technical and educational settings – the transition was more difficult. Second, the authoritarian politics of some countries led to the irrelevancy of the constitutional provisions regarding language (indeed, often to the irrelevancy of the constitutions as a whole). Kazakhstan, because it suffered from both of these problems, provides an example where the constitutional provisions – although symbolically significant – have little effect on the actual practice.

Taken together, Chapters 1 and 2 raise a series of interesting questions concerning the role of constitutions in dealing with language difference. First, they suggest that there is a broad range of issues that a constitution may address regarding language. One issue is whether to choose a single official or national language. This issue can generate conflict between competing language groups (as in India), highlight the practical limitations of a language that has been marginalized for generations (as in Kazakhstan), and connect to issues of nationalism and subnationalism (in both countries and in the Central Asian region generally). A second, related issue the constitution may address concerns the status and role of the language associated with the colonial power from which the nation has sought independence. This colonial legacy often carries multiple conflicting implications, as both chapters describe. A third issue the constitution may address concerns the other language groups within the country and their claims for recognition and accommodation. This issue may, in turn, be handled in a variety of ways, including through federalism (as in India) and through the use of individual rights (both in India and in the constitutions of Central Asian countries). In addition to highlighting these specific constitutional choices on language, Part I also raises a question concerning the more general understanding of the role of the constitution in dealing with language: Is the constitution primarily a pragmatic tool for managing linguistic difference or is it essentially a symbolic statement with little or no practical effect?

Part II addresses rural/urban differences. In Chapter 3, Paul Hutchcroft traces the failure of efforts to deal with corruption and patronage by shifting power and resources away from the national government and toward the provinces in the Philippines. This strategy, which has its roots both in the history of U.S. policy and in an ideology of local virtue, has led only to a system of poor governance and restricted democracy. Professor Hutchcroft suggests that the types of reforms necessary to address these problems would not focus on the issue of decentralization (i.e., on the rural/urban divide), but rather on electoral reforms and party development intended to address the interlocking system of patronage that ties local and national government together and makes it fundamentally unaccountable to the people.

In Chapter 4, Huong Thi Nguyen analyzes the use of constitutional arguments in the recent political dialogue in Vietnam surrounding the regulation of rural migrants who have been moving to urban areas at great rates. Despite the fact that Vietnam is an authoritarian regime in which the Constitution has little practical effect in limiting government – and in which there is no constitutional court or other independent enforcement mechanism – Nguyen finds that the Constitution plays an important role in the public dialogue. In particular, the specific rights to housing, freedom of movement, education, health care, work, and equality were all mobilized in the public response to recent household registration laws intended to restrict movement from rural to urban areas. In the course of this public discussion, the Constitution was used both to emphasize certain negative rights that would restrict the government's ability to control people and to assert a consensus on certain rights regardless of one's position on the ultimate issues of democracy and one-party rule.

Part II highlights several important ways in which a constitution or constitutional ideology may be mobilized around rural/urban difference. On the one hand, in the Philippines, the localist strategy born of a particular decentralizing ideology has failed to address the crippling problems of patronage. Thus, a focus on a particular difference – the urban center versus the rural hinterlands – has been a poor basis for addressing the underlying problem of corruption. On the other hand, in Vietnam, a universalist view of rights has been used not only to enlist public support for the claims of a relatively powerless group (rural-to-urban migrants) but also to generate some limits on the government even in the absence of democratic accountability. In this case, focusing on the common commitment to rights shared by both urban and rural people has provided an important rhetoric for curbing government abuse of power. These two cases suggest the complex interplay of ideology and institutions, each of which is shaped by the constitution, in determining whether social problems are more effectively addressed through the mobilization of difference or its elision.

Part III of the book addresses the issue of ethnicity or race. Race is, of course, a contested concept,[6] but, for our purposes, any difference that is understood by some of the people involved in either racial or ethnic terms (as opposed to, for example, linguistic, geographical, religious, or gendered terms) fits within this section. In Chapter 5, David C. Williams offers a taxonomy of different reasons for federalism and suggests that these reasons would lead to different types of federal systems. He then assesses the situation of ethnic minority groups in Burma, showing how their contexts and motivations would lead them to want and need different types of federalism. Thus, a federal system that would satisfy all of the different minority groups would need to be asymmetrical and potentially very complex. There is, however, an important shift taking place right now: as they have fought and worked together over the decades of civil war in Burma, the ethnic minority groups are coming to see things more the same way. Their cooperation is shaping their views in ways that push them toward greater coherence. As a result, a simpler, more symmetrical system might work for them in the future. This dynamic illustrates the important point that the needs and desires of the parties to constitutional

---

[6] *See* Richard Delgado and Jean Stefancic, "Introduction," in *Critical Race Theory: The Cutting Edge*, eds. Richard Delgado and Jean Stefancic (Philadelphia: Temple University Press, 2000); V. Satzewich, "Race, Racism, and Racialization: Contested Concepts," in *Racism and Social Inequality in Canada: Concepts, Controversies, and Strategies of Resistance*, ed. V. Satzewich (Toronto: Thompson Educational, 1998).

negotiations are, in part, a product of the constitutional process, not just an independent input in that process.

Chapter 6 by Gardner Bovingdon examines a recent and surprising turn in Chinese policy that suggests a possible abandonment of the *minzu* system of autonomy for certain areas dominated by non-Han ethnic groups. He outlines the historical and legal roots of the *minzu* policy and the political struggles over it within the Communist Party. As a result of such struggles, there has almost never been a real experience of autonomy for ethnic minorities under this system. The chapter then canvases the recent unrest in Tibet and Xinjiang and the current proposals to abandon the *minzu* system in the name of a "melting pot" vision of universal citizenship. It concludes that such a shift would actually be simply a new version of the old pattern of Han dominance over other groups. As a result, he suggests, the best path would be for China to make a more meaningful commitment to ethnic autonomy.

This part of the book raises several important issues about the relationship between constitutions and ethnic difference. First, it points out that the ideological commitments of the constitution – for example, to ethnic autonomy – may be inconsistent with the actual practice in law and politics. In China, the texts of the laws seem to promise autonomy, but, for political and cultural reasons, there has never been meaningful control by ethnic minorities over their own affairs. Second, both Chapters 5 and 6 indicate that the details of institutional arrangements are crucial to making protections for ethnic minorities work. In Burma, different sorts of federalism would be required to meet the needs of different ethnic groups, and in China, much more institutional structure is necessary to provide real autonomy. Third, Part III raises interesting questions about the interaction between constitutional ideologies and the concerns of ethnic minorities. In China, we see an ideology of universal citizenship being mobilized against the claims of ethnic groups. In Burma, we see that there is a dialectical relationship between constitutional processes and ethnic groups' goals: their goals are part of what shapes the process, but at the same time, the constitutional process may itself shape the groups' goals and self-understandings as well.

Part IV looks at religious differences and their relationship to constitutions. In Chapter 7, Feisal Amin Rasoul al-Istrabadi traces the divide between Shi'a and Sunna in Iraq over the issue of federalism and the ironic switch in their positions over time. In this sad and powerful story, many opportunities to reduce the divisions over this issue were missed. The role of specific historical and even personal elements in determining the outcome of the constitutional negotiations highlights the contingency of such results – and counteracts, to some extent, the attitude of inevitability that outside commentators sometimes bring to constitutional failures. The chapter also provides a sobering account of the role of international players in constitutional processes. In this case, Chapter 7 argues that the United States, with its own agenda and its ignorance of basic cultural and political conditions, bears a great deal of the responsibility for the failures in Iraq.

Ran Hirschl explores the significance of the constitutionalization of religion in Chapter 8, arguing that, contrary to the assumptions of the Enlightenment paradigm, putting religion into the constitution may be a mechanism for state control over religion rather than the reverse. In Israel, for example, the state is defined as both democratic and Jewish. One of the areas of jurisprudence in which the meaning of a Jewish state has been developed concerns who qualifies as a Jew. The chapter describes the case law on this question and demonstrates that the courts have played an important role in restraining the influence of religious authorities by bringing them under the general principles of the rule of law. In Malaysia, Professor Hirschl argues, a similar pattern appears in the use of federalism as a mechanism to restrain the power of Shari'a courts in this Islamic state. Thus, the constitutionalization of religion is a two-edged sword: it may be sought by those wishing to strengthen religion relative to the state, but it may also result in the state taming religion.

The chapters in Part IV highlight several different ways in which religion and constitutions interact. First, specific constitutional mechanisms or provisions can become focal points for division and conflict between religious groups even if they are not explicitly concerned with religion, as federalism has in Iraq. Second, particular constitutional provisions can shore up or undercut the political power of different religious groups (or of specific authority figures within such groups).[7] Third, ironically, constitutionalizing religion may facilitate the taming of religion by state authorities, particularly courts, which have an incentive to bring this competing authority center under control. All of these interactions raise a series of more general questions. How can a constitution deal with

---

[7] Another example of this sort of effect on the power of religious authorities, which is not discussed in detail in the chapters, is the inclusion of provisions concerning the role of Shari'a in the law, which is the subject of so much controversy in the post-Arab Spring countries right now. *See* Bassam Tibi, *The Sharia State: Arab Spring and Democratization* (London: Routledge, 2013).

religion in a way that defuses religious strife rather than exacerbating it? How can a constitution reflect the religious identity of a country's people (if that is what they wish) without either violating the rights of religious minorities or putting the power of the state behind particular (always contested) religious authorities? More generally, how can a constitution avoid blending religion and the state in ways detrimental to both?[8]

Part V deals with gender and sexuality. Although it is conceivable that a country might lack one of the other lines of division discussed (i.e., it might be completely homogeneous religiously or ethnically), every country has at least two genders (and possibly more, as the final chapter points out). Gender and sexuality have not usually been the engines of civil unrest – in the way that the other divisions discussed sometimes have – but these differences have important constitutional implications nonetheless. The struggle for recognition and equality across lines of gender and sexual difference has been a major engine for constitutional change in many places, as each of the chapters in this part demonstrates.

Kim Rubenstein and Christabel Richards-Neville begin Chapter 9 by reviewing a range of feminist views on the nature of gender difference, focusing on equality, difference, and dominance as the crucial issues. They canvass the history of women in constitution-making and in government generally in Australia, pointing out the very limited participation of women in these spheres. The authors then explore two areas of constitutional jurisprudence that might be fruitful for expanding women's roles in politics: the meaning of representative government and the understanding of federalism. Finally, they suggest a series of future constitutional possibilities for increasing women's political voice: electoral quotas, judicial quotas, "twinning" of electoral districts (so as to have male and female representative from each), and alternating males and females as the head of state.

In Chapter 10, Asma Afsaruddin explores the recent phenomenon of Islamic feminism. Professor Afsaruddin finds that these movements are characterized by their focus on the Qur'an rather than on the jurisprudence built around the holy text. Islamic feminists seek a religious foundation for gender equality, rather than a secular one, and they use exegesis and literary techniques to uncover male bias in many traditional interpretations of the Qur'an. The chapter places Islamic feminisms in context, relating them to other modernist movements in Islam, and it provides

---

[8] This formulation of the question is intended to leave open the possibility that there may be some forms of blending that are not detrimental to either.

two detailed examples of feminist theorists – one in Malaysia and one in Indonesia – including descriptions of the legal issues they worked on, the political mechanisms they used to seek reforms, and the success or failure of their efforts. The portrait of Islamic feminism that emerges from this chapter is a picture of women claiming power, respect, and equality within their own traditions.

Chapter 11, by Sean Dickson and Steve Sanders, describes the jurisprudence of India, Nepal, and Pakistan on issues relating to discrimination on the basis of sexual orientation and gender identity (SOGI). The authors find that these courts are developing an approach very different from the one prevalent in Western countries, where the focus has been on the ways in which SOGI minorities are the same as heterosexuals and where sexual orientation is foregrounded and gender identity is secondary. In South Asia, by contrast, the focus is on the ways in which certain traditionally recognized gender identities, such as *hijras*, are distinctive and deserving of protection against discrimination. Thus, instead of the Western tendency to universalize, the South Asian approach highlights local cultural categories. One result of this difference is that gender identity has been the engine of change, with sexual orientation (and concomitant protection for same-sex sexual activity) following or even missing, as in Pakistan.

The chapters in Part V illustrate some of the many ways in which gender/sexuality difference informs and is informed by constitutional values and structures. In all three chapters, we see the ways in which disadvantaged groups (women and SOGI minorities) can and do use the resources of their cultures – whether those resources are the values of federalism and representative government, the values of the Qur'an, or the existence of traditional third-gender categories – to argue for equality. This appropriation of cultures that have traditionally been used to marginalize them is one distinctive aspect of their contribution to constitutional development.

The chapters also highlight the importance of institutions for supporting ideologies of equality. In Australia, certain changes in political institutions could dramatically increase women's roles in governance. In South Asia, changes in the way the government identifies a person's gender on official documents were necessary to pave the path to equal treatment for *hijras*. In Malaysia and Indonesia, changes in the family law and personal status code – along with giving women greater access to Islamic education – are necessary to move toward a more equal status. Thus, an ideology of equality is insufficient without the institutional structures to support it.

Finally, all three chapters raise interesting questions about the types of arguments that are most effective in mobilizing change in a certain context: sometimes universalizing arguments that build on commonality and sameness are most effective, whereas in other situations, arguments about distinctiveness and cultural specificity are more useful. The challenge is to develop an understanding of equality in terms of gender and sexuality that can encompass both types of arguments.

Because of its conceptual organization around types of difference, this book offers several important advantages. First, the geographical range of the book provides some powerful comparisons and contrasts in the ways that each type of difference plays out in different parts of the world. For example, in Part I on language, Benjamin Cohen's chapter on India provides an example of a constitution that managed to skillfully defuse a potentially explosive political issue. William Fierman's chapter on Kazahkstan, on the other hand, describes the irrelevance of the constitutions to the issue of language in Central Asia. These two examples mark points on a continuum along which one might map constitutions in countries with significant linguistic divisions. Each part, taken as a whole, provides such a map of the issues concerning a particular type of difference and the responses of a range of countries within the region to those issues. In the earlier summaries of each part, this introduction has outlined a few of those issues for each form of difference.

Second, this conceptual organization allows the reader to see patterns across various types of difference and to focus on the similarities and differences in the ways constitutions deal with various types of divisions. For example, one striking similarity across all the categories is the salience of federalism as a constitutional tool for managing (or enflaming) difference. Benjamin Cohen sees federalism as one part of the successful constitutional program for dealing with language difference in India. Paul Hutchcroft describes the failure of localist strategies – shifting power and resources from the center to the regions – for dealing with corruption in the Philippines. David Williams explores the different types of federalism that might be mobilized to deal with ethnic divisions in Burma. Feisal Istrabadi sees federalism as the central constitutional issue around which religious division is organized in Iraq. Ran Hirschl sees federalism as central to the management of religion in Malaysia. Kim Rubenstein and Christabel Richards-Neville explore the relevance of federalism in Australia from a gender equality perspective. In other words, certain constitutional mechanisms – such as federalism – play out in a variety of ways across multiple forms of difference. This observation suggests that constitutional drafters need to consider multiple axes of difference when they are thinking about including such a mechanism, rather than focusing only on the particular type of difference that might be most salient to them at the moment.

Finally, the conceptual organization draws attention to the interaction of types of difference. The book is divided into conceptual categories, but, of course, these categories are not neatly separated in the world. Rather, one type of difference will often be related to or have consequences for another type. For example, language difference is often closely connected to ethnicity. One of the central concerns of the ethnic minorities in Burma, discussed by David Williams, is the preservation of their languages. It would not be possible to satisfy these groups with protections against ethnic discrimination if they did not also have the power to educate their children in their own languages. The nature of their ethnic identity, in other words, is intimately connected to their linguistic identity: it is not possible to adequately deal with one without also dealing with the other. Similarly, Ran Hirschl notes the connection between religion and ethnicity in Malaysia and the complex legal issues about ethnicity that arise when someone changes his or her religious affiliation.

Conversely, some forms of difference are in tension with other forms. For example, constitutional mechanisms for accommodating religious difference sometimes cause or exacerbate gender inequality, as Asma Afsaruddin describes in her chapter. The same can be true for constitutional accommodation of ethnic differences in the form of recognition of customary law.[9] If cultural or religious groups (minorities or majorities) are protected in the practice of traditional customs that treat women unequally, then one type of difference is being accommodated at the cost of damage to another. The conceptual organization of the book is not intended to suggest that these categories are neatly severable, but rather to highlight the areas of overlap, influence, and tension between them.

A FRAMEWORK FOR THINKING ABOUT CONSTITUTIONS AND DIFFERENCE

So, in light of these multiple and crosscutting interactions, how might we conceptualize the relationship between difference and constitutionalism? I would like to offer some thoughts about a framework that might

---

[9] *See* Susan H. Williams, "Democracy, Gender Equality, and Customary Law: Constitutionalizing Internal Cultural Disruption," *Indiana Journal of Global Legal Studies* 18 (2011).

encompass the many issues raised in the chapters of this book. I have spent over a decade working with constitutional drafters and reformers in several countries around the world, including Burma, Liberia, South Sudan, Vietnam, and Libya.[10] I will draw on my own experience as a constitutional advisor and on the chapters in the book to suggest a framework for thinking about the issue of difference in the context of constitutions.

Constitutions and constitutionalism can contribute to the management of difference in two overarching ways: ideologically and institutionally. Within each of these broad categories, there are several different subsets. The framework I will suggest provides a set of inquiries; asking these questions about any given constitution in relation to a particular type of difference will highlight the range of interactions between them. I will outline the inquiries, using examples from the chapters of the book and my own experience. The goal is to provide a method for canvassing the complicated landscape of constitutional interactions with difference in a way that is both clear and thorough.

Ideology

The first way in which constitutions can affect difference is by defining the basic ideology or underlying conceptual commitments of the legal order. Thus, we sometimes speak of democratic constitutions, socialist constitutions, or Islamic constitutions. Even in the absence of such labels, one of the central functions of a constitution is to express the fundamental values and commitments of a society. As a result, constitutions can be powerful cultural symbols, providing recognition to certain forms of difference (sometimes at the cost of reifying them), while devaluing or breaking down the significance of others.

Sometimes constitutions have these effects explicitly, as when the constitution specifically addresses the type of difference at issue. From the perspective of a Western legal tradition committed to neutrality and individualism, it might seem obvious that the way to avoid exacerbating difference is to refuse to mention it in the constitution. Experience in the many countries discussed in this book suggests, however, that the path is not so simple or straightforward. The Indian Constitution on language

---

[10] The Center for Constitutional Democracy at the Indiana University Maurer School of Law, which I direct with David C. Williams, studies constitutional design and advises constitutional reformers in countries around the world. For information about the Center's work, *see* http://ccd.indiana.edu.

and the Israeli approach to religion provide examples of constitutional ideologies that address specific differences explicitly, but with opposite results. In India, the effect of these provisions recognizing certain languages has been to reduce the tensions and violence around language difference, whereas in Israel, religious lines are hardened by the legal recognition of specific identity categories. Constitutions that single out a particular ethnic group as the national identity, such as Malaysia's, may have a reifying effect on identity categories. On the other hand, a constitutional ideology that recognizes certain historic lines of difference as the basis for social disadvantage and commits to redress them can move a country toward greater equality and stability, as in South Africa's constitutional commitment to a non-racialist and nonsexist society[11] or Nepal's constitutional commitment to the equal recognition of all gender identities. Thus, the choice is not simply between addressing or eliding the relevant differences, but rather between approaches that will help manage the difference productively and approaches that will harden lines of division and tensions between groups. Ideological commitments that explicitly recognize certain forms of difference can fall into both sorts of approaches.

Moreover, even when the constitution does not specifically mention a particular type of difference, the basic ideological commitments of the constitution may have important implications for that difference. The constitution helps define the nature of politics and political interaction within a society. Constitutions create political cultures with certain characteristics, and those characteristics, in turn, affect the social roles – and even the identities – of groups.

On the one hand, constitutions can promote a transformative political culture: they can provide an engine for the transformation of traditional institutions to make them more reflective of the experience of excluded groups. For example, the constitution may interact with difference by functioning as a resource in public dialogue that draws people together across their differences and creates pressure for limitations on the power of authoritarian regimes, as Huong Thi Nguyen explores in her chapter on Vietnam. The political culture created by a constitution can also ground the emergence of new identities that cross the traditional lines of division, creating complex and interpenetrating identities that challenge the old categories, as David Williams suggests is possible in Burma.

---

[11] *See* Constitution of the Republic of South Africa, Art. 1(b) (1996).

These are powerful, positive opportunities created by the political culture shaped by a constitution (or, in the case of Burma, a constitutional process).

On the other hand, the constitution can also create political cultures that have a negative effect on issues of difference, even if the particular provision at issue never mentions those differences explicitly. For example, as Gardner Bovingdon describes, the dominance of the Han group, although never explicitly authorized by the Constitution of China, is implicit in the political culture assumed by that document, to the detriment of the many ethnic minority groups in China. Similarly, the formal model of equality implicit in the U.S. Constitution – which sees equality primarily in terms of avoiding government discrimination against particular individuals – makes it difficult to adequately address the social roots of gender or racial inequality.[12] By creating or facilitating a certain type of political culture, the constitution can support either productive or destructive understandings of difference.

Indeed, sometimes a constitution has only an ideological effect, because it is never implemented in practice and therefore generates no institutional consequences. As William Fierman has described in the case of language policy in Kazakhstan, political realities may make the constitution little more than a statement of ideology. We should not assume that such practically ineffective constitutions are meaningless, however. They may still have important effects on political culture and, thereby, on difference.

Thus, the first set of questions that should guide an inquiry into the relationship between a constitution and a particular form of difference concerns the ideological/cultural impact of the constitution. First, does the constitution explicitly address this form of difference? If so, how does it construct the difference? Does that construction work to reduce or exacerbate tensions and conflict across that difference? Second, whether or not the constitution addresses this form of difference explicitly, does the constitution create or facilitate a political culture that has implications for this difference? While asking these questions, one must keep in mind that those implications can range from reifying difference and exacerbating tensions across these lines, to making people more comfortable

---

[12] *See* Mary Becker, "Patriarchy and Inequality: Toward a Substantive Feminism," 1999 *University of Chicago Legal Forum* 21 (1999); Joan Williams, "Do Women Need Special Treatment? Do Feminists Need Equality?" *Journal of Contemporary Legal Issues* 9 (1998).

living with lines of difference (for example, by reducing the inequalities associated with them), to facilitating the transformation of identities and relationships.

Institutions

The second way in which constitutions affect difference is by establishing the basic institutions and practices of government. In this role, the constitution can have enormous effects, both direct and indirect, on the meaning and operation of difference. I will suggest that there are at least three different kinds of institutional effects that should be examined: the flow of material resources, the distribution of decision-making authority, and the creation of incentives.

These three kinds of effects are deeply interrelated and intertwining. For example, power over material resources almost always translates into certain forms of decision-making authority, such as deciding whether or not to exclude others from those resources. It would be possible to draw the lines between these categories differently or to assign any given impact to more than one of the categories. Thus, I am not arguing that these three categories are independent, nor that they are the only possible way of organizing the effects here, nor that any particular impact must be seen as in one category rather than another. The categories need not be conceptually distinct, uniquely justified, or mutually exclusive to serve their purpose.

These three categories have a very limited purpose in my argument: they are simply intended as heuristic devices to help us think about the widest possible range of effects that institutional arrangements have on difference. Thinking about effects in all three of these categories should help us draw a more complete picture of the many and complex ways in which the institutions created by a constitution affect difference. If the categories achieve this goal, then they have served their purpose.

Material Resources

The legal institutions established by the constitution can control the flow of resources both into and within the country in ways that ease or exacerbate tensions along lines of difference. Constitutional provisions relating to property ownership and citizenship, particularly if they are cast in racial or ethnic terms, provide one of the clearest examples of such distributional effects. For example, in Liberia, the constitution limits citizenship to those who are "Negroes or of Negro descent" and limits real property ownership to Liberian citizens.[13] This provision obviously affects the distribution of material resources as between different races.[14]

However, even provisions that do not mention race, ethnicity, or other lines of difference can have such distributional effects. For example, constitutional provisions concerning which level of government gets the benefit of the exploitation of natural resources can affect the material resources available to different groups, robbing local communities of the benefits of development and exacerbating rural/urban (and, often, also ethnic) divisions.[15] Paul Hutchcroft's chapter on the Philippines provides another example of the distributional effects of constitutional provisions: moving resources from one set of patronage networks to another, without improving the accountability of government. Sometimes such effects flow from provisions that do not seem to have much to do with material resources at all. For example, a constitutional provision guaranteeing a free education, and thereby eliminating the school fees that keep many parents from educating their daughters, can lead to a higher socioeconomic status for women.[16]

Thus, in thinking about the institutional impact of a constitution on a particular form of difference, one set of questions to consider includes: Does the constitution explicitly allocate certain material resources to certain groups? Even if it does not do so explicitly, does the institutional

---

[13] Constitution of Liberia, Art. 27(b)(on citizenship) and Art. 22 (a) (on property ownership) (1986).

[14] The actual effect may not, however, be the one intended or expected. In Liberia, many of the businesses are owned by Lebanese and Asian people who are not citizens because of their race, although some of them have lived in Liberia for generations. See "Liberia: Economy," *Global Edge* (Michigan State University Broad College of Business), last accessed June 1, 2013, http://globaledge.msu.edu/countries/liberia/economy. They cannot own the real property on which their businesses are located, but long-term leases have been used to avoid that problem. *See* David C. Williams and Jallah Barbu, *A Treatise on the Meaning of the Liberian Constitution* (manuscript on file with the author, 2010).

[15] *See* Nicholas Haysom and Sean Kane, "Negotiating Natural Resources for Peace: Ownership, Control, and Wealth-Sharing" (Center for Humanitarian Dialogue Briefing Paper, October 2009), last accessed May 30, 2013, http://www.constitutionmaking.org/files/resources_peace.pdf.

[16] School fees are one of the biggest barriers to girls' education, *see* "School Fees Barrier for Girls," *BBC News*, September 5, 2005, http://news.bbc.co.uk/2/hi/uk_news/education/4215934.stm. Education, in turn, is one the primary determinants of socioeconomic status, and the income and educational level of women is also an important factor in the welfare of children. For information about the impact of school fees on girls' education and the United Nations' School Fee Abolition Initiative (SFAI), *see* http://www.ungei.org/infobycountry/247_712.html, accessed May 30, 2013.

arrangement created by the constitution result in distributional patterns that follow lines of difference? Do such distributional patterns promote equality? Do they increase connection and/or harmony across those lines, or do they exacerbate tensions between groups?

Decision-Making Power

In addition to the allocation of material resources, constitutions also allocate decision-making power over certain issues to certain people. Obviously, the allocation of decision-making power is one effect of the provisions identifying who can serve in political office and which powers each office holder will have. However, the allocation of decision-making power is also an effect of two other categories of constitutional provisions: (1) those provisions giving groups certain forms of recognition and autonomy and (2) rights provisions, which reserve certain decisions to the right holder as opposed to the government. Constitutions, through the allocation of decision-making power, can directly or indirectly interact with lines of difference.

A constitution directly interacts with difference in relation to this power when it explicitly allocates decision-making responsibility on the basis of such difference. For example, many constitutions around the world provide seats in the legislature for the representatives of groups defined by language,[17] religion,[18] or gender.[19] Allocation of political representation on the basis of these identity categories has a range of effects on difference. On the one hand, it may give voice and influence to a group that has traditionally lacked them, as gender quotas sometimes do, and it may encourage such a group to organize in ways that will increase its power.[20] However, such schemes also tend to harden the lines of division between groups by placing a premium on identifying who counts as a member. Ethnic identity, for example, can be extremely complex because of intermarriage and cultural mixing. Using ethnicity as a qualification for political office can build walls rather than bridges between groups.

---

[17] *See, e.g.,* Constitution of Belgium, Art. 43, 67 (1994).
[18] *See, e.g.,* Constitution of Lebanon, Art. 24 (1926, as amended).
[19] *See, e.g.,* Constitution of Rwanda, Art. 9(a) (guaranteeing women 30% of all decision making posts), Art. 76 (reserved seats in the Chamber of Deputies) (2000). For a general discussion of the global movement toward gender quotas, *see* Drude Dahlerup, *Women, Quotas, and Politics* (London: Routledge, 2005).
[20] For a fascinating look at some of the consequences of gender quotas, *see* Susan Franceschet, Mona Lena Krook, Jennifer Piscopo, eds., *The Impact of Gender Quotas* (Oxford: Oxford University Press, 2012).

Arrangements such as this may encourage the leaders of such groups to emphasize their differences and exacerbate hostility against other groups as a mechanism for shoring up their power base.[21] Thus, within the category of constitutional mechanisms for allocating government power along lines of difference, the effects are complex and sometimes contradictory.[22]

Decision-making power does not need to be governmental power, however. A different form of decision making is allocated according to lines of difference by constitutional provisions that authorize certain communities – generally religious or cultural communities – to exercise power over their own members, for example, by recognizing systems of customary or religious law for family and personal status issues.[23] Here, too, the effects are multiple and complicated. Such community autonomy can be an important protection for a minority group that would otherwise find itself forced to conform to the majority culture.[24] However, the way in which the constitution chooses to recognize such autonomy can have important implications for power struggles within the group: either shoring up the control of traditional authority figures or empowering the challenges posed by those who may have been marginalized even within the minority community, such as women or sexual minorities.[25]

Finally, as mentioned, the decision-making power allocated by a constitution can also take the form of individual rights. Thus, a right to reproductive autonomy empowers women relative to both the state and, possibly, their partners or families.[26] Similarly, a right to interact with

[21] *See* Sven Gunnar Simonsen, "Addressing Ethnic Divisions in Post-Conflict Institution-Building: Lessons from Recent Cases," *Security Dialogue* 36, No. 3 (September 2005).

[22] They are also the subject of a large and contentious literature in political science. Compare Horowitz, *Ethnic Groups in Conflict, supra* n. 4, and Lijphart, *Patterns of Democracy, supra* n. 4, on the utility of such arrangements.

[23] *See* Susan H. Williams, "Democratic Theory, Feminist Theory, and Constitutionalism: Models of Equality and the Challenge of Multiculturalism," in *Feminist Constitutionalism: Global Perspectives*, eds. Beverley Baines, Daphne Barak-Erez, Tsvi Kahana (Cambridge: Cambridge University Press, 2012).

[24] *See* Will Kymlicka, *Multicultural Citizenship: A Liberal Theory of Minority Rights* (New York: Oxford University Press, 1995); Kymlicka, ed., *The Rights of Minority Cultures, supra* n. 3; Eisenberg and Spinner-Halevy, eds., *supra* n. 3.

[25] *See* Williams, "Democratic Theory," *supra* n. 23. *See also* Schachar, *Multicultural Jurisdictions, supra* n. 3; Sarah Song, *Politics of Multiculturalism, supra* n. 3.

[26] *See, e.g.*, the South African Constitution, Article 12(2), which protects "the right to bodily and psychological integrity, which includes the right – (a) to make decisions concerning reproduction; [and] (b) to security in and control over their body." Because this constitution also creates the possibility for horizontal enforcement of rights, see Art. 8(2) and (3), it offers potential protection against private persons who might interfere with the right as well as against government interference.

government in your own language, as Ben Cohen describes in the Indian Constitution, empowers members of linguistic minorities. A right to the free exercise of religion that entitles a person to a religiously based exemption from a generally applicable law that violates his or her beliefs is a powerful mechanism for protecting the decisional autonomy of religious minorities.[27] Thus, decision-making power allocated explicitly by a constitution can take a variety of forms – including representation in government, rights, and community autonomy – and can have a wide range of effects on difference.

Moreover, decision-making power can also be the result of provisions that do not explicitly refer to the type of difference at issue. The institutions created by the constitution can have the effect of empowering or disempowering specific groups without ever mentioning them. Thus, proportional representation electoral systems, even without any explicit provisions for gender balance, tend to produce a substantially higher percentage of women in the legislature as compared to first-past-the-post systems.[28] As discussed by David Williams, federalism – without any reference to ethnic identities – can often create meaningful autonomy for ethnic minority groups who live in certain areas.

Thus, the second set of inquiries focuses on the allocation of power over decision making. As the earlier examples illustrate, we need to ask not only about the ways in which the constitution explicitly allocates decision-making power to certain groups through political representation, rights, or community autonomy, but also about the ways in which the institutions created by the constitution might have the effect of distributing decision-making power along lines of difference, even if they are not explicitly cast in those terms.

Incentives

Finally, constitutions also create systems of incentives that can have the effect of helping a country deal with difference or making it more difficult to do so. These effects can be more subtle than some of the direct allocations of resources or decision-making power described in the first two

---

[27] This was the approach taken in the United States under the Sherbert model, *see* Sherbert v. Verner, 374 U.S. 398 (1963), which was abandoned by the Supreme Court in the Smith case: *see* Employment Division v. Smith 494 U.S. 872 (1990). *See generally* Susan H. Williams and David C. Williams, "Volitionalism and Religious Liberty," *Cornell Law Review* 76 (1991).

[28] *See* Pippa Norris, "The Impact of Electoral Reform on Women's Representation," *Acta Politica* 41 (2006).

subsections, but they are often extremely important. Incentive effects do not require anyone to do anything, nor do they directly give anything to anyone, but they create situations in which people are much more likely to act in certain ways. As a result of those patterns of behavior, certain lines of difference may be softened or hardened, and certain groups may be advantaged or disadvantaged.

Electoral systems are one of the clearest examples of institutions with such incentive effects, although they tend to be little understood by anyone other than political scientists. For example, in many countries, the rise of ethnically or religiously identified political parties is thought to exacerbate tension and violence across these lines. To prevent such parties, some constitutions simply prohibit them, but such prohibitions raise difficult theoretical and practical problems.[29] A much more effective method is to design the electoral system to create a disincentive for such parties. Thus, a simple majoritarian system for choosing a president, for example, creates no incentive for a majority group to seek common ground with minorities because it can win the office without them. Alternatively, an electoral system that requires the president to get a certain percentage of votes in all areas of the country (assuming that the minority groups are majorities in some places) will create an incentive for majority candidates to reach out to those minority groups to get the necessary percentage in their region. These sorts of electoral systems are, for this reason, an effective way of discouraging the creation of ethnically or religiously identified parties.

Many of the chapters in this book include reflections on the incentive effects of constitutional arrangements. For example, Ran Hirschl observes that courts often try to use constitutional recognitions for religion as a way to bring religious authorities under the control of the courts. This insight illuminates a set of incentives that motivate a pattern of behavior on the part of courts affecting the legal status of religion. Similarly, Paul Hutchcroft argues that localizing strategies have not worked to reduce corruption in the Philippines. He attributes this failure to the networks of patronage and the party system that are facilitated by the constitutional arrangements and that create incentives that maintain these patterns of behavior. To change the behaviors, one would need to change the systems that encourage them. David Williams observes that the process of building

[29] For a very interesting discussion of such prohibitions in African constitutions, *see* Matthias Basedau, Matthijs Bogaards, Christof Hartmann, Peter Niesen, "Ethnic Party Bans in Africa: A Research Agenda," *German Law Journal* 8, No. 6 (2007).

a consensus on the necessary constitutional reforms has created incentives for the ethnic minorities in Burma to reconceive their interests in ways that bring them closer together.

When assessing institutional incentives, however, one cannot simply assume that the constitutional mechanism will be effective. Even if the institution creates certain incentives, people may fail to conform their behavior to the expected pattern because of cross-cutting or contrary pressures. As Feisal Istrabadi describes in Iraq, culture, politics, violence, and other pressures may lead people to behave in ways that are contrary to their interests, given the incentive structure created by legal institutions. Institutional incentives are only one factor in shaping behaviors, but they will often determine the consequences of the behavior (e.g., a lack of Sunni representation in the constitutional drafting process in Iraq) even when they are not effective in generating the desired behavior (i.e., getting Sunna to participate in the election for the drafting body).

Thus, the third set of questions about institutions and their effect on difference focuses on incentive effects. This set looks at the institutional arrangements created by the constitution and asks: What incentives are created by these institutions for cooperation across lines of difference? What incentives are created for exacerbation of difference? Do the institutions incentivize extremism or moderation? Do the institutions incentivize focusing attention on equality, disadvantage, and injustice, or do they obscure such issues? Given other social forces (such as culture and politics), how likely is it that these incentives will generate the expected behavior?

All three of the types of institutional effects discussed in this section are fundamentally about power. Control over material resources, decision-making authority, and incentives that create advantage for certain groups of people are all forms of power. Indeed, one might suggest that the ideological issues are also, at their root, a matter of power: certain ideologies are sources of power for certain people. Of course, there are no simple lines dividing one sort of power from another, and people who enjoy one form of power are often able to convert it into other forms as well. Thus, ideologies tend to be reified in the form of institutions, and institutional structures tend to generate ideologies that support them. As a result, where a particular interaction belongs in this framework is often simply dependent on whether one chooses to describe it as a matter of ideology or of institutions, of material resources or decision making or incentives.

As a result, the important point about the framework is not which box a particular interaction goes in, but whether the framework leads us to consider all of the important interactions between constitutions and difference. The framework is intended to organize the many and varied types of interactions we encounter in the following chapters in a way that would allow an observer (or a designer) to think through systematically the ways in which a particular constitution might interact with a particular form of difference. By asking the sets of questions outlined here, it is possible to illuminate the many ways in which constitutions create, elide, reify, manage, exacerbate, ameliorate, and transform difference.

CONCLUSION

In short, there is no simple answer to the question of how constitutions relate to difference, but this relationship provides fertile ground for exploration and cultivation. It is only possible to see this complicated terrain, however, if one looks through the lenses of multiple national experiences and multiple disciplines. The chapters in this book offer a variety of such geographical and disciplinary perspectives for those seeking to explore this fascinating landscape. This introduction suggests that, by asking a series of questions organized around the ideological and institutional effects of constitutions, it is possible to get a bird's eye view of this whole terrain. Together, then, the book is a travel guide for those who wish to explore the many and varied ways in which constitutions affect difference.

Part I

Language

Negotiating Differences:
India's Language Policy

Benjamin B. Cohen

India is a country of vast differences and bewildering diversity. Its geography ranges from the humid tropics of the south to the snow covered mountains in the north. Spiritually, India is home to four of the world's great religions – Hinduism, Buddhism, Jainism, and Sikhism – as well as being the home to a vast Muslim community and a sizeable number of Christians. India's society can be divided along class lines, which have been made even more prominent since the country liberalized its economy in the early 1990s. Its populace has not two gender groups (male and female), but three – the *hijras*. Further, for most of the populace, a vast myriad of caste differences not only helps regulate social affairs (birth, marriage, death, profession, etc.) but also is now a driving force in politics. In the last decades, politics has both cleaved along caste lines and diversified as local and regional political parties have come to dominate the national political scene. Woven into the warp and weft of these many differences is language.

Linguistically, modern India is divided into roughly two spheres – one north and one south – with the Vindhya Mountains in central India serving as the rough division between the two. In the north, most Indian languages derive from Sanskrit (itself a branch of Indo-European languages) – for instance, Hindi, Punjabi, Marathi, and Bengali. In the south, languages such as Telugu, Tamil, Kannada, and Oriya are derived from the Dravidian language family. In addition, there are other language groups such as the Sino-Tibetan and Austric groups. All of these languages have their regional dialects, numbering at least 22,000 in sum.[1] Over time, other languages brought to the subcontinent have enriched

---

[1] Shashi Tharoor, *India: From Midnight to the Millennium* (New York: Arcade Publishing, 1997), 113.

the two great language families of the North and South. The Mughals brought Persian and the Perso-Arabic script, which together with local Sanskritic languages merged into the "camp" language of Urdu. The British brought English, which acted as a widespread unifying force, both by allowing them to rule much of the subcontinent and by giving Indians a language that was at once accepted by many but belonged to none.

By the time of India's nationalist movement and independence, the country's constitutional framers faced at least two overarching challenges: India's vast linguistic differences, often linked to ethnic differences as well, and the role of English. Ethnic differences manifested themselves not only along social, geographic, and religious lines, but, vitally, along linguistic lines as well. As Esman has written, "There are few issues, aside from religion, that can mobilize and sustain such passion as the status of language because it is central to collective identity."[2] India's political elites sought a solution in the Constitution that would satisfy the demands of ethnic communities (often called sub-nationalists) who sought recognition of their local language and nationalists who favored a unilingual policy. For many of them, this policy meant the national adoption of Hindi. At the same time, others sought protection from, or at least negotiation with, a dominant national language by supporting plans for a multilingual language policy. India's constitution, in essence, split the difference between a unilingual and multilingual policy: it both recognizes Hindi as a sole official language and recognizes many of India's other major languages. Unlike Pakistan and Sri Lanka, India's language policy, as constructed through the Constitution, is a remarkable example of success, demonstrating the ways in which a country's constitutional underpinnings can successfully accommodate vast and competing differences.

A second major theme surrounding the development of India's language policy in the Constitution was the role of English. English had been the language of the British. As such, it was common to India's political elites; thus, a Telugu speaker from the South could communicate with a Hindi speaker from the North in English rather than in Hindi or Telugu (mutually unintelligible to each other). English could thus be, to borrow concepts from Robert Putnam, both a bridging force between people who spoke different languages and a bonding force among English speakers.[3]

---

[2] Milton J. Esman, "The State and Language Policy," *International Political Science Review* 13, no. 4 (1992): 382.

[3] *See* Robert D. Putnam, *Bowling Alone: The Collapse and Revival of American Community* (New York: Simon & Schuster Paperbacks, 2000), 22.

Shashi Tharoor has written on the role of English as a national language in India:

> [I]t is the language in which two Indian government officials would naturally converse, in which two teenagers might discuss cricket or music, in which a Madras journalist might instinctively address a Bombay businessman, and in which the "national media" (those publications aiming at a countrywide audience) are published. It is undoubtedly the language of a small minority, but its speakers feel no "minority complex" at all.[4]

Staunch nationalists who saw the end to British rule argued that the new country should drop the use of English as quickly as possible and replace it with an Indian language – Hindi being the prime choice. For moderates and for those whom the nationalists' emphasis on Hindi was an anathema, retaining English held some value.[5] As Tharoor suggests, although a relatively small number of India's 1.3 billion citizens speak English, it is a language that belongs to none but can be used by many without upsetting regional or ethnic pride. Through strategic compromise, India's elites were able to manage this axis of difference – pivoting between the former colonial language and regional Indian languages – by compromise.

To tease apart the making of India's constitution, we will see first the ways in which South Asia's colonial legacy shaped ideas about language, and second, the actual crafting of India's constitution as the country neared independence. This is followed by an exploration of how the framers of India's constitution handled the diverse language requirements of the country and the result of those deliberations in the modern Constitution's section on language. India's language policy as framed by the Constitution should ultimately be seen as one of success: able to accommodate vast and often competing differences among its people.

PRE-INDEPENDENCE LANGUAGE POLICY

As the British East India Company expanded its control in the subcontinent during the eighteenth century, its leadership – a governor general in India, his council, and a board of control in London – addressed the array of languages their servants faced. For much of the eighteenth century, the Company pursued a two-pronged approach. On the one hand, many

---

[4] Tharoor, *India, supra* n. 1, 114.
[5] Esman, "Language Policy," *supra* n. 2, 386.

of the Company's officials were enamored with India's Oriental culture and embraced its languages. For instance, Sir William Jones established the Asiatic Society in 1784, which, in part, was devoted to the teaching and spread of Indian languages. In another example, sixteen years later, the East India Company established the College of Fort William in Calcutta. The College boasted a Professor of Hindustani, John Borthwick Gilchrist.[6]

By the nineteenth century, however, the Company had shifted to the second trend: the implementation of English as the Company's language of choice. After 1858, the British Crown followed suit. The first half of the century saw a great push for the spread of English as the language of the Company and the role of English and Western culture as that which should dominate educational institutions. No better example of this is that of Thomas Babington Macaulay's famous "Minute on Indian Education" from 2 February 1835. Macaulay was a law member during the tenure of Governor General William Bentinck. By Macaulay's time, attitudes towards Indian languages had significantly changed from earlier rose-colored visions of India held by Orientalists like Jones. Macaulay wrote, "All parties seem to be agreed on one point, that the dialects commonly spoken among the natives of this part of India contain neither literary nor scientific information, and are, moreover, so poor and rude that, until they are enriched from some other quarter, it will not be easy to translate any valuable work into them."[7] Of course, the "other quarter" Macaulay advocated was the widespread use of English.

However, the emphasis on English and Western learning also had an opposite effect, generating regional linguistic renaissances. Some British Anglicists helped nurture these sentiments. Bengali, Oriya, Tamil, Telugu, Marathi, and other languages all enjoyed a kind of renaissance. Many linguistic groups formed associations to promote their language.[8] At the same time, such a renaissance also fostered new and deepening linguistic and ethnic pride that took root in specific regions of India and in regional movements. As Judith Brown has written, "Linguistic regionalism became a market phenomenon of provincial public life in some

---

[6] Ganpat Teli, "Revisiting the Making of Hindi as a 'National' Language," *Language in India* 12, no. 1 (2012): 3.

[7] G. M. Young, ed., *Speeches of Lord Macaulay with His Minute on Indian Education* (London: Oxford University Press, 1935), 348.

[8] Jyotirindra Das Gupta, *Language Conflict and National Development* (Berkeley: University of California Press, 1970), 69–97.

parts of India. It bonded speakers of the same vernacular, and generated hostility towards other Indian groups who appeared to 'colonize' areas outside their own linguistic regions because of their education and consequent access to administrative employment."[9] Both the cultivation of Indian languages and the spread of English largely affected Hindu and Muslim elites and the upper castes and classes. The poor, low castes and women continued to use their mother tongue with little or no exposure to English.

The mid-nineteenth century saw the Indian Mutiny of 1857 and the change from Company control in India to Crown control the following year. A viceroy with an executive council to advise him replaced the governor general. From London, British Parliament, in part, controlled India through the Secretary of State for India. The Council of India in turn advised the secretary. From the post-Mutiny years to the 1930s, the British government in India passed innumerable acts that refined their control. Some of these began to extend rights to Indians and lay the foundation for the creation of India's constitution. Among these was the 1861 Indian Councils Act. In recognition of India's vast differences (linguistic, ethnic, religious, and otherwise), this act gave legislative powers to the regional Bombay and Madras councils and granted new councils to Bengal, the Northwest Province, Burma, and Punjab. All of these areas had large ethnic communities with their own regional languages. Further, the act allowed Indians, for the first time, to participate in government. Lord Canning added three Indian elites (Maharaja of Patiala, the Raja of Benares, and Sir Dinkar Rao) to his legislative council in 1862. The act provided an administrative structure that would frame Indo-British rule to its end. In 1892, the government passed a second Indian Councils Act. This expanded the number of people participating in the Governor Generals Legislative Council, thus marking an increase in Indian participation in government.

By the twentieth century, the British government in India was trying to both address growing tensions among different religious and ethnic groups across the subcontinent and at the same time respond to increased pressure from India's political parties, especially the Indian National Congress (established in 1885) and the All India Muslim League (established in 1906). A third incarnation of the Indian Councils Act passed in 1909, also known as the Morley-Minto Reforms, made progress

---

[9] Judith Brown, *Modern India: The Origins of an Asian Democracy*, 2nd ed. (Oxford: Oxford University Press, 1994), 177.

in addressing both of these areas of concern. The act provided for elections of Indians to different legislative councils, paving the way to greater shared governance and eventually a democratically elected parliamentary form of government.

This expansion of power granted to Indians, although still limited, was given a fillip by the 1919 Government of India Act (known also as the Montagu Chelmsford reforms). Now, in the larger provinces, power was shared through a system of diarchy whereby provincial councils handled some aspects of government (education, health, and agriculture), whereas others remained in the hands of the viceroy. In 1935, a new Government of India Act came into force. This replaced the earlier system of diarchy, granting greater powers to the provinces. It also established several new provinces in recognition of growing regional and linguistic claims. For instance, Bihar and Orissa were separated into two provinces. The act allowed for direct elections of legislative members. The 1935 Act was arguably the last major act passed by the British government in India. The Indian Constitution replaced it. Thus, from the 1860s on, we see a gradual devolution of power from exclusively British hands to those of Indians. Although not perfect, this process set the stage for India to form its own legislative assembly that would in turn draft the Constitution.

We must now backtrack some years and pick up the thread of language in the mix of Indian politics in the early twentieth century. In 1905, Lord Curzon divided the Bengal Province into smaller units for administrative convenience. At this point, the Indian National Congress opposed the division and argued for the use of language and linguistic states as a better way to reshape India's map. From this year on, Congress recognized the value in linguistic reorganization.

By the early 1920s, Mahatma Gandhi entered the debates over the role of language and linguistic states. When Gandhi assumed leadership of the Congress Party at Nagpur in 1920, he recognized the power of regional languages as a tool to inspire national movements and thus reorganized local congresses along linguistic lines.[10] Further, the issue of language was penultimate in Gandhi's list of items for a constructive program to ready India for freedom. The first was Hindu-Muslim unity, followed by other items such as prohibition, *khadi* (homespun), and village sanitation. The language issues – *rashtrabhasha* (national language) and regional

---

[10] Sugata Bose and Ayesha Jalal, *Modern South Asia: History, Culture, Political Economy* (London: Routledge, 1997), 139.

language – were eleventh and twelfth in a list of thirteen. Thus, for Gandhi, language was a tool to mend communal tension between religious groups. He recognized the linguistic diversity of India but did not foresee that tension between language groups, regardless of religion, would pose one of the greatest threats to independent India.

In 1921, following Gandhi's statements concerning language, the Congress Working Committee issued a statement that "as far as possible, only Hindustani in both Devanagri and Urdu scripts should be used and that all proceedings should be conducted in Hindustani." However, not wanting to offend non-Hindustani speakers, the statement continued: "The Committee considers it premature to set down any hard and fast rules imposing Hindustani on members of various Congress organisations."[11] Although the debate over Hindustani would continue until 1949, another theme of the Congress' struggle with India's language is clear at this early date: the role of provincial or regional languages. The 1921 resolution stated, "The Committee is, however, emphatically of opinion [sic] that all provincial proceedings should be conducted and provincial publications should be printed in the vernaculars of the respective provinces."[12] In 1928, the Congress accepted a report (the Nehru Report) that put linguistic states on the party's platform agenda. Thus, the recognition and protection extended to local language – later enshrined in the Constitution and the Eighth Schedule – were visible at this early date.

In 1940, Gandhi addressed a meeting of the Indian National Congress. In his speech, he linked his moral philosophy of *swaraj* (self-rule) with concrete steps to be taken across the country. Among these was his belief in the value of language, both a *rashtrabhasha* and local or regional language. He said:

> Without a common language no nation can come into being. Instead of worrying himself with the controversy about the Hindi-Hindustani and Urdu, the village worker will acquire a knowledge of the *Rashtrabhasha*, which should be such as can be understood by both Hindus and Muslims.
>
> Our infatuation about English has made us unfaithful to provincial languages. If only as penance for this unfaithfulness the village worker should cultivate in the villagers a love of their own speech. He will have equal regard for all other languages of India, and will learn the language of

[11] November 1921. "Resolutions on States Reorganisation 1920–1956," ed. Indian National Congress (New Delhi, 1956), 2.
[12] Ibid.

the part where he may be working, and thus be able to inspire the villagers there with a regard for their speech.[13]

Gandhi's overwhelming concern in this and other writings was with Hindu-Muslim unity. He clearly frames the idea of a national language as one that is not embroiled in what had become a Hindu-Muslim division over Hindi or Urdu. In addition, the *rashtrabhasha* should be one that both Hindus and Muslims could use; in north India this might have devolved into fights over Hindi versus Urdu, the Devanagri script versus the Perso-Arabic script. In other parts of the country, both Hindus and Muslims spoke the same language – for instance, in parts of Telugu or Tamil speaking areas where Hindi and Urdu were not the lingua franca.

THE CONSTITUTIONAL DEBATES ON LANGUAGE

In the mid-1940s, as India's independence neared, members of the Constituent Assembly faced the Herculean task of outlining and framing India's governmental structure. Among the tasks was what, if any, national language should be chosen, let alone questions of the language of the government, courts, primary and secondary schools, interstate communication, and so forth. As Granville Austin has argued, the result was a "half-hearted compromise" manifesting itself in the Constitution's language section.[14]

Within the Constituent Assembly were a group of radicals who believed in the primacy of Hindi and a group of moderates who were either less enamored with Hindi itself (such as those who spoke languages from India's south) or felt that the elevation of Hindi would damage a fragile Indian unity. The radicals included Balkrishna Sharma, Purushottam Das Tandon, Govind Das, G.S. Gupta, Dr. Raghuvira, Algurai Shastri, V.D. Tripathi, and S.L. Saxena. Many of them shared a similar background: they were educated at Hindu universities at Allahabad or Benares; a few had attended Christian missionary schools in their youth, perhaps preparing them for a distaste of English and Western culture; and of course, they were all Hindi speakers. None had received an education outside of India or outside of the Hindi-speaking north, unlike

---

[13] Dennis Dalton, ed., *Mahatma Gandhi: Selected Political Writings* (Indianapolis, IN: Hackett, 1996), 110.

[14] Granville Austin, *The Indian Constitution: Cornerstone of a Nation*, 1999 ed. (Delhi: Oxford University Press, 1966), chapter 12.

Gandhi, Jawaharlal Nehru, B.R. Ambedkar, Muhammad Ali Jinnah, and others who had substantial educational experiences in Europe or North America.[15] The pro-Hindi group wished to cleanse Hindi of any Urdu words, which were tinged with a relationship to Islam and, thus, Pakistan and seen as anti-national. Further, they desired that Hindi be stripped of any English words, which was the language of India's most recent masters, the British, a painful memory of colonial rule, and at the same time considered a foreign language.

For the moderates like Nehru and Ambedkar, there were other issues. First, the pro-Hindi lobby threatened to damage an emerging and fragile national unity. No one argued against the value of having some form of national language and its importance in promoting unity, but the moderates saw a radical pro-Hindi position as dangerous.[16] Second, many moderates, including Gandhi and Nehru, favored Hindustani rather than Hindi as a candidate for the national language. Hindustani drew vocabulary from Hindi and Urdu and thus served as a link language between Hindus and Muslims. Advocates of Hindustani felt that it could be taught and learned using both the Devanagri and Perso-Arabic scripts – again, an important bridging tool across the growing chasm between Hindus and Muslims.[17] In addition, many of the moderates spoke languages other than Hindi or Hindustani and thus both argued against Hindi and in favor of keeping English as a compromise choice. South and east India were filled with millions of Telugu, Tamil, Oriya, Kannada, and Bengali speakers who all chaffed at the possibility of Hindi being imposed as a national language and felt equally wary of Hindustani. For them, neither language bore any resemblance to their mother tongues, and the push for their adaptation was threatening and offensive.

Before India's independence in August 1947, the Constituent Assembly and some subcommittees debated the role of Hindi, Hindustani, and the other languages of India. The issue arose in late 1946 when the Rules Committee determined that the proceedings of the Assembly itself be conducted in Hindustani or English. A debate ensued because whatever language the Assembly and Parliament used – some people felt – would be

---

[15] Ibid., 284.

[16] India's first year's of independence have been considered its "most dangerous." *See* Selig S. Harrison, *India the Most Dangerous Decades* (Princeton: Princeton University Press, 1960), 55–95.

[17] On the development of Hindi and Urdu, *see* Amrit Rai, *A House Divided* (Delhi: Oxford University Press, 1991).

the de facto national language. Although debated, the rule never changed during the Assembly era.[18]

By July 1947, the partition of the subcontinent had been announced and was underway. Each day, news of communal violence and death streamed into New Delhi. As Austin has written: "In the two months between the third and fourth sessions, the Assembly had passed a watershed in the language controversy. This watershed was Partition. Partition killed Hindustani and endangered the position of English and the provincial languages in the Constitution."[19] Under this shadow, the Assembly once again convened. With the aftermath of partition unfolding around them and a strong anti-Muslim sentiment growing beneath the surface, the pro-Hindi group launched fresh attacks against both Hindustani and English as part of the constitutional fabric. Amendments included the substitution of Hindi for Hindustani and the prevention of English being used at the provincial level governments.

Among the pro-Hindi camp, Das spearheaded and eventually succeeded in changing all but one mention of Hindustani in the Constitution. Das and others continued to make amendments to any proposal put forward concerning the languages of India. At the same time, because of their increasingly extreme views, they lost the support of many non-Hindi speakers who feared a kind of linguistic fanaticism. Several temporary coalitions formed between members from different parts of India as well as members of different faiths. Some south Indian members of the Assembly advocated the use of English for a period of time as a bridge to the national incorporation of Hindi. For them, keeping English bought them time to stave off a Hindi onslaught. Thus, when Das and others moved to change language references in the draft constitution from Hindustani to just Hindi, the southerners largely did not object. Muslims in the Assembly objected to changing Hindi to Hindustani and wanted the continued use of both the Devanagri and Perso-Arabic scripts to be acceptable. They, however, did not opine on the role of English. As some issues began to seem settled (the use of Hindi rather than Hindustani and the continued acceptance of English for a period of time), another rose to the fore. The pro-Hindi lobby sought to have the Constitution adopted in Hindi. However, the version they presented was so heavily influenced by Sanskrit, even sympathetic colleagues complained that it was unintelligible.[20] On this front, the pro-Hindi group was

---

[18] Austin, *The Indian Constitution, supra* n. 14, 274.
[19] Ibid., 277.   [20] Ibid., 281.

not successful and the official version of India's constitution remains in English.[21]

By October 1948, pro-Hindi advocates had further radicalized. They made suggestions that not only established the primacy of Hindi as an official language but also failed to even recognize Urdu as a language of India. The moderates and some former pro-Hindi Assembly members began to grow wary of the increasingly extreme positions being suggested. Austin sums up their response: "Speakers referred to the intolerance, thoughtlessness, and fanaticism of the Hindi campaign."[22] As matters had reached a pitch, then president of India Rajendra Prasad and Prime Minister Nehru both sought a cooling off period, and for a time, debate on the language issue was quelled.

In the first half of 1949, debates on India's languages resumed in the Assembly with new rancor. Members again picked up the idea of a constitution written in Hindi. Prasad argued that the original version of the Constitution be in Hindi with an accepted English translation, whereas Nehru wanted the exact opposite: an English constitution that was professionally translated into Hindi. Perhaps sensing that this issue was ultimately not at the core of the language debate or seminal in the drafting of the Constitution, when Prasad took the idea to the Assembly's Steering Committee, they wisely set it aside, perhaps sensing that this issue was ultimately not at the core of the language debate or seminal in the drafting of the Constitution.[23]

The second half of the year began on 5 August 1949, when the Congress Working Committee published a report on the bilingual areas of India. Throughout India, substantial numbers of language speakers found themselves embedded in states and provinces where they formed a minority. For instance, a large number of Telugu speakers mingled with Oriya speakers along India's Coromandel Coast. The Telugus protested in 1948 and 1949 because Oriya-speaking court officials were not accepting petitions written in Telugu. Thus, the Telugus and others sought some protection from the Constitution for their language and basic linguistic rights. The Working Committee report attempted to provide some principles for linguistic minorities, including the right of a mother tongue and freedom from discrimination based on language.

The report produced a firestorm. Purushottam Das Tandon and others argued vehemently against regional language rights and for the use of

---

[21] The Hindi version was authorized in 1987.
[22] Austin, *The Indian Constitution*, *supra* n. 14, 283.
[23] Ibid., 286.

Hindi as a national language – the latter heavily drawing on Sanskrit when necessary. Das thundered, "Those who oppose acceptance of Hindi as the national language and Nagari as the single national script are still following a policy of anti-national appeasement and are catering to communal aspirations."[24] The debate returned to old themes: Should English have a role as a language of India, and if so, for how long? Further, at the end of a proposed transitional period (when English or Hindi could both be used), could English be entirely replaced? To what end was Hindi to be promoted? Both sides, however, were able to agree that Hindi was to be the official (not national) language of India with Devanagri as the script.

As this debate continued, a new front opened: numerals. The pro-Hindi lobby wanted numerals expressed using Devanagri, whereas the moderates wanted at first to use "Arabic numerals" and then later – again, responding to a simmering anti-Muslim sentiment left from Partition – suggested "international numerals."[25] The latter was accepted. The pro-Hindi group continued to push for the end of English after a transitional period and held to their demand for numerals in the Devanagri script. Finally, with Prasad and Nehru leading the moderates, a draft compromise was offered. This followed what has been called the Munshi-Ayyangar formula (for K.M. Munshi and Gopalaswamy Ayyangar). In this, the official language was Hindi with numerals in the international form. English would be used for fifteen years and then be revisited by later committees. Regional languages would be recognized in the Constitution itself (the Eighth Schedule), and the choice of language would be left up to the states. The pro-Hindi lobby attacked this position (which resembles India's current constitution). They submitted amendment after amendment that would have essentially wiped away all the ground that had been won. After three more days of debate, the final vote took place on 14 September 1949. A draft that would be acceptable contained much of the Munshi-Ayyangar plan but had five amendments added to appease the pro-Hindi group. These included Sanskrit being listed as a language of India; the role of English and numerals in Devanagri could be revisited by Parliament after fifteen years; the High Court could use Hindi if sanctioned by the president; and states' languages could be used to issue bills, acts, and so forth if an English version were made available.[26] Again, Austin sums up the nature of the language section of the Constitution:

[24] *The Hindustan Times*, August 8, 1949, in ibid., 291.
[25] Ibid., 293.   [26] Ibid., 305.

"Hence the Constitution makes clear what the national ideal is, and then, realistically, compromises, laying down how the nation is to function, linguistically speaking, until the ideal is achieved."[27]

DEBATES OVER LINGUISTICALLY BASED PROVINCES

This ideal, however, was to be shaped not only by the wrangling taking place in the Parliament but also by events unfolding far from Delhi. To begin, we must backtrack to 1948 – in the midst of the Hindi/anti-Hindi debates. In that year, Rajendra Prasad established the Linguistic Provinces Commission (better known as the Dar Commission named after its chairman, S.K. Dar) to look into the agitation for redrawing state boundaries, primarily along linguistic lines. For decades, linguistic communities anchored in specific regions around India had pressed for a redrawing of India's political map along linguistic lines. This was largely ignored by the British and was now potentially being ignored by the framers. The Dar Commission Report marks the Indian government's first post-colonial involvement in the linguistic reorganization of states. It is a fascinating report, clearly stating the need for national unity to trump regional demands. The Commission saw regionalism, or even sub-regionalism, as a harbinger of nationalism and separatism.

The report makes several revealing statements about the condition of India's "nation-ness" and the possible effects of linguistic reorganization. The creation of linguistic states would "bring into existence provinces with a sub-national bias at a time when nationalism is yet in its infancy and is not in a position to bear any strain."[28] Some of those in favor of linguistic reorganization argued that linguistic diversity would allow citizens to be better Indian nationalists, but the Commission rejected this, stating, "We are convinced that this is a mistaken view." Reorganization would lead to the "disintegration of the entire country."[29] The Commission felt that "the first and last need of India at the present moment is that it should be made a nation." The Commission thus soundly rejected the idea of any linguistic reorganization of the states. However, Dar recognized that at a future time this reorganization might occur but suggested that "administrative convenience" should be the primary factor in such a

[27] Ibid., 307.
[28] Linguistic Provinces Commission of India, *Report of the Linguistic Provinces Commission* (New Delhi: Government of India Press, 1948), 29.
[29] Ibid., 31.

decision, and language considerations secondary.[30] The Dar Commission Report placed Indian nationalism as the guiding ideology in the decision-making process. Regional aspirations were a threat to the nation and thus should be repressed. The Commission opined:

> We feel that the present is not an opportune time for the formation of new Provinces. It would unmistakably retard the process of consolidation of our gains, dislocate our administrative, economic and financial structure, let loose, while we are still in a formative state, forces of disruption and disintegration, and seriously interfere with the progressive solution of our economic and political difficulties.[31]

Second, the report saw language-based aspirations as the seeds of national or separatist aspirations. However, linguistic communities such as the Telugu speakers of south India (found split between the Madras presidency and the princely state of Hyderabad) did not aspire to nationhood, but instead to statehood. Finally, in recognizing that the states might reorganize in the future, language was not to be the primary force in shaping states, but instead, it would be administrative convenience. As Bose and Jalal have written, "In the immediate aftermath of independence the proponents of a linguistic reorganization of states, as well as communists fighting for poor peasants' rights in Telangana, could be tarred by the sweeping Nehruvian brush of anti-state terrorism."[32]

To study the Dar Commission Report, the Congress Party established a committee comprised of Jawaharlal Nehru, Vallabhbhai Patel, and Pattabhi Sitaramayya, dubbed the JVP Committee. The Committee's response was that linguistic reorganization was not in the nation's best interest at the time but might be considered at a later date. In short, the Committee "revoked the seal of approval that the Congress had once put on the principle of linguistic provinces."[33] However, the move towards linguistic provinces had now crossed a precipice.

Leading the charge towards a redrawing of the map were the Telugu speakers of south India. After Hindi, Telugu was the second most spoken language in India. In 1952, widespread violence erupted in south India, especially in those areas where Telugu speakers formed a majority. In October 1952, a Gandhian named Potti Sri Ramulu began a fast to pressure the central government to create a Telugu state, Andhra. His

[30] Ibid., 29.
[31] Brown, *Modern India, supra* n. 9, 343.
[32] Bose and Jalal, *Modern South Asia, supra* n. 10, 195.
[33] Ramachandra Guha, *India After Gandhi* (New York: HarperCollins, 2007), 192.

fast continued to 15 December, when he died. Again, riots erupted across the Telugu-speaking south. For Nehru, who had wavered on the creation of linguistic provinces, his hand was now forced. On 18 December, three days after Sri Ramulu's death, the cabinet announced that a new state, Andhra Pradesh, would be created on the basis of linguistic lines.[34] Andhra Pradesh came into existence the next year.[35] However, this was just one linguistic group, and the issue remained central to many others across the country.

In October 1955, a three-man commission comprised of Fazl Ali, H.N. Kunzru, and K.M. Panikkar submitted to the Government of India the Report of the States Reorganization Commission. This report would ultimately lead to the redrawing of India's map on the basis of linguistic difference. However, as noted by Arora, the Commission's work "was most certainly weakened when (even before it had commenced its investigation) the Congress Party and Government of India had given their blessing to the creation of Andhra State and thereby accepted the first linguistic state."[36] The report was not done in haste, and the thoroughness of its compilation lent its findings a certain gravitas. The commission members had travelled nearly 40,000 miles to more than 100 different locations, interviewed nearly 10,000 people, and reviewed more than 150,000 documents.

The Commission made several recommendations that attempted to address the vast linguistic differences across India and the volatile mix that these differences posed when combined with a fledgling democracy. First, the Commission suggested that the map of India be redrawn to have sixteen states – loosely designed along linguistic lines. Of the sixteen, Bombay and Punjab would be the only two bilingual states, which recognized the thorny issue of linguistic minorities embedded within larger linguistic groups. Second, some areas were to be federally administered and outside of the state paradigm. These included parts of the Northeast, Delhi, and some islands off the coast. Third, it recommended the redrawing of the former Hyderabad State, replacing that princely bastion with three new states centered on Marathi, Kannada, and Malayalam. The report

[34] *The Constitution of India* (New Delhi: Government of India Ministry of Law and Justice, 2011), 218.

[35] Lisa Mitchell, *Language, Emotion, and Politics in South India* (Bloomington: Indiana University Press, 2009).

[36] Satish Kumar Arora, "The Reorganization of the Indian States," *Far Eastern Survey* 25, no. 2 (1956): 29.

provoked an outcry among certain language groups: the strongest came from Marathi speakers.

Maharashtrians, led by Shankerrao Deo (a former Congress Party leader) agitated for a *Samyukta Maharashtra* (United Maharashtra). Within this united Maharashtrian State, Bombay would be its capital. However, Gujaratis largely dominated that city, especially its business networks and feared becoming an immediate minority in a new Marathi-dominated state. Tensions rose and culminated in riots and violence in the streets of Bombay. Ultimately, both linguistic communities were rewarded with their own states – Maharashtra and Gujarat – however, Bombay was passed over as the capital city for Pune.[37] Because of the sheer number of people it touched and the consequences of its outcome, the States Reorganization Commission report, as Ramachandra Guha has argued, was one of the most "influential reports ever commissioned by a government anywhere."[38]

The States Reorganization Commission and the 1956 States Reorganization Act brings the issue of language back to the Indian Constitution. The act came as an amendment to the Constitution and was coupled with a restructuring of the territories that India had inherited from the British in 1947. This act, more than any other, reshaped the map of India. The act removed distinctions between provinces, presidencies, and princely states and renamed most territories as states, whereas a few were called union territories. Fundamentally, the way in which these new states and territories were created was along linguistic lines. Linguistic reorganization did not solve every problem created by India's vast differences, but it went a long way towards addressing them fairly. Although some argued that the redrawing of India's map along linguistic lines would promote the disintegration of the country, as Guha has noted, "linguistic reorganization seems rather to have consolidated the unity of India . . . on the whole the creation of linguistic states has acted as a largely constructive channel for provincial pride."[39]

REVISITING THE ROLE OF ENGLISH

The early 1960s again saw the issue of language come to the fore across India. Although the map had been redrawn and new linguistically

---

[37] These states came into existence on May 1, 1960.
[38] Guha, *India After Gandhi, supra* n. 33, 603.
[39] Ibid., 208.

defined states had come into existence, the issue of a national language was still a major debate. The primary reason was that the role of Hindi and English had, in a sense, been put on hold from 1950 (when the Constitution was ratified) until the fifteen-year trial period for English came to an end in 1965. Leading up to that, fears of Hindi domination still plagued the South. For instance, to quell such fears, in 1960 then president of India Rajendra Prasad delivered the independence day speech that was entitled "No Imposition of Hindi: Plea for Unity and Understanding."[40] At the same time as Hindi fears dominated the South, other language-based fears spread in the east. For instance, East Pakistani refugees in Assam wanted their children educated in Bengali. Local Assamese speakers resisted, fearing being "drowned" by Bengali speakers, and rioting broke out. Frustrated by the continuing conundrum of language, Nehru addressed Parliament: "How superficial is the covering of that we call 'nationalism' which bursts open at the slightest irritation?"[41]

To address the issue, India's central government devised a plan that would quell linguistic strife through a three-language policy. Individuals would use their mother tongue in primary school education but learn Hindi and English in their secondary school period. This policy "constitutes a striking success of its [India's] federal structure."[42] In April 1963, Nehru ushered through the Parliament the Official Languages Act. This act stated that English "may" continue to be used, but state legislatures were divided on how to interpret this phrase, some seeing *may* as in "may not," whereas others, including Nehru, saw the term to mean "shall." Regardless, the act was necessary as mandated by Article 343 of the Constitution. It was one of several extensions crafted to prolong the use of English.

After Jawaharlal Nehru's death in 1964, the pro-Hindi lobby once again tried to impose Hindi on the nation. As the Constitution had come into effect in 1950, and English was granted a fifteen-year trial period, the celebrations surrounding Republic Day in 1965 took on extra meaning. Members of Parliament from the South wanted the official use of English

[40] Granville Austin, *Working a Democratic Constitution: The Indian Experience* (New Delhi: Oxford University Press, 1999), 155.

[41] Jawaharlal Nehru, September 3, 1960, *Jawaharlal Nehru's Speeches*, vol. 4 (New Delhi: Ministry of Information and Broadcasting, 1963), 7–9.

[42] Sumit Ganguly, "Six Decades of Independence," *Journal of Democracy* 18, no. 2 (2007): 31. Three years later, Parliament extended the use of English, responding to the mandate established by Article 343 of the constitution.

to be extended, fearing dominance by their pro-Hindi counterparts of the North. Leading the group for the retention of English were members of the Tamil DMK Party who organized anti-Hindi rallies across south India.[43] On 26 January 1965 Parliament passed a bill mandating that Hindi be the sole official language of communication between provinces, removing English as an option. In response, two young men took their lives in the name of the Tamil language. Riots erupted in several parts of the country. Then Prime Minister Lal Bahadur Shastri appealed for calm, and within weeks the bill was revoked and the use of English continued. Ultimately, Hindi has perhaps found greater success in becoming a more dominant national language through non-governmental means. For instance, India's vast film industry – releasing over 500 films per year – is conducted mostly through Hindi (although regional language films are also very popular).

India's leadership and the flexibility of its constitution have managed the differences in language to a point where the topic is no longer a major issue. As Austin has remarked, "Language, as a nationally disruptive issue, has progressively disappeared, although sensitivities persist."[44] Indeed, things have moved far beyond the fears and violence of the 1940s, 1950s, and 1960s. As an example, in 1996, then Prime Minister Deve Gowda delivered a speech from the ramparts of the Mughal Red Fort in Delhi. The speech was in Hindi, but the text he read was written for him in the Kannada script. The prime minister did not speak Hindi.[45]

THE CONSTITUTION TODAY

How then does India's current constitution address the issue of linguistic difference and language?[46] The Indian Constitution is the longest in

---

[43] On the negotiation over "troubled states," *see* James Manor, "Center-State Relations," in *The Success of India's Democracy*, ed. Atul Kohli (Cambridge: Cambridge University Press, 2001), 87–91.

[44] Austin, *Working a Democratic Constitution, supra* n. 40, 155.

[45] The flexibility of the Constitution and its ability to recognize new claimants again showed itself in 2000. In that year, the Indian Union again accommodated its differences in the creation of three new states – this time more along administrative and cultural lines. These were Uttaranchal (from Uttar Pradesh), Chhattisgarh (from Madhya Pradesh), and Jharkhand (from Bihar).

[46] Bringing the story of India's language policies up to date, *see* Jyotirindra Dasgupta, "Language Policy and National Development in India," in *Fighting Words Language Policy and Ethnic Relations in Asia*, eds. Michael Brown and Sumit Ganguly (Cambridge MA: MIT Press, 2003), 21–50.

the world. It has 448 articles in 25 parts. Following these are 12 schedules: technical lists that enumerate certain details of the Constitution. The Eighth Schedule of the Constitution concerns India's official languages and is comprised of articles 344 to 351.[47] In addition, there are 97 further amendments.

The authors of India's constitution had the advantage of being able to benefit from the experience of many other countries. By 1946, many other nations had viable constitutions that could serve as models. For instance, from Australia's constitution came the idea of a preamble; from Canada, the idea of a strong federal structure with power spread to the states; from Germany, the ability to suspend citizen's rights during a time of emergency; from the United States, the judicial review of the constitution by a Supreme Court; and from Ireland, the concept of a directive principle. As Sumit Ganguly has written, "the federal structure that India's constitutional dispensation enshrines has often shown a remarkable capacity for innovation."[48]

This innovation (or at least compromise) manifests itself in the language sections of the Constitution. Part XVII of the Constitution has nine articles that comprise the language section. Within the part are four chapters, each with articles that detail the government's language policy. The first chapter is "Language of the Union." India is a *union* of states and peoples rather than a nation or country. The term is technical and at the same time implies an optimistic overtone of unity that the constitutional authors desperately sought. The official language of the union is Hindi in the Devanagri script. The Devanagri script uses letters for consonants and vowels, has no upper- or lowercase, and denotes individual words by a line, or bar, across the top of the letters connecting them. India has no national language specified in the Constitution, only an official one.[49] The authors of the Constitution, having weighed numerous arguments about Hindi, other Indian languages, and English, compromised and gave Hindi official status, but not the pan-Indian rank of national language.

India inherited nearly two centuries of contact and use of the English language, and thus the Constitution needed to address how this foreign language – hardly foreign by 1947 – would or would not be integrated into the union's fabric. Rather than dismiss English entirely or embrace

---

[47] *Constitution of India, supra* n. 34, Arts. 344(1), 351.

[48] Ganguly, "Six Decades of Independence," 31.

[49] Austin, *Working a Democratic Constitution, supra* n. 40, 154.

it fully, the Constitution takes a middle path of continuing to recognize English for "all the official purposes of the Union for which it was being used immediately before."[50] For fifteen years after the Constitution was adopted, English would continue to be used. After that period expired, Parliament would assess the role of English as a language of India. As we have seen, the end of that fifteen-year grace period was marked by violence and ultimately an extension of the use of English. Balancing the powers of the President and the Parliament, the former was given the option to authorize the use of Hindi in addition to English, while the latter was given the option to renew the use of English when the fifteen-year period expired. The Constitution thus affirms the role of Hindi as the official language, but not the national one, and it recognizes English as both part of India's colonial past and part of its future. The choice of Hindi was clearly a victory for Nehru and the north Indian members of the Parliament, while English gave southerners a language other than Hindi to use in official correspondence, if they should choose, thus sweetening an otherwise bitter pill.

Not satisfied with the idea of an official language, Article 344 of the Constitution created a commission to further take up the matter. The President was to organize a commission between the fifth and tenth year after the Constitution came into force that would assess the role of language in India. The commission's mandate was to assess "the progressive use of the Hindi language for the official purposes of the Union" and examine "restrictions on the use of the English language for all or any of the official purposes of the Union."[51] Whereas the first article recognized the maturity of English through its historical context, the second article and its commission explored "restrictions" on the use of English. The role of Hindi, on the other hand, was framed in terms of "progressive use." Clearly, the hope was that over time Hindi's fortunes would rise, while those of English would fall. In its study, the Commission was to take into account the "industrial, cultural and scientific advancement India."[52] Nehru's strong desire to forge India into a modern state can be read into the prominence (first in order) given to industry and science, with culture nestled between the two. Further, to appease the vast non-Hindi speaking portions of the country, the Commission was to hear "the just claims and the interests of persons belonging to the

---

[50] *Constitution of India, supra* n. 34, Art. 343.
[51] Ibid., Art. 344   [52] Ibid.

non-Hindi speaking areas in regard to the public services."[53] A committee would evaluate the work of the Commission and make its recommendations to the President. This committee was to be comprised of thirty members, twenty from the House of the People and the remaining ten from the Council of States. The President could then "issue directions" for any or all of the committee and commission findings. The Commission issued a report in 1955 in which it largely followed the outline of the Constitution: it recognized the importance of Hindi as a unifying Indian language; it recognized the importance of sustaining and supporting regional languages; and it recognized that English was not about to disappear, but would remain a vital language in India, even if it was not of India.[54]

India's constitution in regards to language is in many ways very pragmatic. On the one hand, the Indian Constitution – like many others – establishes the ideals of the Indian Union and the roles and structures of its organization, whereas on the other, it spells out in great detail certain pragmatic necessities.[55] These articles and their mandates remain in the Constitution, serving as an outline to the historical procedures that were followed as well as adding heft to the overall document.

The second chapter, "Regional Languages," addresses the role of languages in the states. These are referred to as "regional languages," but the term *region* is immediately refined by specific mention of the states. The Constitution allowed that states could choose a language in use in that state, or choose Hindi. Again, for the South, Hindi would be an anathema. The states could continue to use English for official purposes in the way it had been used prior to the adoption of the Constitution. For interstate communication, the Constitution allowed states to use English (although it is not specifically mentioned as such), or if two states agree, they might use Hindi between them.

Immediately after independence many of India's states were large and unwieldy and contained a variety of different linguistic groups. These states were leftovers from the British period and contained within them not only different linguistic dialects of the same language but also,

---

[53] Ibid.

[54] "Official Language Commission, 1955-Report," in *Committees and Commissions in India 1947–73*, ed. Virendra Kumar (New Delhi: Concept Publishing Company, 1976), 53–67.

[55] On India's "prudent handling" of the language issue, *see* Ayesha Jalal, *Democracy and Authoritarianism in South Asia* (Cambridge: Cambridge University Press, 1995), 166–68.

in some cases, large numbers of people who spoke entirely different languages. Recognizing the diversity of India's new union, the Constitution provides that if a "substantial portion" of a state's population petitions the president, he or she may officially recognize that language of those people.[56] Here, the question of linguistic dialect would come into play. If one region of a state felt that their language or dialect was distinct enough, that region had a doorway into the halls of official recognition by the President.

The third chapter of the language policy section is "Language of the Supreme Court, High Courts, Etc." These courts were all to be in English. Although English served as a binding language between northerners and southerners, it remained a language of the educated and elite. The millions who were affected by court decisions would need a different way to access that information. Thus, a state governor had the right to have proceedings in the governor's own High Court conducted in the chosen language of the state, or in Hindi. If a state legislature chose to use a language other than English, the Constitution mandated that "a translation of the same [bill or act] in the English language published under the authority of the Governor of the State in the Official Gazette of that State shall be deemed to be the authoritative text thereof in the English language under this article."[57] Although the Constitution was supple enough to allow states to use local languages, it fell back on English and English translations to be the authoritative text of a particular bill or act. Article 349 is again a return to the pragmatic. This article, "Special Procedure for Enactment of Certain Laws Relating to Language," states that for a fifteen-year period no bill or law could be introduced in Parliament without previous consent of the president. The Constitution's authors, well aware of the volatility of the language issue, sought a pragmatic fix. A fifteen-year hiatus on language policy questions would allow the commission and committee to complete their tasks. It would also allow for some of the heat and light generated by the language debates to cool.

The final chapter of the language policy section is entitled "Special Directives." The first article (350) indirectly returns to the earlier articles regarding the language of government, bills, and acts. If those were generally to be conducted in English, Article 350 provides the individual right

---

[56] *Constitution of India, supra* n. 34, Art. 347.
[57] Ibid., Art. 348.

of citizens to redress the government in "any of the languages used in the Union or in the State."[58] In other words, the Constitution shifts from union and state level matters down to every person in India, protecting their right to use a language most comfortable for them. Perhaps the key word here is *used*. The Constitution does not specify that the language of redress must be officially recognized, but rather one that is simply used by a citizen of India. As such, for the millions of Indians who speak a dialect that is not officially recognized, their right of redress in using that particular dialect is protected.

Article 350A continues to spell out certain rights and protections for linguistic minorities. India faces a tremendous challenge in not only educating its populace, but also finding a way to educate people using a language familiar to them. The task is more burdensome in the need to introduce less familiar languages – for instance, Hindi and English in the South. As such, Article 350A states that state and local authorities should "provide adequate facilities for instruction in the mother-tongue at the primary stage of education to children belonging to linguistic minority groups." This directive allowed for a three-language system to develop whereby basic education was in the local language, and Hindi and English would be introduced as well but would not serve as the medium of education until higher grades, or not at all. The following article (350B) provided some bureaucratic weight behind the previous articles in that it created a special officer who would "investigate all matters relating to the safeguards provided for linguistic minorities."[59] This person would report directly to the President of India.

The final article of the language section returns to the role of Hindi. The article, "Directive for Development of the Hindi Language" is worth citing in full:

> It shall be the duty of the Union to promote the spread of the Hindi language, to develop it so that it may serve as a medium of expression for all the elements of the composite culture of India and to secure its enrichment by assimilating without interfering with its genius, the forms, style and expressions used in Hindustani and in the other languages of India specified in the Eighth Schedule, and by drawing, wherever necessary or desirable, for its vocabulary, primarily on Sanskrit and secondarily on other languages.[60]

---

[58] Ibid.
[60] Ibid., Art. 351.

[59] Ibid., Art. 350B.

Hindi was to be developed to serve as a bonding language for all of India. Here, the term *Hindustani* appears – only once in the language section of the Constitution. Hindustani is generally accepted to mean the lingua franca of much of north India. It contains a mix of vocabulary drawn from Urdu and Hindi and other north Indian languages. It remains the language of north India's film industry, Bollywood. For those who supported Hindi as India's national language, the Urdu influences (linked to Muslims) in Hindustani were to be carefully controlled. To that end, when Hindi needed new vocabulary, this article of the Constitution specifically mentions Sanskrit as the language from which vocabulary was to be taken – not Urdu or any Perso-Arabic languages. Although this section of the Constitution belies some of India's Hindi and Hindu nationalists sentiments, it ultimately has little actual force. The article proscribes the "spread of the Hindi language" but has no concrete action specified to promote this.

In the making of India's constitution and its language policy, the Constitution's authors chose to create a list of languages spoken within India in the Eighth Schedule. Although the list is by no means complete – thousands of regional dialects exist but are not listed – the twenty-two languages listed require some explanation. The reason for the Eighth Schedule appears to have been more psychological than practical. The languages in the list are not official or national languages. As Granville Austin has demonstrated, the languages were put on the schedule for psychological and status purposes. The psychology was in part a way for regional language speakers to see their language listed in some way in the Constitution. This was a small countermeasure against the pro-Hindi group, whom regional language speakers feared would ultimately overcome them. Moreover, to have a language in the Constitution conveyed a certain status to that language.[61]

The schedule, written in English, lists the languages in alphabetical order. Since 1950, as new linguistic groups have lobbied the government for inclusion on the list, their languages have been added. For instance, in 2003, Bodo, a language spoken in India's northeast, was added to the schedule. Others include Konkani, spoken along India's west coast, and Maithili, spoken in Indian regions bordering Nepal. Also on the list is Sanskrit. This was part of the original schedule of languages and was a concession to the pro-Hindi lobby that argued so vociferously for a purified Hindi as the official language of India with Sanskrit as the well

---

[61] Austin, *The Indian Constitution, supra* n. 14, 298.

from which it would draw new vocabulary. It should also be noted that Sanskrit is not really a spoken language of India, and perhaps never was. No one orders a cup of tea using Sanskrit; however, for instance, when Indian officials needed a new (Indian) word for "atom bomb" (*paramanu bam*), it was to Sanskrit they went. The schedule also contains Nepali and Urdu. Both of these are intriguing in that they are not only languages of India, but also the official languages of Nepal and Pakistan. The inclusion of Urdu was a concession made by the pro-Hindi lobby to the moderates during the contentious Assembly years. Finally, conspicuously absent from the list is English. Here the pro-Hindi lobby and others who were anti-English succeeded in keeping English off the list of languages in India. Ironically, the list itself and the Constitution are both in English.

How have India's neighbors faired vis-à-vis their own language policies? Compared with India, the region is a story of less success.[62] Pakistan was a nation created along religious lines. The East and West wings of the country were joined in a shared faith, but not in a shared language. From its inception, Pakistani leaders – including Muhammad Ali Jinnah – speaking from West Pakistan pursued a unilingual language policy. Jinnah made it very clear that Urdu and Urdu alone would be Pakistan's sole national language.[63] As Alyssa Ayres has shown, "The decision that Urdu should be Pakistan's national language was therefore invested with religious significance by decision makers in the Muslim League, a significance likely not attached to Urdu by other supporters of the partition."[64] The policy would be a major factor in the split of East and West Pakistan into Bangladesh and Pakistan. For instance, in February 1952, police in East Pakistan clashed with rioters in Dacca over the imposition of Urdu language in a dominantly Bengali-speaking location. The Bengali language had its first martyrs. East and West Pakistan split into Pakistan and Bangladesh in 1972.

The island nation of Sri Lanka has also faced difficulties surrounding its language choices. The majority of the population is Buddhist and speaks Sinhala. In the north of the island, closest to India, however, a large Hindu community speaks Tamil. In 1956, the same year India

---

[62] For Afghanistan, not discussed here, *see* Harold F. Schiffman, ed. *Language Policy and Language Conflict in Afghanistan and Its Neighbors* (Leiden: Brill, 2012).

[63] Alyssa Ayres, "The Politics of Language Policy in Pakistan," in *Fighting Words Language Policy and Ethnic Relations in Asia*, eds. Michael Brown and Sumit Ganguly (Cambridge Massachusetts: MIT Press, 2003), 56.

[64] Ibid., 56.

unveiled its state's reorganization plan, Sri Lanka moved to a unilingual policy whereby Sinhala would be the official language of the country.[65] For Tamils, this added to separatist sentiments. The country was later plunged into a civil war from 1983 to 2009, dragging India into the fray for a period of time.

India's constitution has largely and successfully managed the country's vast linguistic differences. By its independence in 1947, India had a bewildering array of linguistic groups whose demands needed to be addressed in the Constitution. In the North, languages derived from Sanskrit such as Hindi were dominant, whereas in the South, a different set of Dravidian-based languages existed. Washing over both of these were Persian, brought by the Mughals, and English brought by the British. The Constitution has deftly accommodated the linguistic diversity of India's citizenry. Hindi has emerged as a dominant official language, but to appease the southerners, English continues to be a vital language of India.[66] Other languages appear in a constitutional schedule, granting them and their speakers psychological, if not legal, status. India has redrawn its map on multiple occasions to accommodate language claims, and it is likely to do so again. This pragmatic flexibility should not be seen as weakness or the impending balkanization of the country, but rather as a testament to the strength of the Constitution in recognizing and accommodating India's great linguistic diversity.

[65] For an overview, *see* Neil DeVotta, "Ethnolinguistic Nationalism and Ethnic Conflict in Sri Lanka," in *Fighting Words Language Policy and Ethnic Relations in Asia*, eds. Michael Brown and Sumit Ganguly (Cambridge Massachusetts: MIT Press, 2003), 105–140.

[66] One aspect of retaining English in India that few could have foreseen was its contribution to India's economic rise. When Western companies have sought inexpensive call-center outsourcing, India – with its fluent English speakers – was a natural choice. Further, in advance of the West's Y2K fears, Indian computer experts dominated the need for well-trained, English-speaking technicians to come to Europe and North America to help stave off the problem.

2

Constitution and Language in Post-Independence Central Asia

William Fierman

INTRODUCTION

Language status and language rights were among the most important issues that emerged in the USSR in the era of glasnost during the tenure of Mikhail Gorbachev as first secretary of the Communist Party of the Soviet Union. Throughout the USSR, members of the non-Russian elites pleaded for (and later demanded) measures to support their ethnic groups' traditional languages. In most cases, the non-Russian spokespeople called for a change in laws that would raise the status of their languages relative to the USSR's lingua franca, Russian. Indeed, some of the USSR's constituent units challenged the central government's right to dictate language policy to constituent republics. From the perspective of nationalist elites – and, increasingly, national communists who were obliged to keep up with the rapidly changing political situation – the republics were entitled to adopt laws regulating the use of language within the borders of their respective units.

Although calls for language rights were eventually made on behalf of the titular nationalities in all Soviet republics (as well as many other nationalities that did not have Union republics named for them), proponents in some areas of the USSR made demands earlier and more forcefully than in others. Overall, we might envision the Baltic republics (Latvia, Lithuania, and Estonia) as the "locomotive" of the language rights train; to continue with this analogy, the republics of Central Asia were the "caboose."[1] In the case of locomotive republics, the legislation that eventually was adopted quickly led to a real increase in the role of the

---

[1] Although there are also grounds to consider that the republics of the south Caucasus (Georgia, Armenia, and Azerbaijan) were at the head of the train, language issues were somewhat less prominent for the nationalist movements there than in the Baltic.

titular languages (and a corresponding decline of Russian). Even in the caboose republics, however, where the shift was slower, language served as a strong symbol of power.

With the exception of the three south Caucasus republics, all of the USSR's Union republics adopted language laws in 1989–1990.[2] Just months later, in 1991, all fifteen republics of the USSR became independent states. All of them adopted constitutions that privileged the language of the former republic's titular ethnic group. Despite the vastly different conditions in the former locomotive and caboose republics, both the language laws adopted in the USSR's waning months and the treatment of language in the subsequently adopted constitutions were remarkably similar. However, regardless of the similarities in laws and constitutions, the language situations in Central Asia differed radically from those elsewhere, especially in the countries of the Baltic, south Caucasus, and Moldova.[3]

This paper will consider those differences and the relation of those differences to constitutions and subsequent legislation. I will attempt to demonstrate that the language guarantees and other rights provided in constitutions (and law more generally) in Central Asia have relatively little relation to practice. Although the Central Asian republics hooked their "cars" to the independence-bound "engine" that brought independence to five new states in the region, and although elites in Central Asia articulated their goal of raising the status of the titular languages in ways that paralleled those in the "engine republics," their objectives of language change were far beyond reach in two major ways. For one, the languages of the Central Asian republics could not take on the role

---

[2] As will be explained, the reason for no laws of the same type at this time in the south Caucasus was the special status of language already incorporated into the respective Armenian, Azerbaijani, and Georgian constitutions.

[3] It is worth emphasizing that not everyone in the non-Russian republics supported the language laws. Above all, the non-titular population as a rule had little mastery of the titular language and preferred a privileged role for Russian, which was the Soviet lingua franca and had been touted for years as a bond uniting all Soviet people. However, even among the titular populations in the non-Russian republics, there were mixed feelings about the sudden rise in status of the titular language. This is because in some republics – among them the Central Asian republics – the elite was Russian-language dominant, studied in Russian-medium schools, and sometimes had scant knowledge of "their own" language. For these people, the rise of the titular language and replacement of Russian may have been welcomed for symbolic purposes, but it posed many practical problems. To the extent that public communications would shift to the titular language, the Russian-dominant titular population stood to lose power and opportunities for upward mobility.

of national language because they were relatively underdeveloped and – for a variety of reasons – could not quickly become the channel for communication in many domains where Russian had long dominated. (In this regard, Central Asian countries differed from those of the Baltic and south Caucasus.) Beyond that, however, the Central Asian countries did not develop in ways conducive to language being regulated by law. In one sense, this practical irrelevance of the constitution is simply a continuation of the Soviet approach to constitutional rights in general. More significantly, the political systems in the Central Asian republics remained authoritarian and were led by elites whose dominant language was Russian. The following comments will focus on Kazakhstan, the wealthiest of the Central Asian countries. After the analysis of Kazakhstan, I will illustrate some of the ways in which its experience resembles and differs from the other countries in the region.[4]

Language in Soviet and Independent Kazakhstan

Before discussing the relation of Kazakhstan's Constitution to its language, it is necessary to give a brief sketch of language status in late Soviet-era and independent Kazakhstan. As for the Soviet era, from one perspective, Kazakh was a privileged language: Kazakhs, unlike many other ethnic groups inhabiting the USSR, had a Union republic named after them. Thanks to this, Kazakhs benefitted from the Soviet practice which (to oversimplify) was more generous in the case of linguistic rights with ethnic groups having Union republic status than with those with lower-level units or lacking any territorial designation. Such privileges, among other things, applied to mass media as well as educational and cultural institutions. Thanks to this policy, for example, approximately two-thirds of the ethnic Kazakh children in Kazakhstan attended primary and secondary classes in the Kazakh medium, and along with Kazakh book production, the Kazakh literary community produced a weekly literary newspaper and a "thick" monthly literary journal. Such practices were less common among ethnic groups without Union republic status. In the late Soviet era, many such groups had education only for the first few primary grades in their group's traditional language. On the other hand, however, Kazakh was one of the most disadvantaged languages among ethnic groups with Union republic status. Kazakhstan's urban areas had

---

[4] Although constitutions and other laws dealt with languages other than Russian and titular republic languages, my comments do not address other languages.

few Kazakh-medium schools, higher education was overwhelmingly in Russian, Russian-language radio and television were generally superior to Kazakh equivalents, and Kazakh was widely associated with the backwardness of the village or, at best, with a great historical past and a very murky future.

Combined with privilege, demographic factors profoundly affected the linguistic environment in Kazakhstan. In this regard the republic was unique in the USSR. Although by the time of independence Kazakhs had reacquired a plurality in their republic and constituted about 40 percent of the population, in urban areas Slavs outnumbered them by a factor of more than two to one.[5] Almost none of the Slavic population (accounting for almost half of the total) could understand Kazakh, let alone speak or write it. Many urban Kazakhs, especially young people, also knew little Kazakh. Overall, at the time of independence, about 90 percent of the Kazakh SSR's population knew Russian, whereas the number knowing Kazakh was only 30 percent. However, in 1989 Kazakhstan adopted a law making Kazakh the sole state language in the republic.

Space does not permit a detailed examination of the dynamics in the language balance over the last two decades, so I will limit my comments to a few points for comparison with the Soviet era. Symbolically, Kazakh has grown tremendously in the last twenty years: today, unlike in the Soviet era, many public signs, especially those posted by government institutions, are in Kazakh (often in Kazakh alone). The share of Kazakh-language mass media has grown, and Kazakh is in much wider use in education than it was twenty years ago. In part, these changes are related to a shift in the country's demographic composition: official data indicate that Kazakhs now comprise almost two-thirds of the country's population, including a majority in urban areas. Many of today's urban Kazakhs were born in rural areas where Kazakh remained strong. The Kazakh army, of which a large share of draftees comes from those same rural areas, has reportedly largely shifted from Russian to Kazakh.

Nevertheless, the limited growth of Kazakh in a series of domains is clear. Kazakh-medium education and mass media continue to be viewed

---

[5] In the 1989 census, Kazakhs accounted for only 27.1 percent of the Kazakh SSR's urban population, whereas Russians comprised 50.8 percent, Ukrainians accounted for 6.2 percent, Belorussians 1.2 percent, and Poles 0.3 percent. Agenstvo Respubliki Kazakhstan po statistike, *Itogi perepisi naseleniia 1999 goda v Respublike Kazazhstan. Natsional'nyi sostav naseleniia Respubliki Kazakhstan*, vol. 4, pt. 1, *Naselenie Respubliki Kazakhstana po natsional'nostiam, polu, i vozrastu* (Almaty, 2000), 6–11.

as inferior to those in Russian. Although Kazakh government offices are supposed to be operating in Kazakh, this is often accomplished by composing documents in Russian and adding poor quality Kazakh translations underneath. Despite widespread criticism by Kazakh nationalists, proceedings in the Kazakhstan legislature are generally in Russian, and almost all legislation is prepared in that language, and although Kazakh language has been a mandatory school subject in non-Kazakh-medium schools since the early years of independence, pupils completing Russian-medium secondary schools in many parts of the country have notoriously poor Kazakh. The real relation of the status of Russian and Kazakh is also illustrated by the fact that in recent years annual addresses to the country by Kazakhstan's President Nazarbayev have usually been spoken about 20 percent or less in Kazakh and 80 percent in Russian.[6]

In such case it might seem that giving Kazakh special constitutional and other legal status would not be supported among those Kazakhs who continue to use Russian for so many purposes. Indeed, as suggested, some Russian-dominant Kazakhs are not enthusiastic about the growing status for Kazakh. It is, however, highly politically incorrect to doubt publically that Kazakh should eventually be the dominant language in Kazakhstan. The superior role for Kazakh (even if not realized) is a central part of the Kazakh patriotic narrative. Despite the generally low level of Kazakh skills among Russian-medium school graduates, it is telling that many elite Russian-dominant Kazakh parents who choose Russian schools for their children (because they believe them to be of higher quality) nevertheless hire Kazakh language tutors to be sure that their offspring are prepared for the future. Finally, it should not be forgotten that the Kazakh countryside is heavily Kazakh dominant, and with the migration of rural Kazakhs to urban areas, the ethnic and linguistic balance on the streets of Kazakh cities (above all Almaty and Astana) is changing.

Constitution and Language in the Late Soviet Era

Although the Soviet Union collapsed in 1991, many of the institutions (although often under new names), practices, and personnel have shown a striking continuity into the post-independence years. This is especially

---

[6] Bazilkhan Jumabay, "Qazaq tili synaghynan prezidentting birden orysshasy kobeyedi," *Azatttyq Radiosy*, February 11, 2011, accessed August 12, 2013, http://www.azattyq .org/articleprintview/2306178.html.

the case in Central Asia where the post-independence presidents in four of the five countries were former Communist Party leaders in their respective republics.[7] Although one of these former communists was forced to step down because of civil war (in Tajikistan, being replaced by a former collective farm chairman who still is in power), one of the other four (in Turkmenistan) served as president until his death at the end of 2006, and two others (in Uzbekistan and Kazakhstan) are still at the helm of their respective countries.

Along with other factors, the continuity in leadership and the authoritarian nature of the systems over which former communist officials have presided means that many of the attitudes towards law and institutions in Central Asia today are similar to those of the Soviet era. Soviet constitutions promised a very wide range of rights and freedoms. These included, for example, freedoms of speech, press, assembly, and demonstrations (Article 50), as well as freedom to conduct religious worship (Article 52). Despite the constitutional guarantees, these freedoms, of course, were generally not observed in the USSR.

A number of provisions in the 1977 Soviet Constitution concerned language. These included Article 34's provision that all citizens of the USSR were "equal before the law, without distinction of origin, social or property status, race or nationality, sex, education, language, attitude to religion, type and nature of occupation, domicile, or other status." The same article guaranteed citizens equal rights "in all fields of economic, political, social, and cultural life." Article 36 granted citizens rights to "use their native language and the languages of other peoples in the USSR"; Article 45 granted rights to "attend a school where teaching is in the native language." The degree to which the communist regime violated these constitutional provisions was less than for freedoms of speech, press, and so forth.[8]

I would argue that most Soviet citizens, especially prior to the Gorbachev era, did not view the Constitution as a document that in reality defined their rights; and to the extent that Soviet citizens were aware

---

[7] The one exception was Askar Akayev who, although not an apparatchik, was also an active party member, having joined in 1981 and becoming a member of the Central Committee of the Communist Party of the Kirghiz SSR in 1986. *See* http://www.informacia.ru/facts/akaev/1.htm, accessed May 23, 2013.

[8] The other important constitutional provision involving language was Article 159, which dealt with language in judicial proceedings. Article 116 provided for publication of laws in the languages of the Union republics, and Article 169 described the use of the Union republic languages on the USSR's state emblem.

of rights, they recognized that they were guaranteed not by the Constitution, but by everyday practice. Although language rights were not as curtailed as freedoms of speech or assembly, most citizens probably also understood that language rights were based in common practice rather than the Constitution or any other written law. This is suggested, among other ways, by the fact that although the Russian language was not even mentioned in the Soviet Constitution, Communist Party ideologues had promoted it as the second mother tongue of all non-Russian ethnic groups in the USSR. Virtually all Soviet citizens recognized the fact that, regardless of what the Constitution said, Russian enjoyed a de facto superior status.

This is not to imply that, in the case of language, constitutional law was irrelevant. Constitutional provisions concerning language had a profound symbolic significance during this time. This significance is vividly illustrated by events at the time that new constitutions were being prepared for all Soviet republics during the Brezhnev era. Unlike the situation in all other republics, the previous constitutions of the south Caucasus republics named the titular languages of the respective republics as state languages. The drafts of new constitutions, published in early 1978, lacked this designation. Protest demonstrations broke out in Georgia and later in Armenia; as a result, the reference to language was reinstated, not just for Georgia and Armenia but also for their neighbor Azerbaijan.[9] This suggests that even though it was mostly symbolic, language was relevant in the case of the (republic) constitutions.

Although the language was not mentioned in the Brezhnev-era constitutions in Kazakhstan or any of the other Central Asian republics, a detail about the Kazakhstan language law (adopted in 1989) illustrates the delicacy of language questions in legislation and the importance of the symbol in the late Soviet era. The Russian- and Kazakh-language versions of this Kazakh SSR law (modeled on the legislation of the engine republics referred to above) differ from one another. In Russian this legislation is called the law "on languages" (*Zakon o iazykakh*). In Kazakh, however, the legislation is titled the law "on language" (*Til turaly zang*).[10]

---

[9] Craig Whitney, "A Second Soviet Republic Wins Its Language Fight; Exceptions in Linguistic Policy," *New York Times*, April 19, 1978.

[10] In Turkic languages the singular form of nouns is unmarked, meaning that it can refer to more than one object. In conversations with Kazakh linguists, I have been told that the difference in names was intentional. Indeed, it would have been possible to indicate that the law was on languages, by naming it "*Tilder turaly zang.*"

Language, Constitutions, and Hyper-Presidentialism
in Independent Kazakhstan

When the USSR collapsed, Kazakhstan's Declaration of Independence barely touched on the language issue, merely stating that "one of the most important obligations of the state is the rebirth and development of culture, traditions, and language of the Kazakh nation [*natsiia*] and of representatives of other nationalities [*natsionalnosti*] living in Kazakhstan." The first draft of independent Kazakhstan's constitution appeared less than six months after the Declaration of Independence, in June 1992. However, the adoption of the Constitution did not take place until January 1993. One of the main reasons for the delay was the bitter debate about how the document should treat language and, in particular, whether there should be one state language (Kazakh) or two (Kazakh and Russian). In the end, this constitution (like the 1989 language law) made Kazakh the sole state language but kept Russian as the "language of cross-ethnic communication." Among other things, the 1993 Constitution also provided that "the state guarantees the preservation of the sphere of use of [Russian] and other languages and looks after their free development." Although this constitution forbade any restriction of rights and freedoms because of a lack of knowledge of Russian or Kazakh, it also stated that only citizens with a mastery of Kazakh could become president, vice president, or chair of the legislative chamber.[11] In a section of provisions to cover a transition period of unstated length, this constitution mandated that conditions be created to study Kazakh for free and (again, during the transition) for office work to be conducted in Russian as well as Kazakh.[12]

Although symbolically important, these provisions had no significance in practice for three reasons. First, the January 1993 Constitution was quickly supplanted by still another, approved by national referendum in August 1995. Second, as will be explained, Kazakhstan – unlike the countries of the Baltic or south Caucasus – lacked necessary conditions to make Kazakh de facto the state language. Finally, and of greatest importance, the second constitution significantly enhanced the powers of

[11] *See* Konstitutsiia Respubliki Kazakhstan Ot 28 Ianvaria 1993 Goda [Constitution of the Republic of Kazakhstan of January 28, 1993], http://www.carudo.kz/647, accessed August 12, 2013, Arts. 65, 114. The eighth provision of the section entitled Foundations of the Constitutional Order (*Osnovy Konsmimutsionnogo Stroia*) states that Kazakh is the state language. Ibid.

[12] Ibid., Perekhodnye polozheniia.

the president, who has had much greater say over language policy than either of the constitutions.[13] The power of the president is particularly relevant because he has consistently attempted to avoid politicization of the language issue and sought to maintain social harmony among the country's diverse ethnic groups. Had President Nazarbayev placed a higher priority on linguistic Kazakhization of the country, the practical status of the Kazakh language would have been advanced more than it actually has in the first twenty years of independence.

Inasmuch as the topic of this chapter is the relevance of constitutionalism to language, it is worth noting some of the provisions on language adopted in Kazakhstan's second constitution and ways in which it differed from the first constitution. Kazakhstan's 1995 Constitution maintained Kazakh as the single state language; however, it dropped the first constitution's formulation about Russian as the language of "cross-ethnic communication." Although some participants in the discussion of the draft constitution proposed that Russian be given the status of official language, this was rejected. Instead, the new constitution included the following opaque statement: "In state organizations and organs of local administration the Russian language is officially used on a par with Kazakh" (Art. 7).[14]

No authoritative interpretation of this provision has ever been made. Individuals who want to see Kazakh replace Russian in various domains have claimed that this provision simply means that Russian may be used along with Kazakh in government office work and official communications, but that Kazakh texts are in any case obligatory. Others, who support a broader domain of use for Russian, maintain that this provision means that because Russian is used "on a par" with Kazakh, it may be used instead of Kazakh.

The continued confusion on this matter is in large part a function of the fact that in practice it has hardly mattered – except symbolically – what Kazakhstan's constitution says about language. A demonstration of the weak relevance of the Constitution to language matters is the fact that – contrary to the Constitution or subsequent language legislation – it is widely believed in Kazakhstan that Russian remains the country's "language of cross-ethnic communication;" furthermore, despite the very

---

[13] Indeed, all evidence suggests that President Nazarbayev jettisoned the first constitution because it did not concentrate enough power in his hands.

[14] This same formulation was adopted in a new language law adopted in 1997. *See* Law of the Republic of Kazakhstan on Languages, July 11, 1997, accessed August 12, 2013, http://www.usefoundation.org/view/780 (English translation).

vague formulation about Russian's role in the Constitution (carefully not calling Russian Kazakhstan's official language), the press regularly refers to Russian as the country's official language. In numerous informal conversations in Kazakhstan I have argued with well-educated interlocutors who have insisted that the Constitution indeed does make Russian the country's official language and "language of cross-ethnic communication." Perhaps this is not so surprising, given that President Nazarbayev himself has publicly stated the same things.[15]

The central reason for the irrelevance of the Constitution on language policy is that the president has effectively unchecked power to set such policy. Since the early 1990s, President Nazarbayev has ruled in increasingly autocratic fashion. One of the boldest recent manifestations of his power was an initiative to extend his term by referendum until 2020. Although Kazakhstan's Constitutional Court rejected this idea in February 2011, the decision not to proceed with the referendum appears to have been largely a result of international pressure on Kazakhstan rather than a decision based on the constitution. In place of a referendum, Nazarbayev announced an early election for president and became a candidate. As a result of these sorts of extensions of presidential power, the ability of any other political entity to use the Constitution to check the president has been gradually eroded.

In addition, the President has used his power to set language policy in a way that also contributes to the irrelevance of the Constitution. The vague nature of formulations on language in Kazakhstan's constitution (and other major documents) is at least in part a reflection of President Nazarbayev's policy, attempting to balance demands of Kazakh nationalists and non-Kazakhs, especially Slavs, who see Kazakhstan primarily as a bi-ethnic and bilingual state. In his attempts to defuse potential conflict in Kazakhstan, President Nazarbayev has heralded his country's great tolerance and its being home to 130 different nationalities.[16] Kazakhstan has indeed witnessed a high degree of ethnic tolerance, and representatives of 130 nationalities do live in the country. However, as Pål Kolstø has argued, Kazakhstan more closely resembles a bipolar than a multipolar society;[17] besides Kazakhs and

---

[15] Interv'iu Prezidenta RK N.A. Nazarbaeva vedushchim avtorskikh programm kazakhstanskikh telekanalov, *Press Service of the President of RK*, April 10, 2007.

[16] "Nazarbaev pozdravil kazakhstantsev s Dnem edinstva naroda," *Tengri News*, May 1, 2010, accessed August 12, 2013, http://tengrinews.kz/news/49017/.

[17] Pål Kolstø, "Bipolar Societies?" in *Nation Building and Ethnic Integration in Post-Soviet Societies*, ed. Pål Kolstø (Boulder, CO: Westview Press, 1999), 18.

Slavs,[18] who together comprise almost 90 percent of Kazakhstan's population, only four ethnic groups account for more than 1 percent of the population: Uzbeks (2.9 percent), Uyghurs (1.4 percent), Tatars (1.3 percent), and Germans (1.1 percent).[19]

The way in which President Nazarbayev's lead on ethnic policy is more important than the Constitution is also evident in his creation of an "Assembly of the People of Kazakhstan."[20] Kazakhstan's leaders claim that this "consultative [*soveshchatel'nyi*] organ," created in 1995, is democratic, for it gives representation to the country's diverse ethnic groups. In fact, however, the members of the Assembly are not elected but, rather, appointed by the president. A number of representatives of Kazakhstan's ethnic minorities have criticized the organization on these grounds.[21] In any case, whatever the Assembly's representative function may be, it also contributes to a closed circle of power dominated by the president. In 2007 Kazakhstan's constitution was amended to give this Assembly the right to select nine members of the lower chamber of Kazakhstan's legislature: therefore, in addition to the ninety-eight "popularly elected" members (all of them members of the president's party), the new *majlis* opened its session in the fall of 2007 with nine "representatives" from the Assembly.[22] Not by coincidence, the constitutional changes introduced with creation of these "Assembly seats" included a provision that would allow Nazarbayev (but no future president of Kazakhstan) to run for an unlimited number of terms.[23]

[18] Although besides Russians, "Slavs" also includes large numbers of Ukrainians and Belorussians, plus smaller numbers of several other Slavic groups, many Slavs are linguistically and culturally assimilated into Russian culture.

[19] According to the 2009 census figures, Kazakhs accounted for 63.1 percent of the population, and Slavs 26.4 percent (Russians, Ukrainians, Belorussians, and Poles accounting for 23.7, 2.1, 0.4, and 0.2 percent). Agenstvo Respubliki Kazakhstan po statistike, *Perepis' naseleniia Respubliki Kazakhstan 2009 goda. Kratkie itogi* (Astana, 2010), 10.

[20] Until 2007 the name was "Assembly of the Peoples [plural] of Kazakhstan."

[21] Bruce Pannier, "Ethnic Minorities Guaranteed Seats in Parliament," *RFE/RL*, June 29, 2007, accessed August 12, 2013, http://www.rferl.org/content/article/1077396.html.

[22] On the undemocratic nature of the Assembly, *see* Doklad Nezavisimogo eksperta po voprosam men'shinstv. Dobavlenie. Missiia v Kazakhstan (6–15 iiulia 2009 goda) (UN General Assembly Human Rights Commission Document A/HRC/13/23/Add.1), accessed August 12, 2013, http://www2.ohchr.org/english/bodies/hrcouncil/docs/13session/A-HRC-13-23-Add1_ru.pdf.

[23] "Kazakh President Signs Office-for-Life Amendments," *RFE/RL*, May 22, 2007, accessed August 12, 2013, http://www.rferl.org/content/article/1076624.html.

Kazakhstan Against the Background of the Baltic and South Caucasus Countries

It is instructive to look at the language situation in Kazakhstan as well as the relation of language and constitution in Kazakhstan against the background of the Baltic countries and the south Caucasus. Two factors are relevant to this comparison: the status of the titular language and the authoritarianism of the political environment. First, the titular languages were much stronger in the Baltic and Caucasus than in Kazakhstan. Compared to both the Baltic and south Caucasus countries, in Kazakhstan the language environment in most urban areas – especially for high-status language domains – continues to be dominated by Russian. Unlike in Kazakhstan, in these other countries it is, for example, unthinkable that lawmakers would submit legislation to the national legislature for consideration in any language other than the state language. It is likewise unthinkable that the president of the country would make his annual address to the people in Russian. Furthermore, unlike the greater prestige of Russian- over Kazakh-language education in Kazakhstan, Russian-language education in these other countries is not associated with high prestige.

The reasons for this are complex, but most importantly, they relate to the history of language use prior to independence. In the Baltic and south Caucasus (with the partial exception of Azerbaijani), the state languages have long been used as standardized means of communication in a wide variety of domains; moreover, the speakers of these languages have a much longer history of widespread literacy than the peoples of Central Asia. Related to the widespread literacy is the fact that the languages of titular groups in the Baltic and south Caucasus countries were used in high domains that titular languages in Central Asia were not. Thus, for example, in the late Soviet period, higher education was available entirely or almost entirely in the titular language in the Baltic and south Caucasus republics. On the other hand, in Kazakhstan, even in Kazakh-language streams, much of the training in higher educational institutions after the first year – especially in the hard sciences and technical fields – was in Russian.

This provides much of the explanation why, unlike in the Baltic and south Caucasus, in Kazakhstan it was impossible to implement provisions of language laws and constitutions that would have in fact rapidly expanded the use of the titular languages. To explain why in Kazakhstan the Constitution has so little relevance for language issues, however, we must also take account of a second factor: the political environment.

In Kazakhstan, the political system is authoritarian in nature and the Constitution is little more than window dressing. In this regard it is useful to distinguish between the more democratic countries of the Baltic and those in the south Caucasus, particularly Armenia and Azerbaijan. A critical difference between these countries is apparent in the Freedom House rankings of political rights and civil liberties for 2011.[24] In the rankings on a seven-point scale, the countries with the most freedom receive a score of one, with seven reserved for the least free. The countries of the Baltic have sought greater integration with Europe and have been sensitive to demands to develop democratic political systems, including the adoption and observance of democratic constitutions.[25] The situation in the Caucasus is quite different, where Armenia and Azerbaijan continue with authoritarian political systems manifesting many features of the Soviet system.[26] Thus, for historical and cultural reasons in both the Baltic and south Caucasus, the titular language's practical status is much higher than in Kazakhstan; however, in the Baltic the practical status is influenced by a very different sort of political environment than the environment of the south Caucasus.

Table 2.1 illustrates that, for all the similarities between the Baltic and Caucasus in terms of practical use of the titular language, the political environment in the two regions is very different.

Language and Constitution in Kazakhstan: A Central Asian Regional Perspective

If we use the Freedom House ratings as some indication of the importance of constitutions for language practice and rights in individual Central Asian countries, they suggest that constitutions in most of the region are

---

[24] Freedom House, *Freedom in the World 2011*, accessed May 23, 2013, http://www .freedomhouse.org/report/freedom-world/freedom-world-2011.

[25] *See, e.g.*, Uldis Ozolins, "The Impact of European Accession upon Language Policy in the Baltic States," *Language Policy* 2 (2003): 217–38.

[26] The case of Georgia is more complex: at least since 2004 the Georgian regime, seeking greater integration with Western Europe and the United States, has undertaken considerable political and administrative reforms, including moves toward legal guarantees of minority rights. However, as noted in a 2006 report, the work of establishing a framework for the promotion of minority rights in Georgia was an issue "often addressed for reasons of perceived obligation, rather than true will." Johanna Popjanevski, "Minorities and the State in the South Caucasus: Assessing the Protection of National Minorities in Georgia and Azerbaijan" (Central Asia-Caucasus Institute and Silk Road Studies Program, 2006, accessed August 12, 2013, http://www.silkroadstudies.org/new/docs/ Silkroadpapers/0609Popjanevski.pdf): 49.

TABLE 2.1. *Freedom House rankings of*
political rights and civil liberties for 2011

Regions	Political rights	Civil liberties
Baltic		
Estonia	1	1
Latvia	2	2
Lithuania	1	1
South Caucasus		
Armenia	6	4
Azerbaijan	6	5
Georgia	4	3
Central Asia		
Kazakhstan	6	5
Kyrgyzstan	5	5
Tajikistan	6	5
Turkmenistan	7	7
Uzbekistan	7	7

generally no more relevant than in Kazakhstan.[27] This seems particularly true in Turkmenistan and Uzbekistan. In fact, by most measures these two neighbors of Kazakhstan are the most repressive in the region; they also happen to be the states pursuing the strongest nationalizing policies.

Turkmenistan's constitution (adopted in 1992) addresses language issues very sparsely; it merely states that Turkmen is the country's state language (Art. 13), provides for use of other languages in the courts for those who do not know Turkmen (Art. 106), and guarantees citizens equal rights regardless of their language (Art. 17). This last item is not observed in practice: for example, with one exception, all non-Turkmen-medium schools have been closed.[28]

Like in Turkmenistan, Uzbekistan's constitution (adopted 1992) contains provisions regarding languages in the courts (Art. 115) and also promises equal rights to all citizens regardless of language (Art. 18); however, Uzbekistan's constitution also stipulates a language requirement

---

[27] This link might not always exist because, in theory, language rights could be protected by well-established and widely accepted practice. In post-Soviet Central Asia, however, this seems highly unlikely.

[28] There is also a small number of Russian-language groups in mixed-language schools. However, no schools operate to serve the Uzbek or Kazakh populations. The one Russian-language school, in the capital, is administered by Russia, and many of its students are children of Russian expatriates working in Turkmenistan.

for candidates to be Uzbekistan's president (Art. 90). Uzbekistan's constitution combines the declaration of Uzbek as the state language with a guarantee of a "respectful attitude toward the languages, customs and traditions of all nationalities and ethnic groups" living in the country and the creation of "conditions necessary for their development" (Art. 4). Despite what is implied in the Constitution, Uzbekistan's regime has also been limiting educational and cultural opportunities in minority languages, particularly other Turkic languages of the region and Tajik (but not so much for Russian).[29]

Tajikistan's constitution contains provisions like Uzbekistan's in terms of courts (Art. 88), language requirements for the president (Art. 65), and equal rights for all citizens regardless of language (Art. 17); in addition, however, Tajikistan's constitution forbids propaganda and agitation that inflames language enmity (*iazykovaia vrazhda*) (Art. 30). Although the Constitution makes Tajik the state language, it not only declares that all ethnic groups enjoy the right "freely to use their native language," but also keeps Russian as the "language of cross-ethnic communication" (Art. 2). Nevertheless, and despite the fact that Tajikistan is arguably less authoritarian than Turkmenistan and Uzbekistan, there is little relation of the Constitution to provision of language rights. In addition to the political dynamics in the country, this is likely also a result of Tajikistan's severe poverty: even by Central Asian standards, Tajikistan is poor, and it is the only country to have suffered a civil war. Funds for education in any language are particularly scarce.

Let us now turn to Kyrgyzstan, which in important aspects related to constitution and language is an outlier for the region. This is partly rooted in the fact that after independence Kyrgyzstan has had two revolutions (in 2005 and 2010). Consequently, it has adopted three constitutions (1993, 2007, and 2010). It is also worth noting once more that Kyrgyzstan was the only Central Asian country whose first president, Askar Akayev, was not a communist apparatchik. Furthermore, Akayev – not unlike Nazarbayev in Kazakhstan's early years of independence – initially appeared to be leading a political system more based on law than was the case in Uzbekistan, Turkmenistan, or Tajikistan.

All three of Kyrgyzstan's constitutions state that Kyrgyz is the state language and (particularly the second and third constitutions) give

---

[29] For allegations concerning Tajik, *see* Bakhtiyor Ergashev, "Tashkent Targets Tajik Minority" (Institute for War and Peace Reporting, RCA 49, February 21, 2005), accessed January 3, 2013, http://iwpr.net/report-news/tashkent-targets-tajik-minority.

Russian a special status.[30] Likewise, all three constitutions guarantee rights to preserve native languages.[31] Another common clause in all constitutions concerns the need for the president of the country to know Kyrgyz.[32]

The 1993 Constitution devotes the least attention to language. In addition to the features common to all constitutions (as described immediately above), the only other references to language in the first constitution concern prohibition of infringement of rights and freedoms because of a lack of knowledge of the state language (Art. 5) and discrimination based on a citizen's language (Art. 6).

The 2007 Constitution maintained the prohibition on discrimination from the 1993 Constitution (Art. 13) but expanded the "no infringement" clause to include Russian as well Kyrgyz (Art. 5). The 2010 Constitution eliminated this clause entirely: it contains no clause prohibiting infringement of rights as a result of lack of knowledge of Kyrgyz or Russian.

Finally, unlike the 1993 document, the 2007 and 2010 Constitutions specify guarantees with regard to teaching languages. The 2007 Constitution states that "the State will create conditions for teaching the state language and two foreign languages" from preschool through secondary education (Art. 32). The 2010 Constitution makes a significant modification, indicating that beyond Kyrgyz, the conditions for teaching languages extend specifically to Russian and an "international" (*mezhdunarodnyi*)

---

[30] *See* Constitution of the Republic of Kyrgyzstan, May 5, 1993, Art. 5(2), accessed August 12, 2013, http://unpan1.un.org/intradoc/groups/public/documents/untc/unpan003682 .htm; Constitution of the Republic of Kyrgyzstan, October 21, 2007, Art. 5(2), accessed August 12, 2013, http://www.sras.org/constitution_of_the_kyrgyz_republic; Constitution of the Republic of Kyrgyzstan, June 27, 2010, Art. 10(2), accessed August 12, 2013, http://aceproject.org/ero-en/regions/asia/KG/kyrgyzstan-constitution-27-june-2010/view.

[31] The 1993 Constitution guarantees "the preservation, equal and free development and function of the Russian language and all other languages used by the population of the Republic" (Art. 5), whereas the 2007 and 2010 Constitutions (Art. 5 and Art. 10, respectively) do not single out Russian in this regard, instead simply guaranteeing "representatives of all ethnic groups forming the people of Kyrgyzstan the right to preservation of their mother tongue and creation of conditions for its study and development."

[32] *See* Constitution of the Kyrgyz Republic, May 5, 1993, Art. 43(3), accessed August 12, 2013, http://unpan1.un.org/intradoc/groups/public/documents/untc/unpan003682 .htm; Constitution of the Kyrgyz Republic, October 21, 2007, Art. 44(1), accessed August 12, 2013, http://www.sras.org/constitution_of_the_kyrgyz_republic; Constitution of the Kyrgyz Republic, June 27, 2010, Art. 62(1), accessed August 12, 2013, http:// aceproject.org/ero-en/regions/asia/KG/kyrgyzstan-constitution-27-june-2010/view.

language. It is worth noting that although all of the Central Asian constitutions guarantee equal rights to citizens regardless of language, the only language besides the titular language mentioned by name in any constitution is Russian. (It is mentioned in the Constitutions of Kazakhstan, Tajikistan, and Kyrgyzstan, but not Turkmenistan or Uzbekistan.)

As in all of Central Asia, the issue of the proper balance of Russian and titular language has been politically salient in Kyrgyzstan. Especially in the wake of the 2010 revolution, nationalist forces have pushed for Kyrgyz to displace Russian in spheres of public life.[33]

However, among minority languages in Kyrgyzstan, the most politically sensitive questions have related to the role of Uzbek rather than Russian. This sensitivity should be understood in the context of violence that broke out between Uzbeks and Kyrgyz in 1989, resulting in hundreds of deaths. At that time open calls were made for Uzbek to have a special status in Kyrgyzstan; such calls have resurfaced on a number of occasions, including the late 2000s. Generally the calls have been for Uzbek to have special status in Kyrgyzstan's south, where the Uzbek population is concentrated. Kyrgyz authorities have vehemently opposed such a move. Some Kyrgyz see special status for Uzbek in the South as a first step toward regional autonomy, secession from Kyrgyzstan, and possible unification with Uzbekistan.[34]

Violence again erupted from the tense relations between Uzbeks and Kyrgyz in Kyrgyzstan's south in spring 2010, still in the wake of the revolution. The Uzbeks suffered disproportionately: many Uzbek homes, schools, and businesses were destroyed, and hundreds of Uzbeks were killed. Tens of thousands even fled temporarily to Uzbekistan for refuge.[35]

There was some basis to view the 2010 revolution as the first step on a path that might lead to a more democratic political system in Kyrgyzstan.

---

[33] *See, e.g.*, "Driving the Russian Language from Public Life," *Eurasianet.org*, February 17, 2011, accessed December 16, 2012, http://www.eurasianet.org/node/62916. Legislation has even been proposed to fine civil servants who do not know Kyrgyz. Dar'ia Podol'skaia, "Parlament Kirgizii ustanovil shtrafy za neznanie kyrgyzskogo iazyka," *24kg.org*, December 14, 2012, accessed December 16, 2012, http://www.centrasia.ru/newsA.php?st=1355429460.

[34] Joldosh Osmonov, "Uzbek Community in Kyrgyzstan Want Uzbek as Official Language," *CentralAsia-Caucasus Institute Analyst*, June 14, 2006, accessed August 12, 2013, http://www.cacianalyst.org/?q=node/4020/print.

[35] Myles G. Smith, "Southern Kyrgyzstan Tinderbox Awaits Next Spark," *Jamestown Foundation Eurasia Daily Monitor* 9, no. 75, April 16, 2012, accessed August 12, 2013, http://www.jamestown.org/single/?no_cache=1&tx_ttnews[tt_news]=39273.

Those who took power not only made declarations about democracy but also designed a new constitution, one that provided for a new balance of power among the branches of government. Kyrgyzstan replaced the presidential authoritarian system with a mixed presidential and parliamentary system.[36] The division of powers among branches of government was designed to impede action by a president who might seek to create an authoritarian system as had existed in Kyrgyzstan before the revolution.

Did the 2010 revolution's democratic elements and the new constitution lead to greater protection of linguistic and other rights for minorities, in particular the Uzbeks? Unfortunately the answer is negative and clearly demonstrates that the overthrow of an autocratic ruler and the introduction of a constitution with a more balanced division of powers do not in themselves lead to protection of linguistic minorities. In the case of Kyrgyzstan the reasons for this include the history of tense relations between Uzbek and Kyrgyz communities (and, not unrelated) virulent Kyrgyz nationalism fueled by the widespread belief among Kyrgyz that Kyrgyzstan is for the Kyrgyz. Another important factor has been the weakness of the central Kyrgyzstan government (located in the North of the country) and the power of local nationalist leaders in the South to resist political directions from the center.[37]

Many Uzbeks have left Kyrgyzstan because of their experience during the 2010 violence or in anticipation of discrimination and poor prospects for employment and protection of their property and out of fear of future violence. A large number of Uzbek schools have reportedly been closed, and others apparently shifted to Kyrgyz as the language of instruction.[38] Perhaps some Uzbek parents have come to view a high level of competency in the Kyrgyz language as essential for their children's future. However, strong Kyrgyz nationalism and pressure on Uzbek schools from authorities to shift language of instruction are certainly part of the explanation.

---

[36] Carnegie Endowment for International Peace, "Kyrgyzstan's Proposed Constitution" (n.d.), accessed May 23, 2013, http://kyrgyzstan.carnegieendowment.org/2010/06/kyrgystan%E2%80%99s-new-constitution/.

[37] In particular, the mayor of the city of Osh, Melis Myrzakmatov, resisted orders from Bishkek. *See* "Controversial Osh Mayor's Fate Hinges on Elections," *RFE/RL*, March 2, 2012, accessed August 12, 2013, http://www.rferl.org/content/osh_mayor-_fight_for_survival/24502714.html.

[38] Dan Wisniewski, "Uzbek Language Disappearing in Kyrgyzstan," *RFE/RL*, October 1, 2012, accessed January 3, 2013, http://www.rferl.org/content/uzbek-minority-language-under-threat-in-kyrgyzstan/24725665.html.

CONCLUSION

The discussion in this chapter shows that the constitution does not serve as a guarantee of language rights in Kazakhstan, Tajikistan, Turkmenistan, or Uzbekistan. In those countries it appears that it is autocratic presidents who make the most important decisions relative to language, whereas the constitutions are no more than window dressing. Today there is one country in the region without an autocratic leader. Perhaps, over time, constitutional guarantees of language rights will be observed there. To date, however, despite Kyrgyzstan's division of powers and free elections, the constitutional guarantees of minority language rights do not appear to protect those rights on the ground. This suggests that not only can authoritarian governments impede the application of law to language status issues (because the government or branch of the government is so powerful) but also weak governments may not have the strength to ensure the observance of the constitution on language issues.

Part II

Urban/Rural

3

Dreams of Redemption: Localist Strategies of Political Reform in the Philippines*

Paul D. Hutchcroft

"My idea was to . . . [promote] values and clean up the government as you go up the ladder. . . . Start at the barrio, then the municipalities, then the provinces, and then go to the national Senate and Congress."

– Ramon Binamira, Presidential Assistant for Community Development (PACD), 1953–1961[1]

"[The 1991 Local Government Code] was by far one of the most revolutionary pieces of legislation that radically transformed the very nature of the Philippine politico-administrative system at the national and local levels. . . . [It] set off the process of reinventing and defining the discourse of local government in the Philippines. . . . [T]he implementation of devolution and autonomy has further strengthened my conviction and resolve that local autonomy is indeed the key to development in the countryside."

– Aquilino Q. Pimentel, 2000

"Federalism would be the logical and practical culmination of decentralization and local autonomy. . . . Governance will be improved and corruption will be reduced by the new division of powers and functions between the Federal Government and the States, and by the transparency of governance and its accessibility to the people in the regions, cities, provinces, and municipalities."

– Jose V. Abueva, Citizens' Movement for a Federal Republic, 2005

* This is a revised and updated version of a chapter first published under the same title in Yuko Kasuya and Nathan Quimpo, eds., *The Politics of Change in the Philippines* (Manila: Anvil Press, 2010). Reprinted with permission. The author gratefully acknowledges the generous research support of the U.S. Department of Education Fulbright-Hays Faculty Research Abroad Program (in 2003) and the Asia Research Institute of the National University of Singapore (in 2004). Thanks also to those who provided comments at a November 2009 conference of Keio University (where this analysis was first presented) and a March 2011 conference of the Pan-Asia Institute at Indiana University. Allison Ley and Thuy Thu Pham of the Australian National University (ANU) provided valuable editorial and research assistance. All errors, of course, are mine alone.

[1] Interview Binamira, March 11, 2003.

At several points over the past half century in the Philippines, frustration with pervasive patronage politics has prompted a range of localist strategies of reform: barrio-level community development programs (beginning in the 1950s), laws on local autonomy and decentralization (passed in 1959, 1967, and 1991), and more recent proposals for a shift from unitary to federal government. In each case, advocates of these strategies frequently view national-level politics as a hopeless morass of corruption, and propose instead to fight patronage and redeem the country's political system by giving more attention to the local level and/or more authority to local officials. Through examination of the thoroughly interwoven character of patronage structures, from the national to the local level, this chapter asserts that a false dichotomy is often drawn between the character of national and local politics. This dichotomy is common not only in Philippine political discourse, but also in much of the scholarly literature on decentralization.[2] Although localist strategies of reform in the Philippines have an important impact on the distribution of patronage, they have not proven effective in curbing the system of patronage politics as a whole. In order to develop a successful strategy for undermining the patronage system, one must first move beyond simplistic dichotomies. Because the patronage system is nationwide in scope, the most effective strategies of reform are those that are national in character – encompassing the entire, interconnected system of governance as it is based in the center and extends outward to the localities.[3]

This analysis begins with a brief overview of the highly dispersed nature of power within the modern Philippine state as it has emerged since the American colonial era. Through a process that I have termed *patronage-based state formation*, substantial administrative functions

---

[2] For a critique of this more general tendency, *see* Paul D. Hutchcroft, "Centralization and Decentralization in Administration and Politics: Assessing Territorial Dimensions of Authority and Power," *Governance* 14, no. 1 (January 2001): 42–45.

[3] A foundational definition of patronage can be found deep in the footnotes of Martin Shefter, *Political Parties and the State: The American Historical Experience* (Princeton: Princeton University Press, 1994): "Patronage ... involves the exchange of public benefits for political support or party advantage" and is given out by politicians to "individual voters, campaign workers, or contributors." It is a benefit that is "divisible" (i.e., particularistic) rather than "collective" in nature. Ibid., 283. Elsewhere, Shefter associates "collective" with orientation to public policies and/or ideology. Ibid., 23. The definition should be amended to reflect the fact that politicians can give huge quantities of patronage to other politicians, e.g., pork-barrel funds provided to national legislators and local politicians.

have long been effectively subcontracted to local politicians throughout the archipelago. For reasons that I will explain, the patronage-based
state endures to the present, despite historical junctures at which it might
have evolved into another type of state. Section II examines how this
system of governance has broad impacts on national cohesion, governance, and democracy. The negative impacts of patronage-based state
formation have engendered a broad array of reform efforts, including, of most importance to this analysis, localist strategies. Section III
details the specific localist strategies that have been attempted from the
Magsaysay years in the 1950s to the present, and demonstrates their
notable lack of success in curbing the basic problem of patronage. In
terms of the standard dichotomy, the interests of "imperial Manila" –
the national capital and by far the largest urban metropolis – have
often been counterposed against the imperatives of rural development
and/or the virtues of bringing governance closer to people. In the first
decade of the new century, prominent scandals have given new attention
to the role of illegal activities within the extensive patronage linkages
between national and local politicians. The horrific Maguindanao massacre of November 2009 demonstrated, in the extreme, the potential
of these linkages to foster local authoritarian enclaves with high levels of coercive capacity. Section IV briefly surveys recent proposals for
reform, both from citizens' groups and national-level political reformers. It concludes by highlighting the primary policy recommendation
that comes forth from this analysis, and that is to caution future political reform advocates against excessive reliance on localist strategies of
change.

THE ORIGINS OF PATRONAGE-BASED STATE FORMATION

The modern Philippine state can trace its origins to the early American
colonial period, specifically to the leadership of William Howard Taft,
who between 1900 and 1913 (first as Philippine governor-general, then
U.S. secretary of war, and later U.S. president) played a central role in
constructing a new polity – building on the residual architecture of the
previous Spanish colonial state and responding to a major revolutionary
challenge from supporters of Philippine independence.[4] Four policies, in

[4] This analysis draws on Paul D. Hutchcroft, "Colonial Masters, National Politicos, and Provincial Lords: Central Authority and Local Autonomy in the American

particular, helped nurture the territorial dispersal of power throughout the archipelago as well as strong patronage ties linking the national and the local. As will be explained further, the sum total is a process that can be characterized as patronage-based state formation.

First and most obviously, Taft and other architects of American colonial rule arrived in the Philippines with a clear desire to promote as much local autonomy as possible (central intervention in local affairs "is foreign to American practice," declared one early report). With fond reference to New England, Taft proclaimed "town government" to be "the practical way of building up a general government."[5] This involved the systematic organization of municipal elections (restricted to a small elite electorate) in 1901 and the election of provincial governors (by municipal officials) in 1902. In promoting local arenas of political endeavor, American colonials were motivated both out of expediency (seeking to undercut elite support for the guerrilla struggle for Philippine independence) and ideals (replicating the spirit of local self-rule practiced at home). In essence, Taft's so-called policy of attraction involved providing greatly expanded opportunities for political power to elites who had already developed a strong economic base throughout major regions in the latter decades of the Spanish era.

This inclination toward local autonomy was in sharp contrast to other contemporaneous colonial powers, which commonly employed the very effective technique of prefectoralism to enhance the capacity of the central government to control territory, subdue provincial rivals, and extract revenues and resources. In prefectoral systems, the central government divides up the national territory and appoints a prefect to take control of all major governmental functions within each district. The contrast between the Americans and their colonial counterparts was thus stark: the former were inclined to promote local politics and local politicians, whereas the latter favored central control through the appointment of officials whose loyalties would remain with the center.

Second, the American colonial system also differed from its counterparts in giving far more attention to elections and the creation of representative institutions than to the creation of a modern bureaucratic

Philippines, 1900–1913," *Journal of Asian Studies* 59, no. 2 (May 2000): 277–306; Paul D. Hutchcroft and Joel Rocamora, "Patronage-Based Parties and the Democratic Deficit in the Philippines: Origins, Evolution, and the Imperatives of Reform," in *Routledge Handbook of Southeast Asian Politics*, ed. Richard Robison (London: Routledge, 2012), pp. 97–119.

[5] Quoted in Hutchcroft, *supra* n. 4, 283, 286.

apparatus. As Anderson explains, "unlike all the other modern colonial regimes in twentieth century Southeast Asia, which operated through huge, autocratic, white-run bureaucracies, the American authorities in Manila... created only a minimal civil service, and quickly turned over most of its component positions to the natives."[6] Taft's policy of "political tutelage" involved ever-greater opportunities for Philippine elites to seek electoral office – first at the municipal and provincial levels, as noted, and later in the National Assembly and Senate (formed in 1907 and 1916, respectively). Taft did not neglect the goal of constructing a reliable civil service, but, for reasons of historical timing, the effort failed. Because representative institutions in the Philippines emerged before the creation of strong bureaucratic institutions, it was easy for patronage-hungry politicos to overwhelm the nascent administrative agencies of the colonial state.[7]

The centrality of patronage was soon apparent in the sphere of territorial politics, when the initial inclination for local autonomy had by 1903 given way to an increasing American desire to promote better performance and curb corruption among local politicians. More often than not, however, these efforts were frustrated and decentralized patterns of power predominated. Although there were changes in formal administrative procedures seeking to promote greater centralization, key Manila bureaus were unable to provide effective supervision because of both the high rates of turnover in bureaucratic personnel and the resistance of increasingly powerful national legislators (who were, in turn, promoting the interests of political allies in their home provinces).[8] Whereas other colonial powers generally set up strong interior (or home affairs) ministries, with the clear goal of promoting administrative control of the territory, the U.S. colonials in the Philippines had only a weak Executive Bureau with little institutional continuity over time.

---

[6] Benedict Anderson, "Cacique Democracy and the Philippines: Origins and Dreams," *New Left Review* 169 (1988): 11.

[7] See Shefter, *Political Parties and the State, supra* n. 3, who explains that the historical timing of the creation of modern bureaucracies and the emergence of mass political participation is of critical importance in determining the relative strengths of a "constituency for bureaucratic autonomy" versus a "constituency for patronage."

[8] Anderson, "Cacique Democracy and the Philippines," *supra* n. 5, 12, gives emphasis to the "the huge proliferation of provincial and local elective offices – in the absence of an autocratic territorial bureaucracy. From very early on mestizo caciques understood that these offices, in the right hands, could consolidate their local political fiefdoms. Not unexpectedly, the right hands were those of family and friends. Brothers, uncles, and cousins for the senior posts, sons and nephews for the junior ones."

Third, Taft actively promoted the rise of provincial politicians, who came to have an enormously powerful role on the national stage. His initial strategy, beginning in 1900, had been to support a group of Manila notables, organized within the Partido Federal, through access to central government patronage and appointments. By 1905, however, Taft instructed his colonial officials to look to provincial governors for a new group of Filipino leaders in order to "strengthen your hold on the entire archipelago."[9] The two leading provincial governors to emerge, Sergio Osmeña of Cebu and Manuel Quezon of Tayabas, had been quick to see that it was possible to combine a provincial base with access to national power. They were the major figures in the newly formed Nacionalista Party (NP), a purportedly pro-independence party that was to dominate Philippine politics for much of the next four decades. Along with the other provincial elites-turned-national politicos who were elected to the National Assembly in 1907, they very deftly responded to the new opportunities created by American colonials and achieved a level of political authority able to obstruct the goals of the U.S. governor-general.[10] The interaction of elites in the new political institutions in Manila led to the emergence of what Anderson calls a "solid, visible 'national oligarchy.'"[11]

Fourth, political party formation is not a normal activity for most colonial masters, but in the Philippines Taft considered it an important element of his larger project of "political education." Not surprisingly, these political parties had many similarities to the patronage-based party system from which Taft, the highly successful Ohio politician, had emerged. At times, the promotion of patronage was a very conscious policy, as when Taft granted special privileges and resources to the Partido Federal, whose growth he wanted to nurture. More important, however, was how the creation of legislative institutions generated the logic of patronage at a point when bureaucratic structures had barely had a chance to consolidate their strength. Unlike political parties in most of the colonial world, which were excluded from the corridors of power as they pressed for the goal of national independence, the NP enjoyed ready access to patronage resources and increasing influence over appointments within the

[9] Ruby R. Paredes, "The Origins of National Politics: Taft and the Partido Federal," in *Philippine Colonial Democracy*, ed. Ruby R. Paredes (Haven: Yale University Southeast Asia Studies 1989), 60.

[10] Michael Cullinane, *Ilustrado Politics: Filipino Elite Responses to American Rule, 1898–1908* (Quezon City: Ateneo de Manila University Press, 2003).

[11] Anderson, "Cacique Democracy and the Philippines," *supra* n. 5, 11.

bureaucracy.[12] The patronage basis of Philippine political parties, which can be traced to the early American period and endures until present, reinforces the territorial dispersal of power throughout the archipelago. As in other settings in which democratic structures are infused with a strong element of patronage, there are many informal avenues for the promotion of local interests and the diminution of central supervisory structure. In the late nineteenth-century U.S. political system that had shaped Taft, patronage-based parties promoted the "broad dispersion of particularistic benefits downward to the localities."[13] In the decades after the 1870 unification of modern Italy, similarly, patronage practices "allowed local elites and national deputies to bargain for local interests against national directives in return for electoral and parliamentary support. Political channels to the center were more important than administrative channels, but in either case the link to the center remained crucial."[14]

In sum, four policies of the Taft era led to a pronounced dispersal of power throughout the archipelago combined with strong patronage linkages between national and local levels: the promotion of local autonomy, greater attention to elections and legislative institutions than to the creation of a modern bureaucratic apparatus, the nurturing of provincial politicians, and the emergence of patronage-based political parties. Together, these factors constitute a process of patronage-based state formation. Defined more formally, this type of state formation (a) occurs within settings that lack strong political institutions, notably effective bureaucracies and/or well-institutionalized political parties; (b) devolves important elements of state administrative functions to local power holders throughout the country; and (c) displays high levels of interconnectedness among the different territorial layers of government via a patronage system that has its apex in the national capital.[15]

---

[12] This analysis draws on Shefter's distinction between "internally mobilized" and "externally mobilized" parties. The NP are in the former category, defined as parties "founded by elites who occupy positions within the prevailing regime and who undertake to mobilize a popular following behind themselves in an effort either to gain control of the government or to secure their hold over it." *See* Shefter, *Political Parties and the State,* supra n. 3, 29–36, quote at 30; *see also* his specific analysis of the NP. Ibid., 23.

[13] Stephen Skowronek, *Building a New American State: The Expansion of National Administrative Capacities, 1877–1920* (Cambridge: Cambridge University Press, 1982), 39.

[14] Robert D. Putnam, *Making Democracy Work: Civic Traditions in Modern Italy* (Princeton: Princeton University Press, 1993), 19.

[15] Although fuller comparative analysis is beyond the scope of this chapter, brief comments can provide further illustration. Strong elements of patronage exist in a range of political

The creation of the patronage-based state in the early twentieth-century Philippines was also very much a joint, compromise venture of both American colonials and Filipino collaborators.[16] But Taft's brand of compromise was clearly motivated not only by expediency but also by ideals. Unlike the rulers of centralizing colonial (and colonial-era) states elsewhere in Southeast Asia, he did not share the same telos of overcoming competing centers of local power and achieving larger degrees of autonomy from (and dominance over) civil society. He and other architects of the new colonial polity were, instead, acting out of distinctly American notions of what a state should be, specifically strong Jeffersonian biases in favor of decentralized governance and limitations on governmental authority.[17]

The patronage-based state remains in place today, and its origins can be traced to the Taft era. Before proceeding, however, it must be emphasized that I am not making an argument based on historical determinism; in other words, it was by no means inevitable that the patronage-based state endure over the past century. There are several historical junctures at which it could have been displaced, of which I will briefly highlight four. First, there are of course diverse strands of political thought within the American tradition – as evidenced by ongoing tensions regarding central control versus states' rights since the founding of the republic (i.e., the Jeffersonian tradition versus the Hamiltonian tradition carried forth in latter years by Abraham Lincoln and Franklin Roosevelt). Colonial

---

systems, but the term *patronage-based state formation* is reserved for those with weak political institutions. To give two examples: Japan and Malaysia each display high levels of patronage flows, but neither should be characterized as a patronage-based state. Administrative channels are at least as important as political channels in linking the capital to the lower levels of government, and patronage flows have historically been dominated by long-standing and well-institutionalized ruling parties. These issues are explored more fully in Paul D. Hutchcroft, forthcoming, "Linking Capital and Countryside: Patronage and Clientelism in Japan, Thailand, and the Philippines," in *Political Clientelism, Social Policies, and the Quality of Democracy*, eds. Diego Abente Brun and Larry Diamond (Baltimore: Johns Hopkins University Press, 2014).

[16] The devolution of administration functions that comes forth from patronage-based state formation has an important analogue in the revenue sphere, specifically in the system of tax farming found in many eighteenth- and nineteenth-century colonial and colonial-era states, including the Netherlands East Indies, British Malaya, and Siam. *See* my earlier version of this analysis in Yuko Kasuya and Nathan Quimpo, eds., *The Politics of Change in the Philippines* (Manila: Anvil Press, 2010), 426–27.

[17] *See* Paul D. Hutchcroft, "The Hazards of Jeffersonianism: Challenges of State Building in the U.S. and Its Empire," in *Colonial Crucible: Empire in the Making of a Modern American State*, eds. Alfred W. McCoy and Francisco Scarano (Madison: University of Wisconsin Press, 2009).

state formation in the Philippines began just as what Skowronek calls a "new American state" was emerging at home; this process of state reformation involved "new national administrative institutions... free from the clutches of party domination, direct court supervision, and localistic orientations."[18] The reformed U.S. state was not, however, the state that was exported to the new colony in the Philippines. Because the major builders of the colonial state were – by the standards of the day – conservatives rather than reformers or progressives, the major political and bureaucratic reform impulses of the metropole were generally not replicated in Manila.[19] Second, Manuel L. Quezon secured largely uncontested executive authority for himself when he assumed the presidency of the Philippine Commonwealth in 1935. Although he had broad powers of supervision over local governments, and effectively controlled a supine unicameral legislature, he was more interested in centralizing control over patronage resources than building more effective institutions of central government supervision. Third, there was an impulse toward administrative centralization during the Japanese Occupation of 1942–1945, when a ministry of home affairs was put into place. Because Japanese control was challenged in much of the archipelago by other forces, however, these efforts did not get off the ground. Fourth, there were important elements of centralization during the martial-law regime of President Ferdinand Marcos (1972–1986), as will be further discussed. Like Quezon, however, he was more interested in centralizing patronage resources than in centralizing administrative structures.

In sum, a patronage-based polity endures despite multiple historical junctures in which it might have been transformed in other directions. It remains in place across the quarter century since the fall of Marcos in 1986 – albeit with many innovations reflecting the far more complex character of Philippine society, economy, and politics.[20] Although Taft would likely not recognize what has come forth, we can in hindsight trace the evolution of the modern Philippine polity to the process of patronage-based state formation that he set in train more than one century ago. Section II traces the impact of patronage-based state formation on national cohesion, structures of governance, and quality of democracy.

---

[18] Skowronek, *Building a New American State*, *supra* n. 12, 15.

[19] Glenn A. May, *Social Engineering in the Philippines: The Aims, Execution, and Impact of American Colonial Policy, 1900–1913* (Westport, CT: Greenwood Press, 1980), xviii; Frank Hindman Golay, *Face of Empire: United States Philippines Relations, 1898–1946* (Madison: Center for Southeast Asian Studies, University of Wisconsin, 1998), 63.

[20] Hutchcroft and Rocamora, "Patronage-Based Parties," *supra* n. 4.

THE IMPACT OF PATRONAGE-BASED STATE FORMATION

The tone of the analysis thus far may suggest that patronage-based state formation has entirely negative outcomes; there is, in fact, at least one major advantage that must be emphasized. Systems of patronage can be very effective in binding a country together, providing a kind of glue that orients elites of diverse ethnolinguistic heritage in different regions to look to the center for resources. As Scott observed four decades ago, "material self-interest" provided by patronage resources can provide "the necessary political cement" to forge coalitions – particularly in the absence of "a traditional governing elite... [or] a ruling group based on ideological or class interest."[21] In the Philippines, this is best exemplified at the sociocultural margins of the polity in Muslim Mindanao. Abinales traces the late colonial "transformation of Muslim datus from Malay men of prowess into provincial politicians," eventually becoming "Muslim counterparts to the northern caciques." By the early postindependence years, "[a]ll leading Mindanao strong men allied themselves with one of the two [national political] parties.... Many Mindanao leaders attained national prominence via the decentralized structure of national politics, representing one more provincial bloc or network of clans in Congress. *Benefits derived from state access were the main draw for many who ran for office.*" As patronage structures oriented local leaders toward Manila and the resources that it could provide, the frontier of southern Mindanao was "rendered governable" by the "interlacing" of state and society.[22]

The integrative qualities of the Philippine polity are given further emphasis by Landé in the conclusion to his classic 1965 study. After acknowledging that the "system of identical parties" produces a "lack of real choice" for voters, he proceeds to highlight its "important... contribution to national unity":

> The rivalry of parties at election time does not, as it does in some countries, become an occasion for the clash of interests and the exacerbation of hostility between diverse regions and social classes. On the contrary, this is the time when each party, fearing that its rival might deprive it of its

---

[21] James C. Scott, "Corruption, Machine Politics, and Political Change," *American Political Science Review* 63, no. 4 (December 1969): 1151.

[22] Patricio N. Abinales, *Making Mindanao: Cotabato and Davao in the Formation of the Philippine Nation-State* (Quezon City: Ateneo de Manila University Press, 2000), 67, 130, 184 (emphasis added).

supporters in some important region or among some influential group, will go to great lengths to match or outdo the opposite party in catering to every region and every group.[23]

The major disadvantages of patronage-based state formation become clear when analysis shifts to the character of governance structures and democracy. First, farming out the tasks of administration brings huge compromises in the *quality of governance* as local politicians are both acting on behalf of the state and on behalf of their own political (and financial) interests. Some exhibit devotion to public goals, but others find private goals more compelling. Landé, in his analysis of politics in the 1960s, observes that the "power of petty politicians" stems from their influence over local voters: "The consequence in terms of substantive government policy is that to a very considerable degree the national leadership in the Philippines must defer to the consensus among local politicians throughout the country." (This is balanced, he immediately adds, by the power that national leaders derive "from the great quantity of material rewards at their disposal"; these dynamics lead to significant shifts in the relative power of local and national at different points in the electoral cycle.[24])

In his analysis of state-society relations in Mindanao in the early postindependence years, Abinales explains that "the parameters of governance are negotiated and determined." Local strong men "exemplified the administrative capability of this political fusion by their respective roles as strongmen and state actors, here defending their local turf, there executing imperatives of state on their constituencies."[25] This process of negotiation and mutual bargaining has continued into more recent years, leading to both frequent abuse of local office and inattention to the basic needs of constituents. Sidel's analysis of Cavite, a province close to

---

[23] Carl H. Landé, *Leaders, Factions, and Parties: The Structure of Philippine Politics* (New Haven: Yale University Southeast Asian Studies, 1965), 119; *see also* ibid., 38 and 40, where he explains how the "truly nationwide" parties "[exert] a unifying influence by bringing together within each party politicians from all of the islands, whose diverse constituencies include voters representing every type of crop, industry, and linguistic or religious minority." Landé's focus on patron-client relationships should not be confused with my own analysis of patronage structures. The former examines a relationship that may or may not exist within the state, whereas the latter focuses on material resources emanating from the state and deployed for political purposes. Patronage may be present in patron-client ties, but it is not an essential element of the relationship. *See* Paul D. Hutchcroft, forthcoming, "Linking Capital and Countryside," *supra* n. 14.

[24] Landé, *Leaders, Factions, and Parties, supra* n. 22, 79, 82–83 (quote at 79).

[25] Abinales, *Making Mindanao, supra* n. 21, 184.

Manila, speaks of "small-town mayors" who since the 1970s have "used their office, control over state-based coercive and economic resources, and links to provincial and national politicians to perpetuate their own local power monopolies in their respective municipalities." Similarly, a 1990s study of Philippine local governance concluded that "the state tends to be more completely captured by the elite on the local level than on the national level."[26]

Second, the *quality of democracy* suffers enormously within a patronage-oriented state. Voters rarely have any clear choice between contending programmatic or ideological perspectives, as competition centers primarily around the disbursement of pork and patronage. To the extent that policy matters, major policy changes are commonly commercialized – purchased outright via pork-barrel allocations to patronage-hungry politicos. While Philippine democracy has major difficulties delivering goods of a public character, those with favorable access to the state have countless means of milking the system for private gain. For ordinary citizens who derive few such benefits, explains economist Emmanuel de Dios, "government is an abstraction, an alienated entity, whose only palpable dimension is the episodic patronage dispensed by bosses and politicians, which merely reinforces the poor's real condition of dependence."[27] Widespread vote buying undermines democratic participation and accountability, and at the end of the day Philippine democracy does strikingly little to give a voice to those who have long suffered under highly inequitable socioeconomic structures.

To a certain extent, many Filipinos may have grown accustomed to patronage-based governance; after all, it is the only system that has existed in the Philippines as far back as anyone can remember. It might be viewed as politics as usual, or as part and parcel of a democratic polity – or even perhaps Philippines-style democracy.[28] When "provincial godfathers"

---

[26] John T. Sidel, *Capital, Coercion, and Crime: Bossism in the Philippines* (Stanford: Stanford University Press, 1999), 24; Terence George, "Local Governance: People Power in the Provinces?" in *Organizing for Democracy: NGOs, Civil Society, and the Philippine State*, eds. G. Sidney Silliman and Lela Garner Noble (Quezon City: Ateneo de Manila University Press, 1998), 247.

[27] Emmanuel S. De Dios and Paul D. Hutchcroft, "Political Economy," in *The Philippine Economy: Development, Policies, and Challenges*, eds. Arsenio Balisacan and Hal Hill (New York: Oxford University Press and Quezon City: Ateneo de Manila University Press, 2003), 65.

[28] Some commentators mistakenly suggest that patronage politics in the Philippines can be explained by innate cultural traits. Although there is indeed a patronage-oriented political culture that has emerged over the past century, the ultimate origins of the

burst onto the national stage in Thailand in the late 1980s and 1990s and "money politics" began to undermine elements of the bureaucracy that had previously been relatively insulated from patronage pressures, many Thais perceived an aberrant and deeply troubling trend that needed to be reformed via the 1997 Constitution (which, despite its flaws and ultimate failure, did have many virtuous features). In the Philippines, by contrast, there is no point in recent history in which patronage-based governance can be viewed as a new or surprising phenomenon.

Even so, there have been many points at which frustrations over bad governance and low-quality democracy have engendered movements for change – for example, calls for cleaner government, promotion of free and fair elections, efforts to curb the pork barrel, and the like. At times, these attempts are part of a crass electoral calculus in which patronage-oriented politicians *out of office* attack the excesses of patronage politics in order to displace patronage-oriented politicians who are *in office*. In many cases across the decades, however, there have been genuine and well-meaning efforts to undercut old styles of politics, improve governance, and provide a stronger foundation for Philippine democracy. One important strand of these efforts has been localist strategies of reform, beginning most significantly with major barrio-level initiatives under President Ramon Magsaysay in the 1950s. Section III examines some of these strategies, placing them within the broader context of central-local relations as they have evolved from the granting of independence in 1946 to present.

LOCALIST STRATEGIES IN THE POSTINDEPENDENCE PHILIPPINES

When democratic structures were reestablished after the war, the Commonwealth's one-party rule was replaced with a two-party system in which patronage resources were dispersed in a far more decentralized manner. The elite had experienced major divisions during the war and now faced a major challenge from below through the mobilization of peasants in the Huk movement.[29] As Abinales has said of Mindanao,

patronage-based polity can be found in the institutional innovations of the American colonial regime of the early twentieth century. For a fuller analysis of the long-standing recourse to cultural explanations, which commonly blame some combination of Spanish and Malay customs, *see* Hutchcroft, "Colonial Masters," *supra* n. 4, 297–98.

[29] This movement originated during the war as the *Hukbo ng Bayan laban sa mga Hapon* (the People's Anti-Japanese Army) or *Hukbalahap*. After avenues for parliamentary struggle were closed off in the immediate postwar years, the Huks reorganized as a

one can say of the entire country: "World War II halted Quezon's centralizing streak" and presented opportunities for the "reinvigoration" of local power.[30] Although "loose firearms" had already been considered a problem in the colonial period, the country became awash in guns during the Japanese Occupation – with many now in the hands of the "new men" who had emerged in the course of a highly decentralized guerrilla struggle. Compared to the immediate prewar years, politicians in the provinces were in a much stronger position relative to those at the center.

As a result of its distinctive American colonial heritage, the Philippines in the initial decades after independence displayed a complex web of central-local ties in which Manila could seem to be at once overlord and lorded over. Certain aspects of central-local relations were highly centralized: even the most trifling of administrative decisions had to be approved in Manila, and many local and provincial authorities chafed at restrictions on their autonomy. At the same time, Manila displayed weak capacity for sustained supervision of provincial and local officials – and national politicians commonly relied heavily on local power (and the brokering of arrangements with local bosses and their private armies) in order to succeed in electoral contests. As in colonial years, moreover, mayors enjoyed considerable control over local police forces, and the heightened postwar prevalence of guns fostered "warlord" armies that were especially active at election time. Local leaders delivered blocs of votes in exchange for benefits from allies in Manila, while "national" politics itself was often dominated by the need of congresspersons to consolidate local bailiwicks (through such means as rampant pork-barrel spending). Central supervision of local governments was almost entirely ad hoc, oriented to punishing political opponents while providing political allies with effective autonomy. Both local police and the national Philippine Constabulary were highly politicized, frequently deployed in electoral battles on behalf of those who controlled them.

Despite repression from both the state and landlords, the Huks continued to gain strength, and by the end of the 1940s it seemed that the center would not hold. As Frank Golay explains:

> peasant-based guerrilla army that challenged landlords in the countryside (most of all in Central Luzon) and came to be viewed as a major threat to the national government in Manila. *See* Benedict J. Kerkvliet, *The Huk Rebellion: A Study of Peasant Revolt in the Philippines* (Berkeley: University of California Press, 1977).
> [30] Abinales, *Making Mindanao, supra* n. 21, 66.

The government seemed willing to let the military go unpaid and the educational system wither for want of funds, and even to succumb to the Huk rebellion, rather than face up to minimum responsibility for governmental functions. . . . [There was] mounting evidence that the body politic was incapable of action in the interests of all Filipinos. It is a depressing commentary that the reforms, when they did come, were to a considerable extent installed from the outside as a result of [a U.S. mission that] . . . made far-reaching recommendations in the areas of fiscal policy, agricultural development, and social and administrative reform.[31]

The United States perceived a particular deterioration of conditions during the administration of President Elpidio Quirino (1948–1953), and actively supported Ramon Magsaysay in the elections of 1953. Under Magsaysay (1953–1957), a combination of populist counterinsurgency strategy and frustration with national-level corruption led to a "focus on the barrio" and on governance that emanates from the rural grassroots.[32] A central element of this strategy was the formation of the Presidential Assistant for Community Development (PACD), which enlisted a corps of idealistic volunteers to promote barrio-level rural development programs throughout the country. As indicated by the opening epigraph to this chapter (quoting a 2003 interview with PACD founder Ramon Binamira), theirs was nothing less than a missionary zeal. PACD was to "involve people in their own development," Binamira explained.[33] At the national level, his goal was to create a new kind of bureaucracy "that would manage without regard to politics" (2003); within PACD, he proclaimed two ostensibly anti-patronage policies: recruitment of field workers "through a civil service examination and not through political recommendations" and "refusing to use community development as a tool for partisan activity since this would certainly kill community spirit."[34]

---

[31] Frank Hindman Golay, *The Philippines: Public Policy and National Economic Development* (Ithaca: Cornell University Press, 1961), 71–72, 80.

[32] To quote the title of an important volume recording the spirit of the times: Jose V. Abueva, *Focus on the Barrio: The Story Behind the Birth of the Philippine Community Development Program Under President Ramon Magsaysay* (Manila: University of the Philippines Institute of Public Administration, 1959).

[33] Interview Binamira, 2003. Similarly, in the words of a 1957 Presidential Assistant for Community Development report, "Annual Report of the Presidential Assistant on Community Development, July 1, 1956–June 30, 1957," 5: "The main motive force for [implementing community development] should come from the barrio people themselves."

[34] Ramon P. Binamira, "There is Progress in Rural Development" (No publisher; typewritten report, 1957?), 3–4.

PACD did promote change in Philippine politics, but one must question the degree to which it initiated the level-by-level "clean up" of government to which Binamira aspired. The presidential assistant was a highly political position, appointed by the president, and through PACD the Presidential Palace gained a new means of extending patronage support to allies in rural barrios (the lowest level of Philippine governance, where the vast bulk of the voters resided), thereby bypassing as necessary any governors or mayors who may have been political rivals.[35] But for all the focus on the barrio, one contemporary analyst pointed out, the use of national funds and the national-level appointment of personnel "gives a national orientation to the program, and thus continues to foster the people's tendency to look to Manila for all kinds of assistance."[36] Through PACD, there was a new discourse in Philippine politics: according to another contemporary observer, "phrases such as 'community development'... have become potential weapons in the arsenal of politics."[37] Whereas one ostensible purpose of PACD was to curb patronage politics, the end result was in fact the integration of the barrios more effectively into electoral politics as well as into patronage networks that extended from the Presidential Palace in Manila to the furthest reaches of the archipelago. Viewing his achievements many decades later, Binamira asserted that "we changed the politics of this country." After the creation of PACD, "no person ever got elected... without the support of the barrio."

Localist strategies continued in later administrations, after the untimely death of Magsaysay in a March 1957 plane crash. Binamira stayed on as presidential assistant under President Carlos Garcia, whose weaker political stature encouraged particular reliance on the electoral advantage that could come from PACD (indeed, the name of the

[35] In the 2003 interview, Binamira tended to describe governors and mayors who supported PACD as "officials" and those who opposed PACD as "politicians." On the one hand, many barrio, municipal, and provincial "officials" were "reoriented"; on the other, he proudly declared, "We fought the politicians. We could defeat a congressman with PACD."

[36] L. C. Mariano, "Legislative Reform: An Analysis of Current Proposals," *Philippine Journal of Public Administration* 3, no. 1 (1959): 67. Political scientist Jose Abueva, the major chronicler of PACD, explained in an interview that the philosophy of the organization was "aided self-help." Pressed on whether this may be a new form of patronage politics, he spoke of PACD as a kind of "matching patronage." Although "classic patronage is one way," he further stated, aided self-help is a "bargain" in which "people provided their time and local resources" (Interview Abueva, 2003).

[37] Buenaventura M. Villanueva, "The Community Development Program of the Philippine Government," *Philippine Journal of Public Administration* 1, no. 2 (April 1957): 150.

president was directly attached to community development projects in barrios throughout the land).[38] Attention soon turned to the more formal organization of barrio governance, which had previously been a hodgepodge of arrangements centering around a barrio lieutenant (the counterpart of today's barangay captain) who was sometimes elected but more generally appointed by the mayor.[39] Earlier in the decade, in 1955, a law had established elective barrio councils.[40] Binamira worked with Senator Emmanuel Palaez of Mindanao to secure the passage of the Barrio Charter of 1959, which gave barrios formal legal status along with the rights to impose limited taxes and enact ordinances. It was revised in 1963, in part through the efforts of Senator Manuel P. Manahan, a former aide to President Magsaysay, who had long expressed the belief that the barrio was "the solid base of nation-building" and barrio home rule was "the only way to balance the distribution of power between the government and the masses."[41] Through these acts, new local elective positions were added to a political system already notable for the proliferation of such posts. The barrio lieutenant became a uniformly elective post, and provisions were put in place for the election of a six-member barrio council. In the initial years, PACD administered the electoral process.[42]

While Binamira and Manahan may have anticipated popular empowerment, the greater impact was instead a deepening of the connection of the barrio to national politics and an increased appetite for patronage resources at the basis of the political system. "For a decade after 1956," reports Wurfel, "more than P100 million of U.S. and Philippine government funds poured into the community development program.... The barrio lieutenant became a political figure with whom bigger politicians dealt and often the backbone of the mayor's following."[43] In his 1971 analysis of new patterns in Philippine local politics, based on

---

[38] Interview Abueva, 2003.

[39] John H. Romani and M. Ladd Thomas, *A Survey of Local Government in the Philippines* (Manila: University of the Philippines Institute of Public Administration, 1954).

[40] Buenaventura M. Villanueva, "Some Unsettling Questions in Philippine Local Government," *Philippine Journal of Public Administration* 5, no. 3 (1961): 341.

[41] Manahan is quoted in *Manila Times*, November 19, 1958, and February 24, 1959, respectively. Information also drawn from interview Binamira, 2003; Jose V. Abueva, "Bridging the Gap Between the Elite and the People in the Philippines," *Philippine Journal of Public Administration* 8, no. 4 (1964): 341. On the provisions of the act, see Jean Grossholtz, *Politics in the Philippines* (Boston: Little, Brown, and Company, 1964), 130–31.

[42] Abueva, "Bridging the Gap," *supra* n. 39, 341.

[43] David Wurfel, *Filipino Politics: Development and Decay* (Ithaca: Cornell University Press and Quezon City: Ateneo de Manila University Press, 1988), 91.

research in six localities in Luzon and the Visayas, Machado observed
that the head of the barrio had increasingly become

> the man with the best access to outside resources, which in most . . . cases
> means best access to the town Mayor. In a competitive situation, such
> access will be a critical factor in determining who is elected. And if a Mayor
> chooses to keep a barrio non-competitive or to influence the outcome of
> the competition, he will usually have to be fairly generous in channeling
> resources through his choice for Barrio Captain.[44]

Along with attention to the barrio level, a 1959 Local Autonomy Law
gave the provinces and chartered cities greater control over fiscal affairs,
planning, and personnel administration. Villanueva credits "the clamor
of local chief executives and the progressive outlook" of a group of
young senators for passage of the measure, but quickly denounces it as
"at best a misnomer and at worst pretentious." Local officials still had
major restrictions on personnel administration and budget autonomy, he
argues, and weak taxing powers.[45] The rhetoric of the 1960s shifted from
local autonomy to decentralization, a concept that came to be regarded
as a "talisman"; some desired to make local governments more effective,
whereas others saw decentralization merely as a way to cut governors and
mayors into a "patronage game" long dominated by the president and
Congress.[46] "Stripped of all its legal niceties," writes Villanueva, "decentralizing some functional areas to local divisional units actually meant
giving patronage 'to the governors and mayors [who] would be authorized to appoint the officials within their authority.'"[47] Indeed, political
competition played a huge role in controversies over various decentralization bills. One measure, introduced in Congress in 1965 and endorsed by

---

[44] K. G. Machado, "Changing Aspects of Factionalism in Philippine Local Politics," *Asian Survey* 11, no. 12 (December 1971): 1194.

[45] A. B. Villanueva, "Decentralization and Executive-Legislative Relations in the Philip-pines, 1961–1967," *Modern Asian Studies* 12, no. 3 (1978): 379; *see also* Raul P. de Guzman, "Philippine Local Government: Issues, Problems and Trends," *Philippine Journal of Public Administration* 10, no. 2–3 (1966): 235.

[46] Villanueva, "Decentralization and Executive-Legislative Relations," *supra* n. 43, 377–389, quotes at 378 and 379. This leaves aside the irony of the Philippines embarking on a plan for decentralization in the absence of any comprehensive historical process of centralization. Indeed, one can note some element of truth to the old quip that the only two truly national organizations in the Philippines are the Catholic Church and San Miguel Brewery.

[47] Villanueva, "Decentralization and Executive-Legislative Relations," *supra* n. 43, 387. Internal quote from April 5, 1965, *House Congressional Record*, 2:15.

the Leagues of Provincial Governors and City Mayors, sought to transfer to the provinces and cities responsibility for agricultural extension, rural health, and intermediate-level education. President Ferdinand Marcos vetoed the bill in 1967, arguing that it would transfer responsibilities best performed by the national government. Critics charged, however, that Marcos killed the bill because both its supporters and many of its beneficiaries were his political opponents.[48]

Later in the same year, Marcos and Congress did agree on a Decentralization Act that introduced four major changes. First, in the areas of agricultural extension, the provinces and cities were to supplement the activities of the national government. Second, "National approval over a number of local actions was removed." Third, provinces were given larger allocations of national revenues. And fourth, governors rather than the president were given the power to appoint the provincial assessor and agriculturalist.[49] Nevertheless, the 1967 act, like the 1959 act before it, was "saddled with many restrictions, to the extent that the powers that were supposedly granted became at best restrictive and at worst inoperative."[50] To the extent that decentralization entailed sharing the disbursement of patronage resources with governors and other possible rivals, it is not surprising that both the President and members of Congress were often less than generous.

Meanwhile, under Marcos's leadership the patronage potential of PACD was turned to full throttle and used as a well-tuned vehicle for presidential intervention in local politics. As Doronila explains, Marcos used the organization to "[distribute] cash or largesse directly to municipal officials and barrio captains."[51] Headed by the consummate young politico (later senator) Ernesto Maceda, PACD very boldly proclaimed its ties to the President. One PACD brochure, published soon after Marcos was first elected in 1965, had a cover that said "FM [Ferdinand Marcos]: New Patron of Community Development."[52] After Marcos's unprecedented re-election, in 1969, a PACD newsletter was unabashed

---

[48] Villanueva, "Decentralization and Executive-Legislative Relations," *supra* n. 43, 380–81.

[49] Raul P. de Guzman, Mila A. Reforma, and Elena M. Panganiban, "Local Government," in *Government and Politics of the Philippines*, eds. de Guzman and Reforma (Singapore: Oxford University Press, 1988), 213.

[50] Villanueva, "Decentralization and Executive-Legislative Relations," *supra* n. 43, 386.

[51] Amando Doronila, *The State, Economic Transformation, and Political Change in the Philippines, 1946–1972* (Singapore: Oxford University Press, 1992), 132.

[52] "FM: New Patron of Community Development" (Manila: PACD, n.d. [1966?]).

in self-congratulation: "Call it a 'secret weapon,' but CD [community development] has proved once again that it can do wonders in election contests."[53] According to Abueva, who watched the evolution of PACD since its inception, Maceda "in a very raw way tried to convert it into a grassroots campaign organization." If in the early years of the organization there was tension between patronage and self-help, he noted, by the Marcos years one can say that "patronage really won out."[54]

After Marcos declared martial law in 1972, he faced few constraints and had many new opportunities: major political rivals were jailed or in exile, and his regime enjoyed ample support from the United States and foreign donors. For the first time since Quezon, there were many reforms and policies that both tilted the balance of power back to the center and changed the dynamics of local politics. First, local police forces were brought under national control and so-called loose firearms were collected from private armies and the citizenry as a whole. Second, local elections were suspended, thus making local politicians accountable not to electoral dynamics but rather to Ministry of Local Governments (MLG) officials charged with overseeing appointments and dismissals. Third, fourteen new regional planning bodies were organized to coordinate national development policy at a new supraprovincial level. Fourth, the closure of the national Congress in 1972 meant that provincial governors no longer needed to contend with rival local congresspersons. Their role in infrastructural projects was further enhanced by support from the Provincial Development Assistance Program of the U.S. Agency for International Development. Despite these important changes, however, Marcos restructured but did not overturn the local, familial basis of Philippine politics; as already noted, he resembled Quezon in focusing more on the centralization of patronage resources than the centralization of administrative structures.[55]

As he was systematically dismantling the structures of democracy at the national level, Marcos built the facade of democracy at the local level. Local citizens' assemblies were formed in *barangays* (barrios) throughout the archipelago to be convened – as the top official for local

---

[53] Presidential Assistant for Community Development (PACD), Newsletter, November–December, 1969, 3.

[54] Interview Abueva, 2003.

[55] For broader parallels between Quezon and Marcos, *see* Alfred W. McCoy, "Quezon's Commonwealth: The Emergence of Philippine Authoritarianism," in *Philippine Colonial Democracy*, ed. Ruby R. Paredes (New Haven: Yale University Southeast Asia Studies, 1988).

governments candidly explained – "from time to time when the need to hear its views arises."[56] The 1973 Constitution brought forth the rhetoric of local autonomy but made clear that the focus would be on the lowliest and most non-threatening unit of all: the barrio. Barangay brigades, organized by the regime and touted as elements of participatory democracy, encouraged devotion to Ferdinand and Imelda Marcos (with candlelight rituals in which blindfolded initiates were brought one by one into a tent to learn "the principles they should stand for").[57] The MLG doled out resources to barangay leaders who were loyal to the regime, while those who were not faced the threat of dismissal or punishment.

It was not until 1978 that the regime replaced the closed Congress of pre-martial law days with an Interim National Assembly. In preparation for the 1978 elections, the Marcos regime launched its own ruling party, the Kilusang Bagong Lipunan (New Society Movement, or KBL). The rhetoric of a new society and the emergence of new faces notwithstanding, the old, informal patronage politics of the pre-martial law years remained the fundamental basis of the KBL. Throughout much of the country, politicians flocked to the KBL for the benefits that it could dispense. Local officials, who could be replaced at will by the regime, were particularly anxious to join the ruling party. (The head of the KBL, not coincidentally, was simultaneously the Minister of Local Governments.) Three major cronies of Marcos became regional party chairmen, tasked with ensuring KBL victory and at the same time given the opportunity to achieve political dominance over other power holders in their respective regions of the country. The patronage dispensed by this political machine was an important bulwark for the regime, complementing its elaboration of hollow democratic structures and extensive use of coercion.

Since the fall of Marcos, amid the massive "People Power" uprising on the streets of Manila in 1986, many patterns of pre-martial law politics have returned. The reopening of Congress marked the return of democratic institutions after nearly fifteen years of highly repressive and crony-infested authoritarianism; at the same time, however, it has given many old provincial dynasties new opportunities to reassert their influence over national politics. As in the pre-martial law era, political parties have remained weak and poorly institutionalized, more oriented toward

[56] Jose A. Roño, Interview, "DLGCD Focuses on Development Strategy for Local Government," *Local Government Bulletin* 8, no. 1 (January–February 1973): 3.

[57] Interview Victor Sumulong, Philippine House of Representatives, Quezon City, December 9, 2003. (From 1975 to 1985, Sumulong served as assistant secretary for what became the Ministry for Local Governments.)

the pork barrel than toward programmatic appeals. In 1991, a highly respected election commissioner estimated that enough illegal weapons had been smuggled into the country during the previous five years to supply two additional national armies.[58]

The often beleaguered administration of Corazon Aquino showed itself highly accommodating to local power in the provinces (including many so-called warlord figures associated with the previous regime) and very responsive as well to long-standing sentiment in favor of providing more authority to local government units: provinces, cities, municipalities, and barangays. In part out of a strong reaction against previous authoritarian excesses, the 1986 Constitution promised these units "local autonomy," "a system of decentralization," and "a just share . . . in the national taxes which shall be automatically released to them."[59] In addition, it had distinct provisions for autonomous regions in Muslim Mindanao and the upland Cordillera region of northern Luzon.[60]

As part of the emergency powers that she assumed in the immediate aftermath of the fall of Marcos in late February 1986, President Aquino's administration proceeded to appoint officers-in-charge, or OICs, to provincial and municipal posts throughout the country. The immediate concern of administration politicos (most importantly the President's brother, Jose "Peping" Cojuangco) was the creation of a stronger political base throughout the country in advance of the reconvening of Congress in 1987. It was also essential to devote major attention to the January 1988 local elections, which replaced the OICs with elected officials and determined who would continue to control the local political machinery throughout the archipelago.[61]

The most innovative political reform during the Aquino years was the Local Government Code (LGC) of 1991, a decentralization initiative that came forth from the mandate of the 1986 Constitution. Variously lauded

---

[58] Marites Dañguilan-Vitug, "Ballots and Bullets: The Military in Elections," in *1992 and Beyond: Forces and Issues in Philippine Elections*, eds. Lorna Kalaw-Tirol and Sheila S. Coronel (Quezon City: Philippine Center for Investigative Journalism and the Ateneo Center for Social Policy and Public Affairs, 1992), 90–91, quoting COMELEC Commissioner Haydee Yorac.

[59] The 1986 Constitution of the Philippines, Article X, Sections 2, 3, and 6.

[60] The 1986 Constitution of the Philippines, Article X, Sections 15–21.

[61] Several very insightful illustrations of the local dynamics of this process can be found in Benedict J. Kerkvliet and Resil B. Mojares, *From Marcos to Aquino: Local Perspectives on Political Transition in the Philippines* (Quezon City: Ateneo de Manila University Press, 1991).

as "the key to national development"[62] and as a catalyst for greater local democratic participation, the Code gives greater authority and resources to a range of local politicians, some of whom have a genuine agenda of democratic reform (commonly in alliance with civil society organizations) and some of whom seek merely to further entrench their control of local authoritarian enclaves.[63] The most important provision of the Code mandates the central government to provide local units with automatic and greatly increased allotments of internal revenue. The stated goal was to reduce the central government's discretionary power over local governments, and the outcome was a more than quadrupling of transfers (in real terms) between 1991 and 1997.[64] In political terms, this quite obviously strengthened the position of local politicians vis-à-vis congresspersons. Although some may claim that the Code has promoted local autonomy and "radically transformed the very nature of the Philippine political-administrative system,"[65] it can be viewed more cynically as a mere re-slicing of the patronage pie in favor of governors, city mayors, town mayors, and barangay captains.

The passage of the LGC again revealed major competition between congresspersons and local government politicians, and it was only with the support of President Aquino and presidential candidate Ramon Mitra (then Speaker of the House) that the bill became law.[66] Because most congresspersons had political rivals among the governors and mayors in their districts, explains former Speaker Protempore Antonio Cuenco, "it was a natural tendency not to yield powers to these people, who would screw

---

[62] Aquilino Q. Pimentel, *The Local Government Code of 1991: The Key to National Development* (Manila: Cacho Publishing House, 1993).

[63] George neatly summarizes three "particularly striking" elements of the code: increased resources (40% of internal revenue, nearly four times the previous level of 11%), new authority and personnel for local governments (especially in the provision of health services), and enhanced opportunities for popular participation. His four case studies reveal some hopeful signs of "local people power," but he concludes that the LGC "has not been the direct cause of increased civic participation." George, "Local Governance," *supra* n. 25, 248, 250.

[64] Steven Rood, "Decentralization, Democracy, and Development," in *The Philippines: New Directions in Domestic Policy and Foreign Relations*, ed. David G. Timberman (New York: Asia Society, 1998), 118–19.

[65] Aquilino Q. Pimentel, "Pursuing Our Collective Struggle for Local Autonomy: Amending the Local Government Code of 1991" (Opening statements in the Senate Committee hearing on the proposed amendments to the Local Government Code. La Union, August 4, 2000), 1.

[66] *See* Paul D. Hutchcroft, "Paradoxes of Decentralization: The Political Dynamics Behind the Passage of the 1991 Local Government Code of the Philippines," in *KPI Yearbook 2003*, ed. Michael H. Nelson (Bangkok: King Prajadhipok's Institute, 2004).

them." A concern was how increased revenue allotments to local governments would reduce the pork-barrel monies used by congresspersons to build and consolidate their local constituencies. "More money, more power," says Cuenco. "It's that simple." A former President of the League of Cities, Cebu City Mayor Tomas Osmeña, recalled that congresspersons cared little about the issue of decentralization in the abstract, but thought primarily of their rivalries with local officials. Whenever local officials and congresspersons conferred, he says, "the arguments were over money, control over police, and public works."[67] Congresspersons are said to have found decentralization most objectionable when the local officials in their districts were bitter rivals; in some cases, reports Cuenco, congresspersons "were at war with their own relatives... [and] didn't want their brothers to have more power." In other cases, congresspersons enjoyed close ties with officials in their districts, and nurtured plans to run for local office and reap the benefits of the Code.[68]

Another key reform at this time was the 1991 creation of the Philippine National Police, placed under at least the nominal control of a renamed Department of the Interior and Local Governments (DILG).[69] Under President Fidel Ramos (1992–1998), the DILG continued to support decentralization while at the same time seeking (with only limited success) to curb private armies in the countryside. Indeed, many local politicians continued to wield coercive power independently of the central state (even if sometimes nominally on behalf of the state). The worst-ever manifestation of local coercive power led, tragically, into the Maguindanao massacre of November 2009 (as discussed in more detail later in this section).

Although all presidents since Aquino have voiced strong support for the virtues of local autonomy as embodied in the Local Government Code,

---

[67] In the end, the Department of Public Works and Highways was exempted from decentralization. As a central element of congresspersons' pork-barrel spending, it was critical to them that this most important trough of patronage remained under national control. Hill et al. explain that the bulk of the 70,000 bureaucrats devolved from the center to localities were from the Department of Health (65%) and the Department of Agriculture (25%). Hal Hill, Arsenio M. Balisacan, and Sharon Faye A. Piza, "The Philippines and Regional Development," in *The Dynamics of Regional Development: The Philippines in East Asia*, eds. Balisacan and Hill (Quezon City: Ateneo de Manila University Press, 2007), 15.

[68] Interviews, Cuenco and Osmeña, 2000.

[69] *See* Alfred W. McCoy, *Policing America's Empire* (Madison: University of Wisconsin Press, 2009), 450, on the larger context of a "semiformal symbiosis of national police, politicians and jueteng [gambling]."

there have been recurring tensions over the law's guaranteed allotment of 40 percent of all internal revenues to provinces, cities, municipalities, and barangays. This was the most contentious element in the passage of the Code and has turned out to be its most consequential outcome. One can note three major types of tensions related to the internal revenue allotment (IRA). The first is between local politicians and national executives, with occasional efforts since 1998 to make the allocation of the funds less than automatic.[70] Second, already noted, is the tension between local politicians and national legislators, who in response to the LGC sought to regain the advantage by providing themselves with even heftier pork-barrel allocations in the 1990s. A third element of tension is among various layers of local politicians, especially since the formula incorporated into the Code gives a particularly favorable cut to cities relative to other units.[71]

Senator Aquilino Pimentel, often called "the father of the Local Government Code," observes that the IRA is "a lifeblood" of support for the operations of local governments.[72] Indeed, as de Dios points out, "many local government units are almost exclusively reliant on the IRA for financing, treating it basically as a dole."[73] This is a troubling outcome, particularly if one recalls that a central goal of the LGC was to enhance local autonomy. There are two further dysfunctional elements of the IRA, however, that de Dios very clearly articulates. The ready availability of these funds provides "no incentive... either to augment revenues or to use them effectively."[74] In addition, "[a]ssured revenue transfers... have

[70] *See* Rosario G. Manasan, "Decentralization and the Financing of Regional Development," in *The Dynamics of Regional Development: The Philippines in East Asia*, eds. Balisacan and Hill (Quezon City: Ateneo de Manila University Press, 2007), 292. The first case, in 1998, was especially prominent. It was justified on grounds of austerity, amid a fiscal crisis, but successfully challenged before the Supreme Court.

[71] Paul D. Hutchcroft, "Re-Slicing the Pie of Patronage: The Politics of the Internal Revenue Allotment in the Philippines, 1991–2010," *Philippine Review of Economics* 49, no. 1 (June 2012).

[72] Aquilino Q. Pimentel, "Pursuing our Collective Struggle for Local Autonomy: Amending the Local Government Code of 1991," (Manila: Senate, Republic of the Philippines, 2000), xi.

[73] Manasan, "Decentralization and the Financing," *supra* n. 67, 296, provides data on the degree to which the IRA has deepened local government reliance on central resources. From 1992 to 2003, the proportion of income (net of borrowing) derived from the IRA was an astounding 81.3% for provinces (as compared to 38.8% pre-code), 74.1% for municipalities (formerly 38.3%), and 47% for cities (formerly 33.2%).

[74] *See* ibid., 301, for further analysis of revenue disincentives. Additional insights on local government unit (LGU) finances come from Hill et al. "The Philippines," *supra* n. 64: "The widespread perception is that LGU's are invariably controlled by local elites who

not weaned local politics away from the imperative of securing additional resources through typical networks of patronage and vertical transactions with the centre. The patronage relationship remains intact."[75] As with the focus on the barrio in the 1950s and subsequent local autonomy measures in 1959 and 1967, therefore, the LGC has failed as a strategy to undermine patronage. The major outcome of localist strategies to curb patronage politics, we may conclude, is merely to reconfigure the quantity and locus of patronage resources.

The first decade of the new century brought new permutations to the long-standing phenomenon of patronage-based governance in the Philippines. These were years dominated by Gloria Macapagal-Arroyo, who occupied the Presidential Palace from 2001 to 2010 – longer than any president in Philippine history with the exception of Ferdinand Marcos. She first moved from the vice presidency to the presidency in January 2001, when President Joseph Estrada left office amid a "People Power II" uprising in protest against allegations of corruption (including, inter alia, evidence that he was taking protection money from illegal gambling syndicates involving local politicians).[76] Arroyo initially promised to be a champion of anti-corruption efforts, but by mid-2005 had herself became bogged down in corruption charges. In May accusations were made that her husband and son were taking monthly payments from local gambling lords. This had particular resonance because her predecessor had been drummed out of office partly because of similar allegations. Most damaging, however, was the bombshell that hit the headlines in June 2005. This involved the release of tapes of wiretapped conversations that were thought to contain the voice of the President talking to a Commission on Elections (COMELEC) commissioner amid the counting of ballots

are unwilling to tax themselves.... [LGU] financial records are poorly maintained and audited, and lack transparency. Moreover, local governments continue to employ a significant number of 'non-career' staff, an a priori indicator that normal recruitment procedures have been bypassed." According to a 2005 World Bank report cited by Hill et al., 'non-career' staff is 38.6% of local government personnel versus 4.7% of central government personnel. Ibid., 36, 47.

[75] Emmanuel S. De Dios, "Local Politics and Local Economy," in *The Dynamics of Regional Development: The Philippines in East Asia*, eds. Balisacan and Hill (Quezon City: Ateneo de Manila University Press, 2007), 196. Takeshi Kawanaka's analysis of post-LGC Naga City reinforces this point: Mayor Jesse Robredo, a reformer widely regarded for his positive use of the progressive provisions of the LGC, nonetheless depended critically on the patronage ties he nurtured and maintained with higher level politicians in Manila. Takeshi Kawanaka, *Power in a Philippine City* (Chiba: Institute of Developing Economies, 2002), 102.

[76] Hutchcroft and Rocamora, "Patronage-Based Parties," *supra* n. 4, 110.

in the weeks after the May 2004 election. The topic of the conversation was a one million vote margin of victory, and the release of the tape brought forth a firestorm of demands that the President resign. In a nationally televised address, on June 27, Arroyo admitted to improper conversations with the commissioner, unsavory COMELEC veteran Virgilio "Garci" Garcillano, but denied that it was her voice on the leaked tapes. From that point on, Arroyo's presidency was an exercise in regime preservation – with high levels of unpopularity, frequent but ultimately unsuccessful attempts at impeachment, and recurrent crises.[77] Central to her "staying power," argues Abinales, was

> her relationship with provincial governors, city and town mayors, and village councilors, whose confidence Arroyo has maintained through her adept handling of state funds. With these local officials backing her up, and with the *secondary* support of the Armed Forces of the Philippines, Arroyo has been able to deflect fierce criticism and ride wave after wave of opposition attacks on her presidency.[78]

Particularly important, not surprisingly, has been the IRA: by "[keeping] the flow of funds open to all but implacable opponents," she has "gained the loyalty of [local politicians] regardless of party affiliation.[79] It has long been the practice of local politicians to align themselves with the Palace in search of the patronage resources they need for political success, and for the Palace, in turn, to seek out the support of local politicians in order to win elections and survive political crises. Under Arroyo, this practice became more brazen than ever, given her government's perceived need to court local politicians not only for the usual purposes of electoral advantage but also to fight off impeachment challenges. As the spigot of the pork barrel was opened wide – and brazen cash payouts were provided in late 2007 to congresspersons and governors within the walls of the Presidential Palace – one can suppose that there were few expectations regarding "good governance" performance criteria.

---

[77] Based on the initial greeting in the taped telephone conversation, this came to be known as the "Hello, Garci" scandal. (The "Hello, Garci" greeting from the taped conversation, meanwhile, became a popular cell phone ringtone.) For further analysis, *see* Paul D. Hutchcroft, "The Arroyo Imbroglio in the Philippines," *Journal of Democracy* 19, no. 1 (January 2008): 141–155.

[78] Patricio N. Abinales, "The Philippines: Weak State, Resilient President," in *Southeast Asian Affairs 2008*, eds. Daljit Singh and Tin Maung Maung Than (Singapore: ISEAS Publications, 2008), 294, emphasis in original.

[79] Ibid., 294, 298; *see also* Hutchcroft, "Re-Slicing the Pie," *supra* n. 68, 127–28.

Even the brutality of warlord armies could be overlooked as long the votes were delivered up at election time. Allegations of electoral fraud reemerged in the 2007 midterm elections, many focusing on Mindanao's remote province of Maguindanao – where a well-known protégé of Virgilio Garcillano was serving as provincial election supervisor. Thanks in part to implausibly unbalanced vote returns from Maguindanao, the President's political allies were able to deliver a victory sweep to her slate of national senatorial candidates. The key figure in securing this outcome was Governor Andal Ampatuan, who commanded a substantial paramilitary force and had a reputation for using violence against his political enemies.[80]

As elections have become more expensive and appetites for resources thus more insatiable, funds from the underworld and from illegal activities have come to cast a new shadow over Philippine politics. As a former Speaker of the House succinctly explained (amid a controversy that was soon to expel him from presidential favor), "It's the drug lords and gambling lords... who finance the candidates. So from Day One, they become corrupt. So the whole political process is rotten."[81]

On November 23, 2009, the darkest side of Philippine patronage politics was revealed in a horrific massacre. Esmail Mangudadatu, a political enemy of the Ampatuan family, knew the danger of challenging the power of the preeminent local warlord family but was nonetheless determined to contest the governorship of Maguindanao province. He sent female relatives to file his papers of candidacy, and they were accompanied by some thirty journalists. Such a convoy, it was incorrectly reasoned, would be safe from harm. After being intercepted en route by the Ampatuan family's private army, a total of fifty-seven persons were brutally massacred.[82]

The Philippines has never had a more horrendous act of electoral violence, and nowhere in the world have more journalists been killed in

[80] Hutchcroft, "The Arroyo Imbroglio," *supra* n. 73.

[81] *Philippine Daily Inquirer*, October 18, 2007. For further analysis of the "covert netherworld" of Philippine politics, *see* Alfred W. McCoy, "Covert Netherworld: Clandestine Services and Criminal Syndicates in Shaping the Philippine State," in *Government of the Shadows: Parapolitics and Criminal Sovereignty*, eds. Eric Wilson and Tim Lindsey (London: Pluto Press, 2009).

[82] International Crisis Group (ICG), "The Philippines: After the Maguindanao Massacre," *Asia Briefing* No. 98, December 21, 2009, http://www.crisisgroup.org/~/media/Files/asia/south-east-asia/philippines/b98%20The%20%20Philippines%20After%20the%20Maguindanao%20Massacre.ashx, accessed August 19, 2013.

a single incident.[83] In this sense, the massacre was an aberration, and it would be unfair to use it as any sort of characterization of the norm of local power in the Philippines. Nonetheless, the killings took place within a larger context in which national and local politicians cooperate closely toward their mutual ends. As a report of the International Crisis Group (ICG) explains, this context facilitated the outcome:

> Political patronage by successive governments in Manila, most notably the Arroyo administration, allowed the Ampatuans to amass great wealth and unchecked power, including the possession of a private arsenal with mortars, rocket launchers and state-of-the-art assault rifles. They controlled the police, the judiciary, and the local election commission.... The Ampatuans' exercise of absolute authority was made possible not only by political patronage from Manila, but also by laws and regulations permitting the arming and private funding of civilian auxiliaries to the army and police; lack of oversight over or audits of central government allocations to local government budgets; the ease with which weapons can be imported, purchased and circulated; and a thoroughly dysfunctional legal system. The family also took advantage of the conflict between the government and the Moro Islamic Liberation Front (MILF) to position itself as a loyal counter-insurgency force, even though it used the green light obtained for arming civilians more to expand its own power than defend the state.[84]

Prominent events in the first decade of the new century have exposed – more dramatically than ever – how patronage ties between national and local politicians can extend further into involvement in gambling syndicates, engagement with drug lords, collusion in electoral fraud, and the concentration of coercive force in the hands of local warlords. From the gambling scandals of 2001 and 2005 to the electoral fraud scandals of 2004 and 2007 to the massacre of 2009, it became ever more difficult for anyone to continue to put forth the old narrative about redeeming the country's political system through the granting of greater authority to local officials. In the May 2010 elections, the overwhelming sentiment was in favor of reform, and the campaign slogan of victorious candidate Benigno S. Aquino III focused on the need to fight corruption. On his inauguration, the new president proclaimed a new era in Philippine politics: "No more influence-peddling, no more patronage politics, no more stealing . . . no more bribes."

---

[83] Ibid., 6.   [84] Ibid., 1.

A NEW AWAKENING? FROM DREAMS OF REDEMPTION TO CAREFULLY CONSIDERED STRATEGIES OF REFORM

What are the optimal means of curbing the deeply entrenched system of patronage politics in the Philippines? As in previous decades, this system binds the country together – but at the expense of good governance and the quality of democracy.

Faced with huge political problems emanating in large part from a patronage-dominated (and now underworld-infested) political system, many in the Arroyo years came to advocate huge solutions that – in the rhetoric of their supporters – are not uncommonly treated as panaceas. As in the past, these reform proponents emphasized the virtues of localist strategies intended to shift power away from "imperial Manila" and toward officials at the local level. If decentralization was promoted by some as the solution to the country's problems in the 1990s, federalism took a similar appeal in the following decade. The lofty promises had a familiar ring, albeit now sometimes combined as well with the additional panacea of parliamentarism.[85] (If the system is currently presidential, so goes the logic, it should become parliamentary. If it is currently unitary, then federalism is the solution. Better yet, why not go all the way to a federal-parliamentary democracy?) As highlighted in the epigraph at the outset of this chapter, Abueva envisaged that federalism will bring better governance and less corruption.[86] Fellow federalist Rey Magno Teves predicts that "[i]n a federal-parliamentary democracy we shall be better able to achieve a just and enduring peace and accelerate nation-building and development for our people's security, prosperity and welfare, and to enhance our country's ability to participate in the global economy and community."[87] As with other localist strategies, the basis of these assertions is a presumed dichotomy between the character of national and local politics: the former is the problem to be reformed, whereas

---

[85] My own view is that a parliamentary system is, in general, superior to a presidential system. In a setting with weak and poorly institutionalized parties, however, a parliamentary form of government is a recipe for disaster. On the weak and poorly institutionalized character of Philippine parties, *see* Nathan Quimpo, "The Left, Elections, and the Political Party System in the Philippines," *Critical Asian Studies* 37 (March 2005); and Hutchcroft and Rocamora, "Patronage-Based Parties," *supra* n. 4.

[86] Jose Veloso Abueva, *Charter Change for Good Governance: Towards a Federal Republic of the Philippines with a Parliamentary Government* (Marikina City: Citizens' Movement for a Federal Philippines and Kalayaan College Institute of Federal-Parliamentary Democracy, 2005).

[87] Ibid., preface.

the latter provides the ready solution; the former is lacking in virtue, whereas the latter is an untapped reservoir of virtue. Given the repeated failure of localist strategies over the past six decades, there was good reason to examine the federalists' hopes, dreams, and projections with a particularly skeptical eye. From a policy standpoint, this chapter provides a cautionary argument against excessive reliance on localist strategies of reform. Although such strategies can have an important impact on the distribution of patronage, they have not proven effective in curbing the system of patronage politics as a whole.

By the time Benigno S. Aquino III assumed the presidency in mid-2010, the widespread and long-standing faith in the redemptive capacity of the local could no longer be sustained with the same vigor. A former city mayor and prominent reform advocate, Jesse Robredo, was put in charge of the DILG with the mandate both to reform local governments and to curb the local gambling syndicates that had been the source of scandal in the two previous administrations. From the beginning, Robredo spoke in terms of "calibrated decentralization"; local governments should be given more freedom, he announced, "but every freedom will be coupled with accountability."[88] His attempts at improving local government performance came to be institutionalized in three closely related programs: (a) the Full Disclosure Policy, requiring that the budgets and projects of local governments be publicly available; (b) the granting of a Seal of Good Housekeeping (SGH) to those local governments that demonstrate strong performance based on specific criteria; and (c) for those local governments that obtain the SGH and demonstrate strong capacity in other elements of governance (including planning, budgeting and financial management, revenue mobilization, and procurement), the opportunity to apply for a Performance Challenge Fund that provides additional resources for projects related to local development and poverty alleviation.[89] These programs combined both "carrot and stick." Those

---

[88] *Philippine Daily Inquirer*, July 12, 2010.

[89] The details of the three programs are drawn from Ronald D. Holmes, forthcoming, "Moving Forward but for How Long? Assessing the First Two and One-Half Years of the Benigno S. Aquino Administration," in *Mindanao: The Pursuit of Peace and the Challenges Ahead*, ed. Paul D. Hutchcroft (Manila: Anvil Press, 2013); Alex B. Brillantes and Maricel T. Fernandez, "Restoring Trust and Building Integrity in Government: Issues and Concerns in the Philippines and Areas for Reform," *International Public Management Review* 12, no. 2 (2012): 57; Department of the Interior and Local Government, Republic of the Philippines, "LG Sector," 2012, accessed May 25, 2013, http://www.dilg.gov.ph/PDF_File/transparency/DILG-Transparency-20121112–5e96b24862.pdf, 8, 10.

who failed to practice full disclosure were threatened with administrative sanctions, and Robredo announced plans in late 2011 to "up the ante" in the SGH program and "increase the standards of compliance." In early 2012, he announced that "[t]he days of mediocrity are over and from here on, strong performance will be the cornerstone of any support that the government and development partners will provide [local government units]." Absentee local politicians were threatened with suspension from office, and a Local Governance Watch was established as a means of promoting accountability through the active engagement of civil society organizations.[90]

This package of reforms represents an extremely important advance, and was made all the more credible by Robredo's reputation as a straight operator who was more committed to the cause of long-term governance reform than to short-term political advantage. There was an outpouring of grief throughout the country after his untimely demise in an August 2012 plane crash, with one eulogy describing him as an "icon of good governance."[91] President Aquino proclaimed his desire to ensure the continuance of the reforms and installed his 2010 running mate Manuel A. Roxas II in Robredo's old post.[92] The Robredo reforms, skillfully crafted as they were by a former city mayor, have helped move the country away from the unrealistic expectations of previous decades. They put a focus not only on the positive things that can be achieved by local governments, but also on the need for mechanisms to promote accountability and improve performance. At the same time, these laudable policy innovations under the Aquino government have largely failed to move beyond the deeply entrenched dichotomy between national and local politics. As important as it is to promote reform at the local level, such efforts should be conceived of as part of a more holistic process of reform encompassing an entire political system.

From an analytical standpoint, this chapter has urged the careful reassessment of a long-standing dichotomy that seeks to distinguish between the character of national and local politics. This has often led to the problematic assumption that one layer of government is relatively

---

[90] *Philippine Daily Inquirer*, January 20 and October 10, 2011; January 13, February 27, and June 29, 2012. The "carrot and stick" characterization comes from the newspaper column of Solita Collas-Monsod, a prominent economist and former national secretary for economic development (*Philippine Daily Inquirer*, January 8, 2011).

[91] *Sun Star*, August 21, 2012.

[92] *Philippine News Agency*, August 25, 2012; *Philippine Daily Inquirer*, September 9, 2012.

more corrupt and another layer of government is relatively more virtuous. In fact, the different territorial layers of government within the Philippine polity are deeply interwoven via a patronage system that has its apex in Manila and extends outward to provinces, cities, towns, and barangays throughout the archipelago. Since the early twentieth century, important administrative functions of the state have been subcontracted out to local politicians; in the pursuit of localist strategies of reform in the late twentieth century, moreover, the patronage flows from the top to the bottom of the system have both expanded in quantity and moved downward in location. Meanwhile, political institutions – notably the bureaucracy and political parties – have remained weak. As Putnam says of post-1870 Italy one can also say of the Philippines over the past century: "Political channels to the center [are] more important than administrative channels, but in either case the link to the center [remains] crucial." In sum, the dichotomy that has inspired localist dreams of redemption is not a dichotomy that actually exists within a patronage-based state. Similarly, initiatives to reform the local level of government are unlikely to achieve their full potential without a clear recognition of the multifaceted nature of the patronage system as it extends from capital to countryside.

Without in any way detracting from the genuine and well-meaning spirit of reform that has motivated many localist strategies over the past six decades, one must acknowledge that the pursuit of these strategies has frequently diverted efforts from other more promising and well-conceived paths of reform. While the Robredo reforms are far more promising, their efficacy is ultimately limited by the persistence of the dichotomy between national versus local. A fuller exploration of possible reform agendas is beyond the scope of this chapter, but I can very briefly sketch out two possible avenues of change – each of which focus on some aspect of the country's weak political institutions. The first is reform of the electoral system, with the goal of nurturing stronger and more programmatic political parties. This would involve junking the dysfunctional party-list system (which, very oddly, does not allow any political party to gain more than three congressional seats) and replacing it with some element of a more standard proportional-representation (PR) system; following the example of Japan and Korea, the Philippines could consider a mixed system involving both single-member-district seats and PR. The nurturing of better institutionalized, policy-oriented parties would be a long and difficult effort, but even incremental steps toward success could have a positive impact on the entire political system – from the national to the local levels. The second path of reform would be in the long-beleaguered Philippine bureaucracy. No one can pretend to have easy solutions for reforming (and sustaining the reform of) an inefficient, patrimonial bureaucracy, but there can be virtue in focusing on a certain sector of the bureaucracy and combining both bottom-up and top-down pressures for reform. Just as it is a mistake to target the local at the expense of the national, so would it be a mistake to target the national at the expense of the local. The overall goal should be the promotion of a more efficient and less corrupt bureaucracy at all levels, not only in Manila but also in local government units throughout the country. Sadly, the reform measures pursued by President Aquino have not (as of yet) given adequate attention to the underlying institutional deficiencies of the country's political parties and bureaucratic agencies.[93]

Specifics aside, the fundamental argument is that clear understandings of the patronage-based nature of state formation in the Philippines are critical to efforts to curb patronage. If the problem is a patronage system that extends from the Presidential Palace to the smallest localities at the periphery of the state, it is not adequate for reform efforts to focus merely on the lower levels of government. Localist strategies, as dreams of redemption, were heavily discredited by scandals and events in the first decade of this century; more recently, reform measures have sought to develop more fully the capacities of local governments through a combination of both the carrot and the stick. Now that President Aquino has moved into the second half of his single six-year term, it is essential to move toward carefully considered strategies of political reform that can address the pathologies of the patronage system as they exist and interact at both the national *and* the local levels of the Philippine polity.

---

[93] Hutchcroft and Rocamora, "Patronage-Based Parties," *supra* n. 4, 113.

4

Constitutional Rights and Dialogic Process in Socialist Vietnam: Protecting Rural-to-Urban Migrants' Rights without a Constitutional Court

Huong Thi Nguyen

This chapter focuses on the constitutional arguments in public debates that revolve around the Vietnamese authorities' two recent efforts to deal with urban growth and migration: the 2006 Law on Residence and the 2010 draft Capital Law. One of the central issues in these debates was the constitutionality of the household registration system (*ho khau*) – a legacy of the planned economy – as a tool to restrict urban-ward migration flow. The public has successfully made use of constitutional rights as leverage against abusive regulatory proposals. After strong public reaction in favor of constitutional rights of the migrants, the government had to moderate or remove controversial provisions from the bills, and they had to take into consideration constitutional concerns in the drafting process.[1] These phenomena open up new questions for the role of the constitution in general and the role of rights provisions in particular in the sociopolitical deliberation process in the absence of a constitutional court. This paper argues that, first, constitutional rights provisions have inherent value in the sociopolitical dialogic process, which takes place even within formally authoritarian regimes and in the absence of a constitutional court, as they constitute leverage for advocacy efforts to protect the politically disadvantaged from unchecked practices of power. Second, constitutional arguments that were put forth in the Vietnamese debates have revealed how the distinctions between political-civil rights as negative rights, on

---

[1] Public reaction here is understood as (a) opinions raised by members of the National Assembly during legislative debate which were spread by media outlets and (b) public opinions as expressed through comments, interviews, and expert analysis which were published on newspapers.

the one hand, and socioeconomic rights as positive rights, on the other hand, are not clear cut and easy distinctions. In the Vietnamese context, arguments in favor of socioeconomic rights and civic rights call for both negative and positive duties of the state. Social and economic rights can acquire a negative duty aspect as the society struggles to move away from an absolute political control of the social sphere. Thus, this paper also demonstrates how constitutional appreciation and understanding is shaped by one country's history, and how constitutionalism should be seen as a process in which we live and learn from our past experience and entrench our lessons by crystallizing them in fundamental laws of the country. Understanding this legacy is important for future constitutional reforms.

In the first part, I will present some theoretical discussion regarding the role of the constitution in deliberative democratic process, as well as the debate on the validity of the distinction between positive rights versus negative rights. In the next two parts, I will discuss the internal migration in Vietnam and the two debates surrounding the 2006 Law on Residence and the Capital Law draft to see how constitutional provisions have been successfully advanced against discriminatory governmental proposals vis-à-vis migrants in the cities. In the last section, I will reflect on the contribution of the findings from the Vietnamese debates to the general discussion of the nature of constitutional rights, the values of rights provision in the sociopolitical deliberative process, and the implication for constitutional design.

I. THEORETICAL DEBATES: CONSTITUTIONALISM, RIGHTS, AND DEMOCRACY

This section will outline two of the current debates in constitutional theory: first, the debate regarding positive rights versus negative rights in Western constitutional scholarship and, second, the discussion on the role of the constitution in the democratic process.[2]

A. *Negative Rights, Positive Rights, and State Duties*

Socioeconomic rights used to be regarded with a great deal of suspicion, especially in the American legal tradition. Opponents used to refer to

---

[2] My goal here is not to take a definite stance in the debate on constitutionalism versus democracy. I merely use these theoretical insights because they offer a useful way to understand and interpret the meanings of the emerging constitutionalism in Vietnam.

socioeconomic rights as positive rights – rights that give the recipient the ability to demand a specific resource or opportunity from the government; whereas a negative right gives recipients the ability to make the government stop interfering with the exercise of their rights in some way.[3] The opponents' objections have two main points: the cost of implementing these rights and the judicial encroachment on the policymaking power of the political branches. These problems provided the basis to object to the incorporation of socioeconomic rights into the constitution; as, it is said, the main focus of the constitution is to limit the government's action instead of calling for its action.[4]

Proponents of socioeconomic rights argue that the distinction between positive rights and negative rights is misleading, as socioeconomic and political-civil rights both have negative and positive duties of state associated with them.[5] Some traditional rights, such as the right to vote, require both negative and positive duties by the state. For example, the state must not interfere when people are voting; however, the state also has the positive duty to organize regular elections.[6] Thus, the rejection of social rights on the basis that they require positive duties from the state is not well grounded.[7] Cecile Fabre thus puts forward the "complementarity thesis," according to which "the two set of rights – negative and positive – complement one another, in that they each protect interests in certain ways, and taken together afford full protection to these interests." In other words, she advocates for an interest-based theory of rights: both negative rights and positive rights are needed to protect various aspects of a given interest.[8] Each right could contain both negative aspects (against interference) and positive aspects (requiring state duties to protect, promote, and realize these rights). In this paper, I suggest that the study of the constitutional rights debate in Vietnam supports proponents' arguments in favor of socioeconomic rights. For both civil/political rights and social/economic rights, the constitutional rights demands in Vietnam

---

[3] *See* Frank Cross, "The Error of Positive Rights," *UCLA Law Review* 48 (2000–2001).

[4] Cecile Fabre, *Social Rights Under the Constitution* (New York: Oxford University Press, 2000), 41.

[5] *See* Fabre, *Social Rights, supra* n. 4; Cass R. Sunstein, *Designing Democracy: What Constitutions Do* (New York: Oxford University Press, 2001), 221–37.

[6] Fabre, *Social Rights, supra* n. 4, 45 ("The right to vote is a right to take part in the political process of one's country, by voting in referenda and by electing representatives in various bodies. The duty of the state in that respect is to organize regular elections, which supposes a whole range of activities, from paying people to take care of each station poll to printing out ballot papers and to rescheduling the parliamentary agenda so as to accommodate the election campaign.").

[7] Ibid.

[8] Ibid., 46–47.

seem to expect the Vietnamese government to perform both negative and positive duties.

B. The Role of Constitutional Rights in Dialogic Political Processes

The second current scholarly debate that informs my analysis concerns the role of rights – claims in the dialogic political process, even where no effective constitutional enforcement mechanism exists. Cass Sunstein suggests that a constitution has a role to play in deliberative democracy: the "internal morality of democracy" requires a state to go beyond majoritarian rule and to adequately protect constitutional rights of individual and groups.[9] I will extend this argument by demonstrating that constitutional rights, both socioeconomic rights and civic rights, have inherent value in the dialogic political process, even where no effective constitutional enforcement mechanism exists. This finding, moreover, should encourage the inclusion of socioeconomic rights in constitutions, for their contribution to the political dialogic process.

Sunstein's notion of "internal morality of democracy" seems at first to be confined to the protection of political and civil rights.[10] The author is more careful when mentioning socioeconomic rights. This skepticism is not a result of the rights[11] but rather from concern about judicial entanglement with managerial issues.[12] Examining the *Grootboom* decision of the South African Constitutional Court, he praises the self-restraint approach of the Court in issuing a decision that is reasonable enough to protect the neediest while still deferring to democratic institutions in prioritizing social policies.[13]

Sunstein is well aware of the "deliberative trouble" which happens when agreement cannot be reached during the societal deliberative process.[14] Thus, he emphasizes the value of "incompletely theorized agreements" – "a process by which people agree on practices, or outcomes, despite disagreement or uncertainty about fundamental issues." This principle is central in constitution-making and constitutional interpretation.[15] Constitutions and constitutional arguments can be

---

[9] Sunstein, *Designing Democracy*, *supra* n. 5, 6–7.

[10] Ibid., 7 (" . . . the right of free expression, the right to vote, the right to political equality, and even the right to private property, for people cannot be independent citizens if their holdings are subject to unlimited government readjustment.").

[11] Ibid., 11.   [12] Ibid., 10.

[13] Ibid., 221–37.   [14] Ibid., 8.

pragmatic, instead of idealized; agreements can be reached on practical issues without a complete agreement on the theoretical standpoints of concerned parties.[16]

Sunstein's work inspires two ideas that shape the way I approach the constitutional debate in Vietnam regarding rights of migrants in the cities. First, the constitution has a role in promoting deliberative democracy, as witnessed by the South African case, where constitutional rights interpretation provides leverage for societal attention and political deliberation in favor of the neediest. Second, a constitution could be regarded as a pragmatic instrument within deliberative democracy, as it provides a minimum platform on which agreement on concrete matters can be reached without a complete agreement on theoretical and abstract issues such as the nature of the political regime (authoritarianism versus democracy; socialism versus liberalism, for instance).[17] Thus, the constitution can be interpreted in an incrementally liberal way as a concrete solution for the most urgent sociopolitical matters.

Sunstein's arguments seem to be relevant to explain the nature of the rights debate in Vietnam, an authoritarian context without a constitutional court. Rights provisions in the Constitution play a role as a shared basis, an accepted starting point, for societal discussion on matters that may be deemed sensitive in an illiberal political context. New interpretation of state duties and citizens' rights can arise naturally from this shared constitutional basis, without an open discussion on the nature of the political regime. The debates on the rights of the rural-to-urban migrants in Vietnam, including civil rights such as freedom of movement and socioeconomic rights such as rights to housing, work, health, and education, in the context of the making of the Residence Law and Capital Law in Vietnam, will demonstrate this use of constitutional rights.

II. BACKGROUND INFORMATION: VIETNAM, MARKET ECONOMY, AND RURAL-TO-URBAN MIGRATION

Vietnam is a unitary state under a one-party political regime.[18] The country's leading party – the Communist Party of Vietnam – embraces Marxism-Leninism as official ideology and has pursued a transition to

---

[15] Ibid., 9.   [16] Ibid., 10.

[17] That is, the value of the "incompletely theorized agreement."

[18] 1992 *Constitution of the Socialist Republic of Vietnam* (amended December 25, 2001), http://publicofficialsfinancialdisclosure.worldbank.org/fdl/sites/fdl/files/assets/law-library-files/Vietnam_Constitution_1992_amended%202001_EN.pdf.

socialism since ending the war with France in 1954 in the North and reunification in 1975 of the whole country. As the planned economy was on the brink of collapse, in 1986, the 6th National Congress of the Communist Party abolished the centralized economic system, adopted a multi-sector economy and opened the country to international trade. In 1992, the Party-State amended the Constitution to redefine the country's "economic regime" as one of a market economy with a socialist orientation.[19] The 1992 Constitution provides for citizens' freedom of movement and residence,[20] right to work,[21] right to education,[22] entitlement to health care[23] and housing ownership,[24] equality before the law,[25] and "right to physical inviolability and to have their lives, health, honor and dignity protected by law."[26] The Constitution also explicitly requires the state to take action to protect people's health,[27] create jobs,[28] and "create favorable conditions for the studies, work, and recreation of young people."[29]

Internal migration existed in the planned economy period under government-led programs. Since the switch to a market economy and the relaxation of the state's population management policies, migration has changed in both its nature and intensity.[30] However, the related legal regimes, notably the household registration system, have changed little, constituting considerable obstacles to migrants' settlement in new places and making everyday life difficult for them. Before analyzing the 2006 Law on Residence and 2010 Capital Law debates, we must examine the changes in prior regulations since 1986, how migrants' lives were affected by the policies, and shifting popular attitudes toward the policies.

A. Household Registration System and the Implication for Migration and Migrant's Situation in the Cities

Although similar systems had existed in Vietnam during the colonial period and during war times, the household registration system was

---

[19] Ibid., Art. 15 ("The State promotes a multi-component commodity economy functioning in accordance with market mechanisms under the management of the State and following a socialist orientation.").

[20] Ibid., Art. 68.   [21] Ibid., Art. 55.

[22] Ibid., Art. 59.   [23] Ibid., Art. 61.

[24] Ibid., Art. 58.   [25] Ibid., Art. 52.

[26] Ibid., Art. 71.   [27] Ibid., Art. 39.

[28] Ibid., Art. 55.   [29] Ibid., Art. 66.

[30] United Nations, *Internal Migration: Opportunities and Challenges for Socio-economic Development in Viet Nam* (2010), 6.

formally introduced in the Democratic Republic of Vietnam in the 1950s[31] and provided the state with a tool to control the population by classifying citizens into different residential statuses with differentiated rights and obligations.[32] In the planned economy, the household registration system was the means for the socialist government to limit social mobility[33] and to acquire socio-economic knowledge about the population, on the basis of which state and local authorities regulated people's access to goods and services at a particular place.[34] It was also a means of identification, which had consequences for a person's civil status and related benefits.[35] To live without household registration was "to live without the rights granted to Vietnamese citizens under the law."[36]

During the period of the economic reforms from 1986 to 2006, the household registration system changed little and maintained strict

[31] Andrew Hardy, "Rules and Resources: Negotiating the Household Registration System in Vietnam Under Reform," *SOJOURN: Journal of Social Issues in Southeast Asia* 16 (2001): 188–89.

[32] United Nations, *Internal Migration, supra* n. 30, 18 ("Prior to 2007, four categories existed where permanent residents enjoyed KT1 status, entitling them to full residential rights, including permission to purchase land-use rights and the ability to access schools and medical services within their district of residence. Those who moved to a different district, but still in the same province, had KT2 status and could purchase land-use rights but were limited to schooling and other social services in the district where they are registered. People who were registered in one province but resided in another were classified KT3 and generally held a temporary residence permit of six to- 12 months which could be renewed fairly easily. These people could also purchase land titles, but could not access schooling unless there was space available after KT1 and KT2 children had enrolled. Those in the KT4 category were registered as individuals without a family, in contrast to the other three categories, and possessed an extendable three-month residence permit. They could not purchase land titles, and like KT3 residence status, they could not access certain social services.").

[33] Consider Measure No. 5 of the Prime Minister of Vietnam's *Circular No. 495 TTG Regarding the Limitation of the Rural Population to the Cities* (October 23, 1957) as an example of an explicit statement of the state vision of regional planning: "Beside propaganda and education, the administrative branches and committees of the cities need to consider appropriate administrative and economic measures *to limit the peasants to go to the cities*, such as: *a strict control of the household registration*, or progressively eliminate street merchandise." (Emphasis added.)

[34] Hardy, "Rules and Resources," *supra* n. 31, 191.

[35] Ibid., 191–92 ("Births, marriages, migrations, and deaths all required registration. This implied that someone whose birth was not declared would not be able to claim rights to services such as education and health (school and hospital places were not planned for), and the declaration of their marriage (the union's registration is conditional on presentation of identification). Even when one died, the *ho khau* was still of importance. Unregistered residents were not entitled to commune land for burial.").

[36] Ibid., 192.

TABLE 4.1. *Household registration's regulatory changes over time*

	Conditions of permanent household registration in cities	Temporary residence registration in cities
Decree 4-HDBT of January 7, 1988, Issuing the Regulations of the Household Registration and Control	Being employed or mobilized by competent state organs (art. 10, cl. 1)	6 months renewable (art. 12)
Decree 51/CP on the Household Registration and Control (May 10, 1997)	• Legal accommodation (art. 11), and • Being employed or mobilized by the competent state organs (art. 12, cl. 1)	12 months renewable (Implementation circular IV-B-2-a)
Decree 108/2005/ND-CP (August 19, 2005), amending Decree 15/CP	• Legal accommodation (art. 11) and being employed or mobilized by the state (art. 12, cl. 1) OR • Legal accommodation (art. 11) and continuous residence of at least 3 years (art. 12, cl. 2)	12 months renewable
2006 Law on Residence	• Legal accommodation and continual residence of at least 1 year (art. 20, cl. 1)	No duration limitation
2010 Draft Capital Law – early 2010 version	• Lawful employment with a salary double that of the minimum wage, and • Proof of legal accommodation, and • Continuous temporary residence of at least 5 years	
2010 Draft Capital Law – February 22, 2010, version	The above requirements were removed, as well as the requirement of a working permit for migrants in the cities. There would be no additional requirement for permanent household registration in the capital (i.e., the 2006 Law on Residence would apply).	

	Conditions of permanent household registration in cities	Temporary residence registration in cities
2012 Draft Capital Law (adopted November 21, 2012)	More restrictive in terms of migration compared to the 2006 Law on Residence: 3 years of temporary residence in Hanoi are required for permanent household registration (in addition to the conditions set out by the 2006 Law on Residence).	

conditions of permanent household registration. According to Decree 4-HDBT of January 7, 1988, Issuing the Regulations of the Household Registration and Control, only those employed or mobilized by the competent state organs could apply for permanent registration in the new place.[37] Ten years later, the constraints remained the same: those who moved to the cities for job purposes and wished to apply for permanent household registration were required to have a legal accommodation (legal house ownership, housing lease, or consent of the household head to permanently live in his/her residence)[38] and be employed or mobilized by the competent state organs.[39] All other categories of migrants (students, free laborers, and those who actually live in the cities but without a permanent registration) were only eligible for temporary residence registration.[40]

Despite the constraining policy, the transition to the market economy has resulted in a rapidly increasing internal migration.[41] Whereas census

[37] Council of Ministers of Vietnam, Decree 4-HDBT Regulating of the Household Registration and Management (January 7, 1988), Art. 10, cl. 1. Those who resided temporarily outside of their place of permanent registration had to register their temporary residence; the duration of the temporary registration was 6 months renewable. Ibid., Art. 12.

[38] Government of Vietnam, Decree 51/CP On the Household Registration and Management (May 10, 1997), Art. 11.

[39] Ibid., Art. 12, cl. 1.   [40] Ibid., Art. 15.

[41] Dang Nguyen Anh et al., "Migration in Vietnam: A Review of Information on Current Trends and Patterns, and Their Policy Implications" (Paper presented at the Regional Conference on Migration, Development and Pro-Poor Policy Choices in Asia, June 22–24, 2003, in Dhaka, Bangladesh), i ("The economic reforms or 'Renovation' [Doi Moi]

data recorded 4.5 million internal migrants between 1994 and 1999,[42] the number reached 6.6 million in the 2004–2009 period.[43] Many people migrated from rural to urban areas, which led to an urban population growth of 3.4 percent each year, compared to 0.4 percent of population growth in rural areas.[44] Among big cities, Ho Chi Minh City and Hanoi held the biggest shares of rural-to-urban migrants in the 1990s, respectively 46 percent and 17 percent.[45]

In the market economy, household registration is no longer an "all-embracing tool" through which one obtains subsidies and commodities from the state.[46] However, the connection between household registration and access to social services and administrative procedures still remains the law today.[47] It has direct consequences for migrants who cannot obtain permanent registration in the place where they work and live[48] and who do not have resources to pay for private schools for their

---

introduced in 1986 affected migration in three main ways. In agriculture, decollectivisation and the introduction of the household contract system have released farmers from the land. In cities, the household registration system continues, but no longer limits the acquisition of essential goods and access to employment. In the emerging industrial sector, Vietnam's incorporation into the global economy has resulted in flows of foreign direct investment attracting migrant workers where such industries concentrate."); United Nations, *Internal Migration, supra* n. 30, 6 ("In Viet Nam, the socioeconomic development resulting from the Doi Moi [Renewal] process launched in 1986 has certainly catalyzed increasing internal migration, by not only making it possible for people to move away from their area of origin, but also by providing the motivation to do so as a result of growing regional disparities. Internal migration has in turn contributed to socio-economic development through the movement of workers to fill demand for labour created by industrial development and foreign direct investment, as well as by impacting large numbers of migrant-sending households.").

[42] Dang Nguyen Anh et al., "Migration in Vietnam," *supra* n. 41, i.

[43] United Nations, *Internal Migration, supra* n. 30, 6.

[44] Ibid. 7.

[45] Liem T. Nguyen and Michael J. White, "Health Status of Temporary Migrants in Urban Areas in Vietnam," *International Migration* 45(4) (October 2007): 130.

[46] Hardy, "Rules and Resources," *supra* n. 31, 205.

[47] United Nations, *Internal Migration, supra* n. 30, 17 ("Even now, a hộ khẩu is required for certain administrative procedures, such as to buy land or build a house, register a motor vehicle, borrow money, access subsidized medical care, water and electricity or to participate in the national targeted programs for poverty reduction.").

[48] Ibid., 32 ("Many administrative activities need to be carried out at the place of registration, such as marriage certificates and access to poverty assistance programmes, thus creating a hostile and difficult living environment for migrants whose permanent registration is at the departure area. The hộ khẩu system thus impacts migrant groups that are already vulnerable.").

children[49] or private health care services.[50] The household registration policy also complicates access to adequate housing for migrants. Newly arrived migrants, especially those who do not have family or social networks in the new place, have to rent accommodation, often in inadequate guest houses or boarding houses. As the law requires proof of legal accommodation (a lease agreement, for example) to register in the new place, newly arrived migrants find themselves dependent on landlords to be able to register. Also, access to social housing provided by the state for migrants requires registration status.[51] Thus, the household registration policy makes life difficult for the most disadvantaged migrants.

The household registration system, with its explicit purpose of "restricting the urban growth" in an era where urban-ward migration was the increasing trend, was increasingly regarded as outdated, reflecting the old-fashioned "socialist economic management, political record determinism, and wartime surveillance."[52] By 2004, discriminatory treatments of migrants in the cities drew a lot of attention. The public was outraged about the absurdities of local regulations that required permanent registration as a condition to apply for all other essential paperwork. A typical example was the connection between household registration proof and house ownership title – "the most effective obstacle Ho Chi Minh city ['s authorities] imposed on migrants."[53] There, local authorities required a legal house ownership title in the city to apply for the permanent residence; however, to apply for certificate of house ownership, a proof of permanent registration in the city was a condition.[54] This

---

[49] Ibid., 33 ("Children with permanent household registration are guaranteed a place in a public elementary school, but public elementary schools are not obligated to provide places to children from households with only KT3 and KT4 [temporary] registration if the schools are already full.").

[50] Ibid., 32 ("By forcing them to resort to private providers for secure social and support services such as health care and loans, which are often more expensive, existing inequalities are exacerbated and urban poverty increased.").

[51] Ibid., 39–40.

[52] Hardy, "Rules and Resources," *supra* n. 31, 207.

[53] Phan Huy Tưởng, "Dân Nhập Cư: Anh Là Ai?" [Migrants: Who Are They?], *Tuổi Trẻ*, March 11, 2004, http://vietbao.vn/Trang-ban-doc/Dan-nhap-cu-anh-la-ai/40023522/478/.

[54] Ibid. Regarding the household registration requirement, the migrants in the city had to "have a stable temporary residence, after 6 months they would need to show the certificate of temporary absence from the locality where they were permanently registered in order to continue their temporary registration in the city for the next 6 months, then after 2 years they would be allowed to reside temporarily for 1 year (KT3 category),

created a vicious circle of marginalization for migrants in the city. Administrative absurdities also created room for corruption, as only money and relationship could help some migrants obtain the paperwork they needed.[55]

In 2004, the debate on the constitutionality of Ho Chi Minh City's regulation was visible in state media. Facing questions from National Assembly members, the then deputy-minister of Natural Resources and Environment affirmed in September 2004, "there has never been a legal requirement of household registration to obtain house ownership," that this practice was wrongfully adopted by local authorities, and that these local regulations "were violating the constitutional provision of the right to freedom of movement of the citizens."[56]

In 2005, Decree 108/2005/ND-CP amended the 1997 Decree 51/CP and loosened the permanent registration requirement: those who had a legal accommodation (owned or rented, or free residence with the owner's consent) could permanently register in the cities.[57] However, for cities of special status such as Hanoi or Ho Chi Minh City, an additional condition applied: uninterrupted residence with a legal accommodation for at least three years.[58] For the first time, employment by the state was not required as a condition for registration. The implementation documents stressed the responsibilities of the competent public securities organ to resolve the applications within deadlines and to not ask for documents other than those required by law.[59] This regulatory shift in 2005 signified an important change in the public and official mindsets

and from then on their temporary registration would need to be renewed every year so that their temporary residence in the city could be deemed legal." Regarding the house ownership condition, "those having a permanent registration could be considered for the certificate of house ownership, but for migrants, usually the answer of the city's authorities were not clear regarding whether or not they could be granted certificate of house ownership."

[55] Ibid.

[56] "Quy Định Của Địa Phương Phải Có Hộ Khẩu Mới Được Mua Đất Là Trái Hiến Pháp" [Local Regulations Requiring Household Registration to Buy Land Violates the Constitution], *VietnamNet*, September 30, 2004, http://vietnamese-law-consultancy.com/vietnamese/content/browse.php?action=shownews?category=&id=45&topicid=27.

[57] Government of Vietnam, *Decree 108/2005/ND-CP Amending Some Provisions of the Decree 51/CP of May 10th, 1997 on Household Registration and Management* (August 19, 2005), Art. 12 cl. 2 as amended.

[58] Ibid.

[59] *See* Public Security Ministry of Vietnam, *Circular to Direct the Implementation of Decree 51/CP and Decree 108/2005/ND-CP* (October 7, 2005).

regarding states' duties and citizens' rights, a shift that continued in the debates in 2006 and 2010.[60]

B. The 2006 Law on Residence Debate

The Law on Residence was enacted in 2006. One of the central issues in the debate was whether the household registration system should be maintained. There were two positions in public opinion at that moment. Some participants argued that the state should abolish the household registration system completely for it had become outdated and been abused by the authorities to impose undue difficulties for citizens. Others argued that the household registration system should be retained because it served the state's population management and urbanization policies. Within the second position, there were two opinions. First, the household registration system should be maintained not only to manage the population's mobility, but also to restrict the urban-ward migration. The other position agreed to maintain the household registration system only for the population management purpose and argued that it should be simplified for the citizens' convenience.

For the purpose of this paper, it is important to stress how constitutional rights constituted the basis for the debate. These rights include not only the right to freedom of movement, but also social rights such as rights to housing, to work, and to health care service and the right of children to education. In the debate, these rights are deemed interconnected. This interconnectedness might be particular to Vietnam – as a legacy of the household registration system and its original function as the basis for social services provisions in a particular locality. In any case, the debate witnessed a shift in the perception of the relationship between citizens and state: because people have rights, the state has correlative duties to respect and promote these rights.[61]

---

[60] Mạnh Cường, "Nhiều Ngành Đang Lạm Dụng Hộ Khẩu Để Hành Dân" [Many Departments Are Abusing Household Registration to Harass Citizens], *Dân Trí*, September 22, 2005, http://dantri.com.vn/dien-dan/nhieu-nganh-dang-lam-dung-ho-khau-de-hanh-dan-78854.htm.

[61] The data for this study is drawn from opinions, interviews, news reports, and expert analyses that were published in newspapers and journals inside the country and that were also published on the web page of these newspapers and journals. These sources might not convey a complete view of different positions of public opinion, but they nonetheless reflect issues people cared about, and a more or less social consensus on certain values,

C. The Law on Residence Discussion: How Constitutional Rights Were Central to the Debate

The law on residence was drafted by the Ministry of Public Security and released to "collect opinions of central state ministries and organs" in February 2006.[62] The draft asserted the right to freedom of residence of the citizens[63] but still required permanent household registration as a condition to enjoy the rights and services provided by local authorities.[64] Some Vietnamese jurists commented that the draft conveyed a "shift in the perception of the value of household registration," which should be seen from then on more as an administrative paperwork than a determinant of the enjoyment of the citizens' rights.[65]

The legislative debate at the National Assembly also revealed the shifting perception of the citizen-state relationship. Opinions ranged from abolishing the household registration system completely and switching to a National Identity Card system for the population management purpose[66] to keeping the registration system but strictly prohibiting all regulations that would require permanent household registration as a condition for the delivery of social services, as such requirements would restrict the rights and freedoms of the citizens.[67] Some opinions suggested that the household registration should not be used as a means to control the migration flow.[68]

---

because public newspapers are controlled by the party-state, and whatever got published can be deemed to be accepted within the political epistemology of the regime.

[62] "Dự Luật Cư Trú: Hộ Khẩu Chỉ Là Giấy Chứng Nhận Cư Trú" [The Draft Law on Residence: Household Registration Is a Mere Certification of Residence], *Tuổi Trẻ*, February 15, 2006, http://moj.gov.vn/ct/tintuc/Pages/thong-tin-khac.aspx&ItemID=2822.

[63] Ibid. (*Residence* was defined as the permanent residence or temporary residence at a particular locality in the Vietnamese territory).

[64] Ibid.

[65] *See* ibid., Lawyer Bui Quang Nghiem's opinion.

[66] *See* Nguyen Dinh Loc's opinion in "Dự Án Luật Cư Trú Tiếp Tục Giữ Quy Định về Hộ Khẩu" [The Draft Law on Residence Maintains Provisions on Household Registration], *Sài Gòn Giải Phóng*, April 5, 2006, http://vietnamese-law-consultancy.com/vietnamese/content/browse.php?action=shownews&category=&id=54&topicid=851.

[67] Xuân Toàn, "Quốc Hội Thảo Luận Về Dự Án Luật Cư Trú: Xóa Bỏ Những Thủ Tục Hành Chính 'Ăn Theo' Sổ Hộ Khẩu" [The National Assembly Debates the Draft Law on Residence: Repealing Administrative Procedures that Require Household Registration], *Việt Báo*, June 9, 2006, http://vietbao.vn/Xa-hoi/Quoc-hoi-thao-luan-ve-du-an-Luat-Cu-tru-Xoa-bo-nhung-thu-tuc-hanh-chinh-an-theo-so-ho-khau/45197072/157/.

[68] "Luật chuyển giao công nghệ và Luật cư trú có lợi cho phát triển kinh tế và hội nhập quốc tế" [Law on Technology Transfer and Law on Residence Are Beneficial to Economic Development and International Integration], *Website Đảng Cộng Sản*, September 26, 2006, http://moj.gov.vn/ct/tintuc/Pages/nghien-cuu-trao-doi.aspx?ItemID=1666.

Two important constitutional arguments emerged from these debates. First, the household registration system violated citizens' rights to freedom of movement and other socioeconomic rights. Second, a constitutional review mechanism was needed to prevent future abuse of the household registration system by local authorities to restrict peoples' rights.

Regarding the first argument, in an interview in early 2006 the former Minister of Justice Nguyen Dinh Loc, then a member of the National Assembly, clearly made the point: the household registration policy limited not only the right to freedom of movement within the country but also other constitutional rights such as the right to education of children and the right to purchase and own housing.[69]

> The household registration problem is not only related to the right to freedom of residence of the citizens, it also creates an abnormality in the citizen-to-citizen relationship. A person having a permanent household registration is deemed to be a citizen with full enjoyment of constitutional rights, and that person enjoys these rights quite naturally as a full-fledged citizen. Yet how about those new comers who do not have permanent household registration? [Their lives] are very difficult. [...] We appreciate the Constitution, regarding the Constitution as supreme [law], yet we do not respect constitutional provisions. This is a systematic problem, not the fault of the Constitution.[70]

Answering the question on whether the management of the population through the household registration system would violate the Constitution, he responded:

> [In principle], if I do not have a permanent household registration, I cannot live here, I have to go back to where I am registered to live. In reality, I still live here normally, I still go to work, earn salary. Yet, without a household registration, other rights of mine are affected. Education is a right, an obligation, yet my children who do not have a permanent household registration cannot go to the school they want, they have to go to a school in a locality where they are not registered. This generates other violations of rights, not only violation of the right to freedom of residence. The right to housing is a solemn right of the individual, yet now people are told that they cannot buy a house without a household registration in

---

[69] "Hộ Khẩu Đã Hoàn Thành Sứ Mệnh Lịch Sử" [Household Registration Have Completed Its Historical Mission], *Tuổi Trẻ*, March 13, 2006, http://vietbao.vn/Xa-hoi/Ho-khau-da-hoan-thanh-su-menh-lich-su/30106293/157/.
[70] Ibid.

the area, and when they apply to get a permanent household registration booklet, they will be asked whether they already own a house [. . .]. All of these are contrary to the spirit of the Constitution, contrary to the text of the Constitution [sic].[71]

An official of the Ministry of Justice in September 2005 also stressed the constitutional aspect of the household registration system:

Decree 108, compared to Decree 51, already relaxed the conditions of household registration, but still reflected the old management mindset. Let just mention the language. Article 11 said: "to be registered at the new location . . . " Just the words "to be" already reveal the patronizing attitude. In fact, it is not that I am registered, but that the police has to come and register the household for me. I exercise my constitutional right, the right to freedom of residence, my accommodation is legal, and the police officer must acknowledge and issue my permanent household registration [sic].[72]

We can see here a clear shift in the perception of the relationship between the state and the citizen. The duty of the state official to register the citizen's residency when required conditions are fulfilled is actually a positive duty of the state, even though the right to freedom of residence is usually considered to be a negative right.

Public opinion went even further to suggest a judicial review mechanism so that citizens can challenge unconstitutional laws. As the newspaper reported, there existed hundreds of local regulatory measures that violated the Constitution; if the competent authorities did not take action to repeal them, there would be no mean for the citizens to directly challenge them. According to Nguyen Dinh Loc:

We have not yet given the people the power to challenge [the constitutionality of] a legal provision. When we will have a constitutional court, a legal document – decree or law – that is contrary to the constitution will be challenged by the people before the court. A constitutional court would consider whether the act would violate the constitution or not. If the court declared the act unconstitutional, it would be invalid. Yet, now we have not yet conferred to the people this power. The people can only outcry to protest.[73]

[71] Ibid.
[72] Mạnh Cường, "Nhiều Ngành Đang Lạm Dụng Hộ Khẩu," *supra* n. 60.
[73] "Hộ Khẩu Đã Hoàn Thành Sứ Mệnh Lịch Sử" [Household Registration Have Completed Its Historical Mission].

Other opinions even laid out visions of this constitutional court, and why the administrative court in Vietnam would not be sufficient to protect the constitutional rights of citizens. Independence must be the key feature of the constitutional court.[74]

The Law on Residence was adopted on November 29, 2006,[75] leaning toward a simplification of the household registration system and emphasizing the duty of the state. The general rule now is after one year of uninterrupted temporary residency, a citizen is eligible to apply for permanent household registration.[76] Household registration should be a mere tool for population management and statistical purposes, not a fiat to restrict enjoyment of rights and social benefits. Thus, the police have the duty to register people on request.[77] The adoption of these measures was praised as a positive step in the struggle for the rights of the people.[78]

There was a clear shift in the language and mindset between the previous decrees and the 2006 Law. Compared to the 1997 Decree 51/CP on household registration and control, the 2006 Law was on residence. The term "residence" (*cư trú*) is progressively used instead of "household registration" (*hộ khẩu*). Even though household registration is still in use, it is intended to be more as a proof of residency than a control on individuals, at least in the public rhetoric. Decree 51/CP in 1997 stressed the authority of the state on citizens to "*determine* the residence of the citizens, to guarantee the implementation of rights and duties of the citizens, to enhance the social management, to firmly *maintain the political security and social order.*"[79] Whereas, the 2006 Law on Residence emphasizes citizens' rights and state's duties. Consider Article 1: "This law provides for the right to freedom of residence of citizens on the territory of the Socialist Republic of Vietnam,"[80] and Article 3: "Citizens satisfying the conditions of permanent or temporary registration *have the right to require the competent state organs to register their permanent or temporary residence.*"[81] There is a clear shift in the perception of the

---

[74] Trần Hồng Phong, "Cần Một Tòa Án Hiến Pháp (phần 2)" [The Need of a Constitutional Court (part 2)], *Hai Mặt*, Sept. 26, 2010, http://www.haimat.vn/article/can-mot-toa-an-hien-phap-bai-2.

[75] National Assembly of Vietnam, Law on Residence of 2006, No. 81/2006/QH11 (November 29, 2006) [hereinafter Law on Residence].

[76] Ibid., Art. 20, cl. 1.   [77] Ibid., Art. 3.

[78] Tương Lai, "Quyền Cư Trú, Quyền Của Dân" [Right to Residence, Right of the People], Pháp Luật TpHCM, June 27, 2007, http://daibieunhandan.vn/default.aspx?tabid=73&NewsId=18413.

[79] Government of Vietnam, Decree 51/CP, *supra* n. 38, Art. 1

[80] Ibid.   [81] Ibid. Art. 3.

duties of the state. Now citizens are not "registered" – an expression that conveys the state's patronizing attitude. Citizens, in the language of the 2006 Law on Residence, have the right to require state authorities to register their permanent residence. Article 4 on the principles of residence and residence management moreover mentioned the need for state regulations to be "in compliance with the Constitution and the law."[82] The reference to the Constitution had been completely absent in the previous regulatory documents.

D. *Debate on the Draft Capital Law: Rights Provisions as the Platform for Deliberation on the Proposals Regarding the Restriction of the Migration to the Capital*

The story of household registration did not end with the Law on Residence. In 2010, the issues of household registration and migration limitation once again resurged with the debate on the draft Capital Law. In 2010, Vietnam commemorated the 1,000-year anniversary of Hanoi, the capital. State and local authorities initiated many big projects to mark this event. The plan to enact a Capital Law was part of these projects, although its contents turned out to reach much farther than mere cultural matters. The Capital Law drafting committee started their work by the end of 2009 and was eager to "establish a specific mechanism so that the city of Hanoi would effectuate its role, its mission as the face of the country [sic]."[83] The first draft was presented to the National Assembly early in January 2010, proposing bold suggestions to confer on the authorities of Hanoi exorbitant powers, including the power to restrict the migration flow by measures stricter than those provided for in the Law on Residence, the power to adopt measures to manage the household registration, and the power to control and limit spontaneous migration to the city, especially seasonal workers and the homeless in the capital. On the conditions of permanent household registration in Hanoi, the first draft of the law required "a lawful employment with a salary of twice the amount of the minimum wage; proof of legal accommodation in the city; and continuous temporary residency of at least 5 years." The

---

[82] Ibid., Art. 4, cl. 1.

[83] "Xây dựng Dự Thảo Luật Thủ đô: Giải pháp gỡ "vướng" cho Hà Nội" [Drafting Capital Law Bill: Solution of "Disentanglement" for Hanoi], *Hà Nội Mới*, December 4, 2009, http://www.cpv.org.vn/cpv/modules/news/newsdetail.aspx?cn_id=375712&co_id=30361.

draft law envisaged working permits issued by the city's authorities as a condition for migrants to work in Hanoi.[84]

Constitutional claims were raised quickly in the media in January 2010 against the initial draft. The news media emphasized constitutional issues in their reports' titles and headings, thereby making the constitutional aspect more central. Constitutional objections to the draft law included lack of a constitutional basis for the exorbitant power of the capital's authorities, violation of the equality principle, and violation of the right to freedom of movement and freedom of residence of the citizens.[85]

One analysis stood out in the debate for its thorough evaluation of the constitutionality of the draft Capital Law. On January 19, 2010, VietnamNet published an opinion article by lawyer La Khanh Tung in which he explained how the draft law violated the citizens' constitutional rights and the international law of human rights. For La Khanh Tung, the draft Capital Law "had provisions that restrict some fundamental rights of the citizens, the right to freedom of residence and the right to freedom of labor." First, on the right to freedom of residence, besides the normal conditions set out by the Law on Residence, the extra requirement for household registration in Hanoi – five years of lawful temporary residency, plus a salary double the amount of the minimum wage – violated not only the right to freedom of residence, but also the right to freedom of movement, as the two rights are closely connected. For the lawyer, these rights are "very important for the development of the individual." They "are not absolute rights, and can be restricted, but to avoid the arbitrary regulations by the authorities, international law has strict provisions on the conditions of the limitation of these rights": restrictive measures on those rights can only be adopted for national security purpose, public order, social health or morality, or rights to freedom of other people, and so forth. However, the Capital Law drafters did not provide any basis to prove that the limitation of the citizens' rights served public order purposes.

Second, for the lawyer, when the draft law imposed a working permit as a condition to work in Hanoi, it clearly violated the right to work and the freedom to choose one's profession, besides other rights to adequate

---

[84] *See* Wendy Zeldin, "Vietnam: Revised Draft Capital Law Made Public," *Library of Congress*, March 2, 2010, http://www.loc.gov/lawweb/servlet/lloc_news?disp2_l205401840_Legislative2opower.

[85] Lê Kiên, "Dự Thảo Luật Thủ Đô Vướng Hiến Pháp" [The Draft Capital Law Has Constitutional Problems], *Tuổi Trẻ*, February 12, 2010, http://phienbancu.tuoitre.vn/Tianyon/Index.aspx?ArticleID=363514&ChannelID=3.

working conditions. These are the rights that are enshrined not only in international human rights instruments to which Vietnam is a signatory, but also in Article 55 of the Vietnamese Constitution and in Article 5 of the Vietnamese Labor Code. Thus, "the State of Vietnam (the whole apparatus from the central to the local authorities, both in the rural and urban areas) has not only the obligation to respect the right to work, but also the duty to create jobs for the citizens." We can see in La Khanh Tung's analysis an emphasis on both the negative and positive duties of the state: regarding the right to work, the state has both the duty to respect it and to promote it.

One month after the first draft, a revised draft was presented in which the controversial measures that restricted migration to the city were removed.[86] In May 2010, the National Assembly rejected a push by the Ministry of Justice – the principle drafter of the bill – to quickly deliberate and adopt the draft law. The legislature postponed the deliberation of the bill to a subsequent session in November 2010 to have more time to consider the executive's proposal.[87] As the debate continued in the media during 2010, it was interesting to note how, again, the Constitution provided the platform on which the government and the members of the National Assembly articulated their arguments. The executive branch, the drafter of the law, had to respond to pro-rights arguments, to justify their proposals in constitutional terms, and, thus, to adopt the logic of the social debate.

In the Report on the Evaluation of the Capital Law project published by the Evaluation Council of the Ministry of Justice, there was an evaluation of the constitutionality of the law, but the evaluation was very superficial. There was almost no serious constitutional analysis. The only constitutional provision that was mentioned was Article 52 of the Constitution (all citizens are equal before the law). The council just said

---

[86] "Hà Nội Bỏ Dự Án Siết Chặt Nhập Cư" [Hanoi Abandons the Plan to Restrict Migration], *Pháp Luật TpHCM*, February 20, 2010, http://vtc.vn/2-239555/xa-hoi/ha-noi-bo-du-an-siet-chat-nhap-cu.htm. Although these concrete measures were removed from the draft law, observers subsequently noticed that the government attempted to reintroduce the removed restrictive measures into the implementation decrees regarding the migration control. Trần Thức, "Hà Nội Muốn Siết Chặt Nhập Cư: Cuộc Sống Mới, Tư Duy Cũ" [Ha Noi Intending to Restrict Migration: New Life, Old Mindset], *Công An Nhân Dân*, November 19, 2010, http://antgct.cand.com.vn/vi-vn/cstctuan/2010/11/54751.cand.

[87] Hồng Khánh, "Lùi Thời Hạn Trình Luật Thủ Đô Đến Cuối Năm" [Postponing the Deadline to Present the Capital Law to the End of the Year], *VnExpress*, May 11, 2010, http://vnexpress.net/gl/xa-hoi/2010/05/3ba1bb91/.

the provisions of the draft are in accordance with Article 52, although the drafting committee might need to review Article 26 of the draft law (on the conditions to recruit public officials of the capital) to make sure of its conformity with the principle of equality.[88]

During the discussion session in which members of the People's Council of Hanoi contributed opinions to the draft Capital Law, Mr. Vo Van Tuyen from the Ministry of Justice found a simplistic excuse for the Capital Law in his interpretation of Article 68 of the Constitution:

> According to article 68 of the Constitution, a citizen has the right to freedom of residence *in accordance with the law.* The drafting committee thinks that the Capital Law is also a law, so the provisions conferring to the Government the power to issue regulations regarding the conditions of residence in the center of Hanoi [...] in accordance with the general planning of the capital is not contrary to the Constitution.[89]

The Minister of Justice Ha Hung Cuong, in a media interview, also raised constitutional arguments:

> To reduce migration is necessary to reduce the population growth of the capital, to limit traffic congestion, to reduce the grubbiness of the capital [sic]. The Constitution provides that everybody has the right to freedom of residence in accordance with the law; it does not mean everybody can reside anywhere [sic]. Thus, one cannot say that the provisions regarding residence in the draft law are contrary to the Constitution.[90]

Even though the arguments of these officials might sound absurd, simplistic, or evasive, the most important thing to note for the purpose of this paper is that constitutionality has become part of the sociopolitical epistemology: the government has had to justify their proposals in constitutional terms and thus admitted the logic raised by the public debate and followed it.

---

[88] The Evaluation Council of the Justice Ministry, Report No. 45/BTP-HDTD on the Evaluation of the Capital Law Project (March 18, 2010).

[89] "Hội Đồng Nhân Dân Thành Phố Hà Nội Góp Ý cho Dự Thảo Luật Thủ Đô: Tiếp Tục Bổ Sung, Làm Rõ Nhiều Vấn Đề" [The People's Council of Hanoi Contributes Opinion for the Draft Capital Law: Continuing to Complete and Clarify Many Issues], *Hà Nội Mới*, No. 14768, March 31, 2010; Nguyên Nhung, "Dự Thảo Luật Thủ Đô: Nhiều Nội Dung Chưa Thống Nhất" [Draft Capital Law: Inconsistent Content], Daibieunhandan.com, April 1, 2010, http://daibieunhandan.vn/default.aspx?tabid=81&NewsId=101265.

[90] "Việc Nhập Hộ Khẩu Theo Tôi Là Hơi Dễ" [For Me, Household Registration Is Too Easy], *VTC News*, November 5, 2010, http://vietbao.vn/Xa-hoi/Viec-nhap-ho-khau-Ha-Noi-theo-toi-la-hoi-de/75269301/157/.

The 12th Legislature deliberated the draft law in the final working session from November 2010 to March 2011. There continued to be strong constitutional objections against a special power for the authorities of Hanoi to regulate migration to the city by fiat, among other exorbitant powers.[91] On March 29, 2011, the National Assembly rejected the draft Capital Law. The executive again submitted another draft for deliberation at the 13th National Assembly in 2012.[92] By October 2012, the debates at the National Assembly and in the media continued to raise constitutional concern about the strictness of the draft Capital Law compared to the 2006 Law on Residence: whereas the 2006 Law allows permanent registration in the cities after one year of temporary residency, the draft Capital Law requires three years.[93] At this point, however, conditions such as lawful employment, salary of twice the amount of the minimum wages, and so forth were clearly out of the question on the grounds that they constituted violations of citizens' constitutional rights. On November 21, 2012, the Capital Law was adopted with only one difference from the 2006 Law on Residence. The 2012 Capital Law provides for an additional requirement of three years of temporary residency for migrants who do not work for the state, do not have a permanent employment contract, or do not have family members who are permanent residents of Hanoi to register for permanent residence in the city.[94]

[91] Vũ Anh Minh, "Dự Thảo Luật Thủ Đô Cần Thêm Thời Gian Nghiên Cứu" [More Time Is Needed to Consider the Draft Capital Law], *VietnamPlus*, November 16, 2010, http://hanoi.vietnamplus.vn/Home/Du-thao-Luat-Thu-do-can-them-thoi-gian-nghien-cuu/201011/3727.vnplus; Chính Trung, "Cần Sớm Thông Qua Luật Thủ Đô" [Need to Pass the Capital Law Soon], *An Ninh Thủ Đô*, January 1, 2011, http://www.anninhthudo.vn/errorpages/404.htm?aspxerrorpath=/tianyon/Index.aspx; Cẩn Cường, "Luật Thủ đô: Khó "đua" kịp Đại lễ 1.000 năm" [Capital Law: Difficult to Meet the 1,000 Years Great Commemoration], *Dân Trí*, February 9, 2010, http://dantri.com.vn/xa-hoi/luat-thu-do-kho-dua-kip-dai-le-1000-nam-378516.htm; Thu Hiền, "Luật Thủ đô phải đảm bảo nguyên tắc hợp hiến, hợp pháp" [Capital Law Must Ensure Its Legality and Constitutionality], *Lao Động*, January 14, 2011, http://laodong.com.vn/Chinh-tri/Luat-Thu-do-phai-dam-bao-nguyen-tac-hop-hien-hop-phap/46629.bld.

[92] "Luật Thủ Đô "Tái Xuất": Vẫn Siết Nhập Cư, Tăng Mức Phạt" [Capital Law Reappears: Still Restricting Migration, Increasing Fines], *VnEconomy*, August 17, 2012, http://vneconomy.vn/20120817103815320P0C9920/luat-thu-do-tai-xuat-van-siet-nhap-cu-tang-muc-phat.htm.

[93] "Luật Thủ Đô: Vẫn Siết Nhập Cư Nội Thành" [Capital Law: Still Restricting Urbanward Migration], *VnEconomy*, October 6, 2012, http://vneconomy.vn/20121006053828890P0C9920/luat-thu-do-van-siet-nhap-cu-noi-thanh.htm.

[94] National Assembly of Vietnam, Luật Thủ Đô [Capital Law], No. 25/2012/QH13 (November 21, 2012), Art. 19.

III. REFLECTION FROM THE VIETNAMESE EXPERIENCE

This chapter has shown how constitutional rights played a role in the Vietnamese debates on law and policy, even in the absence of a constitutional court. The Constitution has become a pragmatic tool in the sociopolitical deliberation process. The case of Vietnam has revealed the potential of constitutional arguments to open the political system and societal dialogue. To borrow from Sunstein's notion of incompletely theorized agreements, rights provisions in the Vietnamese Constitution contribute to political deliberation to resolve the most urgent matters, without requiring agreement on major theoretical points. For example, constitutional rights have been advanced to transform the nature of the household registration system and to shift the relationship between citizen and state – the concrete issues that have upset people. However, fundamental issues of democracy versus authoritarianism were actually not discussed. In other words, articulation of citizens' rights and the state's duties, both negative and positive duties, occurred quite naturally without arguing about the nature of the regime and succeeded in part to transform the public perception of the state-society relationship, at least formally in the law.

Regarding the distinction of positive versus negative rights, the Vietnamese debates revealed how each right was associated with both negative duties and positive duties of the state. There are four rights and one principle that are most relevant in the debates: freedom of residence (which is closely related to freedom of movement), right to housing, right to work, right to education, and the principle of equality.

The right to freedom of residence is usually seen as a civil right. The correlative state's duty is often negative: the state should not restrict people's movement and settlement. However, from the debate in Vietnam, we can see that state duty is also positive: state officials have the duty to register citizens' residence.

The rights to work, housing, and education are usually seen as socioeconomic rights. The correlative state duties are often positive: the state has to create jobs and provide housing and education. However, there is also a negative duty of the state in the Vietnamese context: the state should not restrain the equal opportunity for jobs, housing, and education.

I suggest that the historical-political legacy plays a role in this peculiarity of rights articulation in Vietnam: social and economic rights can require a state's negative duties as the society struggles to move away

TABLE 4.2. *Nature of rights in the Vietnamese debate on household registration regulation*

Right	State's negative duties	State's positive duties
To freedom of residence	To not interfere with the population's mobility by fiat	To register citizens' residency when they move
To education	To not issue administrative burdens to hinder the choice of the school	To provide the education system
To health care	To not issue administrative burdens to hinder the enjoyment of the right	To provide health care services
To work	To not interfere with the freedom to find work wherever the citizens wish	To create jobs

from an absolute political control of the social sphere by the socialist state. In the pre-1986 planned economy, the Vietnamese state's proactive intervention to allocate resources, social services, and employments had been taken for granted. However, once Vietnam switched to a market-based economy, the society started to get used to the law of the market and the sphere of social autonomy such a system brings about (however limited in scope this sphere is in the imperfect socialist market system in Vietnam). Because of the history of proactive yet discriminatory state intervention in sociopolitical life, the articulation of rights, even socioeconomic rights, emphasizes also the negative duties of the state to avoid such discrimination.

This does not mean that in a country such as Vietnam, the state only has negative duties concerning socioeconomic rights. The state's duties in the realization of socioeconomic rights are positive duties. However, in the Vietnamese context, the articulation of some socioeconomic rights also includes negative duties of the state: the state has the positive duties to realize socioeconomic rights, but the state should also restrain from taking measures that are discriminatory in the realization of those rights.

It could also be argued that the negative duties associated with the three socioeconomic rights were justified in the name of the principle of equality: citizens should not be discriminated against because of their place of origin. A unitary state should not hinder citizens' access and equal opportunity to education, jobs, and housing. The household registration system is the measure taken by the state (that is, a positive intervention by the state) to facilitate or restrict citizens' access to basic social services and to the job market in a locality, on the basis of citizens' place of origin. Such measure is out of tune with the new social mindset that stresses the importance of equal opportunity and equal access to state social services.

The finding from the Vietnamese constitutional rights' debates shows how historical experience shapes our constitutional expectations. Thus, a deep understanding of social issues and correlative constitutional demands is necessary to determine the direction of constitutional reforms. For instance, socioeconomic rights are taken for granted in the Vietnamese context, thus arguments against socioeconomic rights should only be taken as warnings of precaution in determining the extent and scope of these rights, not as the basis to completely ignore these rights in the Constitution. Also, the language of the rights provisions, for both civic and socioeconomic rights, should reflect both the negative and positive duties of the state.

CONCLUSION

It might seem self-contradictory to use rights and a deliberative democracy framework to analyze policy debates in a socialist regime, yet, a closer look at constitutional debates in Vietnam has revealed that the logic of deliberative democracy, at least in the way Sunstein conceptualizes it, is there: the use of constitutional arguments to challenge concrete abusive practices of power, leaving aside potential disagreements on other fundamental matters of the nature of the regime. This does not mean this nascent signal of a deliberative democracy in Vietnam is satisfying or sufficient. This is not what this chapter suggests. Rather, the finding of this paper should be seen as a hopeful discovery to understand where we are now and to remind political and legal reformers of the need to take historical legacy and societal demands seriously. At least this is one way to interpret Sunstein's message, that "the route to future advances, in both theory and practice, will lie less through abstractions, and in discussions of the concepts themselves, and more through an appreciation of the concrete contexts in which a nation's diverse aspirations are tested and specified."[95]

[95] Sunstein, *Designing Democracy, supra* n. 5, 11.

Part III

Ethnicity and Race

5

Asymmetrical Federalism in Burma*

David C. Williams

INTRODUCTION

Federalism is often touted as a partial solution for civil wars rooted in ethnic conflict.[1] Under a sensitive federal system, each ethnic group would be allowed to govern itself in those areas of life that matter most to it and with respect to which it is different from the country as a whole. The central government, by contrast, would have jurisdiction only over those areas in which unity and uniformity are necessary and those with respect to which the various groups do not differ. As a result, federalism might seem a good bargain for all the contending groups; they might give their loyalty to the constitutional regime because it satisfies their desire for self-determination.

Nowhere, however, are ethnic groups all created alike: different issues matter to different groups, and the groups differ from the country as a whole with respect to different areas of life. Accordingly, different territorially concentrated ethnic groups make demands for control over different areas of life. In other words, they demand a system of asymmetrical federalism, a system in which different states receive different

---

* Much of this article is drawn from the author's personal experience advising Burmese pro-democracy groups on constitutional reform and drafting between May 2003 and the present. As such, much of the information herein is not footnoted in the conventional manner. Any questions regarding these experiences should be directed to the author.

[1] See, e.g., Nancy Bermeo, "Conclusion: The Merits of Federalism," in *Federalism and Territorial Cleavages*, eds. Ugo M. Amoretti and Nancy Bermeo (Baltimore: Johns Hopkins University Press, 2004), 457–82 (discussing the advantages of federal systems in eliminating ethnic conflict); Baogang He, Brian Galligan, and Takashi Inoguchi, *Federalism in Asia* (Cheltenham, Northampton: Edward Elgar, 2007); Katherine Adeney, "Comment: The "Necessity" of Asymmetrical Federalism?" *Ethonopolitics* 6(1) (2007): 117–20 (examining asymmetrical federalism in various countries).

types and/or different degrees of power. In some countries, such as India, asymmetrical federalism has proved to be invaluable in coping with ethnic tensions.[2]

But asymmetrical federalism also has drawbacks. As has often been noted, asymmetrical systems can be complicated, cumbersome, and difficult to operationalize, especially for those who have had more experience at waging war than at waging peace.[3] In addition, asymmetrical systems frequently lead to intergroup resentment if some groups are perceived to have received a better deal than others.[4] Such resentment can be especially dangerous in countries newly and shakily emergent from civil war and therefore prone to relapse into civil war.

In this essay, however, I want to stress a different drawback to asymmetrical federalism: although it is sensitive to differences among groups at any given time, it tends to be insensitive to changes within any one group over time. Asymmetrical systems are generally quite complicated and detailed so as to recognize that ethnic groups have different needs and demands. Those needs and demands, however, are not static; they change with the years, especially if democracy takes hold and brings the groups into closer and more harmonious contact. War tends to harden differences; peace tends to make them more fluid. Asymmetrical systems can therefore rapidly become a highly detailed snapshot of the ethnic landscape of the past and hence insensitive to the current situation. In addition, if the groups do become more like each other, they may no longer need individualized treatments; the same system of symmetrical federalism might work for them all.

Many think that despite its drawbacks, asymmetrical federalism may be a good approach in certain countries because of its extreme sensitivity to differences among groups.[5] However, its insensitivity to difference over time must be factored into the balance, because it might virtually

---

[2] *See* Alfred Stepan, "Federalism, Multi-National States and Democracy: A Theoretical Framework, the Indian Model and a Tamil Case Study" (Paper read at the 98th American Political Science Association Annual Meeting and Exhibition, 2002 August 29); David Stuligross and Varshney Ashutosh, "Ethnic Diversities, Constitutional Designs and Public Policies in India," in *The Architecture of Democracy Constitutional Design, Conflict Management, and Democracy*, ed. Andrew Reynolds (New York: Oxford University Press, 2002), 429–54.

[3] *See, e.g.,* Jorge Martinez-Vazquez, "Asymmetric Federalism in Russia: Cure or Poison?" in *Fiscal Fragmentation in Decentralized Countries: Subsidiarity, Solidarity and Asymmetry* (Cheltenham: Edward Elgar, 2007), 227–66.

[4] He et al., *Federalism in Asia, supra* n. 1, 44.

[5] *See, e.g.,* Marc Weller and Katherine Nobbs, eds., *Asymmetric Autonomy and the Settlement of Ethnic Conflicts* (Philadelphia: University of Pennsylvania Press, 2011) (discussing the paradox of autonomy and integration in asymmetrical systems).

negate the asymmetrical system's initial sensitivity. As a result, it may be that the drawbacks outweigh the advantages; perhaps a symmetrical system would have been a better choice at the outset. In addition, a less complicated, more open-textured constitutional system might prove more adaptable to changed circumstances. In this essay, I will explore this thesis through a close-grained analysis of Burma's constitutional history.

BACKGROUND TO BURMESE FEDERALISM

Burma is a multi-ethnic country that has suffered civil war for decades. The majority group is called the Burmans; they constitute about two-thirds of the population.[6] There are many minority groups that together make up the remaining one-third. The minorities had never been wholly integrated into the Burman kingdom before the British conquered the area during the nineteenth century. When the British left at the close of World War II, many minorities did not wish to be included in the new country called Burma because they feared that they would be politically and militarily dominated by the Burmans. The Karen went first into revolt in 1948, and eventually they were joined by virtually every other minority group. In the midst of the war, the military seized power in 1962 and held it until quite recently.[7] In other words, the conflict in Burma is not foundationally about democracy versus militarism. It is foundationally about ethnicity, and even if Burma returns to democracy, it will not be stable unless it addresses the underlying ethnic issues.[8]

The prospects for improvement in Burma's ethnic climate have brightened markedly in recent years, although peace is still only a distant dream for many of Burma's minority people. In 2008, the military government's constituent assembly finished a draft constitution, which was ratified by a fraudulent referendum the same year.[9] The new constitution still gives the military a dominant role: the army is not subject to civilian control,[10]

---

[6] *See* David I. Steinberg, *Burma, The State of Myanmar* (Washington, DC: Georgetown University Press, 2001).

[7] For a more detailed history of events leading up to military's assumption of power, *see* David C. Williams, "Constitutionalism Before Constitutions: Burma's Struggle to Build a New Order," *Texas Law Review* 87 (2009).

[8] For a more general discussion of the role of ethnic issues in Burma, *see* David C. Williams, "Ethnicity, Elections, and Reform in Burma," *Georgetown Journal of International Affairs* 12 (2011): 99.

[9] *See* "Burma 'Approves New Constitution,'" *BBC News*, 200 May 15, http://news.bbc .co.uk/2/hi/asia-pacific/7402105.stm.

[10] *See* Constitution of the Republic of the Union of Myanmar, chap. I, § 20 (2008) (translated in *Constitution of the Countries of the World*, vol. 12, eds. Ridiger Wolfrum

and the commander-in-chief appoints 25 percent of the members of the state and union legislatures,[11] as well as the Defense, Interior, and Border Affairs Ministers.[12] As the first election approached, the government revoked all of its ceasefires with the ethnic resistance armies, and so it seemed that the civil war would only spread and intensify under the new constitutional regime.[13] Instead, after the 2010 elections, the new civilian president proved surprisingly open to reform,[14] releasing political prisoners,[15] easing censorship,[16] and allowing a limited number of ethnic minority people to win elections for the state and union legislatures.[17]

The president also reversed course on the civil war: having revoked the old ceasefires, the government now sought to cement new ones.[18] At the time of this writing, the fighting still continues in Kachin State because the Kachin Independence Army and the government have been unable to

and Rainer Grote (New York: Oxford University Press, 2009)) (declaring the rights and responsibilities of the military to include "safeguarding the non-disintegration of the Union, the non-disintegration of National solidarity and the perpetuation of sovereignty" and "safeguarding the Constitution").

[11] *See* ibid. ch. III, § 109(b) (requiring the 440-member legislature to include 110 representatives "who are members of the Defense Services nominated by the Commander-in-Chief of the Defense Services").

[12] *See* ibid. ch. V, § 232(b) (mandating that the president appoint the ministers of Defense, Border Affairs, and Home Affairs from a list of members of Defense Services nominated by the commander-in-chief of the Defense Services and permitting the commander-in-chief to make the appointments himself if he desires to do so).

[13] *See* Brian McCartan, "Myanmar Ceasefires on a Tripwire," *Asian Times Online*, 2010 April 30, http://www.atimes.com/atimes/Southeast_Asia/LD30Ae01.html; Lawi Weng, "Mon Cease-fire Anniversary Passes without Ceremony," *The Irrawaddy*, 2010 June 30, http://www2.irrawaddy.org/article.php?art_id=18839.

[14] *See* Thomas Fuller, "As Myanmar Changes, So Does Its Leader," *New Yorks Times*, 2012 April 3, http://www.nytimes.com/2012/04/04/world/asia/myanmar-president-praises-weekend-elections.html?pagewanted=all&_r=0 (detailing the shift in leadership style of U Thein Sein as he settled into the role of president of Burma).

[15] *See* "Myanmar's President Grants 452 Prisoners Amnesty," *CNN*, 2012 November 15, http://www.cnn.com/2012/11/14/world/asia/myanmar-prisoner-release/index.html.

[16] *See* Thomas Fuller, "Myanmar to Curb Censorship of Media," *New York Times*, 2012 August 20, http://www.nytimes.com/2012/08/21/world/asia/myanmar-abolishes-censorship-of-private-publications.html?_r=0.

[17] *See* "Final Election Results Announced," *Democratic Voice of Burma*, 2010 November 18, http://www.dvb.no/elections/final-election-results-announced/12942 (noting that "despite fears before the polls that any pro-democracy candidates would be altogether sidelined," four oppositions were able to win seats in the closely choreographed election).

[18] *See* Seth Mydans, "Burmese Government and Ethnic Rebel Group Sign Cease-Fire," *New York Times*, 2012 January 12, http://www.nytimes.com/2012/01/13/world/asia/myanmar-signs-truce-with-ethnic-rebel-group.html.

come to terms.[19] The war also continues at a lower level even in some areas governed by the new ceasefires, because the army is still acting independently from the civilian government.[20] Nonetheless, as part of the ceasefires, the union negotiators have promised the ethnic armies that the next step will be open-ended political talks.[21] Constitutional reform will be very much on the table, including what the union negotiators call *constitutional decentralization* rather than *federalism* because they equate the latter term with secession.

For full disclosure, I should reveal that the Center for Constitutional Democracy, which I direct, is advising many of the ethnic armies, and I know many of the leaders personally.[22] I have often walked across the borders to meet with the officers and civilian leaders in the areas that they control. Political conditions have so improved that it is now possible for us to meet openly with our friends in Rangoon itself.

The leaders of the ethnic armies believe that constitutional reform will allow them to achieve self-determination through decentralization, power-sharing at the centre, and individual rights to protect local culture. For the sake of convenience in this essay, I will call this three-part package *federalism*, but I intend it as a purely stipulated usage. I am not trying to intervene into the scholarly controversy over the true meaning of the term – whatever that might mean.[23]

For a long time, outside observers tended to conceive of the conflict in Burma as a simple struggle between democracy and militarism;[24] they

[19] *See* Kocha Olarn and Jethro Mullen, "Myanmar airstrikes on Kachin Rebels Raise Global Concerns," 2013 *New York Times*, January 3, http://edition.cnn.com/2013/01/03/world/asia/myanmar-kachin-violence/?hpt=ias_c2.

[20] *See* "Myanmar: Storm Clouds on the Horizon" (International Crisis Group Asia Report No. 238, 2012 November 12, http://www.crisisgroup.org/~/media/Files/asia/southeast-asia/burma-myanmar/238-myanmar-storm-clouds-on-the-horizon.pdf): 4 (detailing the complicity of security forces in violence against Muslims).

[21] *See* Saw Yan Naing, "Naypyidaw Promises Kachins Political Dialogue," *The Irrawaddy*, 2012 October 30, http://www.irrawaddy.org/archives/17647 (describing union promises of open political dialogue made to the Kachin Independence Organization during recent talks between the two groups).

[22] Further information about the Center for Constitutional Democracy can be found on our Web site, http://ccd.indiana.edu/.

[23] *See, e.g.*, Randy E. Barnett, "Three Federalisms," *Loyola University Chicago Law Journal* 39 (2008) (discussing three variants of American federalism).

[24] *See, e.g.*, "Editorial, Democracy, Burma-Style," *Washington Post*, 2008 May 4, http://www.washingtonpost.com/wp-dyn/content/article/2008/05/03/AR2008050301755.html (characterizing the political situation in Burma as a conflict between proponents of democracy, such as Aung San Suu Kyi, and the military junta); Seth Mydans and Mark McDonald, "Pro-Democracy Leader Goes on Trial in Myanmar," *New York*

showed little awareness of the underlying ethnic roots of the struggle. More recently, organizations such as the U.S. Department of State,[25] the United Nations,[26] and the European Union[27] have shown more awareness that the ethnic minorities have special constitutional needs and make special demands, but they still tend to lump the minorities together as posing a single issue. Outsiders generally have very little sense that the minorities are themselves highly variable. Of course, people recognize that the minorities are not culturally the same: they have different languages, religions, and so forth. However, they are thought to have the same kind of grievances, aspirations, and relationships to the centre, and so the same constitutional solution will work for all of them.

If the minorities really did need the same constitutional treatment, a simple, robust system of symmetrical federalism would serve their ends. In fact, however, the minorities are different not only from the majority but also from each other; they actually need and want different things from their constitution. As a result, finding a constitutional settlement that will work equally well for all is more complicated than might first appear.

The remainder of this essay will advance three claims. The next section will explain that although diverse, many of the minorities do share

---

Times, 2009 May 18, http://www.nytimes.com/2009/05/19/world/asia/19myanmar. html?_r=0 (reporting on the currently ongoing trial of Suu Kyi for violating the terms of her house arrest and casting her as the symbolic leader of all opposition to the government); Lisa Brooten, "Human Rights Discourse and the Development of Democracy in a Multiethnic State," *Asian Journal of Communication* 14 (September 2004): 184 (quoting one Karenni leader's frustrations: "When you go out and visit a diplomat, and you start talking about the Karenni or other [non-Burman] groups, he will say, 'No, we don't know [about that]. We know only about Aung San Suu Kyi and democracy.'").

[25] *See* "Background Briefing on the Secretary's Meetings With Burmese President Thein Sein, Congolese President Joseph Kabila and Rwandan President Paul Kagame by Senior State Department Officials," 2012 September 26, U.S. Department of State Web site, http://www.state.gov/r/pa/prs/ps/2012/09/198284.htm (referring to ethnic issues in Burma).

[26] *See* Permanent Mission of the Union of Myanmar to the United Nations, "Memorandum on the Situation of Human Rights in the Union of Myanmar," 2008 November 5, http://www.un.int/wcm/content/site/myanmar/cache/offonce/pid/2669; jsessionid=905A8738AEA18D1CDE38E8B9D8B39CA2 (detailing a history of ethnic groups in Burma).

[27] *See* The Council of the European Union, "Council Conclusions on Burma/Myanmar," 2012 April 23, http://eeas.europa.eu/myanmar/docs/council_conclusions_april_2012_en. pdf (recognizing a desire to "bring peace and stability to ethnic regions.... as part of national reconciliation.").

some common demands. In different ways and to different degrees, decentralization, power-sharing, and individual rights will help many of the minorities. The minorities, however, tend to desire these features for not one but three different reasons: cultural diversity, distrust of the Burmans, and self-determination for its own sake. In the design of a constitution, however, each of these reasons pulls in different directions: the different reasons for desiring federalism would entail somewhat different constitutional schemes. Although all three would be served by decentralization, power-sharing, and individual rights, each reason would lead to a different particular version of each of those features, conceivably leading to a quite complicated constitution. Even if all the minorities were therefore exactly the same, they would need a complex constitution with a wide variety of constitutional mechanisms.

However, the second claim is that they are not in fact the same, and the third section will examine their differences. Although sharing the common ground laid out in the second section, the minorities also have somewhat different constitutional needs, though they do not always realize that fact. Each part of the federalism package will help (or not help) different minority groups in different ways and to different degrees, and the individual groups desire them in different ways and to different degrees. In the face of this diversity, the Burmese could adopt a very complicated constitution that treats all the minorities differently, according to their own particular characteristics. This option poses the same problems as all asymmetrical arrangements: the Burmese people would find it difficult to make such a complicated constitution work; it might spark resentment if some are perceived to have gotten an especially good deal; and the minorities will continue to change, so that this very complicated constitution might rapidly become obsolete.

The fourth section suggests a different possibility: a new pan-ethnic consciousness is, I believe, emerging among the minorities. Because of networking and fighting together, they have begun to conceptualize their problems in more similar ways. As a result, over time, a constitution that treats the minorities all the same will not be so risky because they will be more the same, and they might learn to accommodate themselves to it. Of course, if the minorities do not become more alike and refuse to accommodate, then there may be continued turbulence and even civil war. For that reason, symmetrical federalism can be at best a calculated gamble, not a sure-fire cure. If it does emerge, however, this new pan-minority identity might even serve as a way station to a pan-Burmese identity that does not suppress the more particular ethnic identities but includes all

Burmese people – Burmans and minorities alike. And without such a broad civic identity, Burma may never shake off the risk of reversion to its bloody past.

WHAT THE MINORITIES HAVE IN COMMON

To understand the future prospects for Burmese constitutionalism, one must first understand the nature of the ethnic conflict. Many scholars of ethnic identity rightly emphasize that ethnicity is a social construction, neither primordial nor natural.[28] Nonetheless, many Burmese minorities experience their ethnicity as real and meaningful, even if it is socially constructed. They believe that the military government is making war on them because of their ethnicity, and they have often felt that they can depend only on co-ethnics when the bullets are flying. Although ethnic identity is sometimes poisonous, many groups in Burma illustrate its upside: despite going through decades of civil war, many of the minorities still form stable communities, with intact authority structures, whose members care for each other. As a result, Burma has not melted down into the sort of war of all against all that other places have. At the same time, because they are socially constructed, ethnic identities have not remained static. James Scott believes that the ancestors of many of the hill people actually were Burmans from central Burma who fled into the hills to escape the ravages of the Burman State and promptly took on a new ethnic identity.[29] More recently, during the fighting of the last fifty years, ethnic identities seem to have hardened, and they might become more fluid if democracy and compromise politics firmly take hold.

For now, however, the minorities experience their ethnicity as real, and most think that it is central to their political perceptions and agendas. As a result, they demand that the union constitution allow them to express it in political space. From my observation, they have three core concerns – three reasons for demanding special constitutional protection.

First, they feel that their culture is different from the majority's, and they do not want to be governed by the majority's culture. The minorities speak different languages, often practice different religions, and have

---

[28] *See, e.g.*, James D. Fearon and David D. Laitin, "Violence and the Social Construction of Ethnic Identity," *International Organization* 54(4) (2000): 845–77.

[29] James Scott, "Hill-Valley Relations in Mainland Southeast Asia, Especially Burma: Why Civilizations Can't Climb Hills" (Keynote address, Burma Studies Conference, Burma-Myanmar Research and Its Future, Gothenberg, Sweden, 2002).

different political structures.[30] The military junta has, on and off, committed campaigns to "Burmanize" the minorities[31]: burning down churches,[32] banning the use of local languages in various ways,[33] and allowing only Burmans to rise to high military office.[34] The minorities worry that even after a transition to democracy, a government dominated by Burmans will continue these methods, and that by virtue of their greater number, the Burmans will be able to do so unless the constitution limits what an electoral majority can do to the minority.

Second, the minorities tend to distrust Burmans considered as a group, although they have great trust in particular Burmans, especially Aung san Suu Kyi.[35] The minorities remember that of old: the Burman kings tried to conquer them, and that during World War II, the Burman army committed atrocities against them.[36] Even today, many minorities believe that most Burmans view the minorities as inferior, assume that Burmans should always be running things, and do not care about the minorities' interests and concerns. Some worry that even in a democratic government, Burmans will actively persecute them – again, unless the constitution limits what an electoral majority can do to the minority.

---

[30] *See generally* Edmund Leach, *Political Systems of Highland Burma: A Study of Kachin Social Structure* (London: Berg, 1973) (studying these differences for the Kachin and Shan populations in North East Burma specifically); Martin Smith, *Burma: Insurgency and the Politics of Ethnicity* (New York: Zed Books, 1999) (identifying hundreds of regional dialects).

[31] *See, e.g.*, Mark Fineman, "Muslims Flee Brutal Effort to 'Burmanize' Myanmar," *L.A. Times*, 1992 February 15, http://articles.latimes.com/1992-02-15/news/mn-1739-1_muslim-refugees (describing military junta's efforts to "Burmanize" 40 million people).

[32] *See* Charlie Campbell, "Burma Among Worst For Religious Freedom: Report," *The Irrawaddy*, 2012 March 29, http://www.irrawaddy.org/archives/1339 (detailing the burning of churches by the military).

[33] *See* Physicians for Human Rights, "Life Under the Junta: Evidence of Crimes Against Humanity in Burma's Chin State," January 2011, https://s3.amazonaws.com/PHR_Reports/life-under-the-junta-burma-chin-state.pdf (describing the military government's policy of appointing village elders to "village headman" almost exclusively on the basis of the ability to speak Burmese, the language of the Burman majority).

[34] *See* Jacob Leibenluft, "Who's in the Junta? The Mysterious Generals Who Run Burma," *Slate Magazine*, 2008 June 2, http://www.slate.com/articles/news_and_politics/explainer/2008/06/whos_in_the_junta.html (describing the background of Burma's most powerful military leaders).

[35] *See* Kyaw Phyo Tha, "Suu Kyi Urges Self-Reliance as Burma Marks Independence Day," *The Irrawaddy*, 2013 January 4, http://www.irrawaddy.org/archives/23122 (identifying Suu Kyi as the "Burmese democracy icon").

[36] *See* Seamus Martov, "Memories of WWII Run Deep for KIO," *The Irrawaddy*, 2012 August 13, http://www.irrawaddy.org/archives/11355.

Third, the different minorities believe that they are distinct peoples, and they want to tell their story, as a collective whole, in political space, through control of a state. In other words, they want self-determination for its own sake, not merely to protect their culture or to avoid Burman bigotry. For many westerners, with their more individualistic epistemologies, this reason may seem more obscure than the others, but it is no less real to the ethnic minorities. Many of them have a strong sense of belonging to a people, and part of what makes their lives worthwhile is the joining with co-ethnics to remember a shared past and create a shared future. Participation in this collective project gives them meaning, purpose, and identity.

Minority leaders generally believe that three constitutional devices – federalism, power-sharing in the union government, and individual rights – are the appropriate mechanisms to meet these three demands. Before the adoption of the 2008 Constitution, the minorities decided to draft proposed or "model" constitutions for each of the states to garner international attention, define their own goals more clearly for themselves, and inform the military regime of their intentions.[37] To that end, committees formed from resistance armies and civil society organizations in each state.[38] Although the primary goal of these constitutions was to outline a government for the state, many also contained provisions dealing with the relationship between the state and the union government.[39] Eventually, under the aegis of the Ethnic Nationalities Council, the state committees came together to form a new umbrella committee, called the Federal Constitution Drafting and Coordinating Committee (FCDCC), to draft a proposed union constitution.[40] These documents provide the

[37] *See, e.g.,* Kachin State Constitution (2006 Draft), http://www.ibiblio.org/obl/docs4/ Kachin-E&B.pdf (identifying the "present military leaders['] . . . [desire to] write [a] military dominated constitution that will give them the chance to pull the string of the regime and the right to seize the power whenever they like" as a basis for the drafting of a state constitution); *see generally* "Online Burma/Myanmar Library," accessed 2013 May 21, http://www.burmalibrary.org/show.php?cat=1140 (database containing draft copies of constitutions for the Shan, Chin, Karenni, Mon, Karen, Arakan, and Kachin states).

[38] *See, e.g.,* "Shan State Congress Formed," *Shanland,* 2008 December 24, http://www .shanland.org/oldversion/shan-state-congress-formed.htm (detailing the five organizations from which the seven-member constitutional committee was formed).

[39] *See, e.g.,* Kachin State Constitution (2006 Draft), *supra* n. 37, ch. 7, Art. 88 ("The Kachin State government and the Federal Union of the Republic of Burma shall interact with and assist each other to implement the tasks of the Federal Union of the Republic of Burma and of Kachin State.").

[40] *See* "Burmese Exiled Activists Complete Draft Constitution," *Democratic Voice of Burma,* 2008 February 14, http://www.dvb.no/uncategorized/burmese-exiled-activists-complete-draft-constitution/1042.

clearest and most reliable evidence of what the minorities want. In the interests of candour, I should again disclose that I advised all these committees at every stage of the proceedings.

These proposed constitutions vary in content, but they are as one in calling for decentralization, super-proportional power-sharing in the upper house of the union legislature, and strong individual rights of special importance to the minorities. Indeed, strikingly, even the military government's 2008 Constitution makes gestures towards these features, although in a much more limited way than the minorities' own proposals.[41] Speaking very generally, constitutional reform along such lines will help a great number of the minorities; this is their common ground, to the extent that they have one.

First, decentralization: the minorities are concentrated in seven hilly states surrounding the Irrawaddy delta, which is the Burman homeland.[42] Each state is named after a titular ethnic group: the Chin, Kachin, Karen, Karenni, Mon, Shan, and Rakhine.[43] To devolve power to these states is therefore to devolve power to the minorities. Decentralization would address all three of the minorities' concerns: to some extent, it would allow them to tell their own tale, insulate them from Burman animosity, and empower them to govern themselves according to their own culture.

However, the three different reasons for decentralization would lead to three different types of decentralization. For example, to protect cultural diversity, the constitution drafters would need to pursue a very particular line of inquiry. They should identify those particular areas of human life, such as language and religion, that share three features: with respect to such areas, the Burmans' culture differs from the minorities' culture; the minorities view such areas as especially important to their distinctive identity; and the minorities reasonably fear that a Burman-dominated central government might fail to protect the minorities' diversity in such areas. The constitution should then reserve power over those areas to the states. By contrast, to address the concern about Burman animosity or

---

[41] *See* Constitution of the Republic of the Union of Myanmar, *supra* n. 10, ch. IV, § 141(a) ("representatives elected in an equal number of 12 representatives from each Region or State inclusive of relevant Union territories"); *see* ibid., ch. 8, § 354(d) ("Every citizen shall be at liberty in the exercise of the following rights . . . to develop their language, literature, culture they cherish, religion they profess, and customs without prejudice to the relations between one national race and another or among national races and to other faiths.").

[42] Martin Smith, *Burma (Myanmar): The Time for Change* (London: Minority Rights Group International, 2002), 9.

[43] *See* Steinberg, *The State of Myanmar*, *supra* n. 6, xv–xx (containing detailed maps and statistical tables on the geographic distribution of Burma's ethnic minority groups).

indifference, the constitution should cabin the power of Burman office holders to injure ethnic minorities. For example, the state governments might have a veto over the use of the army against civilians within their jurisdiction; state governors might be directly elected rather than appointed from the centre; or, as in the German system, the union government could adopt general policies, but only the states would have power directly to implement them and so alone would come into contact with their citizens.[44] Finally, to allow the minorities to tell their story as peoples, state control over immigration and citizenship would become important, as would general independence from the centre and perhaps even a secession right.

In short, the different reasons for decentralization counsel different types of decentralization. However, so long as the different types are not mutually contradictory, a sufficiently complicated constitution might be able to combine them all. The same sort of analysis applies to power-sharing at the centre: each reason for power-sharing would counsel a different type of power-sharing. The most common proposal is that the titular minority states should be super-proportionally represented in the upper house of the legislature. In particular, many minorities believe that each of the seven minority states should send the same number of representatives to the upper house as the more populous states to be carved out of the central Burman areas. The different reasons for power-sharing would assign different jobs to this chamber.

For example, to shelter the minorities' cultural diversity, the drafters should again identify those areas of life that share three features: with respect to such areas, the Burmans' culture differs from the minorities' culture; the minorities view such areas as especially important to their distinctive identity; and the minorities reasonably fear that a Burman-dominated central government might fail to protect the minorities' diversity in such areas. In other words, they should identify those areas that should ideally fall within the purview of the state governments under a decentralization scheme, as noted earlier. However, if any organ of the central government should enjoy any power over those areas, then it should be the upper house; in particular, it might hold an absolute veto against union legislation in those areas. By contrast, to protect against the

---

[44] *See* Dan Hough and Charlie Jeffery, "Germany: An Erosion of Federal-Länder Linkages," in *Devolution and Electoral Politics*, eds. Dan Hough and Charlie Jeffery (Manchester: Manchester University Press, 2006), 119–39 (detailing shifts in the German federal system as a function of this power-sharing between the federal- and state-controlled legislative chambers).

animosity of Burman office holders, the upper house should have power to regulate the interaction between those office holders and people in the minority states. For example, the upper house might have a role in choosing the federal office holders serving in the states, and/or it might have a veto on the use of military force in the states. To ensure that the minorities can tell their stories as peoples, the state legislatures might directly choose the representatives to the upper house, so that the members would serve as delegates from the states themselves.

Finally, the different ethnic demands would lead to different collections of individual rights. For cultural difference, the minorities will want individual rights in those areas of life, such as culture, language, and religion, that share our now familiar three features: with respect to such areas, the Burmans' culture differs from the minorities' culture; the minorities view such areas as especially important to their distinctive identity; and the minorities reasonably fear that a Burman-dominated central government might fail to protect the minorities' diversity in such areas. To the extent that any government should be allowed to regulate such areas, as we have seen, it should be the states, perhaps with the assistance of the upper house. To a significant extent, however, those areas should fall within the control of individuals; although in a state with a strong ethnic identity, the government might have more power over such matters as religion, language, and culture than in a more thoroughly liberal democracy. By contrast, to protect against the animosity of Burman office holders, the constitution should contain very strong anti-discrimination rules and procedural protections, as well as an impartial judiciary to enforce them. To safeguard the ability of the minorities to tell their stories as peoples, the constitution should safeguard rights of political participation in the state government, so that all minority members may have a hand in telling the story.

HOW THE MINORITIES DIFFER

In short, the minorities desire federalism for three different reasons, each of which would lead to different versions of each of the three-part federalism package – for a total of nine different approaches. If we could end the analysis at this point, if the situation were as simple as sketched in the last section, Burma's constitution would already be extremely complicated – although, at least, symmetrical. In fact, however, the situation is more complicated. So far, we have been wildly generalizing; we have been treating the ethnic groups as one large set, as though every member of the set had the same relationship to these various grievances and mechanisms. However, they do not, and as a result, no single set of constitutional arrangements will satisfy all the minority groups. Because some of the groups have power to wreck the peace if they are unsatisfied, this state of affairs is clearly a cause for concern. It may be necessary, then, to contemplate a system of asymmetrical federalism, despite all its familiar drawbacks.

In particular, the different groups experience the grievances in different ways and to different degrees. In addition, because of geography, the different constitutional mechanisms will function differently for different groups; the same device will produce different results – some quite unsatisfactory to some groups – in different neighbourhoods.

The Asymmetrical Effects of Symmetrical Federalism

To understand the way that the different mechanisms will work for different groups in different parts of the country, it is important to understand that Burma's minority states have hugely variable demographics. Some of Burma's minority states contain small, relatively homogeneous populations, such as Chin and Karenni States.[45] Others house populations that are quite large and almost as ethnically complicated as Burma itself, such as Shan and Kachin states.[46] Although the Shan are a plurality in Shan State and the Kachin in Kachin State, those states also contain large numbers of minorities, including Burman people, who, although nationally the majority, are locally a minority.

For these minorities-within-minorities, the three-part federalism package would be an improvement on the current situation, but it would not allow meaningful self-determination. Decentralization will not work, because the minorities-within-minorities are populous enough to elect only a small fraction of their state legislature. Moving to a popularly elected governor would help the locally dominant group – the titular minority – a great deal, because it would wrest control out of Nay Pyi Daw's hands, but it would do nothing for minorities-within-minorities. Similarly, power-sharing would not work, because the minorities-within-minorities are populous enough to elect only a very small number, if that, of the state representatives to the upper house of the union legislature. Individual rights may help some, mostly to blunt ethnic animosity and protect cultural differences at the individual level, but it will not empower

[45] *See* Steinberg, *supra* n. 6.   [46] Ibid.

these small groups to tell their story as peoples in political space; for that, they need control of a government. In addition, individual rights will not help at all unless the judges are both sensitive to the circumstances of the minorities-within-minorities and powerful enough to enforce their edicts, and Burma satisfies neither condition very well right now.

As a result, the FCDCC draft union constitution, some of the draft state constitutions, and the government's own 2008 Constitution provide for the creation of autonomous zones for these smaller groups – essentially states-within-states-within-the-state.[47] This approach might help these smaller minorities secure some very limited self-determination. However, the powers given these third-tier entities will necessarily be limited. In addition, autonomous zones will do nothing to ensure that the minorities-within-minorities have a meaningful share of power in the upper house of the union legislature. The creation of autonomous zones would also further complicate an already cumbersome structure. Finally, and perhaps fatally, there are no obvious boundaries for these autonomous zones: they would have to be crafted out of whole cloth. If they are created, the drawing of their boundaries would likely be highly disruptive and politically contentious. More likely, however, in the absence of clear preset boundaries, few or no zones will be created because no one would know where to start. The constitutional provisions authorizing the creation of autonomous zones would therefore become yet one more empty promise to these small groups.[48]

In addition, because the regime has resettled many Burman people in the minority areas, some titular minority states are probably no longer actual minority states. Mon State, for example, is probably majority Burman, with a large Mon minority, a substantial Karen population, and smaller populations of other minorities. Because the regime has prevented data gathering, it is hard to determine whether other states are similarly situated, but Arakan and Kachin states may be. As a result, the Burmans will likely control both the state governments and the state representatives to the upper house of the union legislature, so those devices will be useless to the minorities. Even where Burmans are not an absolute majority, they may control the election of a significant number of representatives

---

[47] *See, e.g.,* Constitution of the Republic of the Union of Myanmar, *supra* n. 10, ch. II, § 49 (detailing various ethnic regions in addition to named constituted states).

[48] *See* Khin Maung Win, "Designing Constitution as Policy Formulation to Stop Human Rights Violations," *Legal Issues on Burma* 8 (2001): 63–65 (describing minority groups' perception that the central government has made false promises of federalism since 1947).

to the state legislature and the upper house of the union legislature. In other words, symmetrical decentralization and power-sharing may help the titular minorities in some states but not in others.

To be frank, most of the ethnic leaders have paid little attention to these hard facts. When we have pushed them on the subject, they have generally responded with three proposals: remove the Burmans from their states, deny the Burmans state citizenship, or redraw the boundaries of the state to exclude areas where Burmans are concentrated. None of these is a workable option. The first two – removal and denial of state citizenship on the basis of ethnicity – might well violate international norms. The third – redrawing the boundaries – would prove viciously contentious not only with the union and the local Burman population but with other minority groups. In many cases, to exclude Burman concentrations from one ethnic state, it would be necessary to insert them into a different ethnic state where titular minority voters would not welcome such diminution of their voting power. In addition, once the prospect of redrawing boundaries is opened up, many of the ethnic states will press claims for territory in other ethnic states that they believe to have been part of their traditional homeland. For example, the traditional Mon capital, Pegu, is now located in Pegu region, not Mon State, and the New Mon State Party would very much like it back. Again, there is seldom an objective set of standards for redrawing jurisdictional boundaries, so the process is always fraught.

Finally, in reality, the union negotiators would never accept any of these three options. The first two would require them to treat Burman concentrations in the minority states as pariah populations. As to the third option, the 2008 Constitution makes redrawing state boundaries very difficult – an indication of how reluctant Burma's leaders are to make such changes. Under Section 53, before a boundary can be redrawn, the voters in any township affected must vote for the change; the state legislature must vote for the change; and three-quarters of the union level legislators from the affected states must vote for the change.[49] If the state legislature does not vote for the change, the union legislature may override that decision but only by a three-quarters vote.[50]

In fine, things will remain as they are: the state boundaries will not move, Burman voters will not be moved, and they will retain the right

[49] *See* Constitution of the Republic of the Union of Myanmar, *supra* n. 10, ch. II, § 53(a)–(d).
[50] *See* ibid., ch. II, § 53(e)–(f).

to vote. As a result, a symmetrical system will have asymmetrical results: Burman voters will have more power than the titular minorities in some but not all of the ethnic states.

Asymmetrical Demands for a Federal System

The last section has shown that a symmetrical system will have different effects on differently situated minorities – meeting the demands of some but not of others. In addition, different minority groups entertain those demands in different ways and to different degrees, so that a symmetrical federal system cannot accurately reflect the underlying political reasons for federalism. In other words, to meet asymmetrical demands, the constitution must itself be asymmetrical.

First, recall that many of the minorities want federalism so that they can tell their story, live out their identity, as a people in political space – self-determination for its own sake.[51] To do so, each group needs to control a state. Only some minorities strongly desire such a state, however; others do not care as much, in part because they have long become resigned to the fact that for purely practical reasons, they will never control a state.

On this score, we can observe three demographic variations. First, some groups, although small, have reasonable prospects of controlling a state and so desire federalism. For example, groups such as the Karenni strongly desire self-determination, and federalism may give it to them because Karenni State is fairly homogeneous, and the Karenni people have a strong sense of collective identity.

Second, some groups, although large, will not control a state. For example, the Wa also strongly desire self-determination for its own sake, but federalism will not work so well for them. They have always been extremely independent, and they are now extremely militarily powerful, so much so that the Burmese Army leaves them almost entirely alone.[52] The Wa control a large part of Shan State bordering China, and they have close relationships with the Chinese central and provincial governments in part because the Chinese tend to regard the Wa as a Chinese ethnic

---

[51] *See infra* Part I.
[52] *See* Hseng Khio Fah, "Burma Army Shoots Wa," *Shan Herald*, 2012 April 25, http://www.shanland.org/index.php?option=com_content&view=article&id=3011: burma-army-shoots-wa&catid=86:war&Itemid=284 (detailing Burmese Army's subsequent apology to the United Wa State Army (UWSA) for "attack[ing]...the wrong group.").

group.[53] The Wa assume that they will always be running their own show, but they are a minority in Shan State, so they will not control the state government. Worse, there has usually been tension and sometimes fighting between the Wa and the Shan armed groups.[54] If the government of Shan State tries to assert jurisdiction over them, there will be trouble.

Finally, some small groups have long abandoned the hope of controlling a state because they are a small minority in the state wherein they primarily reside. The Pa-O, for example, are a small group, and they have never had much power. They also have a long history of cooperation and involvement with the Shan people; in the old days, many Pa-O people felt deep loyalty to local Shan princes, who often rewarded them with palace advancement.[55] The Pa-O story, in other words, has always been about not just the Pa-O people alone, but also the way that relationships to other peoples have defined them. If there are no Shan people in the immediate vicinity, the Pa-O people cannot tell their story as they understand it. This self-conception is directly reflected in the career of Colonel Hkun Okker, who is clearly the most prominent Pa-O leader and whom I regard as a personal friend. Hkun Okker is the chairman of the Pa-O National Liberation Organization,[56] but he spends most of his time working as a leader of various pan-ethnic umbrella organizations such as the United Nationalities Federal Congress, the National Council of the Union of Burma, and the National Democratic Front. For Pa-O people like Hkun Okker, self-determination has traditionally entailed integration with the surrounding ethnic groups, not separation or isolation. As a result, the Pa-O may feel that their desire for self-determination will be adequately served by their inclusion in Shan State, even though they will not have a state to call their own.

Recall that the minorities also desire the three-part federalism package because they believe that it will insulate them against what they perceive

---

[53] *See* Zin Linn, "Will Burma Hit the Wa Army Next?" *Asian Correspondent*, 2011 July 12, http://asiancorrespondent.com/59837/will-burma-hit-wa-army-as-next-target/ (describing intervention by Chinese defence officials in deteriorating relationship between the UWSA and the military junta).

[54] *See* "Wa, Shan to Avert Another Close Encounter," *Shan Herald*, 2012 July 31, http://www.shanland.org/index.php?option = com_content&view=article&id=4841:wa-shan-to-avert-another-close-encounter&catid=86:war&Itemid=284 (reporting on recent efforts by UWSA and Shan officials to avoid further conflict).

[55] *See, e.g.,* Chao Tzang Yawnghwe, *The Shan of Burma: Memoirs of a Shan Exile* (Singapore: Institute of Southeast Asian Studies, 2010), 164.

[56] *See* "Pa-Oh National Liberation Organization Structure," accessed 2013 May 21, http://pnlo.org/abous-us/structure/.

to be Burman animosity.[57] However, although virtually all the minorities, as groups, distrust the Burmans, as a group, each minority has somewhat different attitudes towards the Burmans, and the military government has treated each slightly differently.

For example, although Burmans have traditionally regarded most ethnic groups as inferior, they have always felt slightly in the cultural shadow of the Mon, who built the great kingdom of central Burma long before the Burmans arrived on the scene.[58] Mon is, by some accounts, the ancestor language of Burmese, and many of the men who are considered to be early Burman kings were actually Mon.[59] Even the other minorities tend to regard the Mon as cultivated and elegant. The Mon know how to use this edge in negotiations not just with Burmans in general but with the military junta in particular. They managed to secure a very good ceasefire agreement giving them control of a substantial part of Mon State.[60]

At the other end of the spectrum, although it may be tendentious to single out any group as the most victimized, it is nonetheless crystal clear that the Karen have suffered at the hands of the regime more than any other group.[61] The military government clearly hated the Karen. Even before independence, during World War II, the Burmese Army committed atrocities against Karen villages.[62] After independence, the Karen were the first to rise up in arms. In the early years, they posed a serious military

---

[57] *See infra* Part I.

[58] *See generally* Ashley South, *Mon Nationalism and Civil War in Burma: The Golden Sheldrake* (London and New York: Routledge, 2003) (identifying a general prestige afforded the Mon across much of Southeast Asia).

[59] *See* ibid., 80 (describing the ethnic make-up of early royalty).

[60] *See* ibid., 166 (discussing ceasefires entered into by several Burmese opposition groups that permitted them to retain their weapons and control over certain territories); Mary P. Callahan, "Political Authority in Burma's Ethnic Minority States: Devolution, Occupation, and Coexistence," *Policy Studies* 31 (2007): 13 ("[T]he junta ... offered these groups quite extensive local autonomy over economic, social, and local political affairs as well as the opportunity to hold onto their weapons.").

[61] *See* Karen Human Rights Group, *Suffering in Silence: The Human Rights Nightmare of the Karen People of Burma* (Parkland: Universal Publishers, 2000) (containing a compilation of reports from various human rights-related groups detailing atrocities committed against the Karen); Benedict Rogers, *A Land Without Evil: Stopping the Genocide of Burma's Karen People* (Grand Rapids: Kregel Publications, 2004), 31 (describing acts committed against numerous ethnic minorities, focusing on the Karen).

[62] *See* Bertil Lintner, "How World War II Shaped Burma's Future," *The Irrawaddy*, August 2005, http://www2.irrawaddy.org/article.php?art_id=4911&page=2 (noting that the Karen still talk "with bitterness about atrocities carried out against them by the [Burmese Army] during the Japanese occupation.").

threat to take over the country; at one point, their forces conquered the Pegu Yoma, virtually within sight of Rangoon.[63] They have never accepted a ceasefire. The Tatmadaw has responded by an extraordinarily brutal campaign of war crimes and crimes against humanity. In recent years, the army has almost entirely given up combat with the Karen National Liberation Army; instead, they have contented themselves with making war on the civilian populations. Among other atrocities, they have used rape as an instrument of policy; mortared and burned villages, so that the villagers had to flee, creating an enormous refugee and internally displaced persons (IDP) crisis; destroyed rice paddies and fields, bringing on starvation; and sown mines in destroyed villages so that if the villagers return to rebuild, they will be blown up.[64] To many, including myself, it seemed that the war against the Karen approached genocide; the regime seemed to want to eliminate the Karen as a player in Burma's future. Even today, after the union negotiators have signed a ceasefire with the Karen National Liberation Army (NLA), the attacks continue, because the regional commanders will not obey the civilian government when it comes to the Karen.[65]

In a country with deep ethnic wounds, constitutions have to aim for two goals: on the one hand, they must protect vulnerable minorities, and such protection usually involves some degree of separation between the majority and the minorities. On the other hand, however, to reduce ethnic tension, constitutions also need to promote contact between the majority and minorities under safe circumstances. To put it another way, constitutions need to ensure as much interaction as possible consistent with the need to shelter potential victims. However, the Karen need shelter much more than the Mon do, so the balance should be different for them – more protection through separation. They will need more and stronger constitutional tools to protect themselves against the military – perhaps ideally, an absolute prohibition on deploying troops in Karen State, or a

---

[63] Ardeth Maung Thawnghmung, "The Dilemmas of Burma's Multinational Society," in *Multination States in Asia: Accommodation or Resistance*, eds. Jacques Bertrand and André Laliberté (Cambridge, New York: Cambridge University Press, 2010), 136–46 (detailing the military junta's "four-cut policies" to eradicate Karen resistance groups from Pegu Yoma and other locations).

[64] *See generally* Brad Adams and Joe Saunders, "'They Came and Destroyed Our Village Again': The Plight of Internally Displaced Persons in Karen State," *Human Rights Watch* 17(4) (June 2005), http://www.hrw.org/reports/2005/burma0605/burma0605.pdf.

[65] *See* Hanna Hindstrom, "Attacks Continue Despite Karen Ceasefire," *Democratic Voice of Burma*, 2012 February 3, http://www.dvb.no/news/attacks-continue-despite-karen-ceasefire/20059 (describing shelling of Karen refugee camps by the union army).

prohibition on deploying without permission of the state legislature, or a prohibition on using troops against the civilian population.

The third reason that the minorities desire federalism is that it might offer protection against Burmanization: they want to control those areas of life that mark a fault line between Burman culture and their own. However, Burman culture differs from different minority cultures in different ways. Language is an obvious example. Virtually all the minorities speak their own languages and want to preserve them.[66] In fact, most would probably say that language is the one fault line that divides them all from the Burmans. In some places, such as Mon and Arakan states, however, most people speak Burmese as well as their own languages, in part because the Mon and Arakanese languages are fairly close to Burmese. By contrast, in isolated, homogeneous areas, such as the hills of Karen State, the minorities speak only their own languages and view Burmese purely as the language of the oppressor. By contrast again, in heterogeneous locales where different sorts of minorities live cheek by jowl, such as Shan and Kachin states, people tend to view Burmese as the local lingua franca – although they might not like it much, and not all speak it. In effect, it is the public language of commerce and government whenever different minorities come together. The Chins are an extreme case. The various Chin languages are mutually unintelligible; there is no single Chin language that could serve as the official language of the state. When Chin people from different parts of Chin State gather, they speak Burmese to each other, even when the only people in the room are their co-ethnics.

As in a country with ethnic wounds, so in one with linguistic divisions, constitutions must seek two goals: protect local languages but also promote a shared language. However, the strategies for securing those two goals will necessarily be different in different places because the language politics are different. Where Burmese is the lingua franca and is not widely disliked, it would presumably make sense to designate both Burmese and the local language as official languages of the state; it might even be tolerable to make Burmese alone the official language of the union government in that state. In places where Burmese is hated and not spoken, however, it would be intolerable to make Burmese the sole

---

[66] *See* AFP, "Ethnic Minorities Struggle to Preserve Languages," *Democratic Voice of Burma*, 2012 October 22, http://www.dvb.no/uncategorized/ethnic-minorities-struggle-to-preserve-languages/24369 (examining efforts by the Shan, Mon, Chin, Karen, and Kachin to preserve local dialects by having them added to school curriculums).

official language of the union government in that state; and it might not even be possible to make Burmese one of the official languages of the state government.

HOW THE MINORITIES ARE COMING TO BE MORE ALIKE

In short, then, the asymmetric circumstances of the various ethnic minorities would seem to call for an asymmetrical system of federalism. As noted earlier, such systems have marked disadvantages, but if the need for them is great enough, sometimes countries must pay the costs. In particular, in Burma, people have virtually no experience of running a democracy or any kind of constitutional system. Running a very complicated asymmetrical system will be extremely difficult for them, and it is not clear that it will work at all. The country might collapse, or office holders might just ignore the complicated and technical aspects of the constitution. If either occurs, it would have been better to go with a simpler and more robust system, despite its insensitivity to local variation.

In addition, as noted, asymmetrical systems are under threat from change over time. Asymmetrical systems treat different groups differently because they are different from the bulk of the population in different, particular ways. As the years go on, however, ethnic groups inevitably change, and they may become different from the mainstream in ways different from the ways that they used to be different from the bulk of the population. For example, a group that once shared the dominant religion may be converted to a new religion, even in a short period of time; in Burma, such mass conversion is far from farfetched because in fact most Chin and Kachin were evangelized at the end of the nineteenth century and the beginning of the twentieth, so much so that they now regard Christianity as part of the basis for their distinctive identity.[67]

When such a change occurs, the constitution no longer fits conditions on the ground. When the constitution was adopted, the group shared the majority religion and so did not need and would probably not be given control over religious policy; but now it very much needs control over religion within its jurisdiction, as protection against the majority's efforts to re-assimilate them to the dominant religion.

---

[67] *See* Chizom Ekeh, "Minorities in Burma," *Minority Rights Group International*, October 2007, http://www.unhcr.org/refworld/pdfid/47298f632.pdf (finding that more than 80% of the Chin and Kachin practice Christianity).

Many of Burma's ethnic groups have remained somewhat culturally static because they have been isolated from outside influences by war and underdevelopment. If Burma's reform path continues, however, the country will likely change rapidly and, with it, the situation and identity of the various ethnic minorities. If the constitution were easy to amend, and if the political will existed, the constitution could of course be altered to reflect the changed circumstances, although that process would be never-ending as ethnic groups never stop changing. Burma's constitution is quite difficult to amend, however, and the central government has traditionally been quite reluctant to make repeated concessions to reflect the country's diversity.

But a different, more hopeful sort of change is also possible: ethnic minorities might become more and more like each other because of the experience of shared resistance to oppression. If so, an asymmetrical constitution might not be necessary at all; a simpler, vaguer, and more robust symmetrical system might suffice.

And in recent years, I believe, Burma's ethnic minorities are coming to think that they share roughly the same problems, aims, and relationships to the centre. In other words, a new pan-ethnic sensibility might be emerging. I should stress the limits of this observation. First, it is difficult to document, because my perception of it is based on a very large number of personal encounters at a very large number of meetings involving members of more than one ethnic group. Second, this growing convergence is far more marked among the leadership of the groups because they meet a lot. The people on the ground still reflect the old differences. On the other hand, because the people tend to respect their leaders, the attitudes of the leadership matter.

It is possible to discern this change in the way that relationships among the minority groups have changed. In decades past, the minority armies fought the Burmese Army, but they also fought among themselves, most frequently for control of trade and resources. For example, the New Mon State Party and the Karen National Liberation Army fought for control of the cross-border trade with Thailand near the Five Pagodas Pass,[68] and the Shan State Army – South fought with the United Wa State

---

[68] *See* Lawi Weng, "Tension Mounts at Three Pagodas Pass," *The Irrawaddy*, 2009 August 13, http://www2.irrawaddy.org/article.php?art_id=16549 (describing clashes among various groups to "gain control of lucrative concessions for logging, commercial trade and taxation" in this area).

Army near Loi Tai Leng in southern Shan State.[69] In addition, during the 1990s, some groups such as the Kachin Independence Army (KIA) and the New Mon State Party entered ceasefire agreements with the regime, whereas others adamantly refused to do so; the latter typically resented the former as sell-outs.[70] Today, some bad blood still remains on this subject even though in the last two years, the military regime revoked all the ceasefires and then the civilian government promptly entered new ceasefire negotiations with all the groups.[71]

In the last ten years, however, the groups have shown a growing sense of unity of purpose, especially with regard to constitutional reform. From early on, they had formed umbrella associations, such as the National Council of the Union of Burma and the National Democratic Front, but they had no power over the member organizations and frequently experienced in-house feuding.[72] Then, as already noted, the resistance armies and civil society organizations formed state constitution drafting committees, and the Ethnic Nationalities Council (ENC) was formed in part to support those efforts. Subsequently, the ENC formed the FCDCC to write a draft union constitution, and by taking part in this process, the member organizations were all implicitly affirming that a single federal arrangement could be drafted that would, in theory, be acceptable to all of them.

Eventually, most of the ethnic resistance armies came together to form the United Nationalities Federal Council (UNFC), and they have demanded that the government negotiate with it, rather than piecemeal with the different armies.[73] The ethnic leaders fear that the government will try to use divide-and-conquer tactics against them, so they have

---

[69] *See* Nyein Nyein, "UWSA Releases Shan Troops Detained for Six Weeks," *The Irrawaddy*, 2012 September 20, http://www.irrawaddy.org/archives/14537 (varyingly describing ongoing tensions between the two groups over issues related to control of the border).

[70] *See* "Chronology for Kachins in Burma," *Minorities at Risk Project*, 2004, http://www.unhcr.org/refworld/docid/469f387014.html. (detailing ceasefire signed by the KIA and the Burmese government in February 1994).

[71] *See* note 18, *infra*.

[72] *See* Norman Robespierre, "Myanmar's Failed Non-Violent Opposition," *Asian Times Online*, 2008 October 23, http://www.atimes.com/atimes/Southeast_Asia/JJ23Ae01.html (discussing efforts by union government to "haunt the opposition [umbrella groups representing such] fragmentation and conflicting interests.").

[73] *See* Lawi Weng, "Ethnic Alliance Issues Conflict Deadline," *The Irrawaddy*, 2012 May 14, http://www.irrawaddy.org/archives/4132 (detailing a conflict cessation timeline issued by this organization, which "represents 12 ethnic groups in Burma").

resolved to come together on a shared platform for constitutional reform. The UNFC is now issuing joint communiqués about its bargaining position.[74] At the time of writing, the various armies are negotiating separate ceasefires, but they intend to unify through the UNFC when the time comes for political talks.

Most recently, the ethnic armies have even formed a joint command structure to co-ordinate resistance to the regime.[75] The soldiers all will wear their army-specific badges (i.e., KNLA, KIA, etc.) on one shoulder and the Federal Army badge on the other. The commanders have pledged that when the Burmese Army attacks any of the armies, all of the others will retaliate to prevent the Tatmadaw from concentrating its forces. All of this co-operation may be more nominal than real at this point, but the very fact that the minorities want to move in such a direction speaks volumes about their mindset: e pluribus unum.

On the government side, the outgoing military regime allowed the election of a certain number of ethnic minority legislators to the union, state, and region legislators.[76] Presumably, the junta imagined that these representatives would merely be tokens, gestures towards ethnic diversity, but the representatives themselves mean to make the most of the opportunity. They have formed the Ethnic Nationalities Brotherhood, so as to caucus and vote in common, and they intend to push for constitutional reform to help the ethnic minorities, considered not as separate peoples but en masse.

A new sensibility has emerged from all this meeting, discussing, caucusing, and organizing – a new conceptualization of the minorities' situation. They have come to believe that because they have all been oppressed by the centralizing, Burmanizing military government, they all share a cause. For that reason, the minority leaders tend to believe that all the minorities want and need roughly the same constitutional system – in other words, symmetrical federalism. The minorities frequently refer to "the ethnic cause" or "the minorities' quest for self-determination" as though

---

[74] *See, e.g.,* "Statement of the United Nationalities Federal Council (UNFC) Regular Meeting," 2012 July 22, http://www.dictatorwatch.org/UNFC%20St-2%20Eng.pdf (rejecting proposals by the union government for armed ethnic organizations to form political parties and contest the 2010 election).

[75] *See* Htet Aung Kyaw, "Ethnic Armies Agree 'Ring of Resistance,'" *Democratic Voice of Burma,* 2011 February 18, http://www.dvb.no/news/ethnic-armies-agree-'ring-of-resistance'/14330 (detailing talks held over four days by twelve ethnic armed to consolidate efforts against the government).

[76] *See* note 17, *infra.*

it were one cause and one quest. They increasingly speak of "minority issues" rather than Chin issues, Karen issues, and so forth. The problems in the different areas are different, but increasingly, the minorities interpret those different problems through a shared frame of reference – as coming from the same causes and reflecting the same dynamics.

Changing attitudes on the issue of secession also reflect this growing sense of unity. Traditionally, the ethnic armies understood their goal to be independence; each of the ethnic states would become its own sovereign nation. The leadership has become aware that given the realities of geopolitics, secession is no longer a meaningful option, and the various groups have all forsworn it as an immediate goal. The exact reasons are numerous, but among them is the understanding that most of the ethnic states are too small to function as a viable sovereign country. Despite this general turn away from secession, however, many still cling to the hope that the ethnic states might all secede together, as one independent nation rather than seven. Clearly, they imagine that they could all happily coexist under the same constitution because they have similar constitutional needs; they are principally different only from the Burmans.

As the minorities come to perceive their problems in the same way, the problems may in fact become more similar because the problems are to some extent the product of perceptions: they are problems only insofar as the minorities perceive them to be problems. If the minority leaders welcome a symmetrical constitution, they will try to make it work, even if they are wrong in believing that they are similarly situated.

In fact, I believe that the leadership is becoming more similarly situated; their shared associational life has caused them to move closer together. To a significant extent, this growing rapprochement may be the product of exposure to outside influences such as donor agencies, representatives of foreign governments, and even the Center for Constitutional Democracy. Of course, it is only the leadership that has been exposed so far to such influences, but in the years to come, that will change; an open market, infrastructural development, and political freedom will bring ordinary people into close contact with the outside world as well.

This observation is wholly based on close interaction with the Burmese leaders over the span of a decade. As a result, it is exceedingly difficult to document or to demonstrate through quantitative empirical evidence. Instead, I can offer only anecdotal evidence, with all of its problems. As one example, I believe that attitudes towards language are clearly changing. As already noted, in the past some groups spoke little Burmese, in part because they hated it as the language of the oppressor – such as the Karen in Karen State. Other groups spoke Burmese and even had some respect for the Burmese literary tradition – such as the Mon. In recent years, however, more Karen have learned to speak Burmese, and many have accepted that it will necessarily be the shared language in a democratic Burma. On the other hand, although the Mon still mostly speak Burmese and still appreciate Burmese literature, more have come to resent it as the language of the oppressor – an attitude that they may have picked up from the Karen. Because of their changed perceptions, these groups are now more closely situated on the issue of language. Therefore, the same constitutional structures might work for both groups; the constitution would not need to be so complicated. And what is true for language might be true for other issues as well.

It is even possible – this would be the dream – that eventually this process of creating a pan-minority identity might lead to the creation of a pan-Burmese identity that includes the Burmans. That identity would be the product not of forcible Burmanization but of peaceful interaction; it would not make Burman identity central to Burmese identity; and it would supplement rather than replace more specific identities. In the long run, Burma will desperately need such a shared civic identity, rooted neither in ethnicity nor language nor religion nor culture but in the shared day-to-day political experience of building a better future for this suffering country.

CONCLUSION

Understanding Burma's constitutional conflict is important in its own right for anyone who cares about the country or freedom in the world. However, it also has broader implications for constitutionalism and difference beyond Burma's borders. Among these is the reminder that although the demands of minority groups are inputs into the constitutional process, they are also outputs.

Typically, at the start of a constitutional process, minority groups bring certain pre-existing demands to the table. Those demands are based on their experiences and perceptions, developed over years, of the ways that they differ from the majority population. Sometimes, those demands are wildly diverse across the groups because the groups are themselves wildly diverse. They advance these demands in a variety of ways; sometimes, they try peaceful negotiation, but when it fails, they sometimes reach for their guns, and in that sense even civil war should be regarded as a part of the constitutional process.

Their demands, however, often evolve as a result of the constitutional process itself; they are not the same going in and coming out. These demands are shaped by the very process of fighting, reflecting, negotiating, and collaborating with other groups in the constitutional process. In other words, they are neither static nor wholly exogenous to the task of coming to a constitutional settlement. Sometimes, when minority groups collaborate in seeking justice from an oppressive regime, they come to see themselves as more alike, and as a result, their demands become more alike. For countries racked by seemingly intractable conflict, that should be welcome news.

6

Hu Wants Something New:
Discourse and the Deep Structure
of Minzu Policies in China

Gardner Bovingdon

INTRODUCTION: RECONSTITUTING MINZU?

This chapter concerns an enduring conundrum at the heart of contemporary Chinese politics: how to manage relations between the country's Han majority and its cultural others, members of the fifty-five groups officially recognized as "minority minzu" (*shaoshu minzu*). Over time the Chinese Communist Party (CCP) has developed a complex of policies, laws, and established practices collectively known by the umbrella term "minzu policies" (*minzu zhengce*); many had been copied wholesale or adapted from those in the Soviet Union.[1] They include the very practice of recognizing the groups, special protections for their languages and customs, extra points on college entrance exams, slightly looser birth limits under family planning policies, and a system of minzu regional autonomy in regions where those groups live in substantial numbers. Whereas official publications have insisted confidently for decades that the minzu policies "solved" the conundrum of intergroup relations, the record of quiet contention, occasional public protest, and sporadic violence in various parts of the country indicates otherwise. Indeed, the Party's substantial tinkering with those policies over the decades suggests that even top leaders have been skeptical of the claim.

Over the last decade several prominent Chinese academics have urged, with increasing stridency, that the Party stop tinkering and simply abandon its minzu policies. Beijing University professor and policy advisor Ma Rong first publicly argued for this radical shift. In Ma's view, the

[1] Colin Mackerras, *China's Minorities: Integration and Modernization in the Twentieth Century* (Oxford: Oxford University Press, 1994); Pitman B. Potter, *Law, Policy, and Practice on China's Periphery: Selective Adaptation and Institutional Capacity* (New York: Routledge, 2010).

policies of recognizing and protecting cultural differences among groups and of endowing cultural differences with political significance had reversed centuries of statecraft in China and, instead of solving the problem of intergroup relations in the country, had made it more internally divided than at the founding of the People's Republic of China (PRC) in 1949. "Chinese people should," he said,

> absorb the valuable experience of their ancestors' traditions of handling ethnic relations over several thousand years, and they should learn the lessons of America's, India's, and the former Soviet Union's strategies and experience in managing racial and ethnic problems. They should abandon the post-1949 trend of "politicizing" ethnic problems and set off in a new direction, "culturalizing" and gradually "de-politicizing" the problem of minority ethnic groups.[2]

Ma chose his examples carefully: culturally diverse India and the United States were prosperous and (in his view) nationally united countries; the Soviet Union, by contrast, had ceased to be a country. Ma therefore urged that the government abandon the minzu policies and return to the time-tested Chinese strategy of encouraging non-Hans to assimilate, allowing the country to follow the successful examples of the United States and India in building a stronger nation.

Questions of belonging and nation-building policies are tightly linked in modern China. Hence, to understand the country's legal and administrative apparatus for managing non-Han groups, we must begin with the seemingly minor matter of nomenclature, for there is deep disagreement within China about the nature of those groups. Are they peoples? Nations? Ethnic groups? Citizens of a multicultural yet unitary "Chinese nation"? This has in fact been one of the most important questions in Chinese politics for the last century, although not always recognized as such. Ma Rong's prescription for "de-politicizing" the relations among culture groups in China began quite literally with renaming them.

Since well before 1949, Chinese scholars and officials have used the term *minzu* to denote both the various groups – Han, Uyghur, Tibetan, and so on – and the "Chinese nation" (*Zhonghua minzu*) that comprised them all. In Ma's view this usage has produced a kind of semantic

---

[2] Ma Rong, "Lijie Minzu Guanxi De Xin Silu – Shaoshu Zuqun Wentide 'Qu Zhengzhi Hua'" [New Thoughts on How to Understand Minzu Relations – 'Depoliticizing' the Problem of Ethnic Minorities], *Beijing daxue xuebao (zhexue shehui kexue ban)* 41, no. 6 (2004).

and political leakage: it has invited confusion about whether the constituent groups too were nations, and thus possibly deserving of their
own states. To clear up the confusion, Ma urged on the Party a new
rectification of names, reserving minzu for the "Chinese nation" and
henceforth referring to Uyghur, Tibetans, and others as *zuqun* – that is,
as ethnic groups. In other words, Ma literally proposed to "reconstitute"
the groups, in the sense both of remaking them and of changing their
legal status. To abandon the term minzu would remove the foundation of
the system of minzu policies itself – and this was exactly what Ma Rong
intended.

In what follows I will briefly discuss the historical background of the
PRC's minzu policies, introduce their basis in law and practice, review
substantial changes made to those policies in the early Reform Era (1979
on), and return to the radical changes advocated by Ma Rong, as well as
still more searching proposals by others. Precisely because of the ambiguity of the official Chinese term, to render it in English as "nation" or
"nationality" or "ethnic group," as many have done, would imply a false
clarity and prejudge appropriate political outcomes. Therefore, I will use
the term minzu throughout the chapter.[3]

As noted , there are fifty-five groups currently recognized as minority
minzu by the Chinese government. Some have populations numbering
only in the thousands, whereas others have large populations but little
or no history of collective friction with the Chinese government. Thus, I
will focus here on Tibetans and Uyghurs, for several reasons. First, both
groups have collective memories of independent statehood, and some
members of each group continue to advocate independence from China on
the basis of that history, to Beijing's great frustration.[4] Second, violence
in Tibetan regions in 2008 and in Xinjiang in 2009 profoundly affected
popular and official attitudes toward those groups and the minzu policies
affecting them. It is important to recognize nonetheless that any dramatic
changes to China's minzu policies would affect all fifty-five groups.

[3] Gardner Bovingdon, *The Uyghurs: Strangers in Their Own Land* (New York: Columbia
University Press, 2010), 16; Stevan Harrell, "Introduction: Civilizing Projects and the
Reactions to Them," in *Cultural Encounters on China's Ethnic Frontiers*, ed. Stevan
Harrell (Seattle: University of Washington Press, 1995); James Leibold, *Reconfiguring
Chinese Nationalism: How the Qing Frontier and Its Indigenes Became Chinese*, 1st
ed. (New York: Palgrave Macmillan, 2007).

[4] I will also set aside the very important and complex history of Mongols, on which see
Christopher P. Atwood, *Encyclopedia of Mongolia and the Mongol Empire* (New York:
Facts on File, 2004).

HISTORICAL BACKGROUND

The constellation of questions described long preceded the accession of the CCP to power in 1949. Chinese intellectuals writing in the waning days of the Manchu Qing Empire in the late nineteenth century elaborated radically different visions of the "Chinese nation" they expected to rise from that empire's ashes. Should all the territories and peoples conquered by the Qing be fused into a "Chinese national empire" in which Hans would dominate other peoples, or should the new state jettison the non-Chinese peoples and their territories, keeping only the lands where Chinese (today we would call them Hans) predominated?[5] In the end the anti-Qing revolutionary and canny politician Sun Yat-sen adroitly adopted both positions in turn: until the Qing empire collapsed he demanded that Manchus be expelled; then as the head of the Nationalist Party (KMT) that ruled the new Republic of China (founded 1911), he reversed himself and urged that the various peoples – Manchu, Han, and others – must combine to form a new unified "Chinese nation."[6] In practice, however, the Hans controlled the KMT and either marginalized frontier peoples or refused to acknowledge their distinctiveness and political aspirations. The independence or Outer Mongolia, the de facto independence of Tibet, and the emergence of two short-lived independent states of "Eastern Turkistan" (parts of today's Xinjiang) illustrated the folly of ignoring those aspirations and insisting that all peoples within the former Qing borders were simply Chinese.[7]

The insurgent Chinese Communist Party (founded 1921) initially followed Marxist orthodoxy in trying to build an urban base and foment a proletarian revolution to overthrow the Nationalist government. The KMT thwarted that effort, driving the CCP first from the cities in the late 1920s and then from the Chinese heartland into the western periphery in the early 1930s. Denied access to urban populations, the CCP sought alternate bases of support among Han peasants and from the non-Han frontier peoples. To recruit the latter, Party officials formally recognized

[5] Pamela Kyle Crossley, *A Translucent Mirror: History and Identity in Qing Imperial Ideology* (Berkeley: University of California Press, 1999), 351, 353.

[6] Edward J. M. Rhoads, *Manchus & Han: Ethnic Relations and Political Power in Late Qing and Early Republican China, 1861–1928*, Studies on Ethnic Groups in China (Seattle: University of Washington Press, 2000), 275.

[7] James Leibold, "Searching for Han: Early Twentieth-Century Narratives of Chinese Origins and Development," in *Critical Han Studies: The History, Representation, and Identity of China's Majority*, ed. Thomas S. Mullaney et al. (Berkeley: University of California Press, 2012), 216; Leibold, *Reconfiguring Chinese Nationalism*, supra n. 3.

them as peoples and acknowledged their distinctive political rights, both of which the KMT had steadfastly refused to do.[8] In this policy, the CCP largely followed the practices of the Soviet Communist Party.

Soviet and CCP leaders justified their policies toward territorially compact culturally distinct groups (which they called minzu by analogy with the Russian *natsional'nost*) in terms of Marxist doctrine but made their policies according to *realpolitik*. When weak and vying for control of the state, officials made generous offers of future independence or free confederation to the groups. For instance, the Constitution adopted by the CCP in 1931, long before it controlled significant territory in China, granted that "*All* Mongolians, Tibetans, Miao . . . and others living on the territory of China shall enjoy the full right to self-determination" including secession. In 1935, Mao Zedong exhorted the Turkic Muslims of Xinjiang (today's Uyghurs) to "organize your own state!" As they gained power, the parties quieted talk of independence and insisted instead on uniting to fight common enemies domestic and foreign. Once fully in control of the state and victorious in war, Soviet and Chinese communists enacted federal states or systems of regional autonomy to keep minorities in the state – that is, from seceding – and minimize the chance they would revolt against the new polity.[9] Over time they sought to strengthen control of contentious peripheries by engineering the large-scale migration of members of the culturally dominant group into those areas (Russians into Central Asia, Hans into Xinjiang), in effect subcontracting some of the security burden to colonists.

MINZU POLICIES: THE CONSTITUTIONAL BASIS

The 1949 Common Program of the Chinese People's Political Consultative Congress, adopted in lieu of a constitution at the founding of the PRC, established the bases of the country's minzu policies. It formally recognized the existence of various minzu, stipulated their formal legal equality, proposed the establishment of autonomous units where non-Han groups lived "in concentration," and specified that their languages, customs, and religious beliefs be protected and allowed to develop.[10] The successive PRC constitutions (1954, 1972, 1975, and 1982, the last

---

[8] Walker Connor, *The National Question in Marxist-Leninist Theory and Strategy* (Princeton: Princeton University Press, 1984).

[9] Ibid., 74, 76, 81.

[10] Jiann Hsieh, "China's Nationalities Policy: Its Development and Problems," *Anthropos* 81, no. 1/3 (1986): 7.

repeatedly amended) specified the same cultural and linguistic protections, institutions of minzu regional autonomy intended to grant groups control over their "internal affairs," and a carefully specified relationship between those institutions and the central government.[11] Notably, the drafters of the constitutions acknowledged from the beginning the importance of having a substantial proportion of the members of representative bodies come from the titular group (that is, the group exercising autonomy in a given unit), yet did not specify that proportion. Section V, Article 68 of the 1954 Constitution directed that such bodies should have "an appropriate number of representatives"; although dropped from the 1975 Constitution, it was reinstated in the much longer 1982 version.[12]

Both the 1952 Program for Implementing *Minzu* Regional Autonomy (hereafter "Program") and the 1954 Constitution decreed that autonomous units at county, prefectural, and provincial levels would have governmental organs broadly similar to those at the corresponding levels in China proper. The units were expected to have the same branches of government as in the rest of China, a People's Congress with elected representatives chosen from the titular group or groups as well as Hans, and conformity to the decisions of higher-level government organs; because it was beyond question, obedience to the Communist Party organs was not specified. Both documents provided that actual institutional forms could be determined by the wishes of the "great majority of the people and leading figures with links to the people" of the titular group or groups.[13]

The first Constitution also committed the government to drawing up a national autonomy law. However, although the Government

[11] For an extensive discussion of the system of autonomy and the PRC Constitution, *see* Pitman B. Potter, "Governance of China's Periphery: Balancing Local Autonomy and National Unity," *Columbia Journal of Asian Law* 19 (2005). The problem with deciding how well China's minzu policies protect the interests of non-Hans is that the definition of "internal affairs" is so slippery, and the Party continues to claim final interpretive authority. Even so staunch a defender of China's current policies as Hao Shiyuan notes that "the 'internal affairs' of a minority minzu are certainly not some 'historical fact' which take shape and then never change," but instead expand and contract in scope over time. Hao Shiyuan, "Zai Shijian Zhong Buduan Wanshan Minzu Quyu Zizhi Zhidu" [Continually Perfect the Minzu Regional Autonomy System through Praxis], *Guangming wang (Guangming daily online)*, May 13, 2011.

[12] English and Chinese versions of the successive constitutions can be found at http://www.hkpolitics.net/database/chicon/, accessed May 1, 2013.

[13] Here "the people" (*renmin*) was understood to denote only a portion of the total population. The Party-state retained the right to determine which citizen belonged to "the people" and who were "non-people" – class enemies or enemies of the state. Michael Schoenhals, "'Non-People' in the People's Republic of China: A Chronicle of Terminological Ambiguity" (Working paper, Indiana University East Asian Studies Center, http://www.easc.indiana.edu/Pages/Easc/working_papers/framed_4A_PEOPL.htm). For

Administration Council had passed the Program in 1952, a formal law would be promulgated only in 1984 and then amended in 2001. In addition to the administrative principles described, the 1984 Autonomy Law affirmed in general terms what had been practices of long duration in the autonomous regions: affirmative action in the recruitment of college students, the hiring of employees at state enterprises, and the training of base-level government cadres.

The articles of the Autonomy Law reveal the limitations built into the system.[14] Article 15 indicates that all autonomous government organs are under the leadership of the state council, and all must "obey the state council." Article 20 grants organs of autonomy the right to "alter or suspend" policies or orders promulgated by higher-level government units, yet makes such actions subject to approval by those superior units. Although it acknowledges the right of autonomous regional governments to draw up locally appropriate "statutes on autonomy and specific regulations," Article 19 also grants the National People's Congress the authority to approve or reject such statutes.[15] In view of the fact that decisions by congresses in autonomous regions are subject to review by the National People's Congress, whereas those of China's provincial congresses are not, the so-called autonomous regions actually have less freedom to legislate than their counterparts in China proper.[16]

The legal treatment of non-Hans, Pitman Potter notes laconically, has "fallen short of international standards,"[17] and provides little scope for members of the various minzu to decide their own "internal affairs,"

the text of the Program, *see Tongyi Zhanxian Wenti Yu Minzu Wenti [United Front Problems and Minzu Problems]* (Beijing: Renmin chubanshe, 1982), 521–26.

[14] References in this paragraph are to the amended 2001 law, although the relevant articles are almost indistinguishable from those in the 1984 law. The most substantial change of interest here is in Article 20, which has added a requirement that the higher-level government organ respond to proposed alterations within sixty days. According to an article in an official journal, the amendment committee made this change because the provision for local modification of national policies had "essentially not been enacted." Higher-level organs presented such proposals by autonomous units routinely "set them aside and ignored them, never providing a response." Ao Junde, "Minzu Quyu Zizhifa Shi Zenyang Xiugai De" [How the Law on *Minzu* Regional Autonomy Was Amended], *Zhongguo minzu (China Ethnicity)*, no. 4 (2001).

[15] Although the Constitution and Autonomy Law explicitly allow autonomous regions to pass such statutes, Xinjiang's government has never done so. Ghalip Isma'il, "Aptonomiyä Nizami Wä Uning Alahidiliki" [The Law on Autonomy and Its Characteristics], *Millätlär Ittipaqi (Minzu unity – Uyghur edition)*, no. 4 (1996).

[16] Human Rights in China, *China: Minority Exclusion, Marginalization and Rising Tensions* (London: Minority Rights Group International, 2007).

[17] Pitman B. Potter, *The Chinese Legal System: Globalization and Local Legal Culture* (London: Routledge, 2001), 91.

however those are construed.[18] Indeed, the system of governance established in the Xinjiang Uyghur Autonomous Region (XUAR) and Tibetan Autonomous Region (TAR) fails to satisfy a single one of five criteria considered fundamental to autonomy by prominent international jurists: an independent local legislature not subject to central veto power, a locally chosen executive, an independent judiciary, local decision making not compromised by the center's "reservation ... of general discretionary powers," and binding power-sharing arrangements.[19] As mentioned above, Beijing retains veto power over the decisions of People's Congresses in the autonomous regions. The center has chosen each of those regions' successive executives, and the Chinese Supreme People's Court retains supervisory power over their courts. Furthermore, Beijing reserves broad discretionary power over the regions' affairs, including how autonomy is implemented; and the center allocates power over resource exploitation, policing, and other matters on its own initiative, rather than being bound by power-sharing arrangements.[20] Even though it has dramatically departed from the Soviet model in many particulars, on this last point the PRC system clearly followed Moscow's example. In relations with the union republics prior to 1991, Moscow "both define[d] the sphere of authority and exercise[d] it."[21]

As slender as the protections afforded by the evolving legal framework were, major political events in the young republic further compromised them. The Great Leap Forward, launched in 1958, was intended to catapult China into a fully socialist future at breakneck speed and to bring the country wealth rivaling first Britain and later the United States. The economic aspects of the leap are fairly well known. As industrial shock

---

[18] Matthew Moneyhon, "Controlling Xinjiang: Autonomy on China's New Frontier," *Asia-Pacific Law & Policy Journal* 3, no. 1 (2002); Barry Sautman, "Ethnic Law and Minority Rights in China," *Law and Policy* 21, no. 3 (1999); Justin J. Stein, "Taking the Deliberative Turn in China: International Law, Minority Rights, and the Case of Xinjiang," *Journal of Public and International Affairs* 14 (2003); Yu Xingzhong, "From State Leadership to State Responsibility – Comments on the New PRC Law on Regional Autonomy of Ethnic Minorities" (Working paper, Chinese University, 2004), http://www.cuhk.edu.hk/gpa/xzyu/work1.htm.

[19] Hurst Hannum and Richard B. Lillich, "The Concept of Autonomy in International Law," *American Journal of International Law* 74, no. 4 (1980): 886–87.

[20] Matthew Moneyhon, "Controlling Xinjiang," *supra* n. 18, 137, 142–44. Moneyhon makes these points with specific reference to Xinjiang. However, the Autonomy Law he analyzes applies to all autonomous regions in China, from the provincial level down, and Beijing has chosen all the executives of the five autonomous regions since 1949.

[21] Gregory Gleason, *Federalism and Nationalism: The Struggle for Republican Rights in the USSR* (Boulder: Westview, 1990), 65.

workers in the cities labored to shatter all previous production records, peasants worked to exhaustion and beyond for bumper harvests to support industrial production. Party officials swept away practices they saw as impediments to this developmental juggernaut, and thus in the non-Han periphery, they urged rapid cultural homogenization to accompany and facilitate the Leap. Officials showed scant tolerance for difference and regarded minzu identity itself as an "obstacle to progress."[22] As is now widely known, the combination of Great Leap policies, bad weather, and the central government's ill-chosen decision to export grain to meet its debts to the Soviet Union brought on a terrible famine. Party leaders temporarily prevailed on Mao to restore a more moderate economic course and modestly relaxed cultural policies, as officials acknowledged linguistic and cultural differences would persist over the long term. Talk of speedy assimilation subsided.[23]

Minzu policies changed course again in the mid-1960s when Mao and his supporters unleashed the Cultural Revolution (1966–1976). Officials appointed to Cultural Revolutionary Small Groups, which replaced the Party committees in autonomous regions for several years, and the initially mostly Han Red Guards raised demands for cultural conformity to a new extreme. Whereas in China's heartland Red Guards collected and destroyed artifacts of the past, in Xinjiang, Tibet, and other non-Han regions they targeted non-Han culture. Difference was again regarded as a sign of backwardness but now also of potential political unreliability. Uyghur, Tibetan, and especially Mongol officials were hauled from their government posts in great numbers and subjected to "struggle" sessions, not only causing enormous personal suffering but dramatically decreasing the proportion of non-Hans in the governments of the autonomous regions.

HU YAOBANG'S LIBERAL EXPERIMENT: GESTURES TOWARD MORE SUBSTANTIVE AUTONOMY

In retrospect it is clear that policies toward non-Hans were most assimilationist and intolerant during the Cultural Revolution. After Mao's death

---

[22] Donald H. McMillen, *Chinese Communist Power and Policy in Xinjiang, 1949–77* (Boulder: Westview Press, 1979), 11; June Teufel Dreyer, *China's Forty Millions: Minority Nationalities and National Integration in the People's Republic of China* (Cambridge: Harvard University Press, 1976), 157–63.

[23] George Moseley, "China's Fresh Approach to the National Minority Question," *China Quarterly*, 24 (1965), 15–27.

in 1976 and the fall of the Gang of Four, Party leaders faced a crisis. The Cultural Revolution had alienated a large segment of the population throughout China. Yet resentment was particularly grave among Uyghurs, Tibetans, and other non-Hans: for them it had been not merely a political and social assault but an attack on their identities. The continuation of hard-line policies seemed certain to provoke increasing discontent and thus instability. However, officials worried that more tolerant policies, by allowing cultural exploration and freer religious practice, might similarly open the door to unrest.

In 1979 the newly ascendant Deng Xiaoping announced a new era of "Reform and Openness." Although Deng's principal concerns were economic, he also consented to a review of minzu policies, implicitly acknowledging that Tibetans, Uyghurs, and other non-Hans had become profoundly alienated from Beijing. Officials responsible for those policies expressed concern about the deleterious consequences of two decades of nearly unremitting assimilationist pressures on non-Hans, and also on the drastic fall in the proportions of titular groups serving in government, by any measure less than the "appropriate number of representatives" specified in the Constitution. They seemed troubled for the first time, too, to reflect that since 1949 nearly all of the top Party leaders in the autonomous regions had been Han. Thus in 1979 Yang Jingren, a Central Committee member and head of the Minzu Affairs Commission, observed that "comrades at the Ministry of Foreign Affairs say they don't know what to say when foreign visitors ask 'if all the party leaders [in autonomous units] are Han, how can you really say this is regional autonomy?' From the looks of it, this is a problem we must resolve."[24]

In urging that the problem be addressed, Yang was clearly expressing a concern shared by some of China's top leaders. He accompanied Hu Yaobang, appointed with Deng Xiaoping's approval to China's highest formal post as Party general secretary, on an inspection trip to Tibet in May 1980. During the trip Hu was horrified by the economic privation and alienation of the population despite decades of substantial financial support from Beijing. To bring about "ample autonomy" and speed development in Tibet, Hu proposed that two-thirds of the cadre positions there be filled with Tibetans, and a large number of Han cadres be retired or

---

[24] Guojia minwei zhengce yanjiushi, ed., *Guojia Minwei Minzu Zhengce Wenjian Xuanbian, 1979–1984 [Selected Documents Concerning the Minzu Policies of the State Minzu Affairs Commission, 1979–1984]* (Beijing: Zhongyang minzu xueyuan chubanshe, 1988), 8.

transferred to China proper.[25] After convening a meeting with members of the Xinjiang Party Committee in July 1980, Hu approved a proposal along similar lines: all Commune Party first secretaryships should be held by minority cadres, half to two-thirds of county Party secretary positions should be held by minority cadres, and those positions at the prefecture level should have one-third to one-half minority cadres. Overall the ratio of minority cadres was to be raised to more than 60 percent.[26]

Hu invited similarly searching proposals to improve governance and economic development in Inner Mongolia, and by August 1981 the Inner Mongolian Autonomous Region Party Committee had promulgated its proposal to all work units and districts in the region. Disappointed with a plan that envisioned no limits on Han immigration, several thousand Mongol students protested in Hohhot and demanded that Beijing both stop that immigration and increase the proportion of Mongol officials in the government. The protests had no palpable effect at the time, although in 1984 Beijing did choose to limit the further inflow of Hans into northern Inner Mongolia by insisting that only herders could settle there, reportedly because of an internal document warning that the region's fragile ecology required it.[27]

Hu mandated these changes despite ferocious resistance from Han officials. He reportedly told Han cadres in Tibet to "carry out the policy even if you do not understand; make decisions first and straighten out later." What is more, the changes were not short-lived but sustained for more than half of the decade. The results were quite substantial: whereas in the early 1970s fewer than one-third of Party committee members, and only one-fifth of leading cadres at the district level had been Tibetans, by 1989 more than two-thirds of the cadres in Tibet were Tibetan. Furthermore, all top administrative heads at provincial and prefectural levels were Tibetans, and so were the Party secretaries in six out of every seven counties. The Han population reportedly fell 42 percent between

---

[25] Melvyn C. Goldstein, *The Snow Lion and the Dragon: China, Tibet, and the Dalai Lama* (Berkeley: University of California Press, 1997), 65.

[26] Wang Lixiong, *"Xinjiang Ben Minzu Miandui Bu Ke Yuyue De Nanguan – 911 Qishi Lu (10)"* [Insurmountable Obstacles Facing Xinjiang's Own *Minzu* – Lessons from September 11 (Part 10)], *Duowei* 124, http://www.duowei.com; Zhu Xiaomin, "Jiefang Hou Zhi 20 Shiji 80 Niandai Xinjiang Yili Fan Fenlie Douzheng Jiaoxun Qianxi" [A Preliminary Analysis of the Lessons from the Struggle against Separatism in Xinjiang's Ili from the Revolution through the 1980s], *Zhonggong Yili zhou wei dangxiao xuebao,* 3 (2006).

[27] William R. Jankowiak, "The Last Hurrah? Political Protest in Inner Mongolia," *Australian Journal of Chinese Affairs* 19/20 (1988): 280, 287.

1980 and 1985; and yet the opening of Tibet to trade and business in 1984 set in motion a countervailing trend of new Han immigration.[28] In Xinjiang, with Hu's imprimatur, more than 7,000 Han cadres were transferred to China proper in 1981 alone, and in the early part of the decade, all first-ranked Han cadres in the villages of southern Xinjiang reportedly moved to cities or administrative positions. Some 200,000 Hans left Xinjiang between 1979 and 1993, although new immigration more than replaced that number.[29]

Despite the substantial nativization of Party and government in Xinjiang and Tibet in the wake of Hu Yaobang's directives, however, Beijing continued to select trusted Han officials as first secretaries of the Regional Party Committees, as it had done with very few exceptions in prior decades. Ironically, all but one of those exceptions occurred before Yang Jingren's 1979 speech. Although Yang had explicitly acknowledged that the choice of Han first secretaries vitiated Beijing's claim that non-Hans enjoyed autonomy and urged that the policy be changed, since 1980 no member of a titular minority has held the top Party spot in any of the autonomous regions. The appointment of Wu Jinghua, a member of the Yi minzu, as Tibet's First Party secretary in 1985 was regarded by many as a signal that the next secretary would be Tibetan, but following the wave of Lhasa protests, Beijing instead selected the Han official Hu Jintao as his successor in 1988.[30] As an expert on minority affairs in the PRC has said, "It is clear to just about everyone in China that the state is a Han creation... [and] its direction and its directors come from the Han."[31]

The liberalization of cultural policies and nativization (*minzuhua*) of administrative ranks under Hu Yaobang pleased many Tibetans and Uyghurs, even if those changes did not extinguish criticism of Beijing. A sizable number of Tibetans reportedly said they "had never had it so good," and Uyghur peasants and traders avowed a satisfaction with the

---

[28] Wang Lixiong, "Reflections on Tibet," *New Left Review* 14 (2002): 99, 103–4; Tsering W. Shakya, *The Dragon in the Land of Snows: A History of Modern Tibet since 1947* (New York: Columbia University Press, 1999), 389–90, 395, 404–5.

[29] Yin Zhuguang and Mao Yongfu, eds., *Xinjiang Minzu Guanxi Yanjiu [Research on Minzu Relations in Xinjiang]* (Urumchi: Xinjiang Renmin Chubanshe, 1996), 222–23; Zhu Xiaomin, "[A Preliminary Analysis]", *supra* n. 26, 62.

[30] Goldstein, *The Snow Lion and the Dragon, supra* n. 25, 74; Shakya, *History of Modern Tibet, supra* n. 28, 429.

[31] Stevan Harrell, "L'etat, C'est Nous, or We Have Met the Oppressor and He is Us: The Predicament of Minority Cadres in the PRC," in *The Chinese State at the Borders*, ed. Diana Lary (Vancouver: UBC Press, 2007), 223.

Party disconcerting to Uyghur nationalist intellectuals. At the same time, Han cadres in both Xinjiang and Tibet deeply resented Hu, feeling that his policies called their political contributions into question, rewarded local anti-Han prejudice, and threatened the very security of Hans living in the regions.[32]

Hu also faced resistance within China's powerful Central Committee from hardliners such as Deng Liqun and the first head of the Xinjiang Uyghur Autonomous Region Wang Zhen, who argued that Hu was only inviting trouble. In his memoirs Deng later remembered that Hu had announced in Beijing that autonomy in Tibet meant the "right to decide for oneself" and proposed to Xinjiang's leaders that the center retain only three powers – control of defense and foreign relations and a veto over regional policies. Deng had privately asked Hu, incredulously, "How can you propose such a resolution in a minzu autonomous region? How can it be all right... to let the autonomous region exercise [all other powers] itself?" He believed Hu understood neither the threat of foreign powers seeking to detach Tibet and Xinjiang from China from the outside, nor that of independence advocates aiming to do the same from within, and he feared that the cession of so much authority to the autonomous regions opened the door to both threats. An unnamed official sympathetic to Wang Zhen reportedly fulminated, in the same vein, that the author of these proposals was a "traitor" aiming to "create an East Turkestan... surrendering Xinjiang to the Soviet Union and Turkey."[33]

Hu Yaobang was held responsible for a series of student protests in the mid-1980s and dismissed as Party general secretary in 1987. Rid of Hu's supervision, Xinjiang's leaders quickly reversed his nativization initiative and again spurred the recruitment and retention of Han cadres for positions in the XUAR; on being appointed Party first secretary in Tibet, Hu Jintao did the same in the TAR beginning in 1989.[34]

---

[32] Zhu Xiaomin, *Jiefang Hou Zhi 20 Shiji 80 Niandai Xinjiang Yili Fan Fenlie Douzheng Jiaoxun Qianxi* (a Preliminary Analysis of the Lessons from the Struggle against Separatism in Xinjiang's Ili from the Revolution through the 1980s); Justin Jon Rudelson, *Oasis Identities: Uyghur Nationalism Along China's Silk Road* (New York: Columbia University Press, 1997); Yin Zhuguang and Mao Yongfu, *supra* n. 29, 222–223; Tsering W. Shakya, *History of Modern Tibet, supra* n. 28, 400, 410.

[33] Michael Dillon, *Xinjiang – China's Muslim Far Northwest*, Durham East Asia Series (London: RoutledgeCurzon, 2004), 36. Dillon cites Ruan Ming, "Missed Historic Opportunity Recalled," *Minzhu Zhongguo* 8 (February 1992): 17–18. Translated in JPRS-CAR-92-039.

[34] Deng Liqun, *Deng Liqun Zishu: Shi'er Ge Chunqiu [Deng Liqun in His Own Words: Twelve Seasons](1975–1987)* (Hong Kong: Da Feng chubanshe, 2006), 205–8; Zhu

Zhao Ziyang, Hu Yaobang's successor as Party general secretary, blamed widespread Tibetan dissatisfaction manifested in a series of uprisings between 1987 and 1989 on "Han ultra-leftism"; Zhao then met a fate similar to Hu Yaobang's, being blamed for the Tian'anmen protests of spring 1989. Soon after Zhao's dismissal, hardliners were quite satisfied to see Beijing reverse the verdict at a crucial meeting of the Politburo in October 1989, which blamed the disturbances on relaxed political controls.[35]

In sum, by the end of the 1980s a coalition of key Chinese leaders had concluded that liberal policies had not only not gained the loyalty of most Tibetans and Uyghurs but also opened the way to protest.[36] From that point forward no prominent leaders would again propose liberal accommodations as a response to protests in either Xinjiang or Tibet.

THE BEGINNINGS OF RETRENCHMENT: QUESTIONING AUTONOMY

Indeed, the fall of Communist regimes across Eastern Europe and the collapse of the Soviet Union in 1991 dramatically strengthened the argument of Beijing's hardliners that further liberal reforms would be not just risky but disastrous for China. In addition, the emergence of independent states in Central Asia bearing the names of groups also found in Xinjiang – Kazakh, Kyrgyz, Uzbek, and Tajik – seemed to provide new inspiration to Uyghurs longing for an independent state of their own. A series of protests, bombings, and violent riots in Xinjiang between 1990 and 1997 dramatically increased concerns in Beijing about sources of unrest both inside the region and in the adjacent Central Asian states, where at least 300,000 Uyghurs lived and a number of Uyghur political organizations operated. The 1990s and early 2000s saw a series of policy retrenchments in Xinjiang. The regional government cracked down on

---

Xiaomin, "[A Preliminary Analysis]," *supra* n. 26, 62; Dillon, *Xinjiang – China's Muslim Far Northwest*, *supra* n. 33, 36; Cao Changqing (Cao Changching), "Minzu Chongtu Keneng Shi Zongguo Bengkui Jieti – Fang Menguzu Xuezhe Ba He" [Minzu Conflicts May Cause China to Collapse and Break up – an Interview with the Mongol Scholar Bache Johngar], *Caochangqing.com* (originally published in Kai Fang [HK] 1997), http://caochangqing.com/gb/newsdisp.php?News_ID=513.

[35] Tashi Rabgey and Tseten Wangchuk Sharlho, *Sino-Tibetan Dialogue in the Post-Mao Era: Lessons and Prospects*, Policy Studies 12 (Washington, DC: East-West Center Washington, 2004), 15; Lixiong, "Reflections on Tibet," *supra* n. 28, 109.

[36] Goldstein, *The Snow Lion and the Dragon*, *supra* n. 25, 92–98; Shakya, *History of Modern Tibet*, *supra* n. 28, ch. 14, 15.

mosque construction, private religious tuition, and religious observance by school-age youths (initiatives all strengthened in the wake of September 11). The educational bureaucracy stepped up pressure on non-Han schoolchildren to begin studying Mandarin earlier and more extensively and began merging minority-language and Mandarin-language schools; this would culminate in the 2002 announcement that postsecondary schools in Xinjiang would offer only Uyghur literature classes in that language and the Party's 2004 decision to merge all schools serving minorities with those teaching Hans, with a mandate to deliver all courses in Mandarin as soon as possible. Finally, the government clamped down on a wide variety of speech and publications it deemed "separatist," casting a very wide net.[37]

Throughout the decade, Party organs maintained a firm rhetorical commitment to minzu policies and the institutions of autonomy, but, as has been shown, political institutions in China under Party control have proven remarkably flexible in the hands of different leaders. After nearly fifty years of working within the rhetorical and institutional confines of the minzu regional autonomy system, by the late 1990s some of China's leaders appeared to have begun to contemplate doing away with that system entirely. Because the Party has seldom announced such contentious initiatives in advance, and because Beijing's leaders have not been in the habit of submitting to probing questions about their policy choices, we must engage in a kind of updated Kremlinology to reveal the origins, contours, and implications of this initiative. Most of our sources for this relatively new initiative are, therefore, official acts and scholarly studies.

A 1998 study published by the elite Chinese Academy of Social Sciences provided a striking example. Reflecting on the lessons of the Soviet breakup, the study urged that China's government

> dilute [danhua] the minzu viewpoint and minzu consciousness. Beginning by diluting minzu self-awareness and consciousness of minzu independence, gradually weaken [xueruo] the principle of minzu regional autonomy.... In a process that will take some time, wait until the circumstances are basically ripe and change minzu regional autonomy into local autonomy, in order to eliminate the basis for minzu separatist activities.[38]

---

[37] Bovingdon, *The Uyghurs, supra* n. 3, ch. 2, 4; Arienne M. Dwyer, "The Xinjiang Conflict: Uyghur Identity, Language Policy, and Political Discourse," *Policy Studies* 15 (2005): 38–41.

[38] Chen Lianbi, "Eluosi Minzu Guanxi Wenti Yanjiu" [Research on the Problem of *Minzu* Relations in Russia], Zhongguo shehui kexueyuan Dongou Zhongya yanjiusuo, http://euroasia.cass.cn/chinese/Production/projects32/010.html.

As striking a departure from contemporaneous official statements as this was, it was by no means the most radical. Other authors proposed doing away with the term *autonomy* altogether. Beginning in 2002 several authors urged that the central government aim for "collective rule" (*gongzhi*), meaning rule by all minzu groups (understood to include Hans) in concert rather than in separate single-group autonomous units; one scholar even opined that it would soon be appropriate to speak of "post-autonomy" (*hou zizhi*).[39] The importance of these scholarly musings should not be underestimated, because academic journals in China continue to be controlled by the Party, and nothing can be published until it has been approved by Party censors trained to distinguish between acceptable and unacceptable ideas. Given the tremendous political sensitivity of the subject matter, we can infer that academics had been encouraged to explore these options by officials.

It was in this context that Ma Rong published his sweeping 2004 indictment of Chinese minzu policies and call to "de-politicize" non-Han groups, discussed in the chapter introduction. After earning a PhD in sociology at Brown University in the 1980s with a thesis on the determinants of cultural assimilation in China, Ma had returned to China and conducted research on intergroup relations in Xinjiang and Tibet in the 1990s. Influenced by the constructivist turn in the study of identity politics, Ma concluded that China's minzu policies and institutions of autonomy had preserved, and in some cases deepened, the distinctions among groups instead of facilitating their fusion into a unified national whole. In addition, the institutions invited non-Hans to identify with their groups and articulate collective aspirations separate from those of China, Ma felt, and thus "politicized" them. By renaming minzu "ethnic groups" (*zuqun*) and dismantling the preferential policies for them, China could transform "minzu problems" into the more limited and manageable "ethnic problems" found (not coincidentally) in the United States and other liberal democracies. If the proximal goal was more harmonious relations

---

[39] Zhu Lun, "Lun Minzu Gongzhi De Lilun Jichu Yu Jiben Yuanli" [A Discussion of the Theoretical Basis and Basic Tenets of *Minzu* Collective Rule], *Minzu yanjiu* 2 (2002). Du Wenzhong, "Zizhi Yu Gongzhi: Dui Xifang Gudian Minzu Zhengzhi Lilun De Xianzheng Fansi" [Autonomy and Collective Rule: A Constitutionalist Reflection on Classic Western Minzu Political Theory], *Minzu yanjiu* 6 (2002); Ma Dazheng, *Guojia Liyi Gaoyu Yiqie – Xinjiang Wending Wenti De Guancha Yu Sikao (the National Interest above All Else – Analysis of and Reflections on the Problem of Stability in Xinjiang)*, ed. Zhongguo shehui kexueyuan Xinjiang fazhan yanjiu zhongxin, Xinjiang Yanjiu Congshu (Ürümci: Xinjiang renmin chubanshe, 2003).

among groups in "multicultural" China, the more distant one was eliminating once and for all the specter of Soviet-style disintegration.[40]

Ma Rong also addressed international concerns. He noted acidly that Western states have regularly used "minority problems" as a pretext to criticize developing countries. Governments in a number of developing states have devoted great effort to raising the socioeconomic status of minorities to blunt such criticism, yet their actions have neither placated Western observers nor quelled indigenous political demands. Instead, Ma found, minorities have used the state's concessions as the basis for further demands; adding insult to injury, Western states have "without exception" supported those new demands.[41] Expanding on Ma's thesis, another scholar argued that the use of the term minzu to describe the fifty-five non-Han groups, and the term's standard translation into English as "nation," had "led foreign scholars to think of [them as] political entities and separatist movements with the right to exercise 'national self-determination' and found 'nation-states,' and this has caused serious misunderstanding in the international community."[42]

Despite Ma Rong's position as a professor at China's top-ranked Beijing University, and the implicit official support that enabled him to publish such a fundamental challenge to more than five decades of CCP policies, his ideas faced substantial, even withering criticism. Indeed, the large volume of scholarly rebuttals seems to suggest that many academics, and presumably many in the Party center, oppose such a radical abandonment of the minzu system. Jin, Jun, and Rui concluded that "writings in support of Ma Rong's proposal are rare," as Ma himself has conceded.[43]

[40] Barry Sautman, "Paved with Good Intentions Proposals to Curb Minority Rights and Their Consequences for China," *Modern China* 38, no. 1 (2012): 11–12; Ma Rong, "[Understand *Minzu* Relations]," *supra* n. 2; James Leibold, "Toward a Second Generation of Ethnic Policies?" *China Brief* 12, no. 13 (2012).

[41] Ma Rong, "Lijie Minzu Guanxi De Xin Silu - Shaoshu Zuqun Wentide 'Qu Zhengzhi Hua'" [New Thoughts on How to Understand *Minzu* Relations – 'Depoliticizing' the Problem of Ethnic Minorities], *Beijing daxue xuebao (zhexue shehui kexue ban)* 41, no. 6 (2004), 130.

[42] Xiong Yanqing, "Ma Rong: 'Wenhuahua' Zuqun Guanxi" [Ma Rong: 'Culturalizing' Ethnic Relations'], *Zhongguo jiaoyu he keyan jisuanji wang*, http://www.edu.cn/renwu_6123/20071103/t20071103_263091.shtml.

[43] Jin Binggao, Sun Jun, and Xiao Rui, "Minzu Wenti 'Qu Zhengzhi Hua,' 'Wenhuahua': 'Xin Silu' Haishi 'Lao Tao Lu'? Minzu Lilun Qianyan Yanjiu Xilie Lunwen Zhi San" [The 'Depoliticization' and 'Culturalization' of Minzu Problems: A 'New Avenue of Thought' or the 'Same Old Road'? Third in a Series of Theses on Cutting-Edge Research on Minzu Theory], *Heilongjiang minzu congkan [Heilongjiang minzu series]* 3 (2012).

A number of scholars have suggested that merely by proposing to substitute "ethnic group" (*zuqun*) for minzu, Ma Rong showed that he misunderstood, or else was intentionally misrepresenting, the true nature of non-Han groups in China. Qin Wenpeng argued that the "political attributes" of *minzu* could not be ignored, and simply renaming the groups would achieve nothing. It made no sense, Qin argued, to propose strategies inappropriate to China's actual circumstances, "weakening minzu problems into cultural ones owing to qualms about acknowledging their political attributes."[44]

In a similar vein, Miao Li and Pei Shengyu observed that Ma Rong offered no precise definition of "depoliticization." Nonetheless they understood him to mean that "minzu problems must be separated from politics, so that the management of minzu problems no longer has any political significance at all."[45] Like Qin they argued that Ma conjured this ideal in reference to American politics and that it was completely unsuited to China's historical or current circumstances.

Despite the volume and vehemence of criticisms of Ma Rong's proposal, his stature as a policy advisor and public intellectual in China unquestionably changed with the eruption of a series of violent protests in Tibetan areas in 2008 and Xinjiang in 2009.

UNREST IN CHINA'S PERIPHERY AND THE "REHABILITATION" OF MA RONG'S IDEAS

In Tibetan areas in March 2008 and then in Xinjiang in July 2009, episodes of widespread protest and violence demonstrated the continued contentiousness of China's western periphery and seemed to lend new credibility to Ma Rong's dire warnings.

The protests in Tibetan areas were the most serious since the Lhasa demonstrations of 1989, in terms of both their violence and the number of participants. They began with a protest by a group of monks at a monastery, demanding the release of other monks held in jail since fall 2007. Police quelled the protest with teargas and gunfire, which precipitated riots in the streets of Lhasa several days later on March 14.

---

[44] Qin Wenpeng, "Lun Minzu De Zhengzhi Shuxing [On the Political Attributes of Minzu]," *Heilongjiang minzu congkan [Heilongjiang minzu series]* 5 (2009).

[45] Miao Li and Pei Shengyu, "Qian Tan Minzu Wenti 'Qu Zhengzhi Hua' Yu Minzu Quyu Zizhi Zhidu" [A Brief Discussion of the 'Depoliticization' of Minzu Problems and the System of Minzu Regional Autonomy], *Chengde minzu shizhuan xuebao (Journal of Chengde Minzu Pedagogical Institute)* 4 (2011).

Rioters looted shops and reportedly attacked ordinary Hans and Huis in the streets. The government responded by deploying the People's Armed Police to prevent further rioting, but over the next two weeks demonstrations quickly spread to culturally Tibetan areas in Qinghai, Gansu, and Sichuan, and new protests broke out in Lhasa two weeks later, on March 29. Crackdowns on these protests were swift and often bloody, with tallies of dead ranging from dozens to hundreds. Police jailed over 2,000 participants in Tibet and the neighboring provinces and broadcast orders that other participants turn themselves in. Whereas the Chinese government blamed the Dalai Lama for the protests, Tibetan exile groups attributed them to China's mismanagement of Tibet. Representations of the events abroad became a second point of contention, with Beijing and many Chinese citizens arguing that foreign media highlighted police brutality toward Tibetans while concealing Tibetans' violent treatment of Hans and others owing to anti-Chinese bias.[46] The angry crowds that greeted Olympic torch relays in London, Paris, and San Francisco in April indicated that the international community continued to have an active interest in Tibetan affairs and further inflamed Chinese nationalism at home.

The following year on July 5, 2009, Uyghurs in Xinjiang's capital city, Urumci, marched to protest the government's handling of a brawl several weeks before between Han and Uyghur workers in a Guangdong factory in which several Uyghurs died. The protest devolved into a night of terrible violence under circumstances still not well understood. According to official tallies, 197 people died and 1,721 were injured, most of them Hans. Even though Beijing quickly ordered police and soldiers into the city to quell the violence, two days later on July 7 Han vigilantes armed with clubs and other weapons took to the city's streets and clashed with Uyghurs they encountered. Although the violence subsided soon thereafter, a tense atmosphere persisted in the capital city through August and September, when rumors of Uyghurs attacking Hans with syringes precipitated a demonstration by tens of thousands of Hans in the city center on September 3. Participants criticized the government for failing to protect ordinary citizens and demanded changes of policies and personnel.[47]

---

[46] Robert Barnett, "The Tibet Protests of Spring, 2008: Conflict between the Nation and the State," *China Perspectives* 3 (2009).

[47] James A. Millward, "Introduction: Does the 2009 Urumchi Violence Mark a Turning Point?" *Central Asian Survey* 28, no. 4 (2009); Thomas Cliff, "The Partnership of Stability in Xinjiang: State–Society Interactions Following the July 2009 Unrest," *China Journal* 68 (2012).

These outbreaks of unrest, and in particular the reports of attacks on Hans by Uyghurs and Tibetans, led to a much higher volume of popular critiques of "*minzu* policies." Members of the Han majority have become more openly critical of China's minzu policies for several reasons: One is resentment of the special privileges of minorities (much like the backlash against affirmative action in the United States), combined with the conviction that undeserving minorities are crowding out deserving Hans from important opportunities. A second reason is anger that far from being grateful for those special privileges, Tibetans and Uyghurs have (in their view) instead violently attacked Hans and their property. Predictably these two stances combine to support one thesis: the privileges should be taken away to restore Hans' equal rights and to punish minorities for rioting, attacking Hans, and in these ways souring intergroup relations.

THE CURRENT DEBATE: OPEN SEASON ON MINZU POLICIES?

The 2008 violence in Tibet and the 2009 violence in Xinjiang presented the perfect opportunity for hardliners to press Ma Rong's argument that the problems with China's policies toward non-Hans stemmed from too much recognition, not too little. Ominous warnings about the Soviet Union gained currency again, and Ma Rong reiterated his case that China's minzu policies invited a Soviet-style disintegration.[48]

In 2011 Ma's advocacy leapt from the academic realm to the political when Zhu Weiqun, vice director of the United Front and for some time the top PRC official engaged in discussions with the Tibetan Government in Exile, wrote candidly about what he regarded as failings of the country's minzu policies. Zhu argued that it was time to overcome the taboo against discussing "assimilation," which was different from "Sinicization" (*Hanhua*) in that the resultant amalgamated group would absorb the best qualities of all its constituents; urged that the government create no new autonomous units and should mix Hans and non-Hans in schools; and, most significantly, proposed doing away with the minzu designation on the National Identity Card – a symbolic step that, if enacted, would markedly reduce the role of minzu identity in China's public sphere.[49] Some observers saw it as a confirmation of Ma Rong's

[48] Ma Rong, "Minzu Zhuyi Sichao Xia De Zhongguo Minzu Wenti" [China's Minzu Problems under the Influence of the Nationalist Wave], *Xinhua Yuebao [Xinhua monthly]* 4 (2011).

[49] Zhu Weiqun, "Dui Dangqian Minzu Lingyu Wenti De Jidian Sikao – Zhongguo Gongchandang Xinwen" [A Few Reflections on Current Problems in the Minzu Sphere – CCP News], *Xuexi shibao [Study times]*, February 13, 2012.

influence on the Party leadership – or perhaps that he had expressed views held within the Party's inner sanctum.[50]

The most radical proposal for change to date, however, emerged from the pens of two scholars in 2011. Titled "Second-Generation Minzu Policies: Spurring Minzu to Blend and Flourish Together," the article argued that the Party must abandon the autonomy system altogether, cease recognizing minzu difference, and induce all Chinese citizens to assimilate in the service of state security. The authors picked up the argument of previous authors that the Soviet nationalities policies on which the CCP had modeled its own were an unworkable mishmash that had led to the state's disintegration and urged that Beijing now opt for the "melting pot" (*da ronglu*) policies of Brazil, India, and the United States. They argued, further, that the separate identities of China's fifty-five minority minzu were not a temporary indulgence but a threat to the long-term survival of the state. Beijing ought to adopt linguistic and other policies that stripped the various groups of their differences and induced them to identify solely with the Chinese nation. Although the authors nowhere mentioned Ma Rong, they had clearly taken inspiration from his work. At the same time they borrowed authority from Central Committee Work Forums on Tibet in January 2010 and on Xinjiang in May of the same year – meetings convened to address the intergroup frictions and still-enduring poverty in those regions – and claimed to see in these symposia a transition from "first generation" to "second generation" minzu policies.[51]

The authors of the article, Hu Angang and Hu Lianhe, are professors in the School of Management at Qinghua University, one of the two or three top-ranked universities in China. Hu Angang also heads the university's Institute (formerly Center) for Research on National Conditions and has long published the authoritative periodical *Report on National Conditions*, circulated to top Party leaders throughout the country.[52] The multiple republications of the authors' proposal for major changes

---

[50] Learning of Zhu Weiqun's proposal, Tibetan dissident Woeser sent out a sarcastic message on Twitter (February 14, 2012): "Professor Ma Rong has done meritorious service (ligongle)!" – meaning that Ma had now concretely affected Party policy discourse. Accessed June 4, 2013, https://twitter.com/degewa/status/169388942490206209).

[51] Hu Angang and Hu Lianhe, "Di Er Dai Minzu Zhengce: Cujin Minzu Jiaorong Yiti He Fanrong Yiti" [Second-Generation Minzu Policies: Promoting Minzu Blending into One Body and Flourishing as One Body], *mzb.com.cn*, April 10, 2012, http://www.mzb.com.cn/html/Home/report/293093-1.htm.

[52] The enterprise of Hu Angang's Institute *(guoqing yanjiu)*, often translated blandly as "research on national conditions," is better rendered in English as "China national exception studies" according to Geremie Barmé, because officials and scholars in China frequently adduce "national conditions" to justify policies at odds with international norms or make the case that outsiders "misunderstand" China.

in minzu policies indicate that they have enjoyed "clear support in certain segments of the party state and the broader society."[53]

Despite enormous policy swings over the last sixty years, the Communist Party has steadfastly maintained that its policies are "correct" in nearly every context. Open criticism of Party policies and discussion of alternatives are rare, and indeed it has been the principal task of China's enormous force of official Internet censors to squelch such discussions as soon as they emerge on the Web.[54] It was therefore a remarkable departure from past practice, and an indication of strong official support for Hu Angang, when the Web site of the Minzu Affairs Commission openly invited readers to view arguments for and against "Second Generation Minzu Policies" by clicking on hot links marked "pro" and "con."[55] Among the most forceful arguments against were those of Zhang Haiyang, Hao Shiyuan, and Jin Binggao.

CRITIQUES OF THE REFORMERS: SERIOUS DEBATE

In December 2011 Zhang Haiyang, professor at Beijing's Central Minzu University (the flagship institution for the ethnographic and policy-relevant study of non-Hans), published a lengthy critique of the ideas of Ma Rong, Hu Angang, and Hu Lianhe, including a mordant parable:

> A few kids from the great Han clan left [China] village to study abroad. They saw that there were a few single-surname villages, immigrant villages, and colonial villages elsewhere in the world, and began to suffer pangs of jealousy. Returning to their village they mouthed off about how multiple-surname villages didn't measure up to single-surname ones, shouted that they wanted to rip up the village compact, that they wanted to "de-surname"[56] the minor lineages, and insisted that the Han clan language serve as the standard village language. They even said that if members of minor lineages didn't speak the language of the Han clan, didn't adopt its surname, or had the temerity to refuse intermarriage with the Han clan,

---

See, e.g., http://www.thechinastory.org/key-intellectual/hu-angang-%E8%83%A1%E9%9E%8D%E9%92%A2/, accessed June 4, 2013.

[53] Leibold, "Second Generation of Ethnic Policies?" *supra* n. 40, 5.

[54] For a regularly updated and cumulating list of key words forbidden by the CCP's powerful Ministry of Propaganda (Xuanchuan bu), see http://chinadigitaltimes.net/, accessed June 4, 2013.

[55] The site can be found at http://www.mzb.com.cn/html/Home/folder/292573-1.htm, accessed May 1, 2013.

[56] This odd coinage is clearly a mocking reference to Ma Rong's proposal to "de-politicize" (*qu zhengzhihua*) minzu status in China.

the refusals indicated a desire to split the village or sell out the village. Thus it was necessary to keep watch over them and compel them to reform, in order to accelerate the process of homogenization. The formerly balanced and harmonious relations among neighbors in the China village were thus destroyed [by the kids' actions].[57]

Zhang's mocked the high-sounding theories of Ma, Hu, and Hu by reducing them to a parochial dispute about who belonged in the village (read China) and who in the family (read the nation). Concluding his very funny parable, Zhang questioned the reference value of the "India village" and the story of the collapse of the "Soviet village," going on to note that Hong Kong, Macao, and Taiwan villages are all successfully carrying out "one village two systems" without disintegration. After delivering his comic jabs, Zhang continued with deadly serious criticisms, condemning Hu Angang's "Second generation policies" as a "minzu Great Leap Forward" and a redeployment of "concentration camp logic." Zhang further objected that Ma and Hu were disingenuous in insisting on an assimilative "melting pot" model for China: knowing full well that the United States (and the West more generally) had gone through phases of "exclusion," "melting pot," and "tossed salad" and arrived at the "mosaic," they nonetheless insisted on arresting the state of the field at "the melting pot." In his view Chinese elites, although writing in the twenty-first-century East, had been saddled with nineteenth-century ideas by the national education system and thus have as little capacity as early twentieth-century Western elites to enjoy the fruits of multiculturalism.[58]

Hao Shiyuan, head of the Institute of Anthropology and Minzu studies at the Chinese Academy of Social Sciences, challenged the proposals of Ma Rong and Hu Angang in a similar vein. In a series of articles in 2012, Hao criticized the "theoretical and practical errors" of the "Second Generation policies" and argued that none of the examples touted by Hu and Hu – India, Brazil, or the United States (the last of course praised

---

[57] "Zhang Haiyang to Cong shehui fazhan shi dao wenhua shengtaixue" [From the history of social development to cultural ecology], December 2, 2011, http://blog.sina.com.cn/s/blog_48c6994f01010wpl.html.

[58] Title of Weblog. Zhang might have missed the irony that in defending the soundness of the CCP's current minzu policies, he is indirectly affirming the theories of Lenin and Stalin, quite modern in their day but also belonging to the early twentieth century, and more distantly, the nineteenth century ideas of Karl Marx and Lewis Henry Morgan. *See* Dru Gladney, *Muslim Chinese: Ethnic Nationalism in the People's Republic* (Cambridge: Harvard University Press, 1991), 72–73; Erez Manela, *The Wilsonian Moment: Self-Determination and the International Origins of Anticolonial Nationalism* (Oxford; New York: Oxford University Press, 2007).

by Ma Rong) – provided a plausible model for China.[59] Another scholar pointed out that the intention to homogenize the population in the service of state security does not in any way indicate that it is possible, or even desirable, to achieve that goal. Reducing "minzu problems" to a matter of local administration and assimilation might be the preference of advocates of state unity, but it is no guarantee of success. Citing the examples of Mexico and Spain, Qin Wenpeng noted that a stubborn emphasis on assimilation might backfire politically.[60]

It is notable that many of the most prominent academic critics of Ma Rong (who incidentally is Hui) have themselves been members of non-Han groups: Zhang Haiyang is Manchu, Hao Shiyuan is Mongol, and Jin Binggao is Korean. One need not be an essentialist to make sense of this. A prominent American historian of the Qing Empire put the matter plainly after discussing the "policy debates" with numerous colleagues in China: "Every single person I speak to who is not Han opposes this idea, for obvious reasons. They see it as the dismantling of those policies that have provided them with some measure of autonomy . . . and some measure of protection for their different indigenous languages, religions and customs, and what have you."

Although these scholars have mounted a serious challenge to the abandonment of the minzu system, the struggle is not an equal one. The publication of a Web site inviting readers to choose between supporters and opponents seems remarkably balanced and evenhanded, but, in fact, it is

---

[59] Hao Shiyuan, "Yindu Goujian Guojia Minzu 'Jingyan' Bu Zhide Zhongguo Xuexi – Xu Ping 'Di Er Dai Minzu Zhengce' De 'Guoji Jingyan Jiaoxun' Shuo" [India's 'Experience' in Constructing State and Nation Does Not Merit Study by China – a Continuation of a Critique of the Doctrine of 'the Lessons of International Experience' in the 'Second-Generation Minzu Policies'], *Zhongnan minzu daxue xuebao (renwen shehui kexue ban) [Journal of South Central Minzu University – Humanities and social science edition]* 6 (2012); "Ping 'Di Er Dai Minzu Zhengce' Shuo De Lilun Yu Shijian Wuqu" [A Critique of Theoretical and Practical Errors in the Doctrine of 'Second-Generation Minzu Policies'], *Xinjiang shehui kexue [Xinjiang social sciences]* 2 (2012); "Meiguo Shi Zhongguo Jiejue Minzu Wenti De Bangyang Ma? Ping 'Di Er Dai Minzu Zhengce' De 'Guoji Jingyan Jiaoxun' Shuo" [Is America a Model for Solving China's Minzu Problems? A Critique of the Doctrine of 'Lessons from International Experience' in 'Second-Generation Minzu Policies'], *Shijie minzu [Minzu of the world]* 2 (2012); "Baxi Neng Wei Zhongguo Minzu Shiwu Tigong Shenme 'Jingyan' – Zai Ping 'Di Er Dai Minzu Zhengce' De 'Guoji Jingyan Jiaoxun' Shuo" [What 'Experience' Can Brazil Provide in Regard to China's Minzu Affairs? Another Critique of the Doctrine of 'Lessons from International Experience' in 'Second-Generation Minzu Policies'], *Xibei minzu daxue xuebao (zhexue shehui kexue ban) [Journal of Northwest Minzu University – philosophy and social science edition]* 4 (2012).

[60] Qin Wenpeng, "[Political Attributes of Minzu]," *supra* n. 44.

neither. One side is argued by scholars defending Party orthodoxy, and as just noted most of them non-Hans, which any reasonably Web savvy Chinese reader can learn with a few mouse clicks. This position is more likely popularly supported only by a minority.

The other side involves an explicit root and branch dismantling of the full sixty years and more of CCP policy, unprecedented in Party history. So radical a rejection of Party policy could probably only occur without profound damage to the premise of infallibility that justifies CCP dominance by the novel mechanism of a popular mandate for change. It is probably supported at this point by the vast majority of Hans, if only a small number of academics and an even smaller number of officials on record.

Notably, although the Web site invites readers to compare the arguments of the two sides, it provides no opportunity to vote or explicit method of aggregating responses, which might have provided a precedent for direct popular participation in policy making. Instead, Party officials may well be reviewing repostings and commentaries on blogs to test popular opinion behind the scenes, in a CCP-style policy referendum. On reflection the Web site is quite a brilliant stratagem, and what initially appears to be balance resolves, on closer inspection, into strong and bold support for Ma and Hu's dramatic proposals from the apex of the Party.

CONCLUSION: REALITIES AND RHETORIC

Chinese scholars have begun to concede in print that autonomy was not a beneficent gift to non-Hans, but instead a response to widespread political demands from particular groups, such as Uyghurs and Tibetans.[61] Outside China it has long been understood that the CCP's special political arrangements for China's distinct ethno-national groups after 1949 were never intended to satisfy the political aspirations of the largest and most mobilized groups, and indeed they have not. The system of autonomous units assigned to various groups and the legal framework of autonomy above all served the goal of keeping peripheral territories part of China.

[61] Wang Xi'en, "Ye Tan Zai Woguo Minzu Wenti Shangde 'Fansi' He 'Shi Shi Qiu Shi' – Yu Ma Rong Jiaoshou De Ji Dian Shangque" [More Talk About 'Reflection' and 'Seeking Truth from Facts' with Regard to Our Country's Minzu Problems – a Few Points of Discussion with Professor Ma Rong], *Xinan minzu daxue xuebao (renwen shehui kexue)* [*Journal of Southwest Minzu University – humanities and social sciences edition*] 1 (2009).

Despite periodic warnings that ethno-national conflicts might "erupt" in China's Western periphery and jeopardize the country's territorial integrity,[62] Beijing has long regarded the separatist threat as no more than a minor irritant.[63] In reality, the territories of Tibet, Xinjiang, and Inner Mongolia, as well as other regions with substantial non-Han populations, are more tightly bound to the PRC than ever before. Judging simply from the fact that China's borders have remained intact, we can thus count Beijing's methods for handling separatists a success. This cannot, however, be considered diagnostic of a particularly successful set of policies toward non-Hans. In the latter half of the twentieth century, few groups seeking to secede from established states anywhere in the world have been able to do so, and none without external support. CCP leaders and officially sanctioned scholars have been prone to boast that China's policies have preserved state unity by "solving the national question," and yet it is instructive to consider the global solution to the problem in the latter half of the twentieth century. With a remarkably small number of exceptions, if an ethno-national group seeking independence and the territory it claims are part of an existing state, it is more or less stuck in that state.

In light of the realistic impossibility of independence and the historical ineffectiveness of the minzu system, what is the actual significance of the current debate on abandoning that system? It was once observed that as CCP leaders sought popular support and a path to power in the early 1930s, they played a double game, "simultaneously project[ing] the image of preserver of the territorial borders of imperial China when addressing the Han and of promoter of secession when addressing the minorities."[64] In the course of gaining full control of the country, they shifted to promoting unity to Hans, cultural protection and autonomy

---

[62] Dru Gladney, "Ethnic Identity in China: The New Politics of Difference," in *China Briefing, 1994*, ed. William A. Joseph (Boulder: Westview Press, 1994); Dru C. Gladney, "Rumblings from the Uyghur," *Current History* 96, no. 611 (1997); "Xinjiang: China's Future West Bank?" *Current History* 101, no. 656 (2002); Ross Terrill, *The New Chinese Empire and What It Means for the United States* (New York: Basic Books, 2003); Michael D. Swaine, "Exploiting a Strategic Opening," in *Strategic Asia 2004–05: Confronting Terrorism in the Pursuit of Power*, ed. Ashley J. Tellis and Michael Wills (Seattle: National Bureau of Asian Research, 2004), 69; Tony Saich, *Governance and Politics of China*, 2nd ed. (Basingstoke, Hampshire [UK]; New York: Palgrave Macmillan, 2004), 159.

[63] Yitzhak Shichor, "Nuisance Value: Uyghur Activism in Germany and Beijing–Berlin Relations," *Journal of Contemporary China* 22, no. 82 (2013); Tashi Rabgey and Tseten Wangchuk Sharlho, *Sino-Tibetan Dialogue, supra* n. 35, 12.

[64] Connor, *National Question, supra* n. 8, 76–77.

to non-Hans. Ma and Hu have proposed a still more dramatic shift to advocating a single uncompromising message of national unity, a single rubric of citizenship rights and obligations, to Hans and non-Hans alike. This change would almost certainly earn wide support from the Han majority, but it would be a costly mistake. As Zhang Haiyang, Hao Shiyuan, Jin Binggao, and other Chinese scholars have suggested contra Ma Rong and Hu Anbang, Beijing cannot eliminate minzu problems by changing non-Hans' status with a few pen strokes and the scrapping of minzu policies.

Chen Lianbi in 1998, Ma Rong in 2004, and Hu Angang in 2011 had defended their radical proposals not only on grounds of state security, but also by ostensibly embracing the purported universal norm of individual citizenship, not compromised or muddied by intermediating groups. In reality, however, demanding that everyone in China identify with the Chinese nation and embrace universal citizenship would not depoliticize minzu. It would not in fact help the country move beyond the outworn model of the mononational state; instead, in a move that strikingly recalls the rhetorical moves of early twentieth-century Chinese intellectuals, it would reauthorize and reconstitute that model as envisioned by (overwhelmingly Han) elites. As Jin et al. put it, "the true implication of 'depoliticizing' minzu problems is getting rid of the system of minzu regional autonomy; its target is refusing to recognize minzu status; its aim is establishing a (homogeneous) nation-state."[65]

Hardliners in the Party leadership derived several lessons from Hu Yaobang's experiment with granting non-Hans more substantial autonomy in the 1980s: concessions only invite trouble, and the proper response to popular protests is a firm hand. In fact, these were precisely the wrong lessons.[66] Beijing's best option at the moment is to recognize the promise

---

[65] Jin Binggao, Sun Jun, and Xiao Rui, "['Depoliticization' and 'Culturalization' of Minzu Problems]," *supra* n. 43, 1. Will Kymlicka makes similar points in his theoretical critique of nation-building in general. *See* Will Kymlicka, *Politics in the Vernacular: Nationalism, Multiculturalism, and Citizenship* (Oxford; New York: Oxford University Press, 2001).

[66] Thomas Heberer, *China and Its National Minorities: Autonomy or Assimilation?* (Armonk: M. E. Sharpe, 1989); "China's Nationalities Policies: Quo Vadis?" *Casa Asia*, http://www.casaasia.es/pdf/21904105720AM1077184640713.pdf; Yitzhak Shichor, "Blow Up: Internal and External Challenges of Uyghur Separatism and Islamic Radicalism to Chinese Rule in Xinjiang," *Asian Affairs: An American Review* 32, no. 2 (2005). Gray Tuttle, "Failure of Ideologies in China's Relations with Tibetans," in *Multination States in Asia: Accommodation or Resistance*, ed. Jacques Bertrand and Andre Laliberte (Cambridge: Cambridge University Press, 2010).

of Hu Yaobang's reaffirmation of the original compacts with Uyghurs, Tibetans, and others by strengthening rather than eliminating protections of non-Hans' cultural and religious rights and further safeguarding them by allowing more, not less, scope for group political rights. However, such a move would likely provoke strong dissatisfaction among hard-line leaders and China's enormous Han population.[67] Sadly, although Chinese scholars have been able to acknowledge international calls for more robust group rights,[68] no Chinese scholar or official has dared to argue the case inside China. None is likely to step forward when even individual citizens' rights lack a firm basis: the new Xi Jinping administration promulgated an internal document in August 2013 warning Party leaders to be vigilant against "Western constitutionalism" and advocacy of human rights, suggesting that Beijing is likely to roll back, rather than enhance, the scope of rights protections and legal constraints on governance.[69]

Thus, although the CCP could eliminate the autonomy system, I argue that it should not, for both normative and practical reasons. The abandonment of the system would place even greater stress on already vulnerable communities, their cultures and life ways, and their often marginal status in Chinese society. At the same time, it would likely provoke even more desperate gestures of defiance from those who have previously dared to challenge a state that has plainly threatened to squelch collective protests by non-Hans quickly and forcefully, and repeatedly carried through on the threat. The result would not be good for Uyghurs, Tibetans, or other non-Hans, nor would it be good for China as a whole.

[67] Leibold, "Second Generation of Ethnic Policies?" *supra* n. 40.

[68] Qin Wenpeng, "[Political Attributes of Minzu]," *supra* n. 44.

[69] Chris Buckley, "China Takes Aim at Western Ideas," *The New York Times*, August 19, 2013, sec. World / Asia Pacific, http://www.nytimes.com/2013/08/20/world/asia/chinas-new-leadership-takes-hard-line-in-secret-memo.html (cited 2013/08/20).

Part IV

Religion

7

Sectarian Visions of the Iraqi State: Irreconcilable Differences?

Feisal Amin Rasoul al-Istrabadi *

INTRODUCTION

Iraq's permanent constitution has been unable to form a fulcrum balancing the country's competing interests, despite the support it received from an overwhelming majority of the country's citizens. Nearly 80 percent of the voters who cast a vote in the 2005 referendum supported the document.[1] Why then has a consensus around the Constitution failed to coalesce? Looking behind the numbers, the reasons for this failure begin to come into focus: the 20 percent who voted against the Constitution were Iraq's second largest ethno-confessional group, the Arab Sunna.[2]

This chapter will argue that the constitutional processes that Iraq underwent after the fall of the previous regime were divisive rather than cohesive, principally because the new elites failed to develop a shared, or at least compromised, vision of the future organization of the state in the constitutional discussions.[3] It will make its case through the single most divisive issue during and after the negotiations: federalism. This issue drove the entire agenda of the Kurdish parties in Baghdad and dominated the Shii parties' agenda as well. The two interlocutors, driven by their fears

---

* The author expresses his deep gratitude to Susan Williams, Walter W. Foskett Professor of Law at Indiana University Maurer School of Law, for her grace and especially for her encouragement and patience. Thanks are also due to Sumit Ganguly, Professor of Political Science and holder of the Tagore Chair in Indian Cultures and Civilizations, Indiana University – Bloomington, for his insights.

[1] John Ward Anderson, "Sunnis Failed to Defeat Iraq Constitution," *Washington Post*, October 26, 2005, http://www.washingtonpost.com/wp-dyn/content/article/2005/10/25/AR2005102500357.html.

[2] *See* ibid.

[3] The author has intentionally avoided the word *deliberations*. There was nothing deliberative about the drafting process respecting the permanent constitution in 2005.

of a Sunni return to power in Baghdad heralding renewed oppression, strove to create regional autonomy throughout the country, leaving the Baghdad government essentially devoid of power. Iraq's Sunna broadly rejected this vision of the state, preferring to maintain a centralized state. Compromise was not in the air.[4]

At critical junctures during the negotiations for the permanent constitution, when it might have been possible to slow the process in the hope of expanding the participants or to seek compromises, one or more actor(s) succeeded in pushing the process through. Opportunities for delay arose when an impasse occurred (on the issue of federalism), an eventuality for which the interim constitution provided: it would have extended the drafting period, and, under the right circumstances, required new elections for a fresh constituent assembly. Because the Arab Sunna boycotted the elections for the existing constituent assembly, they had no meaningful voice within the Constitutional Drafting Committee. New elections could have thus expanded the process. Instead, the Arab-Shii and Kurdish parties, with the support of the American embassy, expelled the non-elected Sunnis and expedited the drafting process thus avoiding a need to compromise their respective agendas. They produced the permanent constitution in less than six weeks.

These unfortunate manipulations continued into the post-constitutional period. If the constitutional process was divisive the post-constitutional politics were equally so. The consequence has been arguably a continuous civil war since 2004, with a spectacular explosion of violence in 2006–2008. This chapter concludes that the dysfunctional constitutional and political systems that were engendered in the post-2003 period, particularly the sectarian system of spoils-allocation, are responsible for the ongoing violence in the country. It also concludes that there has been a seismic shift in the positions of the Shii and Sunni polities in Iraq. As the Shia parties have controlled the levers of powers over the past eight years, they have come to favor increasing centralization of the state. Conversely, the Sunna have concluded that the new sectarian

---

[4] This chapter focuses on the cleavages between Iraq's Arab Sunna and the Arab-Shii/Kurdish parties that drafted the 2006 Constitution. There are a number of other cleavages that are evident at this writing, including one between one of the Kurdish factions and the current Shii prime minister, as well as cleavages along other axes. *See, e.g.,* Toby Dodge, *Iraq: From War to a New Authoritarianism* (London: Routledge, 2012), 167–68. Those divisions, however, are beyond the scope of this analysis. The author is well aware of the inadequacy of using broad terms such as the "Sunni position," but uses such generalities reluctantly as a convenient, if somewhat inaccurate, shorthand. Again, the author is aware that there are differences within each of the Iraqi Shii, Sunni, and Kurdish polities. Brevity, alas, dictated the need for generalizations.

dispensation leaves them a permanently disenfranchised minority, such that many local leaders have come to favor creating Sunni regions that allow their constituents autonomy from Baghdad. If another round of a sectarian civil war is fought – and one may be underway at this writing – at least some of the Sunni participants will be fighting for regionalism, whereas the Shia parties will be fighting to re-centralize the state.

After this introduction, the following section describes the increasingly divisive constitutional processes that obtained for the interim and permanent constitutions. The third section deals with the political environment in the post-constitutional period. It argues that this period has further exacerbated tensions between Iraq's Shii and Sunni polities. The last section analyzes how the two antagonists have traded positions on the constitutional dispensation and briefly considers why they have been unable to reach a compromise.

Divisive Constitutional Processes

Iraq's tortured constitutional processes set the country on a destructive path, one from which it has not recovered. It is difficult to imagine a more divisive process or one more likely to engender or intensify conflict than what transpired in Iraq from 2003 to 2005. Not least of its flaws was that a foreign agenda – that is, that of the United States – drove the process along several key points.[5] The deep pathologies of Iraqis, tortured for too long by a despotic regime that inflicted horrific mass suffering, also played a role in the destructive politics that attended the constitutional negotiations.

Of course, from the beginning, many Iraqis, Sunna as well as Shia, may have resented the American – any foreign – occupation, although in the very early days it seemed that the population as a whole was waiting to see how things would transpire. The impression this observer had was that the population of Baghdad, at least, was generally relieved that the despot had been removed from power. The failure of U.S. forces to prevent the looting of government buildings that occurred at epic proportions in the early days of the occupation soured much of the population. That the oil ministry was the only government building protected by American troops[6] only contributed to an impression by some that the United States

---

[5] Feisal Amin Rasoul al-Istrabadi, "A Constitution Without Constitutionalism: Reflections on Iraq's Failed Constitutional Process," *Texas Law Review* 87 (2009): 1633–44.

[6] George Packer, *The Assassins' Gate: America in Iraq* (New York: Farrar, Straus and Giroux, 2005), 138; Ali A. Allawi, *The Occupation of Iraq: Winning the War, Losing the Peace* (New Haven, CT: Yale University Press, 2007), 116.

really was only in the country to "rob Iraq's oil."[7] Regardless of the
objective merits of this view, the fact that many Iraqis held it placed into
question the legitimacy of the transformative enterprise from the beginning. A few months after the invasion, the population was evenly split
on whether they regarded the American invasion as truly an attempt to
democratize the country.[8]

Within two months of his arrival in Baghdad, Paul Bremer, the U.S.
administrator in Iraq, appointed a twenty-five-member advisory body
named the Iraqi Governing Council (IGC).[9] Bremer made these appointments along ethno-confessional lines. Thirteen members of the IGC were
chosen because they were Shii Arabs, five because they were Sunni Arabs,
five because they were Kurds, one because he was a Christian, and one
because she (one of only three women) was a Turkmen.[10] Events after
the U.S. intervention would follow this pattern of ethno-confessional
quotas.

Ten of the thirteen Shia appointed to the IGC came from the religious
parties, and another, although nominally non-sectarian,[11] often sided
with the religious parties.[12] Ayad Allawi maintained a strictly secular,
nationalist outlook among the Shii members of the IGC.[13] The discourse
of the Shii parties was also decidedly sectarian: among their first acts
was to form the so-called Shia House in the IGC.[14] In time, the Shia
House would repeatedly flex its muscles, causing the quorum to fail in
the IGC at critical junctures, including when the interim constitution was
being drafted.[15] Such moves must immediately have given the Sunna an
impression that they were being quickly disenfranchised. In the event, of

---

[7] Larry Diamond, *Squandered Victory: The American Occupation and the Bungled Effort to Bring Democracy to Iraq* (New York: Times Books, 2005), 25–26.
[8] Ibid.
[9] *See generally* L. Paul Bremer, *My Year in Iraq: The Struggle to Build a Future of Hope* (New York: Simon & Schuster, 2006), 82–98 (describing the process he went through in selecting each of the members of the IGC).
[10] Diamond, *Squandered Victory, supra* n. 7, 42–43.
[11] *See* Michael Isikoff and David Corn, *Hubris: The Inside Story of Spin, Scandal, and the Selling of the Iraq War* (New York: Three Rivers Press, 2006), 49–54.
[12] *See* Diamond, *Squandered Victory, supra* n. 7, 143–44.
[13] *See, e.g.,* Vali Nasr, *The Shia Revival: How Conflicts Within Islam Will Shape the Future* (New York: W.W. Norton, 2006), 199; Allawi, *The Occupation of Iraq, supra* n. 6, 205.
[14] Allawi, ibid., 205–206. The thirteenth was the head of the Iraqi Communist Party, who, in Bremer's strange calculus, nonetheless counted as a Shii. Dodge, *New Authoritarianism, supra* n. 4, 42.
[15] *See, e.g.,* Diamond, *Squandered Victory, supra* n. 7, 172.

the five Sunnis, one was from a Sunni religious party, the Iraqi Islamic Party – in effect the Muslim Brotherhood.[16]

The initial American plan for drafting a permanent constitution could not have buoyed the Sunna. Under Bremer's plan, each of the twenty-five members of the IGC appointed a member of a constitutional preparatory committee designed to propose a way forward for the drafting process.[17] The glaring lack of legitimacy in having a foreign occupier indirectly appoint a constitutional preparatory committee in the heart of the Arab and Islamic worlds in 2003 seems to have detained neither Bremer nor his senior staff. Compounding the problem was that an American academic, Noah Feldman, who was serving as an advisor to the drafting process, assumed a very public role, rather than remaining in the background.[18]

With only five Sunni representatives on the IGC and thus on the initial constitutional drafting committee, the Sunna sense of disenfranchisement must only have increased. If they regarded the American transformative mission in Iraq with suspicion from the beginning, the appointments Bremer made could not have been calculated to calm their fears. Nor were the Sunna the only ones to object to the proposed mechanism for drafting the constitution. The senior-most Shii cleric, the Grand Ayatullah Ali al-Sistani, issued a *fatwa* – a juridical ruling under Islamic law – declaring that only an elected assembly could draft the constitution.[19] Regardless of the merits of holding an election in a country where the security situation was deteriorating on a daily basis, the American occupation forces could not ignore the spiritual leader of well over half the country, a man who was at the zenith of his political powers, and one whose legitimacy as a leader of this community could not be questioned.[20] Given that no Iraqi had any electoral legitimacy at this time, Sistani's view on so fundamental an issue could not be gainsaid by Bremer, and this initial constitutional preparatory committee simply ceased to function.[21]

---

[16] Ibid., 43.

[17] Bremer, *My Year in Iraq, supra* n. 9, 97–98.

[18] *See, e.g.,* Jennifer R. Lee, "American Will Advise Iraqis on Writing New Constitution," *New York Times*, May 11, 2003, http://www.nytimes.com/2003/05/11/world/aftereffects-the-law-american-will-advise-iraqis-on-writing-new-constitution.html.

[19] *See* Noah Feldman, "The Democratic Fatwa: Islam and Democracy in the Realm of Constitutional Politics," *Oklahoma Law Review* 58 (2006): 6.

[20] Allawi, *The Occupation of Iraq, supra* n. 6, 207 (Sistani's position as the undisputed head of the Shii religious hierarchy was "unassailable").

[21] *See* ibid., 211.

The Sunna's fear of disenfranchisement could only have grown. All Iraqis did, but Sunnis must have noted especially the Americans reeling in the face of Sistani's fatwa. The symbolism of Bremer backing down to a Shii cleric was itself significant. It was unimaginable that Bremer would have backed down to a Sunni cleric. The fatwa clearly had much greater significance, however, than merely knocking the Americans back on their heels: an elected assembly would almost certainly consist mostly of Shia. For many in the Sunni community, these first missteps in the drafting of a constitution were objective proof of the sectarian transfer of power that was under way in the country. For the Americans, they were in a no-win situation with the Sunna either way: if they proceeded with their plan for a constitution, the drafting process was heavily weighted in favor of the Shia. If they did not, they were backing down to a Shii cleric.

A transfer of power in the direction of the Shia was inevitable in any process leading to the democratization of the country. Iraq had been ruled by a single family, supported by a single clan, for thirty-five years. Yet it was all too easy for at least some Shia to identify the family and the clan with their religious affiliation,[22] even though for most of the life of the Iraqi Baathist regime, it had been quite secular.[23] Regardless, a narrative of Sunni oppression of the Shia had emerged among the Shii exile community prior to the war.[24] The American occupation authority accepted this narrative, placing "much emphasis on Iraqi sectarian dynamics and identities."[25] Thus, it seems, officials of the Coalition Provisional Authority (CPA), the occupation authority, had no time for a nationalist, pan-Iraqi discourse. That such a discourse might have assuaged much of the Sunna's fears seemed not to matter. The CPA could seemingly only see the country in reductionist terms.

If CPA officials were unable to avoid elections entirely for a constituent assembly, they were not through trying to delay them.[26] In fairness, there are many valid reasons to delay elections after the fall of a long-lived and tyrannical regime. Political parties may not have had adequate time to organize, and, in the context of a country such as Iraq, where the political parties were organized on ethno-confessional lines, many, including

---

[22] *See* ibid., 137–38.

[23] Phebe Marr, *The Modern History of Iraq* (Boulder, CO: Westview, 1985), 281.

[24] *See* Fanar Haddad, *Sectarianism in Iraq: Antagonistic Visions of Unity* (London: Hurst, 2011), 148.

[25] Ibid.

[26] Diamond, *Squandered Victory, supra* n. 7, 51–52.

this author, feared that early elections would contribute to the further polarization of the country. Indeed, that polarization process was already under way.

In the fall of 2004, a plan emerged designed to transfer authority to the Iraqis before a permanent constitution would be drafted. In keeping with Sistani's view, that meant elections for a constituent assembly in a year-and-a-half, but the CPA proposed a complicated process from which a legislative body would emerge to reassert Iraq's sovereignty. The IGC, the eighteen governorate councils, and local councils within the governorates would each appoint five representatives for a fifteen-member organizing committee in each governorate. Each organizing committee would in turn select between 100 and 200 citizens who would in turn hold caucuses around the governorates. From these caucuses, they would appoint individuals to serve in the National Transitional Parliament.[27] Its complexity aside, there were several problems with this proposal.

To begin with, there is no Arabic word for *caucus*. Explaining the concept to any non-Anglophone Iraqi was, to say the least, cumbersome. Linguistic questions aside, there was a fundamental issue affecting the perceived legitimacy of the resulting assembly as well. The three bodies appointing the organizing committees had each been appointed by the CPA; the IGC, the eighteen provincial councils, and the local councils had all been appointed by Bremer.[28] Thus the foreign occupation authority could not avoid the impression of trying to control the political process, even after Iraq reasserted its authority. Once again, Sistani totally rejected this proposal, insisting that the transitional legislature be elected and that it must pass on any draft constitution.[29]

Thus the CPA abandoned this plan, too. Instead, a two-step process of transitioning to an elected Iraqi government was negotiated with the IGC. An interim government, which would reassert Iraq's sovereignty, would hold elections for a transitional legislative body. That body would in turn oversee the drafting of a permanent constitution.[30] Significantly, Sistani agreed to this proposal.[31]

The first step in establishing a sovereign government and dissolving the CPA was to negotiate a document under which the various political parties would agree to govern the country until an elected assembly

[27] Ibid., 80–81.
[29] Ibid., 84–85.
[31] Ibid.

[28] Ibid., 81.
[30] Ibid., 137.

could draft a permanent constitution. That document, the Law of Administration of the State of Iraq for the Transitional Period (TAL), was negotiated over a four-month period among the members of the IGC and the CPA. During this period, an Iraqi identity as a unifying force at least for the non-Kurdish citizens of the state palpably evanesced. It would not recover; indeed, time would deepen the divisions. Over the months during which the TAL was negotiated, the insurgency gained momentum.

The TAL was specifically not designated as an interim constitution for several reasons. First, the involvement of foreign powers in its drafting (i.e., the United States and the United Kingdom) meant that no party to the negotiations wanted to identify the document as a "constitution" of any sort, because of the obvious legitimacy problem.[32] Equally affecting its legitimacy, the Iraqi drafters of the TAL were all too aware that none of them were elected. This fact raised not only an inherent legitimacy problem; it also implicated Sistani's fatwa requiring an elected assembly. Finally, by designating it as merely a document that would allow Iraq to reassert its sovereignty quickly and allow the administration of the state until a permanent constitution could be drafted, the temperature of the negotiations was lowered. Still, the TAL was in all functional respects an interim constitution.[33]

The single most highly contentious issue during the negotiations for the TAL (and the constitution later) was the issue of federalism.[34] There was in general a broad division in which a common position was adopted by the Shii religious parties, even though the driving force behind that position originated from only one of the parties, which was then called the Supreme Council for the Islamic Revolution in Iraq (SCIRI; later changed to the Islamic Supreme Council of Iraq, ISCI).[35] The common position advocated by the Shia House (with the notable exception of Allawi) adopted the Kurdish model for regionalism throughout Iraq, whereby each of the three major ethno-confessional groups would be largely autonomous within their respective geographic areas – essentially

---

[32] Feisal Amin al-Istrabadi, "Reviving Constitutionalism in Iraq: Key Provisions of the Transitional Administrative Law," *New York Law School Law Review* 50 (2005–2006): 270.

[33] Ibid.

[34] Al-Istrabadi, "Constitution Without Constitutionalism," *supra* n. 5, 1629; Diamond, *Squandered Victory, supra* n. 7, 161 ("The most vexing nexus of issues concerned the status of the Kurds and the future structure of the state of Iraq.").

[35] Al-Istrabadi, ibid., 1632.

a consociational federalism.[36] The government in Baghdad would have only limited portfolios, such as foreign affairs, national defense policy, and equitable distribution of resources.

The five Sunni members of the IGC rejected this strong regionalist model.[37] They, joined by Allawi, argued for a stronger government in Baghdad. This position acknowledged that special circumstances obtained in Iraqi Kurdistan and the Kurdistan Regional Government (KRG) should be recognized as the autonomous regional government in areas under KRG control from March 19, 2003, the date of commencement of hostilities.[38] They argued, however, that the rest of the country should continue to be governed during the transitional period directly from Baghdad, without the possibility of further regions forming.[39] In the end, the Shii-Kurdish view prevailed, and the TAL provided for a relatively weak federal government in Baghdad and the possibility of the formation of other regions, although the latter process was cumbersome.[40] This issue would recur as a divisive issue between the Shia and Sunna, and many Sunna and nationalists accused the framers of the TAL of advocating the breakup of the country.[41]

There was a possibility during the negotiations for the TAL that the Shii religious parties might find common cause with the one Sunni religious party on the IGC, but that possibility did not materialize. At one point during these negotiations, one of the Shii parties asserted that Islamic principles should be "the principal source" of legislation.[42] After protracted negotiations that took multiple turns, the Shii bloc agreed to language making Islam "a source" of legislation, meaning that there

---

[36] Ibid.

[37] *See* Diamond, *Squandered Victory*, *supra* n. 7, 167 (noting that it was the Kurds and Shia parties that drove the federalism issue).

[38] *See* al-Istrabadi, "Constitution Without Constitutionalism," *supra* note 5, 1630.

[39] Diamond, *Squandered Victory*, *supra* n. 7, 167–68. While Diamond is not mistaken that this author argued this point of view on behalf of Pachachi, Pachachi himself had coordinated this view with others who agreed with it.

[40] Qānūn 'Idārat al-Dawlah al-'Iraqiyyah lil Marḥalah al-'Intiqāliyyah [Law of Administration of the State of Iraq for the Transitional Period] Arts. 25 and 53(C) (hereinafter TAL).

[41] *See* Diamond, *Squandered Victory*, *supra* n. 7, 163.

[42] Feisal Amin Rasoul al-Istrabadi, "Islam and the State in Iraq: The Post-2003 Constitutions," in *Constitutionalism in Islamic Countries: Between Upheaval and Continuity*, eds. Rainer Grote and Tilmann Röder (Oxford: Oxford University Press, 2012), 595. Although the author refers to "religious parties" in this description of the negotiations, it would have been more accurate to say the "Shii religious parties" as is clear from the context.

could also be other sources of equal authority.[43] Only after the Shii parties agreed to this compromise did the Sunni religious party raise the issue again, insisting that "the principal source" be reinserted. By waiting until after the other twenty-four parties had agreed to the compromise, this party found itself isolated and quietly dropped the issue. This author wondered at the time if the Sunni religious party could not bring itself to join the Shii parties initially because the divisions over federalism were too great to allow common ground, even where it might otherwise be found.

The resultant two-step transitional process required the CPA to hand off its authority to an unelected Iraqi interim government,[44] which would be formed in cooperation with the United Nations. The principal function of the interim government was to prepare for elections that would occur seven months after it assumed office. The resultant parliament would act as both legislature and constituent assembly, although precisely how it would perform the latter function was left intentionally ambiguous.[45] The TAL was silent on whether the entire assembly of 275 members was to act as a joint drafting committee, or whether a smaller drafting committee could be appointed that would later report to the full assembly.

The course of events did not run quite that smoothly. The elections themselves became quite contentious, and the divisions that surfaced were again along sectarian lines. The Sunni clerics, some of whom argued that continued military operations by a foreign power would taint any such elections, called for a boycott of the elections.[46] For their part, the Shii clerics continued to insist on holding timely elections, sensing that the Shia could capture the balance of power for the first time in Iraq's history.[47]

Adnan Pachachi, Iraq's elder statesman who had served on the IGC presidency, warned that civil war could erupt were elections held under these circumstances. He argued that many Sunna would not vote, either because of their clerics' call for a boycott or because many of the Sunni areas were simply too unsafe for people to take the chance to vote. The resulting situation would find those who prevailed claiming a mandate to draft a constitution, whereas those who had been prevented from voting would regard the election results as illegitimate.[48] Stanford scholar and

[43] Ibid., 596.   [44] TAL, *supra* n. 40, Art. 2(B)(1).

[45] Ibid., Arts. 2(B)(2); 30(A); and 60.

[46] *See* Allawi, *The Occupation of Iraq, supra* n. 6, 334, 340.

[47] Ibid., 340–41.

[48] Adnan Pachachi, Editorial, "Delay the Elections," *Washington Post*, January 2, 2005, at B7.

leading democratization expert Larry Diamond also warned that Iraq was headed for a sectarian civil war if the elections were not delayed.[49] That advice was ignored both in Washington and in Baghdad.

Though the overall turnout in the country approached 60 percent, as Pachachi and Diamond had warned, there was a dismal turnout in the predominately Sunni areas.[50] In Anbar governorate, only 2 percent of eligible voters went to the polls.[51] Whether the turnout was poor because of the boycott, the ongoing violence, or the fact that Sunni areas lacked adequate polling stations, the result was the same. The United Nations had recommended, and the CPA had promulgated, a single-district, closed-list, proportional-representation system in Iraq.[52] Diamond had recommended against this system, noting that it had the potential of eviscerating Sunni representation in the constituent assembly.[53] That is precisely what occurred. Anbar, for example, not only had a low turnout, but its total population was under one million. It was thus unlikely that any of the candidates from Anbar could have obtained a sufficient number of votes to be elected to a seat. In the event, only seventeen Sunni representatives were elected, accounting for no more than 6 percent of the representatives.[54]

The situation would have been very different if Bremer had listened to Diamond, and rather than treating Iraq as a single district the CPA had created eighteen districts based on Iraq's eighteen governorates. The central objection to doing so had been that there was no recent, reliable census, so that there was no reliable way of ascribing a number of representatives for each governorate.[55] Diamond could overcome this objection, in lieu of a census, by assigning the number of representatives in each governorate based on the number of food-ration cards that had been issued there.[56] These ration cards provided food to the overwhelming majority of Iraq's population in light of sanctions that were imposed

---

[49] Larry Diamond, Editorial, "How a Vote Could Derail Democracy," *New York Times*, January 9, 2005, at C13.

[50] Allawi, *The Occupation of Iraq*, *supra* n. 6, 392 (stating that the Sunni boycott was "near universal").

[51] Patrick Cockburn, *The Occupation War and Resistance in Iraq* (London: Verso, 2006), 187.

[52] Diamond, *Squandered Victory*, *supra* n. 7, 269.

[53] Ibid.

[54] Jonathan Morrow, *Iraq's Constitutional Process II: An Opportunity Lost* (Washington, DC: U.S. Institute of Peace, 2005), 6, *available at* http://books.google.com/books?id=6B714n-zx40C&printsec=frontcover&source=gbs_ge_summary_r&cad=0#v=onepage&q&f=true.

[55] Diamond, *Squandered Victory*, *supra* n. 7, 268.

[56] Ibid.

by the United Nations Security Council on Iraq after its 1990 invasion of Kuwait.[57] By rejecting Diamond's advice, the elections themselves and the election results became an independent basis for furthering the sectarian divisions in the country.

Interestingly, the Sunni boycott of the 2005 elections echoed an earlier boycott dating from the foundation of the modern state of Iraq. In the early 1920s, the Shii clerical establishment called for a boycott of elections and participation in the organization of the new state under British auspices.[58] As a result, Shii participation in the political life of the country was largely delayed, and it was only in 1948 that the first Shii (Salih Jabur) was elected prime minister.[59] This initial boycott no doubt contributed to feelings of Shii disenfranchisement that lasted well into the current century.[60] That the Sunni clerics should have repeated this same self-destructive course eighty years later was a blunder of monumental proportions.

Once the new assembly was convoked, it set about the task of establishing a Constitutional Drafting Committee (CDC). Parliament chose fifty-five members from among its ranks to constitute the CDC, which was chaired by Sheikh Humam Hamoudi. Hamoudi belonged to SCIRI/ISCI, the Shii religious party most strident in advocating a weak national government in Baghdad.[61] The selection of Hamoudi itself thus sent a strong signal to those hoping for a stronger national government. Equally telling, only two of the fifty-five members of the CDC were Sunnis.[62]

U.S. Ambassador Zalmay Khalilzad, who had also guided the constitutional process in his native Afghanistan as U.S. ambassador, took on the task of recruiting Sunna to the drafting committee.[63] That it was a foreign ambassador who sought to ensure representation of Iraq's second largest ethno-confessional group was startling. As far as the Shia parties were concerned, they recompensed Khalilzad for his efforts by giving him the sarcastic sobriquet "Abu Omar."[64] It literally meant "Father of Omar,"

---

[57] Allawi, *The Occupation of Iraq, supra* n. 6, 122.

[58] Philip Willard Ireland, *Iraq: A Study in Political Development* (New York: Macmillan, 1938), 391.

[59] Marr, *Modern History of Iraq, supra* n. 23, 102.

[60] *See* Allawi, *The Occupation of Iraq, supra* n. 6, 205–06.

[61] Ibid., 404.   [62] Ibid.

[63] Ibid., 399.

[64] Edward Wong, "U.S. Envoy Says He Had Meetings with Iraq Rebels," *New York Times*, March 26, 2007, http://www.nytimes.com/2007/03/26/world/middleeast/26zal.html?pagewanted=all&_r=0.

but its connotation was "Father of the Sunna." The very act of expanding the representation of those charged with drafting a new constitution thus resulted in sectarian derision.

Khalilzad did find a few men he took to be the "representatives of the Sunna"; although how representative they were – and why he chose them – remains largely unclear.[65] Their bona fides as legitimate representatives of the Sunna aside, these men immediately had another legitimacy problem. In contradistinction to the other members of the drafting committee, they were not elected, resulting in resistance from the elected members.[66] Nonetheless and to his credit, Khalilzad worked out an agreement that decisions of the expanded CDC respecting the new constitution would be by consensus.[67] That promise would prove much easier to make than to keep.

The central fissure in the constitutional politics through the drafting period, of course, remained the issue of federalism. Prior to 2003, the parties in opposition to the ancien régime had ostensibly agreed that Iraq's highly centralized structure should devolve into a federalized state; however, they had never formed a consensus of what *federalism* meant.[68] As described earlier, the Kurds, joined by SCIRI/ISCI, wanted an anemic national government, with few if any prerogatives. These parties shared a distrust of Baghdad and wanted to ensure that the capital could never dominate the political life of the country again. Baghdad would act essentially as no more than a cashier, temporarily holding and distributing the country's material riches to regional governments that would hold the residuum of power. Each ethno-confessional community would largely be in charge of its own affairs, with very little interference from Baghdad. This view posited that Iraq would be divided into symmetric regions, each standing in equipoise to Baghdad. Indeed, late in the negotiations, the head of SCIRI/ISCI called for the creation of one large Shia region, consisting of all the governorates south of Baghdad combined into a single entity.[69] That that super-region would control the vast bulk of Iraq's known oil reserves was not lost on the Sunna.[70]

Although no other regions have been formed hitherto, the SCIRI/ISCI view prevailed in the Constitution. The nexus of the Shii-Kurdish alliance

---

[65] Allawi, *The Occupation of Iraq*, *supra* n. 6, 405.
[66] Ibid.   [67] Ibid.
[68] Ibid., 53.   [69] Ibid., 408.
[70] Ibid., 409 (the possibility that the country would be divided into two regions, while the "resource-poor" predominately Sunni section of the country would be left to fend for itself "confirm[ed the Sunni negotiators'] worst fears about the new constitution").

was SCIRI/ISCI, because it was this party – and this party alone in the Shii bloc – that actually shared almost verbatim the Kurdish outlook for federalism in the new Iraq.[71] The views of other Shii parties were far more divergent than the resultant constitutional text indicates. For example, Muqtada al-Sadr espoused a discourse that had a nationalist tone, albeit one strongly informed by a Shii religious identity.[72] Indeed, after the Constitution was approved, the Sadrist bloc rejected federalism outside Kurdistan.[73] Others such as the Dawa Party – from which Iraq's two elected prime ministers since 2005 were drawn – and the Fadhila Party took an intermediate position on the issue of federalism, favoring a stronger government in Baghdad.[74] Why then did SCIRI/ISCI's view come to dominate the Shii parties?

SCIRI/ISCI being one party in a large coalition, there was a priori no reason for its view to dominate the drafting of the new constitution.[75] Given the real divisions within the Shia bloc, it was conceivable that the more extreme position favoring regionalism could have been used as a negotiating stance with the Sunni representatives. With the Kurds and SCIRI/ISCI on one extreme of the federalism deliberations, and the Sunna attempting to hold on to a more unitary state, it should have been logically possible for the remainder of the Shia bloc to broker the compromises for a text that would have struck a balance between the competing views and perhaps entice the Sunna to join in the compromise.

That such a compromise did not occur related to the fact that, by 2003, the Shia political elites believed that much of the history of the Iraqi State was the history of the oppression of the Shia.[76] Whether this view has merit or not, this conception of history became widely believed by them. The writings of Iraqi sociologist Ali Wardi, for example, gained a new life especially among the Shia, who emphasized his view concerning the fragility of the Iraqi polity with its numerous fissures

---

[71] *See* Reidar Visser, "Beyond SCIRI and Abd al-Aziz al-Hakim: The Silent Forces of the United Iraqi Alliance," *Historiae.org*, January 20, 2006, http://historiae.org/UIA .asp (noting that it is "more accurately" referred to as a Kurdish-SCIRI "deal" than a "Kurdish-Shiite accord," noting also that the concept of federalism that prevailed among the Shii parties was that of SCIRI/ISCI).

[72] Haddad, *Sectarianism In Iraq, supra* n. 24, 113.

[73] Kirk H. Sowell, "Federalism Delayed Amid Sunni, Sadrist Opposition," *Threats Watch*, September 19, 2006, http://threatswatch.org/inbrief/2006/09/federalism-delayed-amid-sunni/.

[74] Ibid.

[75] *See* Allawi, *The Occupation of Iraq, supra* n. 6, 392.

[76] Haddad, *Sectarianism in Iraq, supra* n. 24, 148.

and divisions always hiding just beneath a very thin veneer.[77] The Shii parties were thus motivated during the constitutional discussions by a fear of a Sunni reascendancy and a concomitant return to Shii alienation. This fear almost certainly militated in favor of Shia unity, rather than the parsing of political positions. For SCIRI/ISCI's partners to have asserted nationalist views at that time would have put that unity at risk. It would risk what a Shii polemicist, Hassan al-Alawi, said when recalling the 1920s, that "Shia ultra-nationalism cost them [control over] the nation."[78]

It could be objected that the Shia, being a majority, should not have feared being oppressed in the new democratic order. The rejoinder is that there was no guarantee that a democratic order would in fact effloresce. In the event, the previous regime had found no difficulty in committing mass-murder against this self-same majority over much of the previous thirty-five years. It must also be recalled that these events were occurring very early in the transitional period and that the electoral politics of the country were still in great flux. To the extent SCIRI/ISCI appeared to be ascendant, it would have been to take a risk for any of the other Shii parties to contradict its vision of the state.

Finally, by maintaining SCIRI/ISCI's position, the Shii parties ensured the efficacy of their alliance with the Kurdish parties, thereby assuring their domination over the drafting process. Moreover, to the extent the Kurdish-Shii alliance held, the two sets of political leaderships could claim to be speaking on behalf of the overwhelming majority of the population. To undermine SCIRI/ISCI's position threatened the leverage the two larger blocs wielded through the drafting process. Indeed, if the alliance held, the two blocs could also reasonably anticipate maintaining that leverage through the post-drafting political phase.

These considerations, and perhaps others, were percolating underneath the surface, yet the Sunni representatives seemed to have been wholly oblivious to their own impuissance. These men, who had mostly lived inside Iraq, simply did not understand how politics were played. Politics had largely come to an end in Iraq – in any meaningful measure – shortly after 1968, the year of the Baathist *coup d'état*. Unlike their Shii and Kurdish interlocutors, the Sunna were not expatriates nor veterans of the negotiations that lasted until dawn day after day in hotels in Vienna, London, or Washington. It may be as simple as that they

---

[77] *See, e.g.,* Allawi, *The Occupation of Iraq, supra* n. 6, 12–15.
[78] *Cited in* ibid., 206.

were unaccustomed to negotiating: Under the previous regime they were accustomed to taking orders. Now, having been summoned by the American ambassador, they seemed to believe they could dictate to their far more powerful interlocutors.

Whatever the reasons, the Sunna representatives wholly rejected any notion of federalism.[79] This author was told in a private conversation that Khalilzad had brokered an agreement whereby he believed that the Kurds and the Shia would have accepted the much softer form of federalism that the TAL contained. Even that concept of federalism, which made it much harder for federal regions other than the KRG to form and limited the number of governorates that could form a single region to three,[80] was unacceptable to the Sunna representatives. They dug in their heels, refusing any compromise on dismantling the unitary state.

The fears of these Sunnis must also be placed in context. They knew – it was common knowledge – that many or most of the Kurds might well opt for independence if it were a politically viable choice. Federalism, then, seemed to them as a step toward the disintegration of the country.[81] In truth they were not alone. Throughout the early post-invasion period, in this author's dealings with them, Turkish diplomats reacted very negatively to the issue of federalism in Iraq. With a substantial Kurdish population of its own – some of whom were in open rebellion against it – the last thing the Turkish government wanted was to establish the conditions for a potentially future independent South Kurdistan. It is likely that some of Iraq's other neighbors had similar misgivings. In Saudi Arabia, for instance, the petroliferous Eastern Province is predominately Shii. The precedent on its border of a consociational regionalism potentially leading to independence, therefore, must have been quite unsettling in the kingdom. As the Sunna representatives were traveling to Turkish and Arab capitals, it is unlikely that the advice they heard would have been in the direction of compromise on the issue of federalism.

In the end, therefore, an impasse was reached. These Sunni representatives might have been buoyed by the TAL provisions that contemplated the possibility of an impasse. In that event, the TAL stipulated that new elections would have to be held, the transitional period would be extended, and the drafting process would have to start anew.[82] They might also have taken comfort in recalling the agreement Khalilzad

---

[79] Allawi, ibid., 409.

[80] TAL, *supra* n. 40, Art. 53(C).

[81] Allawi, *The Occupation of Iraq, supra* n. 6, 409.

[82] TAL, *supra* n. 40, Arts. 61(E) and (G).

negotiated requiring consensus for the new draft. They were mistaken on both counts. When the Sunni representatives refused to agree to terms relating to federalism, their views were simply ignored, and the finalization of the draft proceeded without them.[83] After all, the overwhelming majority of the Sunna representatives were unelected: What possible legitimacy could they have mustered to cause a constitutional impasse?

During the latter stages of the negotiations, the chairman of the parliamentary Constitutional Drafting Committee sought to invoke a provision of the TAL that allowed an extension of the drafting deadlines of up to six months without new elections.[84] He asked for a fifteen-day extension, meaning that the referendum would be held on 30 October rather than 15 October.[85] Quite literally before any member of Iraq's polity responded to this request, Khalilzad responded publicly that no such extension was required.[86] From the time the CDC was appointed to the time a final draft was presented to Parliament, a total of six weeks had elapsed – six weeks to draft a constitution that completely reordered the state and turned back more than a century of history. The interim constitution had taken nearly three times longer to negotiate.

By refusing to countenance an extension Khalilzad lost the last chance he had to influence the process in a positive direction. He should have used the time to bring back the Sunni interlocutors, if for no other reason than for the cosmetics of trying to do so. He might also have had more time to impress on the Shii and Kurdish leaderships that a constitution cannot form a national compact where a country's second largest ethno-confessional group has been not merely marginalized but literally shut out. This was a monumental opportunity lost, both for Iraq and for the American mission in Iraq.

An even more monumental failure, however, was Khalilzad's inability to realize that a technical constitutional impasse was in Iraq's long-term interests. The Sunna of Iraq immediately understood what a colossal mistake they had made in failing to participate in the January elections. This author attended a closed-door symposium on constitutional issues hosted by the United Nations Development Programme and the U.S. Institute of Peace in Jordan in February 2005, barely a month after the

---

[83] Allawi, *The Occupation of Iraq, supra* n. 6, 413–14.

[84] TAL, *supra* n. 40, Art. 61(F).

[85] Craig S. Smith and Dexter Filkins, "U.S. and Iraq to Plan Military Transfer: Iraqis Push to Meet Constitution Deadline," *New York Times*, August 2, 2005, at A6.

[86] Ibid.

elections. A number of senior Iraqis were present, including an influential Sunni from Baghdad who had publicly advocated for the boycott. During a formal session, this author asked him how the Sunna had benefited from boycotting the elections. He looked pained and made no reply at all.

Had Khalilzad encouraged the declaration of a formal impasse rather than pushing through with the process, elections for a new constituent assembly would have taken place in December 2005, as they did for the new parliament.[87] The difference is that the Sunna did vote in large numbers in those elections, and they would have thus elected representatives in the new constituent assembly. Whether the resultant constitutional draft would have been any different is speculative; however, it is self-evident that, even if the Sunna would have failed to alter the draft significantly, it would have mattered that representatives of the Sunni community were present as full voting members of a new constitutional drafting committee. It is one thing to lose a vote in a legislative chamber. It is another thing entirely to be locked out of the chamber before a vote is taken.

To their credit, once they were thrown out of the drafting process, the Sunna began to organize – arguably their most positive political act since the downfall of the previous regime.[88] The TAL provided that the draft constitution could be defeated in the referendum if it was rejected by a two-thirds majority in any three governorates.[89] The Sunna aimed to cause the draft to fail in three Sunni-majority governorates. It was in fact a very positive development, even if the aim was to obstruct the passage of the draft constitution. To begin with, it was obviously as much their right to work against the constitutional text as it was the right of others to support it. The larger point, however, was that they were organizing under the rules of the game – the TAL. It was a step that should have been encouraged as a political opening.

Instead, Khalilzad reacted as if he saw this movement as a threat to the agreed schedule. Perhaps he thought it would be politically embarrassing for the American president if the process did not immediately result in a successful outcome. After all, the American mid-term elections were only a year away. Regardless of his reasoning, Khalilzad brokered one

---

[87] In either case, the TAL set the election date for December 15, 2005. TAL, *supra* n. 40, Arts. 61(D), (E), and (G).

[88] Allawi, *The Occupation of Iraq*, *supra* n. 6, 415–416.

[89] TAL, *supra* n. 40, Art. 61(C).

last agreement ostensibly to placate the Sunna. The final constitutional draft already printed by the United Nations and distributed throughout the country stated that the constitutional text would be frozen with no amendments possible for two parliamentary cycles. Khalilzad mediated an agreement with the Shii and Kurdish parties that a constitutional review process could go forward in the first parliament.[90] That agreement was announced on October 12, 2005, three days before the referendum.[91]

That was not the only effort to manipulate the results of the referendum in the days before the vote, however. The Iraqi Parliament, in an attempt to ensure that there would be no chance of a rejection of the draft constitution, announced special rules on how to count the negative votes. To constitute a sufficient negative vote to defeat the referendum, opponents would have to muster two-thirds of *registered*, not actual, voters.[92] Parliament backed down from this ludicrous rule, but the harm was done.[93] The Sunni leadership was outraged, and some were wondering publicly what the point of participating in the political process was for them and their constituents.[94]

The results of the referendum broke down very much along ethnosectarian grounds. Although 78 percent of the votes cast approved the draft, the results in the predominately Sunni provinces of Salahuddin, Anbar, and Nineveh were telling. In Salahuddin, opponents of the draft constitution garnered 81 percent of the votes.[95] In Anbar, the "no" votes constituted 96 percent of the total vote.[96] Thus, of three governorates targeted by the Sunna to veto the draft, two provided a sufficient negative vote to do so. In Nineveh, however, the negative votes fell just short of two-thirds, with 56 percent of the vote.[97] Of just under 10 million votes cast,[98] a shift of some 83,000 votes in Nineveh governorate – 0.85 percent of the total vote – would have defeated the draft.[99]

---

[90] Jonathan Morrow, *Weak Viability: The Iraqi Federal State and the Constitutional Amendment Process* (Washington, DC: U.S. Institute of Peace, 2006), *available at* http://www.usip.org/files/resources/Morrow_SR168.pdf, 1.

[91] Ibid.

[92] Allawi, *The Occupation of Iraq, supra* n. 6, 416.

[93] Ibid. [94] Ibid.

[95] Anderson, "Sunnis Failed to Defeat Iraq Constitution," *supra* n. 1.

[96] Ibid. [97] Ibid.

[98] Ibid.

[99] Kanan Makiya, "Present at the Disintegration," *New York Times*, December 11, 2005, at C13 ("[I]f a mere 83,283 people in the province of Nineveh had voted no instead of yes, the draft constitution would have been defeated.").

Khalilzad's agreement may have been just enough to persuade a sufficient quantum of Sunni voters in Nineveh not to vote "no" to avoid defeating the draft text. What was lost was far more important, however. Yes, Iraq had a new constitution, but at the cost of its utter rejection by the country's second largest ethno-confessional group, Arab Sunna. Had the text been defeated instead, it would have been a strong signal to both the Shii and Kurdish parliamentary parties that they could not simply ride over the heads of the Sunna. In the next round of elections, the Sunna would have participated (as they in fact did), and a second round of the constitutional process – with the Shia and Kurds somewhat chastened by their use of strong-arm tactics – might have resulted in a compromised text that everyone could live with. Moreover, it would have demonstrated to Iraq's Sunna the efficacy of joining the political process. That chance was lost forever. In the event, the ethno-sectarian nature of the vote did not augur well for forging a post-Baathist constitutional dispensation.

As for Khalilzad's last-minute intervention, it amounted to little more than a sham. The Kurds and the Shia had agreed to allow a review process to go forward after the first round of parliamentary elections. They made no representations whatsoever about actually amending any particular provision of the constitutions. At this writing, Iraq is less than one year away from its third parliamentary elections under the Constitution. No amendments have been passed, and none are in sight. Indeed, there is no discussion at all of a constitutional review process. Any Sunni voter who accepted the draft constitution on an assumption that its many defects would be cured would surely be justified in feeling gulled by the U.S. ambassador and by the leadership of the Kurdish and Shii parties.

A Divisive Political Process

On October 25, 2005,[100] the authorities in Baghdad declared that the referendum had approved the draft constitution, with the results outlined in the previous section. Less than four months later, on February 22, 2006, a powerful bomb destroyed the famed Askariyya Shrine in Samarra.[101] The shrine, an object of reverence by both Islamic sects, is of particular

[100] "Iraq Voters Back New Constitution," *BBC News*, October 25, 2005, http://news.bbc .co.uk/2/hi/middle_east/4374822.stm.

[101] *See* Robert F. Worth, "Blast at Shiite Shrine Sets Off Sectarian Fury in Iraq," *New York Times*, February 23, 2006, http://www.nytimes.com/2006/02/23/world/23iraq.html? ref=alaskarishrine.

theological and historical significance to the Shia of Iraq and the world. The result was a cycle of sectarian violence that was unprecedented in Iraq. None of the accustomed barriers to this explosive violence rose to the task after this bombing.

The state itself was a party to the violence, controlled as it was by the Shia religious parties.[102] Indeed, Shii Prime Minister Ibrahim Jaafari failed to impose a curfew until the third day after the bombing.[103] Shii militias, many of them affiliated with governmental parties, went on a rampage destroying Sunni mosques. On the day of the Askariyya bombing, twenty-seven Sunni mosques were attacked in Baghdad alone, and two were destroyed in the southern city of Basra.[104] Even Sistani, who had often been a voice urging calm on his Shii followers, wavered: "If the government's security forces cannot provide the necessary protection," he stated, "the believers will do it."[105] In the volatile immediate aftermath of the bombing, such a message could easily be regarded as carte blanche.

Whether Sistani intended to unleash the Shii militias on the Sunna, which is unlikely, or whether he did not immediately speak explicitly against violence because he knew such a call would not be heeded, the result was the same. By the end of 2006, the United Nations estimated that over 34,000 people had been killed in what was by now clearly a sectarian civil war.[106] In July 2006 alone, "sectarian violence escalated, particularly in the capital, reaching an astonishing 3,159 civilian death."[107] Indeed, Iraqi scholar Fanar Haddad believes that the sectarian civil war had begun in 2005 and that it merely "escalated and became far less ambiguous in 2006–2007."[108]

The inability precisely to determine prospectively when a civil war began is a phenomenon not unique to Iraq. This author was present in 2004 in the IGC chamber when Lakhdar Brahimi, acting as special envoy to Iraq for the U.N. secretary-general, warned the IGC that Iraq was poised on the verge of a civil war. He recalled that in his own

---

[102] Haddad, *Sectarianism In Iraq, supra* n. 24, 181–82.

[103] "Tense Iraq Extends Daytime Curfew," *BBC News*, February 25, 2006, http://news .bbc.co.uk/2/hi/middle_east/4749308.stm.

[104] Robert F. Worth, "Blast Destroys Shrine in Iraq, Setting Off Sectarian Fury," *New York Times*, February 22, 2006, http://www.nytimes.com/2006/02/22/international/ middleeast/22cnd-iraq.html.

[105] Ibid.

[106] *Cited in* Dodge, *New Authoritarianism, supra* n. 4, 59.

[107] Haddad, *Sectarianism in Iraq, supra* n. 24, 180.

[108] Ibid., 181. *But cf.* James D. Fearon, "Iraq's Civil War," *Foreign Affairs* 86 (Mar.–Apr. 2007): 5 (arguing that the civil war in Iraq started in 2004).

native Algeria, the civil war had begun in retrospect long before the political elites recognized that fact. He stated that he had heard the same from many Lebanese regarding their own civil war. Unfortunately, rather than taking the warning seriously, the response among many of the Shia political leadership, especially Abdul Aziz al-Hakim, was outrage at the suggestion that a civil war was impending.

If Haddad is right that the civil war had begun earlier, then the Constitution and its attendant process would not be per se the cause of the conflict. It would instead be a cause of the escalation of the conflict. It would mean that the Iraqis wrote a constitution during a civil war. Either scenario is equally destructive of a polity: to have written a constitution during a civil war or to have prepared a draft without the participation of one of the major ethno-confessional groups in the countrythereby igniting a civil war.

This was the deteriorating atmosphere in which the elections of December 2005 were held – the first elections for the formation of a government under the new constitution. The sectarian nature of the voting can best be summarized by quoting the words of a seasoned observer of pre- and post-2003 Iraq. Patrick Cockburn warned after the balloting, "Iraq is disintegrating."[109] The Shii coalition that governed throughout 2005 was returned by overwhelming margins in Baghdad and Southern Iraq, while, of course, the Kurdish coalition was returned in the North.[110] Iraq's Sunna turned not merely to Sunni parties but to militant parties that opposed the presence of the United States in Iraq and supported, to one degree or another, the insurgency.[111] Cockburn concluded, "All the parties which did well in the election have strength only within their own [ethno-confessional] community."[112]

Interestingly, the constitutional review process promised by the American ambassador actually did initially go forward. A parliamentary Constitutional Review Committee (CRC) was convened under the chairmanship of Hamoudi, who had chaired the CDC in 2005. It actually produced two reports to Parliament. An interim report was produced in May 2007[113]

---

[109] Patrick Cockburn, "Iraq's Election Result: A Divided Nation," *The Independent (U.K.)*, December 21, 2005, http://www.independent.co.uk/news/world/middle-east/iraqs-election-result-a-divided-nation-520280.html.

[110] Ibid.   [111] Ibid.

[112] Ibid. Cockburn's percentages are approximations, as no census worthy of the name has been taken in Iraq since 1957.

[113] Neil J. Kritz et al., *Constitutional Reform in Iraq: Improving Prospects, Political Decisions Needed* (Washington, DC: U.S. Institute of Peace, 2007), 1.

and a final report in July 2009.[114] On the surface, that a constitutional review process could actually produce reports was a seemingly hopeful moment. Needless to say, however, none of the proposed amendments were actually acted on by the full parliament, much less brought forward in a referendum. Still, it is instructive that a constitutional review process took nearly four years to unfold, whereas the Constitution itself was written in less than six weeks.

The review process itself did very little to assuage the sectarian divisions that had seized the country. For instance, the interim report proposed that the office of the presidency, which was constitutionally almost entirely ceremonial, be granted actual powers. The Shii religious parties objected to any such expansion of the powers of the president, so long as he was not directly elected.[115] They wanted to assure their dominance on the levers of powers at all costs. Even in the face – perhaps because – of a brutal civil war that was raging, the Shii parties would not countenance power-sharing in a meaningful sense of the word. If the president were to be given real powers, he must be directly elected, where the numerical advantage of the Shia would be telling.

The Kurdish coalition rejected several proposals that would have impinged on the prerogatives of the KRG, most notably those dealing with management of oil resources, one of the most troubling issues within the federalism rubric. The Constitution stipulates that existing fields are to be managed by the federal government but appears to leave the management of new fields to regional governments. At this writing, the only regional government is the KRG. This is one of the provisions to which the Sunna had objected, and the CRC interim report included a term giving the federal government concurrent jurisdiction over all oil resources; however, the Kurds rejected this proposed amendment, as it would have required them to cede a measure of their autonomy.[116] Again, no amendments were actually voted out of the full parliament.

At the conclusion of the first parliament, therefore, there was genuine constitutional stalemate. The parliamentary parties sensed the need to take the constitutional review process seriously, and they took up the issues that were at the heart of the Sunni rejection of the constitution. Positions only hardened, however. The leaderships of the Shii and

---

[114] Jason Gluck, "Iraq's Constitutional Review Committee Delivers its Final Report to Parliament," *constitutionmaking.org*, August 20, 2009, http://www.comparative constitutions.org/2009/08/iraqs-constitutional-review-committee_20.html.

[115] Kritz et al., *Constitutional Reform in Iraq, supra* n. 113, 3.

[116] *See* Gluck, "Final Report to Parliament," *supra* n. 114.

Kurdish parties could not countenance making the compromises required of them by their Sunni counterparts, because they would appear to be backtracking on their gains, thereby causing them potentially to lose face. For their part, if the Sunna leaders could not secure any of the changes that mattered to their constituents, they had no raison d'être whatsoever, and certainly not for occupying positions in Baghdad.

Just as the Sunna were tiring of the sectarian representatives they had elected, another subtle change began to occur among at least some in the Shii political class. In advance of the governorate elections that were held in early 2009 and anticipating the parliamentary elections scheduled for March 2010, Prime Minister Maliki, a Shii, began to change his discourse, from that of a sectarian Shii to one of an Iraqi nationalist.[117] Using this discourse in the governorate elections, Maliki's new coalition did surprisingly well in Baghdad and the southern governorates. He bested his Shii rivals, who continued to run under the banner of Shiism.[118] Maliki hoped to mirror that success in the parliamentary elections.

Although Maliki did succeed in decimating the other Shii parties in the parliamentary elections of 2010, Maliki himself was bested by a secular-nationalist list headed by former Interim Prime Minister Allawi.[119] The Sunna of Iraq had voted for this list, called Iraqiyya, even though Allawi was from a prominent Baghdadi Shii family. In so doing, they strongly rejected their own sectarian candidates, people whom they had endorsed only four years earlier. Allawi's list garnered 80 percent of the vote in predominately Sunni governorates.[120] Being a secular-nationalist coalition, Allawi's list was the only bloc to win seats throughout Iraq, with the exception of the three predominately Kurdish governorates,[121] where it fielded no candidates.

By obtaining a plurality of the seats in Parliament, Allawi's list was poised to bring the entire post-2003 "exclusive elite pact"[122] based on sectarian identity into question. The pact was predicated on making a bargain between Iraq's principal ethno-confessional groups – namely, the Arab Shia, the Arab Sunna, and the Kurds. As Toby Dodge observes:

---

[117] See Feisal al-Istrabadi, "Is a Democratic, Unified Iraq Viable?" *Near East Quarterly* 7 (February 2012), http://www.neareastquarterly.com/index.php/2012/03/24/is-a-democratic-unified-iraq-viable/.
[118] See J. Scott Carpenter and Ahmed Ali, "Surprises from Iraq's Provincial Elections" (Washington Institute for Near East Policy, Policy Watch #1472, 2009): 1.
[119] Al-Istrabadi, "Is a Democratic, Unified Iraq Viable?" *supra* n. 117.
[120] Dodge, *New Authoritarianism, supra* n. 4, 152.
[121] Ibid.   [122] Ibid.

[M]ost of Iraq's ruling elite was deeply perturbed that Iraqiyya's election victory could herald far-reaching changes to the whole political system.... Since 2003, and crucially in the aftermath of both elections in
2005, governments of national unity were formed through the application
of muhasasa [sic] (sectarian apportionment), the principle that all of Iraq's
sectarian and religious communities should be given cabinet posts.... The
rise of an overtly non-sectarian vote placed the validity of this system in
doubt. How was Iraqiyya to be integrated into a system that only recognized parties along ethnic and religious lines?[123]

The answer is that Iraqiyya was not treated as a non-sectarian list. Thanks
to two of Iraqiyya's members making their own deal with Maliki in
exchange for government positions – namely, the speakership of Parliament and a deputy prime ministership – the other parties were able to
treat Iraqiyya as though it had merely supplanted the discredited Sunni
representative elected in December 2005.[124] For his part, as soon as he
realized that he might conceivably lose the premiership, Maliki tacked
hard to his political right and returned to his highly sectarian discourse,
thereby hoping to appeal to the broad mass of Shia.[125] Dodge's "exclusive
elite pact" of *muḥāṣaṣah* remains intact.

This author has elsewhere described the sense of loss felt by the Sunna
in the aftermath of the 2010 vote:

For the Sunna, the wrangling after the 2010 elections proved their worst
nightmares. They had always feared, once the US occupation took on a
sectarian overtone, that a Shia-Kurdish alliance would marginalise them
permanently. It must be recalled that after the first 2005 elections, the
ones boycotted by the Sunna, a Kurdish president was elected, along with
a sectarian Shia prime minister. The highest ranking Sunni was a vice
president along with the speaker of parliament. The same configuration
obtained after the second elections, held in December 2005, when the
Sunna vote was scattered and cast mainly in favour of Sunni sectarian
parties.

The Sunna of Iraq learnt from their mistakes. They unified behind a
non-sectarian, nationalist candidate (Allawi, a Shia), and they – together
with non-sectarian, nationalist Shia – managed to pull [off] a stunning
upset over the incumbent. Yet the end result was the same: the same Kurdish president, the same Shia sectarian prime minister, and the same Sunni
vice president along with a Sunni parliament speaker. In other words,

[123] Ibid., 155.
[124] Ibid., 155–56. The two were Usama Nujayfi and Saleh Mutlag, respectively.
[125] Al-Istrabadi, "Is a Democratic, Unified Iraq Viable?" *supra* n. 117.

from a Sunna perspective, whether they boycott the elections, or whether they vote in a divided and sectarian manner, or whether they put aside their sectarianism and vote for a nationalist candidate who actually bests his adversaries, the end result is the same: they can only aspire to symbolic positions in the New Iraq, devoid of any real power. This situation neither constitutes healthy politics nor a recipe for long-term national viability.[126]

Several factors have exacerbated the Sunna's sense of disenfranchisement. To begin with, once the two members of Iraqiyya made it clear they were willing to form a government with or without Allawi thereby assuring Maliki a second term, Maliki signed an agreement that would have allowed Allawi to chair a so-called National Council for Strategic Policy. This council was to have a pivotal role in setting major policy.[127] Maliki also agreed, inter alia, to strengthen the legal chain of command of the armed forces and that Iraqiyya would have the defense portfolio.[128] Once actually confirmed in power, Maliki reneged on the entire agreement.[129] More than three years after the elections, the council has never been formed, and Maliki has rejected each of the candidates proffered by Iraqiyya to the post of defense minister.

Other reasons for Sunni disillusionment with Baghdad also appeared. The government of Iraq has begun to move against prominent Sunni politicians, mostly from the Iraqiyya bloc. Maliki proceeded judicially against the Sunni vice president, Tariq Hashimi. An arrest warrant was issued against him, after his bodyguards "confessed" to Hashimi's supposed involvement in terrorist activities. Maliki's son, Ahmed, executed the warrant, commanding the force of tanks and troops that surrounded Hashimi's house.[130] Hashimi, who is currently a fugitive in Turkey (although still technically vice president) has been tried and convicted in absentia. The court handed down five sentences of death against him.[131] That his guards were tortured during the "investigation" and that one

---

[126] Ibid.
[127] Dodge, *New Authoritarianism, supra* n. 4, 156.
[128] Ibid.   [129] Ibid., 162.
[130] Ibid., 165.
[131] Thomas Whittle, "Iraqi Court Issues 5th Death Verdict Against Fugitive VP Hashimi," *NZWeek*, December 14, 2012, http://www.nzweek.com/world/iraqi-court-issues-5th-death-verdict-against-fugitive-vp-hashimi-37439/. Hashimi faces potentially hundreds of death sentences, as he is accused of involvement in some 150 bombings. *See* "Iraq Vice-President Sentenced To Death Amid Deadly Wave Of Insurgent Attacks," *Guardian (U.K.)*, September 9, 2012, http://www.guardian.co.uk/world/2012/sep/09/iraq-vice-president-hashemi-death-sentence.

of those guards died as a result are widely known in the country.[132] Maliki has also moved to arrest the bodyguards of the popular Sunni former minister of finance, also a member of Iraqiyya. This "investigation" again centers on charges of terrorism.[133]

The effort to denude the non-sectarian Iraqiyya list of its elected leadership started even before the March 2010 elections. Some six weeks before polling began, the Shia-led de-Baathification committee barred some 500 Sunni parliamentary candidates from running for political office, charging that they had been prominent Baathis under the prior regime.[134] The list of those barred included the then sitting minister of defense.[135] It also included seventy-two members of the Iraqiyya list.[136] The de-Baathification process has itself raised sectarian tensions. A study undertaken by the U.S. Army Strategic Studies Institute found that de-Baathification, both in its conception and in its execution, was "deeply flawed" and has resulted in the "alienation of Sunni Arabs, the politicization of sectarian differences, *and the rise of the Sunni insurgency.*"[137]

The goal of the Shii political establishment in this aggressive move to eliminate candidates was not to target sectarian Sunnis running for office. Rather, the goal was to target those lists that were running on a non- or cross-sectarian basis. "Those parties and coalitions trying to maximize an exclusively Sunni vote posed no threat to the prime minister and the other Shia coalition...and were hence left alone."[138] In a real sense, therefore, the Shii political establishment sought to dictate to the Sunna for whom they could vote by eliminating those candidates who could

---

[132] Dodge, *New Authoritarianism, supra* n. 4, 165–66.

[133] Duraid Adnan and Tim Arango, "Arrest of a Sunni Minister's Bodyguards Prompts Protests in Iraq," *New York Times*, December 21, 2012, at A-9.

[134] Dodge, *New Authoritarianism, supra* n. 4, 153. Dodge points out that the two officials responsible for this effort, Ahmad Chalabi and Ali Faysal al-Lami, were both candidates contesting for seats in the upcoming elections. *Id.* Sixteen months after this action, al-Lami was assassinated in Baghdad. *See* "Anti-Baath Committee Chief Ali al-Lami Killed in Iraq," *BBC News*, May 27, 2011, http://www.bbc.co.uk/news/world-middle-east-13571208.

[135] Anthony Shadid, "Iraqi Commission Bars Nearly 500 Candidates," *New York Times*, January 15, 2010, at A4. The de-Baathification order was a procedural nightmare on several levels, not least because it was technically issued by a body that had been legislatively superseded by another body. *See* ibid.

[136] W. Andrew Terrell, *Lessons of the Iraqi De-Ba'athification Program for Iraq's Future and the Arab Revolutions* (Carlisle, PA: Strategic Studies Institute, U.S. Army War College, 2012), 51.

[137] Ibid., 56 (emphasis added).

[138] Dodge, *New Authoritarianism, supra* n. 4, 154.

be (and were) attractive outside the Sunni community. When Maliki's pre-election efforts to isolate the non-sectarian lists failed, he employed other, more direct tactics to eliminate those who posed a threat to the post-2003 sectarian dispensation.

Trading Places: Federalism in the Post-Constitutional Dispensation

There is an evident determination on the part of the Shii ruling parties to consolidate and hold power to the detriment of any threat to the "exclusive elite pact," as Dodge has it. From the perspective of the Shii political leadership, there is a certain obvious logic to doing so: the sectarian pact brought them to, and sustains them in, power. Any threat to the status quo, therefore, logically impels an appropriate response. Accordingly, Maliki is driving the Sunna into accepting this pact and eradicating those who challenge it by positing a nationalist, non-sectarian vision.

Viewed from the perspective of the Arab Sunna, there is an inherent tension in this logic, however. It is true that the Kurds are mostly, although not exclusively, Sunnis, and together with Arab Sunna they would constitute a substantial proportion of the Iraqi population. However, the dominant expression of the Kurdish identity is likely to remain for the foreseeable future Kurdish nationality, not religion. Thus if the Sunna, as a minority, accept the sectarian dispensation, they automatically relegate themselves to the status of a permanent underclass. Of course, had they accepted earlier SCIRI/ISCI's essentially consociational vision of the state, their fears could have been substantially reduced, because they could have minimized Shii domination over them by creating a federated region *á la* the KRG. Instead, they lost a civil war fought largely on the basis of maintaining a centralized vision of the state and maintaining their power in that state.[139]

At this writing, however, matters have changed dramatically. The Sunna have come to terms with the fact that they have lost ascendancy in Baghdad. This occurred in the aftermath of Iraqiyya's inability to remain cohesive and find a path to forming a government. Once Maliki began to

---

[139] Lennox Samuels, "'An Honor I Do Not Claim': Ahmad Chalabi on his Role in Iraq and on the US Withdrawal," *Newsweek*, June 24, 2009, http://www.thedailybeast.com/newsweek/2009/06/24/an-honor-i-do-not-claim.html (quoting Chalabi as saying "The Sunnis lost the battle of Baghdad," as if it were some victory after great armies faced each other, rather than what it mostly was – Militias targeting civilians).

crack down on Iraqiyya and on the Sunna, the governorate councils of three predominately Sunni governorates – the same three that had rejected the regionalist constitution – voted to hold referenda on devolving into federated regions.[140] After having resisted regionalism so ferociously, it was a supreme irony that the Sunna were now themselves demanding it.

It was an equally supreme irony that, despite the Shia religious parties having rushed through a constitutional process in six weeks to secure a regionalist constitution, it was Maliki who absolutely refused to allow the referenda on creating Sunni regions to go forward. His refusal to allow the referenda to proceed, of course, absolutely violated the very constitution supported overwhelmingly by the Shia.[141] There was no legal basis whatsoever for his doing so. He simply intimidated the electoral commission into not setting the referenda, claiming that the attempt to create further regions was a Baathist plot.[142] It is highly significant that Maliki moved against Vice President Hashimi within forty-eight hours of Hashimi's having thrown his public support behind the federalist movements.[143]

The Sunna initially recoiled and took up arms against this essentially consociational rearrangement of the state. It was a vision of the state collectively proffered by the Shii religious parties, whatever internal differences may have existed between them, in an alliance with the Kurds. Whereas the Arab-Sunni majority governorates rejected the consociational constitution by comfortable majorities, even if not enough ultimately to defeat the draft, the majority Arab-Shii governorates each voted by margins exceeding 90 percent in favor of the document.[144] That is where the "exclusive elite pact" lay as of the end of the referendum in October 2005. Indeed, by electing sectarian representatives in December 2005, their Shii interlocutors might well have been sanguine that the Sunna had, if not agreed then at least, acquiesced to the pact.

---

[140] Dodge, *New Authoritarianism, supra* n. 4, 164.

[141] Distūr Jumhūhūriyyat al-'Irāq [Iraq Constitution], Art. 119 (First) (recognizing the right of governorates to hold referenda on the creation of regions on the vote of a simple majority of the governorate council). A report issued at about the time of these events asserted that the votes in these governorates were merely "symbolic." *See* Sean Kane et al., "Iraq's Federalism Quandary," *National Interest*, March–April 2012, http://nationalinterest.org/article/iraqs-federalism-quandary-6512. That interpretation is constitutionally inadmissible. *See* Sean Kane et al., ibid.

[142] Dodge, *New Authoritarianism, supra* n. 4, 164–65.

[143] Ibid., 166.

[144] "Iraq Voters Back New Constitution," *supra* n. 100.

Instead a sectarian civil war broke out or had its ferocity geometrically increased. What explains this behavior?

Stanford political scientist James Fearon asserts that "under some conditions the inability to make credible commitments under anarchy can make it impossible for disputants to locate a bargain that would avoid a costly fight."[145] He calls this the "commitment problem."[146] He posits the existence of two models. The first model involves majority rule, whereas the second assumes that at least some rights have been given to the minority.[147] For reasons that will become clearer, in the case of Iraq, it is only necessary to consider the first case in which the new constitutional order involves majority rule.

In Fearon's model, the minority makes a decision whether to accept the terms dictated by the majority or to fight. If it chooses the former, then the "game" continues, and the majority begins to consolidate its power.[148] A minority might well make a choice to fight, because the state at such a moment of transition is at its weakest. It could calculate rationally that it has the best chance of upsetting the new order and perhaps coming closer to (re)imposing its vision.[149] For its part, a majority, finding itself in nominal control perhaps for the first time, might well wish to preserve its gains by making a bargain averting war. However, it typically finds that it is unable to do so, because, given the majoritarian nature of the new order, it is unable to make guarantees to the minority that there will be no further encroachment on the minority's rights in the future, "once the state has been consolidated."[150]

That the Iraqi Constitution of 2006 created a majoritarian order is a proposition that this author has argued more fully elsewhere.[151] It reduces to four salient facts: First, Hamoudi, the chairman of the CDC and CRC, has opined that, in a democracy, the majority is not required "*to consider* all that is demanded by the minority; this would be the reverse of democracy."[152] It should be noted that Hamoudi used the word *consider*: a majority is not required to consider the views of a minority. That leads to the second fact that, as noted, the majority in fact threw the minority

---

[145] James D. Fearon, "Ethnic War as a Commitment Problem" (Working Paper 6, 1995), http://www.stanford.edu/~jfearon/papers/ethcprob.pdf .

[146] Ibid.   [147] Ibid.

[148] Ibid., 7–8.   [149] Ibid., 8.

[150] Ibid., 10.

[151] Al-Istrabadi, "Islam and the State in Iraq," *supra* n. 42, 615–16.

[152] Humam Hamoudi, "My Perceptions on the Iraqi Constitutional Process," *Stanford Law Review* 57 (2007): 1316 (emphasis added).

out of the negotiations for the constitutional draft at a moment when it founded it suitable to do so. No clearer sign of the majority's view of the minority could be given. Third, there is Sistani's objection to the check on majoritarianism, whereby three governorates could theoretically trump a majority's will by vetoing a draft constitution.[153] Finally, when the Sunna attempted to exercise a right ostensibly guaranteed to them in the Constitution to establish their own regions, the Shii government changed the rules de facto, foiling their right to do so. Indeed, the situation was not so much that the Shia parties could not reassure their Sunni interlocutors, as Fearon might suppose; rather, they were doing seemingly all they could to frighten them.

Confronted with this reality, the Sunna obviously opted to fight in 2006. The only reason for pause in applying Fearon's analysis is that the presence of U.S. troops in Iraq could have been the sort of "third-party presence" that might have deterred the Sunna.[154] The reality is that it was obvious to most observers – and the Sunna could not have failed to realize it – that the United States simply did not have control on the ground and that it could not deal with a widespread insurgency. Thus, American forces were obviously no deterrent whatsoever. Indeed, one of the reasons the Sunna chose to fight was to force the Americans to quit Iraq, as they believed that they could retake the state in the absence of these foreign forces.[155]

Iraq seems now to be perched on yet another Fearonian precipice. The Sunna, perhaps convinced their power in Baghdad has waned permanently, are poised to unleash yet another round of violence. The United Nations Assistance Mission in Iraq announced that April 2013 was the "deadliest month since June 2008," the putative "end" of the civil war.[156] It said the same of May[157] and July 2013.[158] Although the violence never

---

[153] Al-Istrabadi, "Islam and the State in Iraq," *supra* n. 42, 615–16.

[154] Fearon, "Ethnic War," *supra* n. 145, 6. Fearon assumes that the third party could typically be the state itself.

[155] Fearon, "Iraq's Civil War," *supra* n. 108, 5.

[156] "Iraqi Violence Claims 700 Lives in April," *UPI.com*, April 30, 2013, http://www.upi.com/Top_News/Special/2013/05/02/Iraqi-violence-claims-700-lives-in-April/UPI-22761367506986/. Of course, if the civil war started in 2004 as Fearon believes, or in 2005 as Haddad argues, then the war never really ended, as there was always ongoing violence in the country.

[157] Patrick Markey, "Fears of Civil War in Iraq After 1,000 Are Killed in a Month," *NBCNews.com*, June 1, 2013, http://worldnews.nbcnews.com/_news/2013/06/01/18676359-fears-of-civil-war-in-iraq-after-1000-are-killed-in-a-month?lite.

[158] "Iraq suffers its deadliest month in five years," *Guardian (U.K.)*, August 1, 2013, http://www.theguardian.com/world/2013/aug/01/iraq-deadliest-month-five-years.

fully subsided, violence on a larger scale has become a routine occurrence again. It appears that another round of increased violence is under way.[159]

If a new round of the civil war is under way, it may well be that the Sunna will be fighting this time for the consociational rights they fought so bitterly against five years ago. They are no doubt calculating, as Maliki rounds up the representatives they voted for, that in another five years, he will have been able to consolidate power even more effectively, making now the relatively optimal time to re-ignite their insurgency. Maliki, for his part, appears unwilling and unable to make any agreement on consociationalism, in no small part because he and his supporters are attempting to re-centralize Iraq. Just as in 2007, Maliki's priority is not a peaceful and fecund Iraq: it is the unity of the Shia, but now on his terms.

CONCLUSION

The constitutional politics of Iraq have been singularly and literally destructive. Although the Shii and Kurdish political leadership forged an alliance that pushed through a constitutional draft on which they could agree, they were unable to forge an understanding with the Sunna of Iraq to allow the Constitution to serve as a national pact. Instead, they pressed every advantage they could to obtain their maximal goals. In principle, that is the right of any large majority, but in the context of Iraq, the majority failed to take into account that the Sunna could destabilize the country. They have done so almost certainly because they feel disenfranchised.

These two communities have seemingly been at cross-purposes since the fall of the previous regime. At the time of the negotiations for both constitutions, the Shia were still fearful that they would be unable to hold on to the new dispensation. Specifically they feared a return to

---

[159] *See, e.g.,* "Iraq violence: Car bombs in and around Baghdad kill 41," BBC News, August 6, 2013, http://www.bbc.co.uk/news/world-middle-east-23590938, "Bomb Attacks Kill at Least 95 across Iraq," *Daily Star (Lebanon)*, May 21, 2013, http://www.dailystar.com.lb/News/Middle-East/2013/May-21/217813-bomb-attacks-kill-at-least-95-across-iraq.ashx#ixzz2TuBcoJ8R; Mohamad Ali Harissi, and "'War on Mosques' Now Daily Part of Iraq Strife," *Daily Star (Lebanon)*, May 21, 2013, http://www.dailystar.com.lb/News/Middle-East/2013/May-21/217773-war-on-mosques-now-daily-part-of-iraq-strife.ashx#ixzz2TuCmRIek.

power of the Sunna, as they saw it, and therefore a return to oppression of the Shia. Thus they pressed ahead with the first elections, even though prudence might have dictated delaying them until the Sunna could be persuaded to abandon their boycott – or indeed, to ascertain whether perhaps some accommodation could be conceived to allay their concerns.

The Shia were thus behaving very much like an oppressed minority that had been given a chance at power for the first time. Such a minority would press its advantages relentlessly, lest the majority seize power again. Of course, they are the majority, and insofar as their religious parties are likely to constitute a sizeable part of the political class for the foreseeable future, they could have afforded to be more magnanimous in their conduct. Indeed, as the majority, it would have been in their long-term interest to tone down their sectarian rhetoric and to appeal to the Sunna's nationalist sentiments. That would have been their clearest road to securing the peace of the country. They could either have appealed to the Sunna as Iraqi nationalists, or, considering the issues respecting Iraq's Kurdish minority, they might have found common cause with the Sunna as fellow Arab citizens of Iraq.

Nor can one be particularly sanguine that the current Shii leadership understands that it has made strategic errors in its dealings with Iraq's second largest ethno-confessional group. The current prime minister has announced that "power-sharing cannot be the foundation for solving our problems."[160] He has also renewed calls for "majority rule," a term almost certain to be understood not in political, but in sectarian, terms, however he may claim to mean it.[161] The strategy of the Shii political leadership continues to be to bait the Sunna.

The Sunna for their part are understandably frustrated, to say the least. To be sure, the decisions of those among them who opted to support the insurgency brought disaster on Iraq as well as on the Sunna themselves. Still, having fought against the new constitutional order and lost and having contested politically for genuine power-sharing in Baghdad during the 2010 elections and having lost again, they subsequently embraced the

---

[160] *Quoted in* Dodge, *New Authoritarianism, supra* n. 4, 165 (footnote omitted).
[161] Stephen Wicken, "Presidency and Protests Turn Attention to Negotiation" (Institute For the Study of War Iraq Updates, Iraq Update #20, 2013), http://iswiraq.blogspot.com/2013/05/2013-iraq-update-20-presidency-and.html. Maliki has made such calls before. *See, e.g.*, "Shi'ite Maliki calls for majority rule in Iraq," *Reuters*, May 15, 2009, http://www.reuters.com/article/2009/05/15/idUSLF624378.

constitutional vision that the Shia fought to protect. At that moment, they had a right to expect that Maliki would allow the constitutionally sanctioned process of referenda on federated regions to proceed. In light of Maliki's rejection, they already see – even though the state has not yet stabilized – that the Shia are reneging on promises to protect their rights, precisely the incentive to battle Fearon posits.

There are lessons to be learned in Iraq and avoided elsewhere. At this writing, in Syria, a bloody civil war rages that is often cast as a battle between a government consisting of a minority (an offshoot of Shiism) and the Sunni majority. Although the Syrian government seems now to have the advantage, should it fall, the Sunna of Syria may well be tempted to follow the example of the majority in Iraq. It has become quite commonplace to assert that the violence in Syria is exacerbating the violence in Iraq.[162] It is entirely plausible that the reverse may also be the case, however. The ferocity and barbarity with which the Syrian regime and its supporters are fighting for survival may well be because they have seen what awaits a dislodged minority when the majority seizes power.[163] For the sake of regional peace and stability, the international community, to the extent it has influence, should mitigate these instincts. A period of confidence-building measures and political accommodation will be essential to a stable and sustainable democratic constitutional order. Such a "cooling off period" by far trumps any perceived imperative to complete a constitutional drafting process in haste. Similar considerations obtain in places such as Libya and elsewhere.

As for Iraq, the decision – and it was a conscious decision – of the Shii political and clerical elites to interact with the Sunna by stressing their differences is understandable, regardless of how destructive it has proven to be. Understandable or not, however, it was not wise. Rather than reassuring the Sunna that they are full citizens of a common state, they have sent multiple clear signals that the Sunna are in fact a new and permanent underclass. In so doing, the Shia elites failed to calculate the capacity of enough Sunnis to begin and sustain an insurgency that effectively

---

[162] *See, e.g.,* Ali Saray, "Iraqi Speaker Discusses Impact of Syria on Iraq," *AlMonitor*, April 8, 2012, http://www.al-monitor.com/pulse/politics/2013/04/iraq-internal-rifts-syria-nujaifi.html.

[163] *See* Feisal Amin Rasoul al-Istrabadi, "Sectarian War a Two-Way Street for Iraq and Syria," *AlMonitor*, May 28, 2013, http://www.al-monitor.com/pulse/originals/2013/05/sectarian-struggle-iran-syria.html.

destabilizes the state. This was a gross miscalculation and tens of thousands of innocent men, women, and children have paid the price for it. Nor is there any sign of an impending end as Iraqis have grown inured to the seemingly endless carnage, even as the world's attention has moved on.

8

Constitutionalism and Religious Difference in Israel (and a Brief Passage to Malaysia)

Ran Hirschl

Countless books and articles are devoted each year to the study of religion in the West, most notably with an eye to American constitutional law of religion or the accommodation of religious difference (or lack thereof) in the supposedly neutral European public sphere. The reality, however, is that even if we leave aside claims à-la Charles Taylor that Western secularism has never really banished religion, as of 2012, approximately half of the world's population, perhaps more, lives in polities that do not subscribe to the Franco-American doctrine of strict structural and substantive separation of religion and state, and where religion continues to play a key role in political and constitutional life. Of these, approximately one billion people now live in polities that feature a strong establishment of religion (e.g., full constitutional endorsement of Islam as the single state religion and its establishment as "a" or "the" source of legislation in at least thirty of the world's predominantly Muslim polities). Many more live in polities that endorse religion in a more subtle way as a source of national heritage and a marker of collective identity, often alongside preferential treatment of a particular religion (e.g., Thailand, Cambodia, Sri Lanka, Bhutan, Slovakia, or Serbia). Such compound settings of the modern and the sacred offer an ideal testing ground for students of constitutionalism and religious difference.

In this chapter I explore the history, scope, and nature of the existential religion-related tensions embedded in the constitutional order of Israel – a polity that features many of the characteristics of that "other world" of religion-and-state constitutional models. Israel defines itself as a Jewish and democratic state. Much has been written about this duality: that is, how logically plausible it may be, given the fact that non-Jews make up approximately one-fifth of Israel's citizenry, and how these two foundational tenets may be translated into a fairly coherent set of guidelines for public life. To add further complication, Israel sees itself as a homeland for the entire world Jewry and draws on religious ascriptions to assign a nationality marker of identity (*Le'om*; practically meaning "ethnicity") to each of its citizens. This is then used as a legal foundation for the maintenance of what has been labeled "ethnic democracy" – a political system that combines democratic and civil rights to all with a structured dominance of a single ethnic group (Jews) to the detriment of others.[1] The Supreme Court of Israel (SCI) has developed rich jurisprudence on formative questions such as "Who is a Jew?" for conversion purposes, equal treatment of Jewish and non-Jewish religious bodies, the legitimacy of political parties that challenge either the Jewish or the democratic tenet of Israel's constitutional identity, or the tension between general principles of Israeli constitutional law and religious tribunals' jurisdictional autonomy in matters of personal status. However, the close entanglement of state and religion in Israel is perhaps best captured by everyday oddities, familiar to Israelis but quite exotic otherwise.

As any traveler's guidebook about Israel mentions, El Al – Israel's national airline – serves only kosher food and does not operate on Saturdays or on Jewish holidays. Less well known is the fact that the Supreme Court of Israel ruled in 1994 in one of the first and most progressive rulings of its kind in the world (the *Danilowitch* case) that El Al had to provide same-sex employees (and their partners) the same benefits it provided to opposite-sex employees (and their partners).[2] In Tel-Aviv, Israel's largest city and center of business and commerce, public transportation comes to a complete halt on Friday at dusk and does not resume before Saturday nightfall, at the end of the Jewish Sabbath. By contrast, in the city of Haifa – Israel's third largest city, located less than 60 miles north of Tel-Aviv – public transportation is fully operative throughout Friday and Saturday. How so? In 1947 the secular leadership of the Zionist movement in pre-state Israel and leaders of the religious Jewish community concluded an informal agreement that created a framework for the

---

[1] *See* Sammy Smooha, "Ethnic Democracy: Israel as an Archetype," *Israel Studies* 2 (1997): 198–241.

[2] HCJ 721/94 *El Al Airlines Ltd.* v. *Danilowitch et al.*, 48(5) P.D. 749. This act of progressive jurisprudence is not exceptional. In December 2012, for example, an Israeli court has approved the nation's first same-sex divorce even though the country does not officially recognize same-sex marriage. Not allowing the separation, the court reasoned, would violate the couple's fundamental rights. Because Rabbinical courts' refusal to deal with same-sex marriage and divorce is to be honored, ruled the court, an ordinary court can claim jurisdiction over the matter.

establishment of the country. The agreement, known as the "status quo agreement," laid out ground rules for the relationship between state and religion in four major areas: education, Kashrut (Jewish dietary rules), matrimonial law, and Shabbat (including the operation of public transportation). The deal froze the common practice at the time with respect to these four realms, including the operation of public transportation in Tel-Aviv and Haifa. And a third, equally telling anecdote: in 2004 Professors Avram Hershko and Aaron Ciechanover of the Technion in Haifa, Israel, won the Nobel Prize in Chemistry for their discovery of ubiquitin-mediated protein degradation. This was the first-ever Nobel Prize awarded to a scientist working in an Israeli university and undoubtedly a foundational event for Israel's scientific community.[3] The Swedish Royal Academy happened to announce Hershko and Ciechanover's prize on a Jewish holiday. Instead of holding a major press conference at the Technion, as one would expect given the moment's grandeur, Technion authorities had to host the press conference with the two laureates at Hershko's private home. It was later revealed that the Technion's rabbi would not allow the university to hold a press conference on the university's premises during the Jewish holiday because by law all public institutions must remain closed on such days. Not even a historic Nobel Prize could change that divine call. These episodes reveal what is arguably one of the most complex settings for studying the charged relations between religion and constitutionalism.

In the following pages I explore the relations between religion and constitutionalism in Israel. I begin with a brief survey of the relevant social and constitutional framework for understanding the status of religion in Israel. Next, I examine landmark constitutional jurisprudence that deals with the clash between Israel's constitutional principles and religious identity, most notably rulings on foundational questions such as "Who is a Jew?" and conversion to Judaism, the balance between claims of religion and general principles of constitutional law, and the jurisdictional autonomy of religious tribunals in personal status matters. In the third part of the chapter, I draw some comparisons to the manifestations of tensions between religious identity and constitutional principles

---

[3] Israelis had won Nobel Prizes in Literature and Peace; Daniel Kahneman, an Israeli, had won the Nobel Prize in Economic Sciences while he was working at Princeton. Israeli scientists have since won the Nobel Prize on three additional occasions: in Economic Sciences in 2005 and in Chemistry in 2009 and in 2011. In 2013, two Israeli citizens working in the U.S. were among the winners of the Nobel Prize in Chemistry.

in Malaysia – one of the countries that have been grappling with a similar set of existential dilemmas pertaining to religion, ethnicity, nation building, and modern constitutional law. I conclude by offering some general observations about the role of constitutional law and courts in mediating the foundational tension between the rule of law and the rule of God in polities that defy the Franco-American doctrine of strict separation of religion and state. Although the constitutional endorsement of religion may reflect genuine aspirations and affirm religion- or ethnicity-based collective identities, it may also be seen as an effective means for containing or domesticating religion by bringing it under constitutional control. The constitutional enshrinement of religion neutralizes religion's revolutionary sting, ensures state input in the translation of religious precepts into guidelines for public life, helps mutate sacred law and manipulate religious discourse to serve nation building and regime legitimacy interests, and, above all, assists in bringing an alternative, even rival, order of authority under state supervision.

THE SOCIAL AND CONSTITUTIONAL FRAMEWORK

The 1948 Declaration of Independence of the State of Israel created temporary governmental institutions. A Constituent Assembly was simultaneously formed and invested with the power to draft a constitution that would eventually establish permanent governing institutions. In 1949, the Constituent Assembly changed its name to the Knesset and established itself as the legislative body of the State of Israel. After debating for a year over the merits of a constitution, it became apparent that the religious parties were opposed to the idea of an entrenched constitution because it would invest the ultimate source of sovereignty in the citizenry rather than in God or Jewish law. "The Torah is our Constitution!" argued the religious parties. *Mapai* – the primary component of what would become the Labor Party and the unchallenged secular ruling party at the time – was also unwilling to proceed with drafting a constitution. This was partly to avoid jeopardizing the tenuous secular/religious coalition government, partly to maintain the Jewish identity aura of the newly established state, and partly because *Mapai* leaders, notably David Ben-Gurion, had no political incentive to transfer policy-making authority to the judiciary and no desire to impose any limitations on their own power. Thus, in 1950 the first Knesset adopted a compromise known as the Harari Resolution. This enabled the Knesset to evade its obligation in terms of the

Declaration of Independence to compose a written constitution, while at the same time preserving its power to enact one through the adoption of a series of Basic Laws.

Since the establishment of the State of Israel, a fundamental – and unresolved – collective-identity issue has been whether the country is a *medinat hok* (a state based on civil or secular law) or a *medinat halakhah* (a state based on Jewish law). Israel's constitutional system is based on two fundamental tenets: the state is Jewish and democratic. It is this commitment to the creation of an ideologically plausible and politically feasible synthesis between particularistic (Jewish) and universalistic (democratic) values that has proved to be the major constitutional challenge faced by Israel since its foundation. Reaching such a synthesis is especially problematic given that non-Jews – primarily Muslims, Christians, and Druze – constitute approximately one-fifth of Israel's citizenry (excluding the Palestinian residents of the West Bank and Gaza Strip). The tension between a commitment to democratic values and a commitment to religion/ethnicity-based collective identity manifests itself in various aspects of public life, most notably in the area of public funding and allocation of goods and opportunities. One of the main vehicles for pro-Jewish preferential treatment in Israel has been the requirement of military service as a proviso for receiving various government funds and benefits. Because most non-Jews are not drafted while all Jews are (including the exempted ultra-Orthodox, who officially have their draft deferred), military service provides a proxy for ethnic discrimination against Arabs in access to welfare, housing, education, employment, or other forms of direct assistance granted to those who serve.

Even within the Jewish population, the exact meaning of Israel as a "Jewish" state has been highly contested. Not only do opinions differ sharply on whether Jews are citizens of a nation, members of a people, participants in a culture, or coreligionists, but even among adherents of the last opinion – arguably the most established of these constructions – there are widely divergent beliefs and degrees of practice. These adherents range from the ultra-Orthodox to millions who define themselves as "traditional" (*Masorti* or *Shomer Masoret*) and include those who pursue a fully secular lifestyle yet celebrate their children's bar/bat mitzvah and acknowledge the Jewish high holidays.

Nevertheless, for a host of historical and political reasons, the Orthodox stream of the Jewish religion has long enjoyed the status of being the sole branch of Judaism formally recognized by the state. This exclusive status has enabled the Orthodox community to establish a near monopoly over the supply of religious services – a lucrative business entailing countless civil service jobs at the national and municipal levels, monitoring of business compliance with legalized, religion-infused standards, and handling of religious ceremonies ranging from circumcisions to weddings to burials. It has also enabled the Orthodox community to impose rigid standards on the process of determining who is a Jew – a question that has crucial symbolic and practical implications because, according to Israel's Law of Return, Jews who immigrate to Israel are entitled to a variety of benefits, including the right to immediate full citizenship. As mentioned, a contested draft-deferment arrangement that has been in place since the establishment of the state allows Orthodox yeshiva students to receive draft deferments (conscription is otherwise compulsory for Jewish citizens of Israel) as long as they maintain their religious studies. The issue became one of the main items on the public agenda in the months leading to the 2013 general elections, as part of a social struggle for "equality in sharing the burden" (*shivyon ba-netel*).[4] On a related front, the potentially far-reaching law *Hok Yesodot Ha'Mishpat* (the foundations of law) was passed in 1980 making Jewish Law (*Mishpat Ivri*) a formal source of interpretation in instances involving lack of precedent or legal lacunae.[5] All of this has taken place even though more than two-thirds of the world's Jews, on whom Israel relies for essential symbolic, material, and strategic support, continue to live outside Israel and do not subscribe to the Orthodox stream of Judaism.

To further complicate things, over the last four decades there has been a continuous decline in the political power and representation of Israel's

[4] The number of Orthodox yeshiva students receiving such deferrals grew from several hundred in the 1950s to tens of thousands in recent years. In the January 2013 elections, some of the secular resentment against this arrangement was channeled into support for the newly established *Yesh Atid* (Hebrew for "there is a future") Party, whose leader, Yair Lapid, was perceived as an opponent of statutory privileges to the Orthodox community. Following the elections, a parliamentary governing coalition was established that did not include an ultra-Orthodox party. As a result, in July 2013 a new bill was drafted that mandates military or civil service enlistment for most ultra-Orthodox within the next few years. Considering the volatile political market in Israel, the actual implementation of that bill is likely to be protracted, and is dependent to a large extent on whether ultra-Orthodox parties become members of the governing coalition in the coming years.

[5] In practice, Jewish law is seldom used for substantive guidance in Supreme Court cases; when it is referenced by Supreme Court judges, it is done largely for ornamental or decorative purposes. A notable exception is Menachem Elon, a prominent Jewish law scholar, judge of the Supreme Court of Israel 1973–1993, and an advocate of substantive use of Jewish law as a main interpretive source.

historically hegemonic, secular-socialist Ashkenazi constituencies (mostly Jews of European descent, often with Western cultural propensities, and – at least during the first few decades of statehood – better off socioeconomically compared with Mizrahi Jews, who are mostly of North African and Middle-Eastern origin). This decline of the Ashkenazi cultural and political establishment was accompanied by a corresponding rise of new or hitherto marginalized groups, some of which (most notably residents of Jewish settlements in the West Bank and religious Mizrahi residents of development towns and socioeconomically underdeveloped urban neighborhoods) are strong advocates for Jewish tradition.[6] The expansion of the electorate by the addition of approximately one million newly arrived immigrants from the former Soviet Union and elsewhere (roughly 15 percent of Israel's population) – many of whom support extreme nationalist parties – also contributed to destabilizing the labor movement's historical grip on political power. As the largely secular Ashkenazi elite's disproportionate influence over the country's important political decision-making arenas has been increasingly challenged, its willingness (if not eagerness) to transfer crucial religion-and-state questions from the political arena to the Supreme Court has likewise increased.[7] Given the court's record of adjudication, as well as its judges' educational background and cultural propensities, Israel's left-leaning, relatively cosmopolitan bourgeoisie can safely assume that its worldviews and policy preferences with regard to constitutive questions of religion and state will be less effectively contested. This has resulted in the transformation of the Supreme Court of Israel into a crucial present-day forum for addressing the country's most fundamental collective-identity quandaries.

Until 1992 Israel's nexus of Basic Laws did not include an entrenched law dealing with civil liberties and human rights. In the absence of a necessary constitutional framework for actively reviewing primary legislation, the Supreme Court was limited to judicial review of administrative acts, informed by the doctrine of an "implied bill of rights."[8] The

---

[6] On the origins and various legal manifestations of Israel's internal social rifts and culture wars, *see* Menachem Mautner, *Law and the Culture of Israel* (New York: Oxford University Press, 2011).

[7] *See* Ran Hirschl, *Towards Juristocracy: The Origins and Consequences of the New Constitutionalism* (Cambridge, MA: Harvard University Press, 2004); Ran Hirschl, "The Socio-Political Origins of Israel's Juristocracy," *Constellations* 16 (2009): 476–92.

[8] The paradigm for this type of expansive administrative review was established in 1953 in the seminal case of HCJ 73/53 *Kol Ha'am* v. *The Minister of the Interior*, 7(2) P.D. 871.

constitutional landscape in Israel was altered in the early 1990s, when the Knesset initiated and carried out an institutional empowerment of the judiciary. This initiative, tacitly supported by Israel's judicial elite, formally began in 1992 with the enactment of two basic rights and liberties laws – Basic Law: Human Dignity and Liberty and Basic Law: Freedom of Occupation. Although these two new human rights-oriented Basic Laws do not constitute an official bill of rights, they are widely understood to fulfill the functions of such a bill. The Supreme Court swiftly endorsed the new possibility to expand the ambit of its influence. First in the *Meatrael* affair (1993), which reached the court several months after the introduction of the two new Basic Laws, and later in the *United Mizrahi Bank* case (1995) – the "Israeli *Marbury v. Madison*," as observers of the Israeli legal system have described it – the SCI formally asserted its authority to exercise judicial review over acts of the Knesset.[9] A majority of the justices held that the two new Basic Laws had indeed ushered in a new era in the historic quest for a comprehensive constitutional catalogue of rights and active judicial review in Israel. It was recognized that these laws had formal constitutional status and were therefore superior to ordinary legislation, forming what is often referred to as the "constitutional revolution" of the mid-1990s.

CONTEMPORARY CONSTITUTIONAL JURISPRUDENCE OF RELIGION

A comprehensive overview of the Israeli Supreme Court's jurisprudence of religion is obviously beyond the purview of this chapter. What may be said with some confidence is that over the last few decades, the Supreme Court has become a bastion of "reason" and "sanity" for Israel's "enlightened public" – a criterion frequently used by the court throughout the 1990s to determine the "reasonableness" of specific acts. This court-constructed "public" closely conforms to the characteristics of the old Ashkenazi establishment at the center of the Zionist consensus and shares its world views and policy preferences.

Since the late 1980s, the court has pursued a distinctly liberalizing agenda in core matters of religion and state, ranging from the curtailment of the exclusive jurisdiction of the rabbinical courts in matters of personal status and the erosion of the Orthodox monopoly over the provision of religious services, to the liberalization of rules pertaining to

---

[9] CA 6821/93 *United Mizrahi Bank v. Migdal Cooperative Village*, 49(4) P.D. 195.

vehicular traffic bans in religious neighborhoods and commercial activity on the Jewish Sabbath, the solemnization of marriage, *kashrut* (kosher) and *shmita* (land sabbatical) laws. In an important case involving blatant ethnic segregation policy by an ultra-Orthodox all-girl school in the predominantly religious West Bank settlement town of Emmanuel (the segregation was justified by school authorities as addressing the distinct needs of two separate religious streams), the court ruled (2009) that although the right to cultural pluralism in education is recognized by Israeli law, religious affiliation as a basis for autonomous schooling is not an absolute right when it collides with the overarching right to equality.[10] (Curiously, the newly established United Kingdom Supreme Court drew on the same general logic in a case involving a selective, some say discriminatory, admission policy by a North London Jewish school).[11] In 2011, the Israeli Supreme Court held in another landmark case that gender segregation in public buses operating in several ultra-Orthodox towns was unlawful.[12] Bus companies offering services (so-called *mehadrin* buses, meaning "embellished," often used among Jews to signal stringency in the context of following God's commandments) in religious neighborhoods were ordered to carry anti-segregation signs indicating that all passengers were allowed to choose any seat, except seats designated to the disabled. Granted, the actual implementation of some of these rulings has been protracted and often considerably less decisive than the court's rulings. In most cases, political pressures and on-the-ground realities make pragmatic compromises more effective than principled legal reasoning. Realities aside, however, the court's jurisprudential voice has been quite clear.

A cornerstone of the court's liberalizing treatment of religion has been the issue of non-Orthodox conversion to Judaism and the related question, "Who is a Jew?" As explained earlier, the matter has significant symbolic, political, and legal implications resulting from Israel's self-definition as a Jewish state and the importance of the Law of Return. As early as 1969, the court ruled (5–4) in *Shalit v. Minister of Interior* in favor of Binyamin Shalit's claim that the government could not use the strict "who is a Jew" test of the Halakha alone to define a person's nationality.[13] Shalit, a Jew born in Israel and an officer in the Israeli navy,

---

[10] HCJ 1067/08 *Noar Ke'Halacha* v. *Ministry of Education* (2009) IsrLR 84 (decision released on August 6, 2009).

[11] See R(E) v. Governing Body of JFS [2009] UKSC 15.

[12] HCJ 746/07 *Ragen v. Ministry of Transport* (decision released on January 5, 2011).

[13] HCJ 58/68 *Shalit v. Minister of Interior*, 23(2) P.D. 477.

married a non-Jewish woman in Scotland. He brought his wife back to Haifa, where two children were born to them. The Ministry of Interior refused to register the children as Jews on Shalit's request because the Halakha stipulates that the mother's religion is the sole determinant of the children's religion. Following the court's ruling that the Halakhic test may not be the only applicable one, a more pluralistic approach was adopted, whereby specific circumstances may warrant registration of children as Jewish even if their mother is not. Beyond the specifics of the case, the court's ruling in *Shalit* may thus be seen as a major judicial statement on the place of Halakha in Israeli law and policy.

In 1989, the SCI held that for purposes of immigration, any person who converted to Judaism outside Israel, whether under the auspices of an Orthodox, Conservative, or Reform religious institution, was automatically entitled to all the rights of an *oleh* (Jewish immigrant), as stated in the Law of Return and the Citizenship Law.[14] In 1995 the SCI was once again drawn into the muddy waters of identity politics. This time the question before the court was whether a person who underwent non-Orthodox conversion in Israel was entitled to automatic citizenship based on the right of return in the same way in which someone who converted outside Israel would be. The court avoided giving a clear answer while explicitly reaffirming its 1989 ruling validating non-Orthodox conversions made abroad.[15]

Following this ruling, an increasing number of non-Jewish persons residing in Israel (primarily foreign workers and non-Jewish immigrants from the former Soviet Union) went abroad to pursue non-Orthodox conversion to claim the benefits awarded by the state to those newcomers recognized as Jews. In response, the Ministry of the Interior (controlled at the time by the religious Shas Party, representing mainly religious Mizrahi Jews of North African and Mediterranean origin) renewed its refusal to recognize Reform and Conservative conversions to Judaism made abroad, despite the SCI's ruling. In 2002 the court responded with a historic decision (9–2) reaffirming non-Orthodox conversions to Judaism performed abroad.[16] In another landmark ruling on the subject (2005) the court agreed (7–4) to recognize non-Orthodox "bypass" conversions

[14] HCJ 264/87 *Sepharadi Torah Guardians, Shas Movement v. Population Registrar*, 43(2) P.D. 723.

[15] HCJ 1031/93 *Pessaro (Goldstein) et al. v. Ministry of Interior*, 49(4) P.D. 661.

[16] HCJ 5070/95 *Conservative Movement v. Minister of Religious Affairs*, (2002) 1 TakEl 634.

to Judaism performed de jure abroad but de facto in Israel.[17] It held that a person who came to Israel as a non-Jew and, during a period of lawful residence there, underwent conversion in a recognized Jewish community abroad would be considered Jewish. In its judgment the court stated: "The Jewish nation is one.... It is dispersed around the world, in communities. Whoever converted to Judaism in one of these communities overseas has joined the Jewish nation by so doing, and is to be seen as a "Jew" under the Law of Return. This can encourage immigration to Israel and maintain the unity of the Jewish nation in the Diaspora and in Israel." Few could articulate the Zionist-nationalist (and anti-Orthodox) view of Judaism in present-day Israel more potently.

Thus it is hardly surprising that in 2009 the court (in a decision written by the then Chief Justice Dorit Beinisch) went on to apply equal-opportunity principles and order the government to fund non-Orthodox conversion study programs, just as it has been funding Orthodox conversion programs. In 2012, the court confirmed the validity of thousands of conversions to Judaism that had been previously annulled by the Orthodox-controlled rabbinical court system for being allegedly too lenient or insincere.[18] These conversions, mainly by immigrants from the former Soviet Union, were initially validated by special conversion courts established by the government to circumvent the rabbinical courts' stringent requirements that were seen as deterring immigrants from converting. "The Rabbinical Court of Appeals rode roughshod over basic procedural rules and the principles of natural justice," wrote Chief Justice Beinisch in her verdict. "It demonstrated contempt for the special conversion courts, and above all, it hurt and did a shocking injustice to the petitioners and their children."[19]

Another pinnacle of the SCI's liberalizing jurisprudence in matters of religion and state is its subjection of the religious courts' jurisprudential autonomy in matters of personal status to the general principles of administrative and constitutional law, most notably due process and gender equality. This has had far-reaching implications in areas as diverse as family and personal-status law, representation in statutory religious bodies, and gender equality in the religious labor market. In Israel, no unified civil law applies to all citizens in matters of marriage and divorce.

---

[17] HCJ 2597/99 *Thais-Rodriguez Tushbaim v. Minister of Interior*, [2005] IsrSC 59(6).
[18] HCJ 5079/08 *Plonit ("Jane Doe") v. Rabbi Avraham Sherman et al.* (decision released on April 25, 2012; not yet published).
[19] Ibid.

Instead, for various political and historical reasons (the roots of contemporary Israeli family law go back as far as the Ottoman Empire's premodern millet system), the courts of the different religious communities hold exclusive jurisdiction over marriage, divorce, and directly associated personal-status matters. A number of other personal-status matters may be adjudicated through the rabbinical court system (controlled by Orthodox Judaism) if the involved parties consent to such extended jurisdiction. Muslim, Christian, and Druze courts also have exclusive jurisdiction over the personal-status affairs of their respective communities.

Since the mid-1990s the SCI has gradually been attempting to limit the authority exercised by religious courts. The most important SCI judgment regarding these matters was rendered in 1995 in the *Bavli* case.[20] In several earlier decisions, the SCI ruled that religious tribunals must comply with provisions of concrete laws pertinent to their operation and jurisdictional boundaries. In its ruling in *Bavli* the SCI expanded considerably its overarching review of religious tribunals' jurisprudence by holding that all religious tribunals, including the Great Rabbinical Court, are statutory bodies established by law and funded by the state; in principle, all aspects of their judgments are thus subject to review by the Supreme Court. Although the SCI recognized the special jurisdictional mandate awarded to Jewish, Muslim, Christian, and Druze courts by the legislature, it nevertheless asserted its power to impose fundamental constitutional norms on their exercise of authority.[21] Rabbinical court officials have responded by publicly asserting their resistance to the idea that the Supreme Court, as a secular entity, possesses the authority to review their adjudication, which rests on religious law. Some have gone so far as to declare their intention to ignore the court's ruling in *Bavli*, which they perceive as an illegitimate intrusion into their exclusive jurisdictional sphere. The Supreme Court was not impressed.

On the basis of its landmark decision in *Bavli*, the SCI went on to overturn at least two dozen other rabbinical court and Shari'a court

---

[20] HCJ 1000/92 *Bavli v. The Great Rabbinical Court*, 48(2) P.D. 6. On Shari'a court jurisdiction, see CA 3077/90 *Plonit ("Jane Doe") v. Ploni ("John Doe")*, 49(2) P.D. 578.

[21] On the potentially groundbreaking implications of the court's decision in Bavli on women's rights, in particular in the personal-status disputes, see Ayelet Shachar and Ran Hirschl, "Constitutional Transformation, Gender Equality, and Religious/National Conflict in Israel: Tentative Progress through the Obstacle Course," in Beverly Baines and Ruth Rubio-Marin eds., *The Gender of Constitutional Jurisprudence* (New York: Cambridge University Press, 2005), 205–29.

rulings for not conforming with general principles of Israel's constitutional and administrative law, including gender equality, reasonableness,
proportionality, natural justice, and procedural fairness. In *Katz* (1996),
the court held that the rabbinical courts were not authorized to declare
an individual who refused to have a civil matter adjudicated by the rabbinical court excommunicated or ostracized. The majority opinion stated
that because the rabbinical court system is a public organ that exists by
force of law and draws its authorities from the law, it could only exercise
those prerogatives vested in it by law.[22] A year later, the court overturned a rabbinical court decision that held that a divorced father who
had become religious was entitled to decide where his children would be
educated, even though his wife, who remained secular, had been granted
custody of the children.[23] In 1998, the court overturned another rabbinical court decision that had forced a divorcee to send her son to a religious
school at the demand of her ex-husband.[24] In a similar spirit, the Supreme
Court ruled in March 2001 that the rabbinical courts were unauthorized
to decide on a request by a man to prohibit his ex-wife from letting their
children spend time with her lesbian partner.[25]

A fascinating illustration of this trend is the court's ruling in *Plonit*
("Jane Doe") v. The Great Rabbinical Court (2008).[26] Section 5 of the
Property Relations between Spouses Law (*Hok Yahasei Mammon bein
Bnei Zug* 1973, amended in 1995) states that in case of divorce, the couple's assets will be split evenly between the two spouses regardless of the
formal registration status of these assets. However, Section 8 of that law
grants courts the authority to determine "special circumstances" in which
an uneven split may be justified. In *Plonit*, a woman who married her husband in 1985 had an extramarital affair in 2003 that eventually brought
about the breakup of her marriage. The Great Rabbinical Court ruled
that the wife's unfaithful behavior constituted "special circumstances,"
and that the husband was entitled to more than half of the couple's assets,
in this case, pension monies owed to him.

---

[22] HCJ 3269/95 *Katz v. Jerusalem Regional Rabbinical Court*, 50(4) P.D. 590.

[23] HCJ 5507/96 *Amir v. Haifa District Court*, 50(3) P.D. 321.

[24] HCJ 5227/97 *David v. Great Rabbinical Court*, 55(1) P.D. 453. Matters of marriage and
divorce fall under the exclusive jurisdiction of rabbinical courts. Matters of children's
education are not within the realm of the rabbinical courts' jurisdiction, unless it is
"bound up" expressly in the suit to the rabbinical court.

[25] HCJ 293/00 *Plonit ("Jane Doe") v. Great Rabbinical Court*, 55(3) P.D. 318.

[26] HCJ 8928/06 *Plonit ("Jane Doe") v. The Great Rabbinical Court* (decision released on
October 8, 2008).

On appeal, the SCI used its reasoning in *Bavli* to overturn the ruling. It accepted the wife's argument that the Great Rabbinical Court ruling did not comply with earlier SCI decisions, which stated that adulterous behavior may justify neither a departure from the presumption of an even split nor a retroactive negation of the adulterous spouse's rights to accumulated property in the years before his or her extramarital affair. Even more important, the SCI rejected the husband's claim that the law assigned to either the rabbinical court or the general court dealing with the matter the authority to decide what "special circumstances" were in this context. The SCI stated decisively that the two systems are not parallel, but unitary. Rulings of the rabbinical court system, including rulings of the Great Rabbinical Court, are subject to review by the Supreme Court and must comply with pertinent jurisprudential principles established by the SCI over the years. One can hardly think of a greater blow to the rabbinical court system's jurisdictional autonomy. It is little wonder that religious parties, led by Shas, vow to pass laws that expand the jurisdiction of the rabbinical court system and exempt it from the Supreme Court's scrutiny.

But the struggle continues. In 2010, the SCI further expanded the scope of its review of rabbinical courts' application of the Property Relations between Spouses Law. In deciding the financial terms of split following divorce, the Great Rabbinical Court had factored in the gains and losses incurred to the pre-marriage assets of each spouse during the time of marriage. Because the husband's pre-marriage assets suffered a loss (but still far exceeded the wife's assets) while the wife's assets generated a moderate gain (but still fell far short of the husband's assets), the Great Rabbinical Court deviated from the even split rule in the husband's favor. On appeal by the wife, the SCI built on its established tradition of substantive review of religious court jurisprudence. It held that the value of an apartment purchased by the husband during the marriage, and jointly and commonly used by the couple throughout the marriage, is to be split evenly between the husband and the wife, even though the funds used for purchasing the apartment came largely from the husband's pre-marriage assets. Conjugal life in an apartment for a lengthy period of time, held the court, turns it into a joint "nest of the family" regardless of whose funds were used to purchase it.[27]

Although the SCI has pursued a distinctly liberalizing agenda in core matters of religion and state, it has also sought to protect the

---

[27] HCJ 5416/09 *Plonit ("Jane Doe") v. Ploni ("John Roe")* (decision released on February 10, 2010).

Zionist-nationalist version of Israel's "Jewishness" pillar of collective identity. In a landmark ruling in the *Citizenship Law/Family Unification* case (2006), the SCI upheld (in a divided 6–5, 263-page decision) a temporary amendment to the new Citizenship and Entry to Israel Law, which imposed age restrictions on the granting of Israeli citizenship and residency permits to Arab residents of the Occupied Territories who marry Israeli citizens.[28] Because the practice of marrying Palestinians is far more common among Israel's Arab minority, the law limiting family unification and spousal naturalization effectively singles out Arab citizens while maintaining the demographic balance in favor of members of Israel's Jewish population, who seldom marry Palestinians and whose noncitizen spouses are often naturalized by way of marriage to an Israeli (Jewish) citizen. The dividing line between the majority and dissenting opinions was between the six justices who favored the first tenet in Israel's self-definition as a Jewish and democratic state and the five justices (including then Chief Justice Aharon Barak) who gave priority to the second. In 2012, the court upheld (6–5) the law's final version. Chief Justice Beinisch sided with the dissenting opinion, arguing that the law denied Israeli-Arabs' equal opportunity to family life. However, the majority ruled that "the right to a family life does not necessarily have to be realized within the borders of Israel." The court's incoming Chief Justice, Asher Grunis, wrote that "human rights cannot be enacted at the price of national suicide" (referring to what has been termed in Israeli public discourse as "the demographic threat" to the Jewish character of the state).

At any rate, the landmark SCI rulings in the *Citizenship Law/Family Unification* cases were certainly not the first time the nature of Israel's Jewish character has been tested in court against other fundamental constitutional values. In the *Meatrael* affair, one of the first post-1992 cases dealing with the normative foundations of Israel, a prima facie contradiction was raised between the constitutional right to freedom of occupation and Israel's primary character as a Jewish state. Meatrael, a private company that intended to import non-kosher meat products into Israel, appealed to the SCI against the refusal of the Ministry of Religious Affairs to license the company to do so. The company argued that the ministry's decision violated its constitutional right to freedom of occupation. The ministry's refusal was based on the claim that Israel's Jewish character

---

[28] HCJ 7052/03 *Adalah v. Minister of Interior,* [2006] 2 TakEl 1754 (Citizenship Law/ Family Unification case I).

was one of the state's supreme constitutional norms and thus had priority over any other norm.[29]

In its first decision on the case the court declared the refusal of the Ministry of Religious Affairs unconstitutional because it contradicted the principles of the new Basic Law by infringing the company's right to engage in any legal economic initiative. Subsequently, under pressure from religious parties, the Basic Law was amended (in the spirit of the Canadian "notwithstanding clause" – Section 33 of the Charter of Rights and Freedoms) to allow for future modifications by ordinary laws endorsed by an absolute majority of Knesset members. An amendment forbidding the import of non-kosher meat was subsequently enacted in 1994. On the basis of the new 1994 Meat Law the government renewed its refusal to license the import of non-kosher meat. In response, Meatrael appealed to the Supreme Court again, arguing for its constitutional right to engage in any legal economic initiative. This time the court ruled against the company on the basis of the reasonableness of the new Meat Law, in light of the amendments made to the Basic Law. Behind this decision, however, lay immense political pressure for the court to prevent any further erosion of the conception of "Israel as a Jewish state" as the highest constitutional norm. In spite of its somewhat anticlimactic ending – the legislature ultimately managed to circumvent judicial scrutiny of its decision – the *Meatrael* affair clearly illustrated the SCI's commitment to breaking the religious establishment's monopoly over the definition of Judaism and provision of religious services.

A closely related frontier of secular/religious struggle is the scope of religious authorities' prerogative over the issuance of *kashrut* (kosher; meaning "fit" or "legitimate" for consumption according to Jewish dietary and food-preparation restrictions) certificates by the Chief Rabbinate. Historically the Chief Rabbinate has refused to issue *kashrut* certificates for businesses that either deal with both kosher and non-kosher foods or sell only kosher food but violate other religious norms (e.g., they operate on the Sabbath, engage in indecent acts, or deal with businesses that do not keep kosher). This practice draws on a rather expansive reading by the Chief Rabbinate of its legal mandate to consider "exclusively kosher food norms" when issuing such certificates. In a series of rulings in the last two decades the court came to the rescue and compelled the

---

[29] HCJ 3872/93 *Meatrael Ltd. v. Prime Minister and Minister of Religious Affairs*, 47(5) P.D. 485; HCJ 5009/94 *Meatrael Ltd. v. The Council of the Chief Rabbinate of Israel*, 48(5) P.D. 617; HCJ 4676/94, *Meatrael Ltd. v. The Knesset*, 50(5) P.D. 15.

Chief Rabbinate to issue kosher food certificates to businesses that sell kosher food regardless of their other practices. This line of rulings reached a peak in 2002 when the SCI harshly criticized the Chief Rabbinate for its continuous misuse of authority and irresponsible contempt of court rulings in illegally denying *kashrut* certificates to kosher meat producers trading with merchants of non-kosher foods.[30] Once again the court stressed that the Chief Rabbinate and the entire rabbinical court system were, first and foremost, statutory bodies created through state laws, and consequently, the decrees and verdicts issued by these bodies must conform with state laws and constitutional norms, even when they contradicted religious customs.

These jurisprudential outcomes are hardly surprising given the court's personal composition, which with very few exceptions has been similar to the country's historically powerful circles in its demographic characteristics.[31] Put bluntly, jurists who are opera goers, whose mothers knew Yiddish, and who own an apartment or two in an upscale neighborhood are much more likely to get appointed to the Supreme Court than those who celebrate the Mimoona (a Northern African Jewish feast), wear Tefillin (phylacteries) every weekday morning, speak fluent Arabic, were born in the former Soviet Union, or have a close family relative under the poverty line. As it happens, over two-thirds of the Israeli electorate falls into at least one of these latter categories.

In the meantime, and outside the courtroom, the political control over judicial appointments to religious tribunals has tightened. In 2008, for the first time in Israel's history, three new Great Rabbinical Court judges (*dayanim*) were sworn in during a ceremony held at the official residence of the president of Israel and took the same oath of office that is taken by civil court judges. Prior to that event, appointees to the rabbinical court system had been sworn in at the Chief Rabbinate. The "relocation" to the president's home and the justice minister's dominance in the appointments process itself reflect the transfer of ministerial authority over the religious court system from the Ministry of Religious Affairs to

---

[30] HCJ 7203/00 *Aviv Osoblanski Ltd. v. The Council of the Chief Rabbinate of Israel*, 56(2) P.D. 196.

[31] As of 2013, three judges (Rubinstein, Hendel, and Solberg) of the fifteen-member court may be considered moderately religious. Hendel is a U.S.-born career judge. Rubinstein was a career civil servant and attorney general prior to his appointment to the court. Both are considerably closer in their world views to the Zionist mainstream than to any ultra-Orthodox world view. Solberg, appointed in 2012, is the first ever resident of a West Bank Jewish settlement to serve as a Supreme Court judge.

the Ministry of Justice. It also symbolizes the greater significance that the state authorities assign to bringing the religious court system under full, non-sectarian government oversight.

A BRIEF PASSAGE TO MALAYSIA

Israeli and Malaysian jurists alike may begrudge the comparison, but there is a considerable resemblance in the relations between constitutional law and religious difference in the two countries. Akin to Israel, Malaysia provides a captivating yet seldom explored illustration of the subtle religion-taming function of constitutional jurisprudence. Malaysia, despite its vast socioeconomic disparity, is one of Asia's economic tigers and a major tourist destination. Its capital, Kuala Lumpur, is one of Asia's most bustling business centers – home of the landmark Petronas Twin Towers, as well as the Menara Kuala Lumpur, currently the world's fifth-tallest telecommunications tower. Putrajaya, Malaysia's new administrative capital next to Kuala Lumpur, features a fully electronic government, matching with its neighboring planned city Cyberjaya, in accordance with former Prime Minister Mahathir bin Mohamad's vision of Malaysia as the "Japan of the Islamic world."[32]

At the same time, however, the Malaysian political sphere, at both the state and federal levels, has undergone substantial Islamization over the last three decades. The Pan-Malaysian Islamic Party (Parti Islam Se-Malaysia, PAS) has been gaining political support and clout since the 1980s. It enjoys strong support in the overwhelmingly Muslim and largely conservative states of Kelantan and Terengganu and to a somewhat lesser degree in the more mixed states of Kedah (bordering southern Thailand), Penang, and Selangor. In the 2008 general elections, a coalition of PAS and its allies (the Pakatan Rakyat coalition, PKR), won 82 of the 222 seats, whereas the governing National Front (Barisan Nasional, BN) coalition won 140 seats. The difference in actual votes was very slim: approximately 4.1 million votes for the BN coalition (or 50.1 percent) and approximately 3.8 million votes for the Pakatan Rakyat coalition (46.4 percent). The trend intensified in the hotly contested 2013 general elections, when the PKR (led by the colorful and charismatic Anwar Ibrahim) received the majority of the popular vote (approximately 5.6 million votes or 50.9 percent), whereas the BN headed by PM Najib Razak, garnered

---

[32] Osman Bakar, "Malaysian Islam in the Twenty-First Century," in *Asian Islam in the 21st Century*, ed. John Esposito et al. (New York: Oxford University Press, 2008), 84.

approximately 5.25 million votes or 47.3 percent of the popular vote.[33] Nonetheless, as a result of Malaysia's rather peculiar electoral system, the BN has still managed to secure 133 seats in the 222-seat parliament as opposed to 89 seats won by the PKR.

Over the past two decades, PAS has positioned itself as a party that aims to reorient the Malaysian polity and Constitution on Islamic legal theory derived from the primary sources of Islam, the Qur'an, Sunna, and Hadiths. It is viewed as a counter-establishment, "periphery against the center" voice in Malaysian politics. In contrast, the National Front BN coalition, led by the historically hegemonic United Malay National Organization (UMNO) – the establishment party – adopts the more mainstream Islam Hadhari doctrine (a moderate or "civilizational" Islam), which PAS sees as based on a watered-down, compromised, and secularized understanding of Islam. This has brought to the fore the constitutional status of Islam as Malaysia's state religion and as a marker of Malay collective identity.

The rise of political Islam has affected the mainstream moderate establishment. Even politicians affiliated with the BN must now resort to "religious talk" in their appeal to the Islamic vote. The former Prime Minister of Malaysia, Mahathir bin Mohamad of the corporate nationalist UMNO, the largest political party in Malaysia and the pillar of the BN coalition, declared in September 2001 that the country was an Islamic State (*negara Islam*), not merely a country that had endorsed Islam as its official religion. This broad Islamization of public life is also reflected in an increasing number of ultraconservative rulings by the National Fatwa Council, Malaysia's top clerical Islamic body. Two 2008 examples are an edict that girls who act like boys or women dressing and behaving like men violate the tenets of Islam and the more ethnically charged ruling that

---

[33] Interestingly, the PKR coalition was led in the 2008 general elections by Wan Azizah Wan Ismail, the wife of prominent opposition leader Anwar Ibrahim, head of the PKR, who assumed the position of opposition leader in August 2008, having served a prison term for alleged corruption and homosexual conduct. Ibrahim served in several ministerial posts and was deputy prime minister from 1993 to 1998, was initially a protégé of the establishment Prime Minister Mahathir bin Mohamad before emerging as the most prominent pro-Malay critic of Mahathir's administration. During his tenure as education minister, Ibrahim introduced numerous pro-Malay policies in the national school curriculum, most prominently renaming the national language from Bahasa Malaysia to Bahasa Melayu in 1991, thereby implying that Malaysia is first and foremost a Malay country. In 2008, Ibrahim was accused again of sexual harassment of a male intern in his party offices. He went on trial in February 2010 and was acquitted in January 2012. Many observers believe that the repeated allegations against Ibrahim are politically motivated.

the practice of Yoga could corrupt Muslins because it involves not just physical exercise but also includes Hindu spiritual elements, chanting, and worship. Prime Minister Abdullah Ahmad Badawi of the UMNO moved to contain the damage, telling the national news agency Bernama that Muslims could continue doing yoga as a type of physical exercise but should refrain from the spiritual chanting.

Consider another telling anecdote. In accordance with Islam's prohibition of the consumption of alcohol, government regulations in Malaysia prohibit concerts from being sponsored by makers of alcoholic beverages. An exception to the rule was made in 2009 for a concert in Kuala Lumpur by the hip-hop group Black Eyed Peas, who were sponsored by the Irish beer company Guinness. The brewery was celebrating its 250th anniversary by sponsoring celebrations around the world; Malaysian authorities thought that the concert would promote tourism. So the concert did go on, albeit without any Muslim Malaysians – approximately 60 percent of the population – because of another recent government regulation prohibiting ethnic Malays (Muslims) from attending events that promote the consumption of alcohol in public. However, non-Malays (i.e., tourists or non-Muslim residents of Malaysia) aged eighteen and over were encouraged by the Ministry of Information, Communication, and Culture to attend the concert and have fun. This is multilayered Malaysia in the early twenty-first century.

The Constitution of 1963 establishes Malaysia as an Islamic State blended with liberal principles (dare we say "Islamic and democratic"?) where "Islam is the religion of the Federation; but other religions may be practiced in peace and harmony in any part of the Federation" (Article 3), and where "every person has the right to profess and practice his religion and to propagate it" (Article 11.1). Furthermore, "every religious group has the right to manage its own religious affairs" (Article 11.3), whereas state law (and, in the Federal Territories of Kuala Lumpur and Labuan, federal law) "may control or restrict the propagation of any religious doctrine or belief among persons professing the religion of Islam" (Article 11.4). To further complicate matters, and mirroring aspects of Israeli law, Malaysian law draws on religious ascriptions to establish what has been termed *ethnic democracy*, where, despite the existence of some ethnic power-sharing mechanisms and an accompanying façade of interracial harmony, Malay political dominance is ensured. Core elements of the political system are organized so as to benefit members of the Malay ethnic group to the detriment of others, and members of minority ethnic groups are not granted proportional access to power. Although

Islam is constitutionally enshrined as Malaysia's state religion, over one-third of Malaysia's population consists of members of other denominations, mainly Buddhists, Hindus, and Christians. However, ethnic Malays (*Bumiputra* or "sons of the soil"), generally Muslim, are granted constitutionally entrenched preferential treatment in various aspects of public life over members of other ethnic groups (Article 153 of the Constitution). Malay citizens who convert out of Islam are no longer considered Malay under the law and hence forfeit the Bumiputra privileges afforded to Malays under Article 153. In other words, Malaysia is a country of all its citizens yet at the same time a country that privileges its Muslim citizens over the non-Muslim ones, all while fostering a national meta-narrative of inter-ethnic peace and harmony.

In the face of this growing Islamization, Malaysia's establishment-supporting judicial elite turned to constitutional division of powers between the federal and state governments to effectively block religious parties-led governments in the states of Kelantan and Terengganu from instituting Qur'an- and Sunna-based *hudood* and *qisas* (retaliation) law as the basis for their criminal code. Although the Kelantan State Assembly passed the Syariah (Malay for "Shari'a") Criminal Enactment in 1993, it has yet to be implemented, mainly because criminal law is in federal hands. According to the Federal Constitution, Syariah courts do not have jurisdiction over offenses "except in so far as conferred by federal law"; state authorities can only legislate for Islamic offenses "except in regard to matters included in the Federal List" (e.g., criminal law and procedure). What is more, Article 75 provides: "If any State law is inconsistent with a federal law, the federal law shall prevail and the State law shall, to the extent of the inconsistency, be void." Finally, item 4(k) in the list of matters falling under federal jurisdiction provides that "[a]scertainment of Islamic Law and other personal laws for purposes of federal law" is a federal matter.

Although the power to create and punish offenses against the precepts of Islam has been assigned by the Constitution to the states, Syariah courts have jurisdiction only over persons professing the religion of Islam. Further, the enactment of *hudood* as state law runs counter to Article 11 (freedom of religion), which has been interpreted to protect individuals against prosecution on the basis of choice of religion. What is more, Article 8 provides that every citizen is equal before the law, hence rendering the blanket application of *hudood* laws arguably unconstitutional because they discriminate against non-Muslims and women. Finally, as the Malaysian Federal Court – the country's supreme court since 1985 – has observed on numerous occasions, Malaysian public law is secular, and unless the Federal Constitution is amended to reflect the Syariah law as the supreme or basic law, this remains the case. The Federal Constitution has not been amended to reflect that position. Article 4(1) still declares that the Federal Constitution is the supreme law.

The religious-secular duality embedded in the Malaysian legal system is further reflected in the changing jurisdictional interrelation between the civil and Syariah courts. Muslims (and non-Muslims who marry Muslims) are obliged to follow the decisions of Syariah courts in matters concerning their religion, most notably marriage, inheritance, apostasy, conversion, and custody. Historically the civil and Syariah courts existed side by side in a dual court structure established at the time of Malaysia's independence, with the prevalent understanding that Syariah courts were subordinate to the civil courts and that the common law was superior to other laws. In a landmark ruling in 1984, the Federal Court, then known as the Supreme Court of Malaysia, held that the common law had not been ousted or otherwise affected by the introduction of the Federal Constitution and that it would allow secular courts to resolve legal issues even where the parties to the case were Muslims.[34] However, in 1988 an amendment to the Constitution, Article 121(1A), was introduced; it provided that civil courts "shall have no jurisdiction in respect of any matter within the jurisdiction of the Syariah Courts."

Even after the 1988 amendment the civil court system continued to view Syariah courts as subordinates and, at any rate, subject to general principles of administrative and constitutional law. The civil courts consistently interpreted the jurisdictional boundaries between the two court systems so as to prevent the expansion of the Syariah court system. Likewise, the Malaysian Bar Council has continued to argue that Article 121(1A) does not exclude the supervisory review power of the Federal Court. However, because Islam has become a major political force in Malaysia, taking an anti-Islamist stand on the question of jurisdictional boundaries is no longer a feasible option for the court. It has opted instead for a strategy of mixed messages and vagueness. Several landmark rulings illustrate this trend.

With respect to the challenge of religious attire in the public sector, the Federal Court (and the Supreme Court of Malaysia before it) has taken a measured approach. In the leading case on the matter (*Kamaruddin v. Public Service Commission Malaysia*, 1994), the Supreme Court applied

---

[34] Che Omar bin Che Soh v. Public Prosecutor, [1984] 1 MLJ 113.

the "mandatory practice test" to determine that the wearing of *purdah* (a veil-like head and neck cover) by a Muslim woman while on her public service work may be restricted by law since it is not an indispensable practice within Islam.[35] In 2006, the Federal Court of Malaysia upheld the constitutionality of the School Regulation Act (1997), which prohibited the wearing of the turban (*serban*) as part of the school uniform, since "this 'practice' was of little significance from the point of view of the religion of Islam."[36] The court made clear that if the practice in question is compulsory or "an integral part" of the religion, courts should give more weight to it, but that since it is not, they should assign it less weight.

More contested is the matter of conversion. The *Lina Joy* case (2007) raised the question of Syariah courts' jurisdictional authority over apostasy in a case of conversion out of Islam.[37] Ms. Lina Joy, who was born Azalina Jailani, claimed to have converted from Islam to Christianity and argued that her conversion was protected by the right to freedom of religion under Article 11 of the Constitution. Because of this, she claimed that she had the right to convert to Christianity without being designated as apostate. However, the National Registration Department refused to change her name or her religious status as they appeared on her identity card on the grounds that the Syariah court had not granted permission for her to renounce Islam. In other words, Lina Joy questioned the hierarchy of three core tenets of Malaysian constitutional order: Shari'a court jurisdiction over conversion, individual religious freedoms, and the ethnic issue (conversion out of Islam undermines one's Bumiputra status). Following a long legal battle, the case reached the Federal Court of Malaysia, which ruled (by a 2–1 vote) in May 2007 that approvals of conversions out of Islam fall under the exclusive jurisdiction of the Syariah court system. In other words, the court refused to limit the jurisdictional boundaries of Syariah courts in Malaysia, even at the cost of infringing on general principles of freedom of religion or formal gender equality.

However, only two months later the Federal Court sent a somewhat different message in the *Latifa Mat Zin* case (2007), an inheritance dispute that raised the question whether the applicable law was the Islamic law of gifts (*hibah*) or the federal law of banking or contract.[38] Although

---

[35] Kamaruddin v. Public Services Commission Malaysia, [1994] 3 MLJ 61.

[36] Meor Atiqulrahman Ishak et al. v. Fatimah Sihi et al., (2006) 4 CLJ 1. See also Jaclyn L. Neo, "Religious Dress in Schools: The *Serban* Controversy in Malaysia," *International and Comparative Law Quarterly* 55 (2006): 671–88.

[37] Lina Joy v. Majlis Agama Islam Wilayah Persekutuan, [2007] 4 MLJ 585.

[38] Latifa Mat Zin v. Rosmawati Binti Sharibun, [2007] 5 MLJ 101.

the court sided with the claimant, holding that Islamic law should apply in the particular situation under dispute, it also stated clearly that "[i]n case an application to the syariah court is resisted on the ground that the syariah court has no jurisdiction in the matter, let me answer that question right now. Interpretation of the Federal Constitution is a matter for this court, not the syariah court. [If] this court says that the syariah court has jurisdiction, [then] it has."[39]

The court's cautious navigation through this politically charged jurisdictional quagmire continued in the *Subashini* case (2007).[40] The originally Hindu husband of a Hindu woman converted to Islam in 2006 and went on to convert their elder son as well. The husband then applied to the Syariah court to dissolve the couple's civil marriage and to obtain custody of both their sons. The Federal Court, in another 2–1 equivocal ruling, held that the civil court has jurisdiction over marriage and divorce, as well as over custody of children in a civil marriage, even when one spouse has converted to Islam, because the original marriage took place when both parties were Hindus. At the same time, the court held that the consent of only one parent was sufficient for a conversion of the children to be lawful. To support its ruling, as well as to increase the legitimacy of this and several other contested decisions, the court cited several solicited opinions of respected religious scholars. These opinions and their authors' academic credentials (including their postsecondary degrees, the institutions of higher learning they attended, and their main publications) were cited in great detail by the court, presumably to signal the court's respect for sacred law. At any rate, the court granted a partial victory to each side of the dispute, compounding the jurisprudential ambiguity. Or, to be more colloquial, it threw each side a chewy bone, while jurisprudential wishy-washiness reigned. What better way to maintain the court's legitimacy while avoiding the possible wrath of influential stakeholders from both sides?

The matter of single-parent consent for the conversion of a child continues to be a hot-button issue in Malaysian constitutional politics. In July 2013, to pick a recent example, the High Court of Malaya in Ipoh (Perak) voided the Muslim conversion certificates of three Hindu minors, as the certificates had been issued based on a unilateral request of the children's originally Hindu, now convert-to-Islam father, and without their Hindu mother's knowledge or consent. The court cited principles of

[39] Ibid.
[40] Subashini v. Saravanan and other, [2008] 2 MLJ 147.

natural justice, breach of Perak legislation which required the children to be present at the time of the purported conversion ceremony, Malaysia's obligation under international law, and most importantly, the Federal Constitution as prescribing a mother's equal right to raise her children according to her faith. Specifically, the court held that the right to "life" and "liberty" protected by Article 5, and the right to practice one's religion in Article 11(1), included within it a right to determine one's child's religious upbringing and education.[41]

In the same year that both *Lina Joy* and *Subashini* were decided, a Catholic newspaper in Malaysia used the word "Allah" to refer to God in its Malay-language edition. A controversy arose regarding who may use the word "Allah": whether it is an exclusively Muslim word (as some Muslim leaders in Malaysia suggest) or a neutral term referring to One God that may be used by all regardless of their religion as the newspaper argued. A law was enacted in the 1980s to ban the use of the term in reference to God by non-Muslims but had seldom been enforced prior to 2007. On December 31, 2009, the High Court in Kuala Lumpur ruled that the ban on non-Muslims using the word "Allah" to refer to God was unconstitutional as it infringed on freedom of expression and freedom of religion principles. The court went on to state that the word "Allah" is the correct word for "God" in various Malay translations of the Bible and that it has been used for centuries by Christians and Muslims alike in Arabic-speaking countries. This ruling was viewed by radical Islamists as a legitimation of deceitful attempts to convert Muslims to Christianity. Riots and church burning followed. The government appealed the High Court ruling, and the implementation of the decision has been suspended until the appeal is heard. In October 2013, Malaysia's Court of Appeal (in a three-judge, all-Muslim bench) upheld the ban on the use of the term "Allah" in reference to God by non-Muslims.

The blurred jurisdictional matrix in Malaysia has given rise to a jurisdictional "war of courts." Aided by increased public support, Syariah courts in several states have begun to suggest that they are authorized to interpret relevant aspects of the Constitution itself (i.e., to go beyond the interpretation and application of Shari'a law). In its judgment in the *Abdul Kahar bin Ahmad* case (2008) the Federal Court dismissed – in an atypically decisive tone – an argument that the 1988 amendment and, in particular, Article 121(1A) conferred jurisdiction on Syariah courts to interpret the Constitution in matters falling under the jurisdiction of such

---

[41] JR 25/10/2009 M. Indira Gandhi v. Pengarah Jabatan Agama Islam Perak et al. (decision released July 25, 2013).

courts. The Federal Court stated: "Before the jurisdiction of this court is excluded it must be shown that the Syariah Court has jurisdiction over the matter first. That is not the case here. . . . The constitutionality of any law, whether a law made by Parliament or by the Legislature of a State . . . is a matter for this court to decide, not the Syariah High Court."[42] The Majlis Agam Islam of Selangor – that state's Islamic council – argued that Article 121(1A) granted full and exclusive jurisdiction to the Syariah court to decide whether a practice falls within the precepts of Islam regardless of its constitutionality. In other words, the Syariah court suggested that the matter of jurisdiction itself should be decided under Shari'a law. The Federal Court countered by ruling that "nowhere in the Constitution is there a provision that the determination of Islamic Law for the purpose of interpreting the Federal Constitution is a matter for the State Legislature."[43] The court held that Article 121(1A) was not inserted "to oust the jurisdiction of this court in matters that rightly belong to it."[44] The entire realm of the constitutionality of state law, however Shari'a-based it may be, can be decided only by the Federal Court.

In short, the Malaysian Federal Court has used constitutionally enshrined principles of federalism to block attempts to expand the ambit of Shari'a law. Operating within an increasingly Islamic political environment, it has been wrestling with the harmonization of constitutional and Shari'a law on a case-by-case basis. Although it has been sending mixed messages with regard to the scope and nature of the 1988 constitutional amendment that established the exclusive jurisdiction of Syariah courts in personal-status matters, it has also asserted its authority vis-à-vis the religious establishment as the sole and ultimate interpreter of Malaysia's Federal Constitution.

CONCLUSION: THE EFFECTS OF CONSTITUTIONALIZING RELIGION

Constitutional law and courts are important mechanisms for the management of religious difference. As is well known, the eighteenth century saw the emergence of a doctrine of separation of church and state, advocated by Enlightenment thinkers as a means of confining dangerous and irrational religious passions to the private sphere. Whereas the public sphere was portrayed as the realm of reason, the private sphere began

---

[42] Abdul Kahar bin Ahmad v. Kerajaan Negeri Selangor Darul Ehsan, (2008) 4 CLJ 309.
[43] Ibid.   [44] Ibid.

to be regarded as the realm of faith, superstition, and other such non-verifiable beliefs. In creating its characteristic division between secular public space and religious private space, European secularism sought to shuffle religious ritual and discipline into the private realm.[45] This distinction, however reductionist and otherwise problematic, has come to be identified as the secularist state's defining marker.

Perhaps counter-intuitively, the opposite model – strong constitutional establishment of religion – may also be used as a mechanism for the containment of religion. In religious-laden polities, the constitutionalization of religion allows the modern state and its pragmatist leaders to elicit most of the nation-building and legitimacy-enhancing benefits of enshrining religion as an aspirational source of collective identity. At the same time, it brings religion under state (constitutional) control and subjects the translation of religious precepts into guidelines for public life to the overarching authority of the state's constitutional order. In that respect, the constitutionalization of religion "formats" and domesticates religion in a way that maintains its benefits for the aspirational state, while attempting to disarm religion of some of its potentially radical edge. Whether this is done through a friendly takeover, a hostile bid, or through some other way, the constitutional establishment of religion and its interlocutors helps the statist project bring religion under check.

That courts in expressly "separationist" regimes of state-and-religion (e.g., France) take an overall religion-limiting stance is not surprising. A notably harder challenge to the constitutional containment of religion is posed by constitutional orders that feature a central place for religion. However, as this brief exploration of constitutional law and religion in two religion-infused polities indicates, even in such settings the constitutional domain has advanced a relatively moderate understanding of religion's place in law and public life. A look at the actual constitutional jurisprudence of religion in Israel and Malaysia reveals that despite the considerable dissimilarities in context, there are some striking parallels in the way in which the constitutional courts in these (and possibly in some other similarly situated countries) have positioned themselves as important religion-taming forces relative to the political setting within which they operate. This may suggest that the constitutional domain's

---

[45] See Talal Asad, Genealogies of Religion: Discipline and Reasons of Power in Christianity and Islam (Baltimore, MD: Johns Hopkins University Press, 1993); David Scott and Charles Hirschkind, eds., Powers of the Secular Modern: Talal Asad and His Interlocutors (Standford, CA: Stanford University Press, 2006).

antagonism toward alternative interpretive hierarchies, most notably religion and its interlocutors, is a universal phenomenon that manifests itself even in the least likely ("most difficult") of settings.

There are obvious instrumental and overtly political ways in which regimes maintain control over the judicial system so as to minimize the risk to prevalent worldviews and powerful interests. However, there seem to be embedded structural and epistemological reasons for the religion-taming tilt of constitutional jurisprudence, even in polities in which a given religion is granted constitutional recognition as a pillar of collective identity. The very logic of constitutional law, with its reasoned set of core tenets, prevalent modes of interpretation, and embedded emphasis on overarching state authority, makes it an attractive enterprise to those who wish to contain religiosity and assert state authority over religious texts, world views, and interpretive hierarchies. The fact that law emanates from the state is translated into state-appointed judges' principled reluctance to treat the organs of the state as subordinate to non-state, purportedly God-given religious directives.[46] Constitutional courts are inherently unsympathetic toward alternative hierarchies of authority and adjudication, which they constantly strive to bring under check.[47] There is a certain centralizing, "seeing like a state" tilt to their outlook.[48] The important role of rights provisions and jurisprudence in contemporary constitutional discourse, alongside the ever-increasing cross-jurisdictional fertilization in that area and the formation of a transnational epistemic community of jurists, adds to constitutional law's secularist appeal. The combination of a-religious propensities and interests, alongside creative interpretation that leads to religion-limiting jurisprudence, may explain why constitutional law and courts have become a secularist shrine in the post-secularist age. As we have seen, the complex labyrinth of constitutional law and religion in Israel and Malaysia – apparently idiosyncratic in many respects – provides vivid illustration of precisely that trend.

---

[46] *See, e.g.*, Martin Shapiro, *Courts: A Comparative and Political Analysis* (Chicago: University of Chicago Press, 1981); Sami Zubaida, *Law and Power in the Islamic World* (London: I.B. Tauris, 2003); Noah Feldman, *The Fall and Rise of the Islamic State* (Princeton: Princeton University Press, 2008).

[47] Ran Hirschl and Ayelet Shachar, "The New Wall of Separation: Permitting Diversity, Restricting Competition," *Cardozo Law Review* 30 (2009): 2535–60; Robert Cover, "The Supreme Court 1982 Term – Foreword: *Nomos* and Narrative," *Harvard Law Review* 97 (1983): 4–68.

[48] *See, e.g.*, James Scott, Seeing Like a State: How Certain Schemes to Improve the Human Condition Have Failed (New Haven: Yale University Press, 1998).

Part V

Gender and Sexuality

9

Australia's Gendered Constitutional History and Future*

Kim Rubenstein and Christabel Richards-Neville

INTRODUCTION

This volume enables us to think about constitutions and constitutionalism and difference in diverse ways. The countries discussed vary in multiple manners; some are democracies and others not, some are old and others new and they are all influenced in varying degrees by ethnicity, religion and language.

Our chapter draws on a project that has been ongoing in Australia since the publication of Deborah Cass and Kim Rubenstein's article "Re/presentations of Women in the Australian Constitutional System".[1] Underpinning this project is a view that although women and men may share many similar needs and concerns, when it comes to the political process there is the undeniable matter of practical reality that women experience the world differently to men, and they do so regardless of how many different voices women may have. Moreover, there is value in considering women both as a singular group, given that women account for more than half of the population, as well as considering the varying groups and needs within that singular group.

The chapter begins by identifying the various ways that feminist scholars have identified difference in their scholarship more broadly.

---

* This paper draws heavily on earlier work published by Kim Rubenstein as footnoted throughout and later research undertaken by Christabel Richards-Neville.

[1] Deborah Cass and Kim Rubenstein, "Re/presentations of Women in the Australian Constitutional System," *Adelaide Law Review* 17 (1995): 3. During the writing of this chapter we were very saddened by the news of the death of Deborah Cass and we urge readers to view this vale piece written by Kim Rubenstein about Deborah: http://blogs.usyd.edu.au/womansconstitution/2013/07/vale_deborah_zipporah_cass.html

It then turns to look at how women influenced the foundations of Australia's constitutional beginnings. An assessment of two foundational constitutional principles – representative democracy and federalism – follows to illustrate how these constitutional concepts can be viewed as gendered. Finally the chapter concludes with a suggestion about how we might refashion the Australian Constitution to assist in rethinking how best the Constitution caters for men and women in their daily lives, promoting a more egalitarian system and society.

We conclude that there is hope for the future of gender equality in Australia by looking beyond equality as a rights concept and by interrogating the architecture of the Constitution to achieve it. For instance, a natural consequence of the changing character of representative democracy is a need for a greater linkage between the elector and the electorate. This linkage must be achieved through the continuous participation of women in the democratic process. Our conclusion regarding federalism is more nuanced and suggests that its enormous potential to be positively gendered is largely underexploited.

GENDER AND DIFFERENCE

Questions of difference are central to much feminist legal scholarship and internal debate. As Margaret Thornton has explained:

> As with social theory generally, there is no agreed-upon perspective or unified notion of 'feminism' in feminist legal theory; it is multifaceted and heteroglossic, which is at once its strength and its Achilles heel. Overcoming the limitations associated with the unitary category 'woman' has caused an enriched notion of the legal subject to emerge, which is raced, sexualised and differently-abled, as well as sexed.[2]

Within that multifaceted discourse, the suggestion that women experience the world, and therefore the legal system, in a manner fundamentally differently from men has been significant in feminist analysis. In the 1980s Carol Gilligan's extensive fieldwork suggested that, empirically, boys and girls approach justice in different ways. Young girls, she observed, were less likely to approach problems on adversarial grounds with the understanding that the winner takes all. Rather, they tended to negotiate.

---

[2] Margaret Thornton, "Neoliberal Melancholia: The Case of Feminist Legal Scholarship," *Australian Feminist Law Journal* 20 (2004): 7–22.

They were less accepting of fundamental principles that should be applied to every situation and did not prioritize reason.[3] Gilligan's work supported the argument that certain differences have emerged between men and women and suggested that unless these differences were recognized the justice process would remain alienating to women. This approach demands that women's relationship with the law goes beyond formal equality and acknowledges that in some circumstances women should be treated differently. Consequently it legitimizes laws benefitting women because of biologically or socially constructed differences. This 'feminine' understanding of justice has also allowed innovative justice experiments such as South Africa's Truth and Reconciliation Commission, Rwanda's *gacaca* courts,[4] and Australia's restorative justice movement.[5]

However, as the Australian Law Reform Commission's 1994 report *Equality Before the Law* emphasised, this approach is not without controversy. First, women's unequal treatment has often been justified on the basis of their differences from men. There is therefore considerable danger in approaching feminist analysis only from a difference perspective. Another approach that has been useful in certain legal contexts is an equality approach – to enable women to have access to both formal and substantial rights that men enjoy. Both approaches, however, fail to challenge the primacy of men as the benchmark against which women's experiences are measured, by subconsciously retaining a male standard of reference.[6]

Catherine MacKinnon suggests a critique, which rejects both a difference approach and the desire for equality. In her view, the failure of the liberal feminist project is that although it has resulted in two schools of thought, they both offer the same answer when asked: 'What is gender a question of?' Both consider gender to be a question of difference. For the former women can be the same as men, whereas for the latter women can be different from men. Rather, McKinnon's answer is that

---

[3] Radhika Coomaraswamy, "Broken Glass: Women, Violence and the Rule of Law," in *The Rule of Law*, ed. Cheryl Saunders and Katherine Le Roy (Sydney: The Federation Press, 2003), 166.

[4] Philip Gourevitch, "The Life After," *New Yorker*, May 4, 2009, 38.

[5] Coomaraswamy, "Broken Glass," *supra* n. 3, 167.

[6] Australian Law Reform Commission, *Equality Before the Law: Women's Equality*, Report No. 69 (1994), 44 [3.12].

gender here is a matter of dominance, not difference. Feminists have noticed that women and men are equally different but not equally powerful. Explaining the subordination of women to men, a political condition, has nothing to do with difference, because the ideology of difference has been so central in its enforcement.[7]

Within McKinnon's paradigm, gender relations must always be understood as being centrally concerned with hierarchy. Although the top and the bottom of the hierarchy are certainly different, they are different because one is powerless, whereas the other is powerful, not because of engrained gender categories. The two answers offered by liberal feminists maintain men as the standard; women can be the same as men and be equal, or they can be different from men, and then they will be women and relegated to the bottom of the hierarchy.[8]

MacKinnon's challenge to feminist theory to centralize women's experiences and escape a male dictated paradigm has been criticised as upholding an establishment failing of liberal feminism, relying on the experiences of middle-class, white women. Angela Harris suggests that, although MacKinnon's work is "powerful and brilliant in many ways," it falls prey to gender essentialism[9] as it is predicated on being able to isolate a single "women's experience, that exists independent of race, creed, class, sexual orientation or nation."[10] It means "the voices that are silenced turn out to be the same voices silenced by the mainstream legal voice of 'We the People' – among them, the voices of black women."[11] In Australia, Larissa Behrendt reminds us that the experiences of indigenous Australian women and black American women are not analogous; however, Angela Harris' argument resonates within the history of Australian feminism. Behrendt suggests that indigenous women are alienated from a mainstream feminist movement that has traditionally neither fought for them nor shared the same goals.[12] Behrendt agrees with Harris' suggestion that an all-encompassing feminist jurisprudence can only be reached

---

[7] Catherine A. McKinnon, *Feminism Unmodified: Discourses on Life and Law* (Harvard: Harvard University Press, 1987), 51.

[8] Ellen C. Du Bois et al., "Feminist Discourse, Moral Values and the Law – A Conversation" (Paper presented at the 1984 James McCormick Mitchell Lecture, State University of New York, October 19, 1984): 21.

[9] Angela Harris, "Race and Essentialism in Feminist Legal Theory," *Standford Law Review* 42 (1990): 585.

[10] Ibid.   [11] Ibid.

[12] Larissa Behrendt, "Aboriginal Women and the White Lies of the Feminist Movement: Implications for Aboriginal Women in Rights Discourses" *Australian Feminist Law Journal* 1 (1993): 28, 34.

through the telling of individual stories, not the construction of grand single theories.[13]

This discussion highlights the importance of initial framework decisions; when we consider the way women experience difference we do so through many lenses: McKinnon's dominance frame, Gilligan's biological framework and liberal feminism's formal equality lens. It is with these concepts in mind that this chapter seeks to consider Australia's gendered constitutional history and its future, drawing on the individual stories and rethinking how our foundational document can best serve the individual and collective needs of men and women in the community.

AUSTRALIAN CONSTITUTIONAL FOUNDATIONS

Responding to Behrendt's call to tell the individual stories,[14] we begin by showcasing women's involvement in Australia's constitutional beginnings. Indeed, Australian Women's History month has dedicated the year 2013 to 'Finding Founding Mothers of the Australian Constitution'.[15]

Historically women were either grossly under-represented or totally absent from constitutional processes. An understanding of this historical exclusion is also necessary to appreciate the continuing under-representation and gender bias evident in women's interactions with constitutional values. As O'Donovan has noted, "[p]ast exclusions inform present practice. History is not yet abolished."[16]

The building of Australia's constitutional system began with the holding of a series of constitutional conventions in 1891, 1897 and 1898 to draft a constitution. Arguably, women were not only under-represented, but they were not represented at all, at least at the first of these conferences. No women were present at the 1891 Convention, and as none were eligible to vote in colonial elections none could contribute to the process by electing delegates.[17]

By 1894 South Australia had introduced universal suffrage. Consequently, South Australian women contributed to the 1897 Convention process through election of delegates. Notably, Catherine Helen Spence

---

[13] Ibid., 36.   [14] Ibid.

[15] Australian Women's History Forum Web site, accessed May 17, 2013, http://www.womenshistory.com.au.

[16] Cass and Rubenstein, "Re/presentations of Women," *supra* n. 1, footnote 110 (quoting O'Donovan, "Gender Blindness or Justice Engendered?" in *Rights of Citizenship*, ed. Robert Blackburn (London: Mansell, 1993), 19).

[17] Cass and Rubenstein, "Re/presentations of Women," *supra* n. 1, 28.

became the first woman to seek political office in Australia in her bid to be a delegate. She failed, coming twenty-second out of thirty-three candidates despite polling a "creditable" 7,383 votes.[18] Whereas Irving has suggested that Spence fell prey to a voting system that continues to disadvantage women[19] and would have been successful if her proportional representation platform was implemented, Spence herself attributed her failure to comments made by South Australian Premier Charles Kingston.[20] Kingston is illustrative of the complexities of the nineteenth-century suffrage debate. Prior to the convention he cast doubt on Spence's ability to stand, an attitude in keeping with the prevailing legal doctrine that married women, lunatics and children had no civil capacity at common law. However, during the 1894 Convention he was the pre-eminent champion of women's suffrage. In many ways the necessity of having those demands represented by a man undermined the message of autonomy and self-representation suffrage arguments intended to convey. However, as a result, the vote of South Australian, and later Western Australian, women was protected.[21] This ability to be both a reformer and conformist was not unique to Kingston but rather indicative of the complexities of the challenge that suffrage and women's representatives implied.

By 1897, Western Australian women also had the vote. However, there were no women representatives at either the 1897 or the 1898 Convention. Women remained disenfranchised in New South Wales and Victoria.

The next phase in the making of Australia's most basic law was the holding in each colony of a referendum to seek approval for the new constitution. It is a critical moment in the development of any nation, and in the case of Australia, the popular mandate bestowed on our Constitution by the referendum process is often touted as Australia's unique badge of democracy. The only problem with this argument is that the electorate that endorsed the Constitution comprised only half

---

[18] Ibid. (citing Janine Haines, *Suffrage to Sufferance: A Hundred Years of Women in Politics* (Sydney: Allen and Unwin, 1992), 62).

[19] Helen Irving, *Gender and the Constitution: Equity and Agency in Comparative Constitutional Design* (Cambridge: Cambridge University Press, 2008), 23, 125.

[20] Haines, *Suffrage to Sufferance, supra* n. 18, 62.

[21] John Hirst, *The Sentimental Nation: The Makings of the Australian Commonwealth* (Oxford: Oxford University Press, 2000) 161; Kim Rubenstein, "Can the Right to Vote Be Taken Away? The Constitution, Citizenship and Voting Rights in 1902–2002 in *Selective Democracy: Race, Gender and the Australian Vote*, ed. John Chesterman and David Philips (Melbourne: Melbourne Publishing Group, 2003), 100–111.

the population in terms of gender and practically none of the indigenous inhabitants.[22] Not only were women not represented in the Conventions, which drafted the new *grundnorm*, but also they were virtually not represented in the electorate which endorsed it.[23]

However, that does not mean there were no Founding Mothers. Research since the early 1990s has revealed the untold story of women's engagement in federation through the Woman's Christian Temperance Union (WCTU), literary and political discussions groups, such as Western Australia's Karrakatta Club, and philanthropic societies. Irving has documented a paradigm shift in the operation of these clubs that, culminating in the federation era, saw them being run, organised and dominated by women.[24] Irving argues that this "process of beginning to 'experience' themselves as political was pivotal in the emergence of a role for women in the federation movement of the period."[25]

Women did influence the convention debates. First, the women of South Australia and Western Australia, which were the only states that had given women the right to vote, guaranteed their federal vote, through section 41 of the Constitution even though it took another two years to gain national women's suffrage.[26] In addition, the WCTU's campaign to grant states independent control over alcohol sale and importation was successful and resulted in section 114 of the Constitution.[27] This success was undoubtedly associated with the veritable onslaught of petitions from the WCTU and other temperance organisations, as well as the development of innovative campaigning techniques involving publicly assessing

[22] In keeping with Behrendt's point, indigenous women's voting rights were compromised by the move to universal suffrage. The Commonwealth Franchise Act 1902 that gave women the right to vote in federal elections specifically excluded indigenous people from voting in federal elections, disenfranchising those indigenous women who had the vote in state elections. *See* Pat Stretton and Christine Finnimore "Black Fellow Citizens: Aborigines and the Commonwealth Franchise," *Australian Historical Studies* 25 (1993): 521.

[23] Although South Australian and Western Australian women were able to vote in the referendum, given they had the vote in their own states, the opinion of the women of New South Wales, Victoria, Tasmania and Queensland went unrecorded as they were not enfranchised.

[24] Helen Irving, "Fair Federalists and Founding Mothers," in *A Women's Constitution: Gender and History in the Australian Commonwealth*, ed. Helen Irving (Sydney: Hale & Ironmonger, 1996), 2.

[25] Ibid., 3.

[26] Women did not have the right to vote in federal elections until the Commonwealth Franchise Act of 1902. *See* Irving, *Gender and the Constitution, supra* n. 19, 15, and Rubenstein, "Can the Right to Vote Be Taken Away," *supra* n. 21.

[27] Irving, "Fair Federalists," *supra* n. 24, 5.

male candidates on the basis of their temperance position.[28] However, interstate trade had been the "lion in the path" of federation since Parkes opened the 1891 Convention with the resolution that trade between the colonies be "absolutely free".[29] Not only women but also the colonies were eager to preserve this resolution, which suggests that the campaign's success was not wholly a result of an acceptance of women in politics.

It is during the referendum campaigns that Irving most strongly highlights the contributions of the nascent 'political' woman. Federation was a divisive issue, with no clear gender lines. Hence, the establishment of the Women's Federal League by Maybanke Wolstenholme in 1898 to advocate federation was strongly driven by the highly publicised anti-Federalist campaign being waged by Rose Scott.[30] We identify Rose Scott's campaign as interesting to reflect on when we discuss federalism further.

Although Australian women were enfranchised nationally in 1902, it would be four decades before they entered federal Parliament.[31] Diane Sainsbury has suggested that this historical gap was the result of women prioritising suffrage over legislative representation, as demonstrated by the Women's Christian Temperance Union actively disavowing electoral eligibility;[32] the fracturing of a unified front following the success of suffrage campaigns; and the propensity for women to run as Independents and distance themselves from party politics, to their electoral disadvantage.[33] Haines agrees with Sainsbury that women generally remained outside the party system, and those who were inside were given unwinnable seats. The impetus for this separation from mainstream politics was articulated by Rose Scott, post-suffrage, when she argued that the whole point of the vote was "to bring a new element into Political life. Not to accentuate the quarrels of men."[34] Furthermore, Haines suggests there were great family responsibilities for women during this time.[35] Indeed, the effect of female representatives was portrayed as simultaneously dangerous and feminizing. Statements such as "No Government

---

[28] Ibid., 6.
[29] Michael Cooper, *Encounters with the Australian Constitution* (North Ryde: CCH Australia Limited, 1988), 63.
[30] Irving, "Fair Federalists," *supra* n. 24, 8.
[31] Diane Sainsbury, "Rights Without Seats: The Puzzle of Women's Legislative Recruitment in Australia" in *Elections Full, Fire & Fair*, ed. Marian Sawyer (Sydney: The Federation Press, 2001), 63.
[32] Ibid., 67.   [33] Ibid., 75.
[34] Marilyn Lake, *Getting Equal: The History of Australian Feminism* (Sydney: Allen and Unwin, 1999), 13 (quoting Rose, correspondence, April 13, 1904, in *Scott papers*, ML MS 38/41).
[35] Haines, *Suffrage to Sufferance, supra* n. 18, 178.

would be safe against the persistent attacks of a feminine opposition..."
appeared in the *Observer*.[36] Whereas the *Mercury* questioned, "[d]o you
really want them in here with their babies and their bottles?"[37]

This dearth of female representatives was not because of a lack of
candidates; between 1902 and 1943 there were thirty-nine unsuccessful nominations of women to the lower house and five for the upper
house.[38] In 1943 Enid Lyons won a seat in the House of Representatives
and Dorothy Tangney entered the Senate. Rather than being a watershed
moment heralding the beginning of an age of multiple female representatives, this proved to be a singular event. In the next twenty-five years,
women would be federally elected only five times.[39]

Nor is this a situation that has responded to the changing mores of
political thought. The second wave feminists of the 1960s and 1970s
advocated a range of initiatives to improve women's political representation, and although this resulted in women enthusiastically becoming
candidates, it did not translate into electoral results. In the eight years
covering 1969 to 1977, there were 161 female candidates for the House
of Representatives. Only forty-four of these were endorsed by a major
party. Only one, Joan Child, was actually elected.[40] Oldfield's comment
that "the prospect of women occupying their hallowed parliamentary
benches seemed to frighten most nineteenth-century parliamentarians out
of their wits..." seems to be timeless.[41]

The situation has been gradually improving since the 1980s. However, today women account for less than one-third (30.1%) of all parliamentarians in Australia. Federally, out of seventy-six parliamentarians
in the upper house only twenty-nine are women. In the lower house
there are thirty-seven women out of 150 parliamentarians.[42] Since federation, 1,595 parliamentarians have served in both houses of Parliament. Only 162, 10.2 per cent, have been women.[43] The picture becomes
bleaker when one focuses on indigenous women. There has never been an

---

[36] Cass and Rubenstein, "Re/presentations of Women," *supra* n. 1, 34 (citing Audrey Oldfield, *Women Suffrage in Australia: A Gift of a Struggle* (Melbourne: Cambridge University Press, 1992), 179 (quoting *Observer*, July 23, 1885)).

[37] Ibid. (citing Oldfield, *Women Suffrage in Australia*, *supra* n. 36, 179 (quoting *Mercury*, October 9, 1903)).

[38] Ibid.   [39] Ibid., 35.

[40] Ibid. Joan Child died on February 22, 2013, aged 91.

[41] Audrey Oldfield, *Woman Suffrage In Australia: A Gift or A Struggle* (Melbroune: University of Cambridge, 1992), 178.

[42] Joy McCann and Janet Wilson, "Representation of Women in Australian Parliaments" (Canberra: Parliament of Australia, Parliamentary Library, 2012), 2.

[43] Ibid., 11.

indigenous woman elected to federal Parliament.[44] At a state and territory level they remain underrepresented, with Carol Martin becoming
the first indigenous women elected to any Australian Parliament in 2001,
following her successful election in Western Australia.[45]

It is therefore apparent that although superficially discordant to contemporary ears the sentiments expressed by the *Mercury* over 100 years
ago have not faded. Recently a degree of parenting support to parliamen-
tarian mothers has emerged, most notably the establishment of on-site
childcare facilities, breast-feeding rooms and a provision allowing nurs-
ing mothers who are members of the House of Representatives to vote by
proxy (the Senate does not have similar standing orders).[46] Evidently, the
spectre of politicians who are both mothers and parliamentarians continues to haunt both the media and most parliamentary colleagues and
officials. This was controversially displayed when Senator Sarah Hanson-
Young's two-year-old child was removed from the Senate chamber during a division, following a ruling by the President of the Senate expelling
'strangers in the house' for duration of the vote.[47] In the ensuing controversy it became apparent that many parliamentarians and officials still do
not want women, with their babies and their bottles.

CONSTITUTIONAL PRINCIPLES

These stories of women and their involvement in the foundations of
Australia's constitutional story to this day provide one aspect of gender and the system of government. However, our project seeks to go
further and address the historical constitutional imbalance between men
and women in Australia by also looking at the principles that inform our
current constitutional system. This allows us to ask whether the system,
either in practice or in aspiration, meets the theories and assumptions
that are central to its own conception of self.[48] The Australian Constitutional system is underpinned by four central principles or concepts:

---

[44] Ibid., 13   [45] Ibid.
[46] Ibid., 33.
[47] Mark Rodrigues, "Children in the Parliamentary Chambers" (Research paper No. 9,
   Parliament of Australia Department of Parliamentary Services, Politics and Public
   Administration Section, Canberra, November 19, 2009).
[48] Several books have begun to look at issues to do with Gender and Constitutions. *See*
   Susan Williams, ed., *Constituting Equality: Gender Equality and Comparative Consti-
   tutional Law* (Cambridge: Cambridge University Press, 2009); Beverly Baines, Daphne
   Barak-Erez and Tsvi Kahana, eds., *Feminist Constitutionalism* (Cambridge: Cambridge
   University Press, 2010).

these are federalism, responsible government, representative democracy and the separation of powers. These four principles can be found in a variety of sources, including the text of the Constitution, constitutional conventions, case law and lesser tools of interpretation.

These principles are expressed in various ways. Responsible government, for example, is implicit in section 64 of the Constitution requiring ministers be members of Parliament and ensuring that those who administer the Departments of State are also responsible to Parliament. The separation of powers doctrine can be discerned in the division of the Constitution into three chapters covering the legislature, the executive and the judiciary, and the vesting of relevant power in each branch, respectively. The rest of this chapter is predominantly concerned with the principles of federalism and representative democracy. The move to a federal system is apparent in the division of legislative power between the states and the commonwealth, the preservation of state constitutions and state laws, the supremacy of federal law in the case of any inconsistency between state and commonwealth laws and representation of the states in the Senate. The Constitution provides for a representative democracy in which people are chosen to be members of Parliament. Section 7 requires that the Senate be composed of senators "directly chosen by the people of the State," and section 24 likewise provides that the House of Representatives is composed of members "directly chosen by the people of the Commonwealth." Various sections refer to 'elections' and 'electors'. Furthermore, section 41 ostensibly protects the right to vote.[49]

Representation

We have already covered some of the issues about women and representation through the discussion of the fight for suffrage and women's unequal presence to this very day in the chambers of Parliament. We now turn to the way representative democracy has been discussed by the courts. We argue that recent High Court cases affirm that the Constitution is underpinned by various fundamental principles, one of which is representative democracy. Moreover, the character of representative democracy requires the elected to be linked with the electorate and public participation.

---

[49] Kim Rubenstein, "From Suffrage to Citizenship: A Republic of Equals" (Speech delivered at Dymphna Clark Annual Lecture, Manning Clark House, March 29, 2008, http://manningclark.org.au/html/Paper-Rubenstein_Kim-Suffrage_to_Citizenship_A_Republic_of_Equals.html): 9.

We propose that, given this model, the current and historical exclusion of women is a violation of the constitutional project as envisaged by the High Court.

This argument has developed alongside the Court's exploration of representative democracy. Although a complete model of representation has not yet being articulated, the following cases elucidate the guiding principles that have been developed. Cass and Rubenstein's 1995 article argued that the then 'recent' freedom of political communication cases examining representative democracy did so in a way that was different to earlier High Court decisions addressing the concept.[50] Soon after, the High Court re-examined those cases in its joint judgment of *Lange v. Australian Broadcasting Corporation*[51] (*Lange*) confirming that sections 7, 8, 13, 24, 25, 28 and 30 of the Constitution provided for "the fundamental features of representative government."[52] *Lange* was the culmination of that series of judgments recognizing that the Constitution provides for a system of representative government, but neither it nor the preceding cases had been concerned with whether the form of representative democracy provided for by the Constitution required a particular form of electoral system. Rather, they centred on whether representative democracy implied a degree of freedom of communication, and it was a turning point in constitutional interpretation that those cases had identified an implied freedom of political communication in the Constitution. For their purposes, representative democracy was posited in a highly abstract manner, and the phrase 'directly chosen by the people' sufficiently encompassed it.[53]

More recently, the High Court has been concerned with representative government and Parliament's power to disenfranchise its citizens. For our purposes, and as the majority noted in *Roach v. Electoral Commissioner*[54] (*Roach*), the subsequent exploration of these issues is more fruitful then the past debates, because "disqualification from the franchise is, if anything, a subject even closer to the central concept of representative government."[55]

Looking from the perspective of gender, it is also interesting that Vickie Roach, the plaintiff in the matter is an indigenous woman. She was serving

---

[50] Cass and Rubenstein, "Re/presentations of Women," *supra* n. 1, 9–19.
[51] *Lange v. Australian Broadcasting Corporation* (1997) 189 CLR 520.
[52] Ibid., 557.
[53] *Rowe v. Electoral Commissioner* (2010) 273 ALR 1, 51 per Hayne J.
[54] *Roach v. Electoral Commissioner* (2007) 233 CLR 162.
[55] Ibid., 198 [80].

a six-year term when she successfully mounted the High Court challenge against the ban on prisoners voting at elections.[56]

Her case concerned the alteration of the *Commonwealth Electoral Act 1918* (Cth), with the result that under sections 93 (8AA) and 208(2)(c) any person serving a full-time prison sentence, irrespective of its length, could not vote at a federal election. Previously, under amendments made in 2004 prisoners were only disenfranchised if the length of their sentence was three years or more. Vickie Roach was convicted in the County Court of Victoria of five counts of offences under the *Crimes Act 1958* (Vic) and sentenced to six years imprisonment. The case centred around her third submission, that it followed from *Lange* that there is an implied freedom of political communication protecting federal elections and that this was impermissibly burdened by the 2006 Act and that the 2006 Act impermissibly limited the operation of representative government required by the Constitution.[57]

In combination, sections 30 and 51(xxxvi) of the Constitution empower Parliament to provide for the 'qualification of electors of members of the House of Representatives' and section 8 extends this power to the qualification for electors of senators. However, sections 7 and 24 influence this power. These sections demand that, as well as requiring that parliamentarians be directly chosen by the people, all laws controlling eligibility must acknowledge that holistically the electoral system provides for ultimate control of Parliament through periodic elections.[58]

In addition to this reading of the Constitution as a whole, with an understanding of its text and structures, provisions must be construed by reference to the system of representative government, as envisaged by the framers. The majority suggested that representative government involved more than voicing concerns to legislators. It demanded a voice in electing those legislators. The exercise of this power to vote reflects essential notions of citizenship and membership. These notions are not extinguished solely by the fact of imprisonment. To determine whether the legislative disqualification is valid, the majority asked whether it was for a 'substantial reason'? That is, a reason that is "reasonably appropriate and adapted to serve an end which is consistent or

---

[56] For more information about Vickie's interesting story as a young indigenous woman, *see* "Leading the Charge," *Sydney Morning Herald*, May 23, 2009, accessed May 16, 2012, http://www.smh.com.au/national/leading-the-charge-20090522-bia8.html.

[57] *Roach v. Electoral Commissioner* (2007) 233 CLR 162, 185 per majority.

[58] Ibid., 188 per majority.

compatible with the maintenance of the constitutionally prescribed system of representative government."[59] While *Lange* was distinguished from *Roach*, on the basis that *Lange* concerned the ability to cast an appropriately informed vote and *Roach* centred on the entitlement to vote at all, the test posed by the court is an adaptation of the second limb of the *Lange* test. Similarly the majority considered the test interchangeable with notions of proportionality.

To determine whether the amendments were proportionate, the majority examined the class of prisoner likely to be affected. Here they noted that the amendments operated without regard to the culpability of the disenfranchised prisoner. In doing so they fell outside the historical justification for disqualifying both electors and candidates, on the grounds that those convicted of certain crimes were lacking in the fitness and probity of character demanded for civic participation. Moreover, the amendments had the effect of imposing more rigorous standards on electors then those prescribed for electees by section 44(ii) of the Constitution. Importantly it was considered significant that, at the time of judgment, 6.3 per cent of the prison population was imprisoned by public order offences, and 17.6 per cent were serving sentences of less than a year.[60] Gummow J, Kirby J, and Crennan J found the 2006 Act to be disproportionate to the maintenance of representative government.[61] In a separate judgment Gleeson CJ considered that it failed to adhere to the requirements of sections 7 and 24, because by "attempt[ing] to identify prisoners who have committed serious crimes by reference to either the term of imprisonment imposed or the maximum penalty for the offence [Parliament] broke the rational connection necessary to reconcile the disenfranchisement with the constitutional imperative of choice by the people."[62]

In contrast, the earlier 2004 version of the act was valid. Although its provisions disenfranchised prisoners, they did so with regard to the seriousness of the offence committed, thus serving as an indicator of a degree of culpability that meant this class of prisoner was temporarily unfit to exercise civic rights. This approach accords with colonial history that has measured culpability by the length of one's sentence and is compatible with standards of representative government.

The majority judges all examined the class of prisoner most likely to be affected by the legislation and suggested that it was likely to

---

[59] Ibid., 199 per majority.
[61] Ibid.

[60] Ibid., 202 per majority.
[62] Ibid., 182 per Gleeson CJ.

disproportionately affect "a not insubstantial number of people, who by reason of their personal characteristics (such as poverty, homelessness, or mental problems), or geographical circumstances do not qualify for . . . a full range of non custodial sentencing options."[63]

However they neglected to directly address another significant factor that was likely to link those effected. The prison population of Australia, as of June 2012, is 93 percent male.[64] This point was also made by Irving who identified the gendered nature of this ostensibly gender-neutral disqualification.[65] Irving suggested that a total commitment to gender equality would require that those currently, or previously, incarcerated and serving a sentence of more than three years should be able to run for office and vote and that the current legislation is also questionable on those grounds.

The second point to emerge from *Roach* was the distinction drawn by the court between individual rights and a limitation on legislation that eventuates from the text and structure of the Constitution.[66] Given that there is no Bill of Rights in the Australian Constitution, the court is not looking to find provisions in which individuals are empowered or protected by the Constitution but rather, what the limits are on how the government legislates in a way that impinges on rights. While this point was emphasized previously in *Cunliffe*,[67] *Lange*[68] and *Levy*[69] – all concerning freedom of communication – *Roach* represented an extension of the concept to multiple facets of representative government.[70] At a practical level this distinction prevents successful plaintiffs from seeking actions for damages.[71] On an ideological level, Zines suggests that emphasizing immunity from legislative control rather than a positive right serves to reinforce the "consequentialist or incidental nature of the freedom in relation to representative government."[72]

[63] Ibid.

[64] Australian Bureau of Statistics, "Prisoners in Australia 2012," 4517.0, last updated April 2, 2013, http://www.abs.gov.au/ausstats/abs@.nsf/Products/5087123B0CCE48C1CA257B3C000DC7CE?opendocument.

[65] Irving, *Gender and the Constitution, supra* n. 19, 112.

[66] *Roach v. Electoral Commissioner* (2007) 233 CLR 162, 200–199.

[67] *Cunliffe v. Commonwealth* (1994) 182 CLR 272, 326 per Brennan J.

[68] *Lange v. Australian Broadcasting Corporation* (1997) 189 CLR 520, 560.

[69] *Levy v. Victoria* (1997) 189 CLR 579, 622 per McHugh J.

[70] *Roach v. Electoral Commissioner* (2007) 233 CLR 162.

[71] Leslie Zines, *The High Court and the Constitution*, 5th ed. (Sydney: The Federation Press, 2008), 549.

[72] Ibid., 550.

For a feminist constitutional dialogue this represents an interesting way in which to think about gender and constitutions. It forces us to move away from a rights-based discourse. This shift also allows over-looked questions of architecture to be prioritized as relevant to feminist critique, and this focus on architecture requires feminist theory to focus on a point before questions of rights violations. This shift has important consequences for our framework of difference. It poses important questions to each lens of that framework. For Gilligan's gender essentialism the question arises: If we accept that men and women should be treated differently by the justice system, what would that equate to if we are looking beyond rights? If freedom is incidental, not inherent, in representative government, then should women be focussed on constitutional amendment to achieve their goals or legislative change? Perhaps formal equality is the most challenged by this paradigm shift: focused as it is on enlightenment individual rights principles, it is difficult to imagine it reconceptualised around incidental prohibitions. We would suggest that McKinnon's dialogue of dominance would balk at the claim that the history of rights that have generally privileged men should be reinterpreted as a history of legislative prohibitions that has emerged only with the Australian Constitution.

Marrying these feminist lenses of difference to the distinction between rights and limitations drawn by the Australian High Court is fundamentally challenging because the High Court's decisions accord with a tradition of Australian exceptionalism, in which rights have never been emphasised, yet most feminist analysis occurs in a rights heavy dialogue. The *Roach* distinction offers an opportunity for a uniquely Australian feminist discourse of difference to develop, removed from its proximity to rights and concerned with the realities of the constitutional architecture of power in Australia.[73]

The two-step test developed in *Roach* was later applied in *Rowe v. Electoral Commissioner*.[74] *Rowe* also concerned the electoral franchise. For the eight federal elections held between 1983 and 2006, the people who qualified as electors had seven days following the issuing of the writs to lodge a claim for enrolment or a transfer of enrolment. However, in

---

[73] Some interesting scholarship in this area can be seen in the Feminism and Institution-alism International Network Web site, http://www.femfiin.co, and Mona Lena Krook and Fiona Mackay, eds., *Gender, Politics and Institutions: Towards a Feminist Institutionalism* (New York: Palgrave MacMillan, 2010).

[74] *Rowe v. Electoral Commissioner* (2010) 273 ALR 1.

2006 the Electoral Act was amended, so that those wanting to enrol had until 8:00 PM on the same day of the issuing of the writs. Those wishing to transfer their enrolment had three days, instead of seven, to do so. The court received evidence from the deputy electoral commissioner that 100,000 claims for enrolment had been received after the new cut-off dates. These claims would have been made within time as the act stood pre 2006.[75]

A majority consisting of French CJ, Gummow and Bell JJ and Crennan J held that the amendments failed to uphold the requirements of sections 7 and 24 of the Constitution that Parliament be chosen by the people. As French CJ discussed, the decision of *Roach* was not directly applicable to *Rowe*, as it concerned an exception to the universal franchise.[76] However, despite being concerned with an electoral law that was fundamentally procedural, the electoral amendments would substantively affect the entitlement of many Australians to vote and, hence, affected the franchise in an analogous way to *Roach*.[77] The question asked by the majority judges was then whether first, as per Gleeson CJ in *Roach*, the rational connection necessary to reconcile the disqualification with the constitutional imperative had been broken.[78] Secondly, as per Gummow, Kirby and Crennan JJ in the same case, whether there was a 'substantial' reason for the amendment.

> A reason will answer that description if it be reasonably appropriate and adapted to serve an end which is consistent or compatible with the maintenance of the constitutionally prescribed system of representative government. When used here the phrase 'reasonable appropriate and adapted' does not mean 'essential' or 'unavoidable'. Rather, as remarked in *Lange*, in this context there is little difference by what is conveyed by that phrase and the notion of 'proportionality'.[79]

French CJ considered that the practical effect of the amendment, that is the prevention of a significant number of people from having their enrolment claims or transfers considered until after the election, was not answered by the submission that these people were so affected because of their failure to observe the statutory requirements. This failure to consider their claims had established a detriment to the constitutional franchise.

[75] Ibid., 105 per Crennan J.

[76] Ibid., 15 per French C. J.

[77] Ibid.

[78] Ibid., 59 per Gummow and Bell J. J.

[79] *Rowe v. Electoral Commissioner* (2010) 243 CLR 1, 59 per Gummow and Bell J. J. (quoting *Roach v. Electoral Commissioner* (2007) 233 CLR 162, 199, [85]).

Moreover, this detriment was not balanced by Parliament's legitimate purpose in addressing faults in the electoral system.[80] This was explored more thoroughly in Crennan J's judgment. In answer to the Commonwealth's submission that the amendments were necessary or appropriate for the maintenance of the electoral roll's integrity, Crennan J held that, (1) demonstrably the Australian Electoral Commission had no difficulty processing late enrolments, as in the 1993, 1996, 1998 and 2001 elections, respectively, 3.32 per cent, 3.23 per cent, 2.94 per cent and 2.96 per cent of total enrolments were processed in the seven-day period between the issuing of the writs and the closure of the rolls; (2) the commonwealth's stated goal of attempting to discourage the late surge of enrolments through exclusion failed to recognize the centrality of the franchise to full civic life; and (3) the need to maintain the integrity of the rolls by protecting them from systemic electoral fraud was without any evidence that shortening the cut-off period reduced fraudulent activity or even that systemic electoral fraud existed.[81] Hence, there was no substantial reason for the amendments.

These two recent cases accord with Cass and Rubenstein's 1995 conclusions following their earlier case analysis.[82] They affirm that the High Court's approach to representative democracy shows that there are different conceptual levels informing constitutional interpretation. At one level, there is the text of the Constitution containing certain rules – such as requiring members of Parliament to be directly chosen by the people. At another, there is the principle or doctrine of representative democracy underpinning the rule, and at yet another level, there are the theories or assumptions behind the formal principle. The overarching principle to emerge from *Lange, Roach* and *Rowe* is that if Parliament wishes to alter the constitutional franchise, there must be proportionality or a substantial reason. Without this, disenfranchisement cannot be reconciled with the constitutional requirement that Parliament be chosen by the people.

More broadly representative democracy requires some linkage of the elected and the electorate,[83] that it is an ongoing requirement[84] and that

---

[80] *Rowe v. Electoral Commissioner* (2010) 243 CLR 1, 38 per French C. J.

[81] Ibid., 120–121, per Crennan J.

[82] Cass and Rubenstein, "Re/presentations of Women," *supra* n. 1, 19.

[83] *Roach v. Electoral Commissioner* (2007) 233 CLR 162, 198 [83] per Gummow, Kirby and Crennan JJ.

[84] *Mulholland v. Electoral Commissioner* (2004) 209 ALR 582, 625 per Gummow and Hayne J. J.

electoral systems can vary over time.[85] The crucial point in relation to the under-representation of women is whether individuals or groups can nevertheless be represented in the elected assembly without physically being present themselves. Does it matter that less than one-third of the Australian legislature is women in 2012?[86] Is it necessary for women to be present to be actually represented? Has the rational connection been disenfranchisement and choice by the people been broken?

We argue that gender is relevant to representation and the under-representation of women in government makes the system unrepresentative. Four justifications for the view that gender is relevant are identified: the invisibility of gender, the difference between interests of men and women, the injustice of exclusion and the nature of democracy.

This first argument stresses that gender is hidden or made invisible in current notions of representative democracy, but it is nevertheless there, evidenced by the overwhelming numerical imbalance between men and women. The invisibility of women in government means that no challenge is offered to the status quo of imbalance in men's representation. The imbalance appears normal and indeed inevitable and maintains the necessity of natural supportive feminine roles. Often it is reaffirmed by the stance of the women who do succeed in being elected, as Sawer and Simms have noted: "Women in Australian political parties have often found that the price of acceptance is to agree to the sidelining or marginalizing of issues concerning the status of women."[87]

Nor is the situation better for those women in politics who are outspoken concerning women's issues, as ex-parliamentarian Kathy Sullivan reflected:

> It appeared that women MP's could state their views however they liked – tactfully or aggressively, sweetly or stridently, obliquely or bluntly – but if they were expressing views about women, too often a majority of the men in their parliamentary audience automatically closed their ears, believing they are hearing fringe feminist rhetoric, which was to be automatically rejected.

---

[85] *Roach v. Electoral Commissioner* (2007) 233 CLR 162, 197 (quoting *Mulholland v. Electoral Commissioner* (2004) 209 ALR 582, 625 per Gummow and Hayne J. J.).

[86] McCann and Wilson, "Representation of Women," *supra* n. 41, 2.

[87] Rebecca Huntley and Janet Ramsey, "Never Made to Follow, Never Born to Lead": Women in the NSW ALP" in *No Fit Place for Women*, eds. Deborah Brennan and Louis Chappell (Sydney: UNSW Press, 2006), 87, 208 (quoting Marian Sawer and Marian Simms, *A Woman's Place: Women and Politics in Australia* (Sydney: Allen and Unwin, 1984)).

This realization was a painful one – considering the number of years I had spent, I thought, I had been patiently explaining modern women's aspirations.[88]

The second argument concerns whether or not men and women have different interests. We have already broadly canvassed the difference debate and explored the juxtapositions between feminists such as Gilligan and McKinnon. Phillips argues that the very difficulties, complexities and clearly differentiated nature of women's interests and opinions suggest that women themselves ought to represent their views.[89]

On an international level Charlesworth argues:

How or whether women's equal participation in decision making would affect the quality of UN decisions is not yet certain. But whatever the evidence of a distinctive women's influence in political decision making, it is at least clear that the realities of women's lives under the present unbalanced system do not contribute in any significant way to the shaping of UN policy.[90]

The central insight suggested by the justification remains compelling, namely, that women experience the world differently to men as an undeniable matter of practical reality. Moreover, regardless of how many different voices women may have, it does not mean that men can properly represent those different voices. Consequently, the current male-dominated Parliament must fail to represent women.

Thirdly, Anne Phillips has argued that it is unjust to exclude women from political life. She illustrates how lacking in nuance the situation is by imagining a reversal of the gender balance: "What would men think of a system of political representation in which they were outnumbered nineteen to one?"[91] Implicit in this argument is the rejection of that long-held bastion of liberal feminism: formal equality. Phillips' demand for justice is, rather, a demand for substantive equality.

---

[88] Cass and Rubenstein, "Re/presentations of Women," *supra* n. 1, 41 (quoting Sullivan, edited text of lecture in the Main Committee Room of Parliament House September 27, 1993, reprinted in the *Canberra Times*, September 28, 1993).

[89] Cass and Rubenstein, "Re/presentations of Women," *supra* n. 1, 22.

[90] Ibid. (quoting Hilary Charlesworth, "Transforming the United Men's Club: Feminist Futures in the United Nations," *Transnational Law and Contemporary Problems* 4 (1994): 444).

[91] Anne Phillips, *Engendering Democracy* (Pennsylvania: Pennsylvania State University Press, 1991), 2.

Phillips is most in favour of the fourth argument, which is that a revitalization of women's engagement in political life would also result in a resurgent democracy. Phillips favours a participatory democracy, as opposed to the liberal or republican models. The difference between these models centres on the form representation takes. Hence, in a participatory democracy people participate in decision making, which occurs not only in the federal political sphere but also at the local level. This model creates a close link between all the parties. Moreover, of all representative democracy models it accords most closely with the High Court's emphasis on participation as a fundamental part of representative democracy: "[R]epresentative government as that notion is understood in the Australian constitutional context comprehends not only the bringing of concerns and grievances to the attention of legislators, but also the presence of a voice in the selection of those legislators."[92]

This dovetails with our critique of the difference argument. The more complex and divergent interests are, the more need there is for a diversity of representatives. Hence, the involvement of women would enhance participatory democracy for both men and women.

The centrality of representation has been recognized in both democratic theory and through a series of High Court cases. It requires a linkage between electors and the elected, and this linkage is achieved through participation. Moreover, as representation is an ongoing process – that does not cease once a body has been elected – participation must be continuous. Although a broad range of groups and peoples should be involved in this process, it is paramount that women be present. This is because, although many women share many interests and concerns with minority groups, they are not a minority.[93] Women are one-half of the population and represent many other groups within themselves. The invisibility of the current gendered dynamic, the difference between men's and women's interests, the injustice of systemically under-representing women and the need to revitalize democracy compel the conclusion that gender is relevant to representation.

Federalism

Returning to the constitutional foundations in moving to examine federalism and its gendered issues, we argue that federalism has been a

---

[92] *Roach v. Electoral Commissioner* (2007) 233 CLR 162, 198, 24 per Gummow J.
[93] Irving, "Fair Federalists," *supra* n. 24, 35.

contentious area for women since it was proposed. For some it offered the ability to vote with one's feet and achieve prominence in local politics under a vertical power distribution. For others federalism would mean the division of issues into lesser local concerns and greater national interests – a binary in which women's issues would always be categorised as local. However, we suggest that there is a degree of Australian exceptionalism that has prevented the division of powers from adhering to this binary. Moreover, its vertical power system has allowed states to champion issues of concern to women despite a recalcitrant federal government.

In our exploration of federalism we are reminded of Rose Scott and her role in the lead up to federation.[94] Rose Scott, a committed suffragette and one of the Founding Mothers,[95] in her active role during the lead up to federation argued stridently against it. She was one of the most prolific anti-Billite speakers during the crucial referendum years of 1898 and 1899. Her concern centred on the ramifications of federation for New South Wales. She argued that the cost of living and taxation would rise, and it would allow the larger states to be unfairly dominated by the smaller through the undemocratic institution of the Senate.[96] Women, she warned, would be greatly disadvantaged by federation because the commonwealth's powers would not be concerned with the 'private' sphere matters that were women's main concern. Rather, commonwealth legislative power would be limited to public powers predicated on male power and authority, such as war, foreign affairs and the economy.[97] Even Barton's promise in the 1898 draft Constitution for a universal women's suffrage, which consolidated most women's support for federation, would not sway Scott. She supported Belle Golding's sentiment: "How dare Barton now say that Federation would bring about women's

---

[94] This section of the chapter draws heavily from Kim Rubenstein, "Feminism and Federalism" (Speech delivered at Gilbert and Tobin Lecture Constitutional Law Conference, February 24, 2006, http://www.gtcentre.unsw.edu.au/sites/gtcentre.unsw.edu.au/files/mdocs/7_KimRubenstein.pdf), 3.

[95] Rose Scott is featured in the Australian Women's History Month at http://www.womenshistory.com.au with a link to her Australian Dictionary of Biography entry at http://adb.anu.edu.au/biography/scott-rose-8370.

[96] The Australian Senate compromises twelve senators for each state, and two for the territories. This equal representation granted greater voting power to the smaller states and was a contentious issue, exacerbated by a late introduction of proportional representation in 1948 to combat the traditional dominance of the majority party. Irving, "Fair Federalists," *supra* n. 24, 9.

[97] Rubenstein, "Feminism and Federalism," *supra* n. 90, 3 (citing Judith Allen, *Rose Scott. Vision and Revision in Feminism* (Melbourne: Oxford University Press, 1994), 146).

franchise, and hold up to public admiration what he so bitterly opposed and tried to defeat . . . Women of Sydney, be not used as tools."[98]

As discussed earlier in the chapter, the move to federation was an issue that divided the women's movement of the 1890s. Although highly influential and widely reported speakers such as Scott and Mrs. Bateson (who advised Western Australians "to keep Federation out as well as rabbits") opposed the federal ideal, other women such as Maybanke Wolstenholme, founder of The Women's Federal League, avidly supported it.[99]

Helen Irving, in her book *Gender and the Constitution*, comments that, for fledgling nations, the choice of federalism is rarely "at large". Rather, it is normally predetermined by the nature of the would-be nation.[100] Federation seemed a logical form of governance for a group of societies that were so similar and yet intent on retaining certain powers, as the Australian colonies were.[101] Even though this may be so, a feminist examination of federalism reveals again how the basic architecture of a nation can be unobtrusively gendered. Irving suggests that America, Australia and Nigeria are united in allocating powers by assigning traditional masculine powers, such as trade, border control and warfare, to the commonwealth.[102] In contrast, local matters tend to be spheres associated with femininity, for example, education, welfare and family matters.

Notably, the Australian Constitution departed from this proposed binary at its formation, with the federal government being granted power to regulate family law under sections 51 (xxi) and (xxii).[103] Irving accords this departure to the observations by founders, such as Quick and Garran, that the inability of Congress to nationally regulate marriage was the American Constitution's most "conspicuous defect."[104] However, the essentially non-gendered powers of the postal service, railways, weights and measures, discussed by Irving, were the first federal powers proposed. La Nauze suggests that the ease with which not only early Federalists but

[98] Irving, "Fair Federalists," *supra* n. 24, 11.
[99] Ibid., 15, 8.
[100] Irving, *Gender and the Constitution, supra* n. 19, 65.
[101] John Andrew La Nauze, *The Making of the Australian Constitution* (Melbourne: Melbourne University Press, 1972), 5.
[102] Irving, *Gender and the Constitution, supra* n. 19, 68.
[103] Ibid., 75.
[104] Ibid. See also Emily Buss & William Buss, Federalism and Family Law in Australia and the United States (forthcoming in 2014).

also newspaper editorials, named these fields as appropriate for federal governance was one of the strongest arguments for federation.[105]

The lure of federalism for feminists lies mainly in its institutional accessibility and opportunity to participate locally. Federations distribute power vertically; national and regional government have parallel institutions, and it is assumed that women are more capable of success in these local institutions. This assumption accords with the principles underpinning distribution of powers according to a masculine/feminine binary. It is likely that in a nation the size of Australia the ability of women to relocate to Canberra for national politics would be circumscribed by family obligations.[106] A recent analysis of federalism also allows us to understand the manner in which the declining membership of rural populations (now only 10.9% of Australia's overall population) has affected women's ability to engage in politics.[107] Potentially, this increased urbanism has removed the tyranny of distance that may have prevented women from commuting easily as representatives.

However, in contrast to the argument that women enjoy more success in local politics, a 2003 study conducted by Vengroff, Nyiri and Fugiero indicated that the unitary/federal nature of nations was less important than the level of economic development and the proportionality of the electoral system to women's representation.[108] This is supported by a 2011 study in Canada across municipal, provincial and federal levels of government, which concluded that there was no evidence of a linear relationship between the level of government and the presence of female legislators.[109] Rather, women were under-represented in all levels of government and, regardless of the level, occupied no more then 25 per cent of seats.[110] This contrasts to political pipeline theory, which argues that

---

[105] La Nauze, *The Making of the Australian Constitution*, 5.

[106] Former Justice Elizabeth Evatt eloquently reminded individuals that if women had been part of the Constitutional Conventions they would never have allowed for section 125 placing the federal capital within the state of New South Wales but at least 100 miles from the city of Sydney. *See* Cass and Rubenstein, "Re/presentations of Women," *supra* n. 1, 37.

[107] "Rural Population in Australia," World Bank 2012 World Development Indicators, accessed May 17, 2013, http://www.tradingeconomics.com/australia/rural-population-wb-data.html.

[108] Irving, "*Gender and the Constitution*," *supra* n. 19, 83.

[109] Erin Tolley, "Do Women 'Do Better' in Municipal Politics? Electoral Representation across Three Levels of Government," *Canadian Journal of Political Science* 44 (2011): 588.

[110] Ibid., 586.

gains in lower levels of government must eventually translate into gains at a higher level.[111]

The second advantage of federalism is the opportunity it provides citizens to 'vote with their feet' and travel to a jurisdiction with more appealing laws. This advantage is enjoyed, however, by only a few independent people with portable lives. Women, and the majority of men with dependants, are unlikely to be able to jurisdiction-hop because of legal distinctions. Even when those distinctions are as fundamental as abortion laws, women are more likely to remain within their state than to be able to afford even temporary relocation to a state in which abortion is legal. This was graphically demonstrated in *R v. Brennan and Leach*[112] in which Tegan Leach was prosecuted under Queensland law for procuring her own abortion by importing misoprostol from Ukraine. Although a jury unanimously found her not guilty, the prosecution of the case sharply highlighted both survival of laws designed to protect women from themselves and the legal fiction of temporary jurisdictional experimentation.

Are there then links between federal principles and feminist values? Prima facie it would appear that the concepts of federalism and feminism are at odds with one another, as federalism is premised on the dividing power territorially, whereas women's interests are not so necessarily geographically based, or geographically transferable.

However, on a policy rather than a personal level, studies have indicated that Australian federalism has the potential to operate in a gender sensitive manner. Comprehensive studies from the Hawke era to the present day by Louise Chappell and Mayet Costello of domestic violence policy have demonstrated that federalism can be a positive structure for promoting women's policy. Its advantages were displayed clearly when national action was stymied during the conservative Howard era, but territory and state programs continued.[113] The prevention of violence against women is a specific example, as a result of the strong constitutional mandate the states enjoy regarding criminal law. However, Chappell and Costello's work does suggest that Australian federalism is not as centralist as it is often depicted.[114] Moreover, areas associated with women's concerns have traditionally fallen under the states' purview.

[111] Ibid., 589.
[112] 2010 District Court of Queensland Indictment 74 of 2010 (unreported).
[113] Louise Chappell and Mayet Costello, "Australian Federalism and Domestic Violence Policy-Making," *Australian Journal of Political Science* 46 (2011): 644.
[114] Ibid., 645.

Consequently, although the case example may not be extrapolated generally, violence against women is not only a highly pertinent example, but it is representative of many areas of law that are central to feminist concerns.

The situation becomes more nuanced when we consider the consequences of the Commonwealth's lack of federal power in the private sphere at the start of the century, which left it largely unable to legislate in respect to welfare matters and condemned women to an illogical state-based welfare scheme.[115] The result of the misplaced assumption that all matters could be territorially divided was that whether a woman lived in Queensland or Victoria was often determinative of the effect that the issues underpinning social welfare had on her life. To the extent that the Commonwealth had power in these areas, under sections 51 (xxi), 51 (xxii) and 51(xxiiA) it was partial and incomplete. This meant women received piecemeal protection from the federal government in the areas of marriage, divorce and specific welfare issues. Consequently, they had to rely significantly on state legislative action. For example, the Constitution provides the Commonwealth with the power to pass legislation in regards to de facto couples' children's disputes, but not their property disputes. Hence, when de facto couples with children separate, they have to spend considerable time and money navigating both the Federal Family Court and the relevant state court.[116]

Furthermore, federalism and feminism share two very important values: pluralism and diversity. Feminist legal theory focuses on recognizing the diversity and plurality of different women's experiences compared to those of men.[117] Similarly, as Professor Michael Crommelin has stated, federalism is a "species of pluralism, which distributes power among groups that enjoy a measure of autonomy and participate in an ordered and permanent way in the exercise of political power by the central entity."[118]

Federalism is at a crossroads; it can either develop into a flexible system, which allows gendered issues to be effectively pursued at different levels of government but represented at all of them, or it can fulfil Rose Scott's warnings and arbitrarily uphold a public/private split of legislative powers between the Commonwealth and state.

---

[115] Rubenstein, "Feminism and Federalism," *supra* n. 90, 4.

[116] Ibid., 6.   [117] Ibid., 13.

[118] Michael Crommelin, "Federalism," in *Essays on Law and Government, Vol. 1: Principles and Values*, ed. Paul Finn (Sydney: Law Book Company, 1995), 168.

THE WAY FORWARD?

This paper has so far documented a number of ways in which women have been excluded from the political franchise of Australia and the ways in which the principles of representative democracy and federalism impact women. This chapter now moves to identify some options that have been put forward to address some of these issues, although much further work is needed to fully develop this project.

In 1977, one-time Labor candidate Anne Conlon said the landscape of political parties was like that of a tribal territory, where a "ruling group resides and rules, occasionally permitting certain outsiders the pleasure of being admitted."[119] Major political parties have increasingly recognised the role they play in determining candidates' success. As a result, since 1981 the Australian Labor Party has had mandatory preselection quotas which require 35 per cent of winnable preselection seats to be allocated to women. Similarly, the Liberal Party has invested in a network to mentor and encourage women to stand for preselection.

Another suggestion, which aims to directly alter the composition of the executive, is double sex parliamentary representation. In this system, the size of each electorate is doubled, and for each electorate there is a male and a female representative. Proponents of this option argue that it would free women from being forced to operate according to the same competitive standard as men. It is a proposal which is particularly appealing to those adherents of difference theory, who argue that women representatives not only have different interest but also a different voice that is often disregarded out of hand in the present system.

An argument has also been made for constitutional quotas, guaranteeing a certain number of seats for women. In 2005, only thirteen countries worldwide had constitutional quotas, although more than forty had constitutional or legislative quotas.[120] These notions reflect an acceptance that one or two representatives cannot adequately represent women. Rather, they either aim for a gender balance, or a critical minority of 30 to 40 per cent women capable of acting as a significant power

---

[119] "Reinventing Political Institutions," Papers on Parliament No. 27, Department of the Senate, Parliament House, Canberra, March 1996, http://www.aph.gov.au/binaries/senate/pubs/pops/pop27/pop27.pdf (citing A. Conlon, "'Women in Politics,' A Personal Viewpoint," *Australian Quarterly* 49(3) (1977): 14).

[120] Drude Dahlerup, "Increasing Women's Political Representation: New Trends in Gender Quotas" in *Women in Parliament: Beyond Numbers*, eds. Julie Ballington and Azza Karam (International IDEA, 2005), 145–46.

block. Hence, the Rwandan Constitution reserves 30 per cent of seats for women, Uganda reserves fifty-six seats and Tanzania allocates their 20 per cent of reserved seats to parties depending on the proportion of seats won.[121]

Other proposals target the political and legal culture nurturing gender inequality. Therefore, the need for schooling in parliamentary skills for women has received much emphasis. This has been evident both within party politics, through organisations such as the National Labor Women's Network[122] and through those organizations which aim to increase women's membership through training outside of party politics, as is evident in the success of EMILY's list which was established by women of the Australian Labor Party but is independent of that party.[123] EMILY's list becomes involved post preselection, and although much of its emphasis is on campaign donations, it also provides training in essential skills to win and hold office.[124] In addition, there is a continuing need for parliamentary work hours and conditions to be reformed. The Scottish Parliament has been lauded as an example of a family-friendly environment since it was reconceived following the 1989 Constitutional Convention.[125] A system of regular government reporting to review bodies, such as the *Convention on All Forms of Discrimination Against Women* (CEDAW) committee, about percentages of women in parliamentary institutions has also been suggested. This would be appropriate considering both Australia's claims to be a regional leader on such issues and its status as a signatory to CEDAW.

Common to all these proposals is the need to make visible the gendered nature of representation in the current system. This has particular resonance in the context of Australia's debate about amending the Constitution to become a republic.[126] This leads us to consider the

---

[121] Ibid., 142.

[122] For further information, *see* National Labor Women's Network Web site, http://lwn.alp.org.au.

[123] Rebecca Huntley and Janet Ramsey, "Never Made to Follow, Never Born to Lead," *supra* n. 87, 108. *See also* EMILY's List Australia Web site, accessed May 17, 2013, http://www.emilyslist.org.au.

[124] Ibid.

[125] Rodrigues, "Children in the Parliamentary Chambers," *supra* n. 46. *See also* Alice Brown, Tahyna Barnett Donaghy et al., "Women and Constitutional Change in Scotland and Northern Ireland," *Parliamentary Affairs* 55 (2002): 76.

[126] In 1999 a referendum was held. For further details, *see* "1999 Referendum Report and Statistics," Australian Electoral Commission, updated January 24, 2011, accessed

gender concerns that should be central to the ongoing question of whether Australia should become a republic.

WOMEN AND THE REPUBLIC

Any discussion surrounding Australia's move to a republic will need to consider the role of the head of state, given that central to the concept of becoming a republic is that the Queen of Australia would no longer be head of state and an Australian person would be in that position.

Most discussion favours the retention of a non-executive head of state, who would have similar, albeit potentially, more defined powers. The dichotomy of constitutional duties and ceremonial duties performed by the current Governor-General as the Queen's representative has been likened to the public/private divide identified by feminists as underlying the public framework. This analogy suggests that ceremonial duties are aligned with the private (feminine) requirement of individuals to feel joined as a community. What has traditionally been regarded as the royal function is, in Australia, fulfilled by the Governor-General, who appeals to a broader notion of community then the pure public power framework. However, the Governor-General simultaneously serves as a constitutional umpire. Arguably, having both of these roles acted out by one political player offers the unique advantage of synthesising the public/private divide. The head of state thus serves to broaden our conception of public power.[127]

However, great this potential may be, it has been generally underexploited. This is largely because the position has continued to reassert the binary status quo, public or private, through the overwhelming appointment of men. In the 112 years since federation there has only been one woman Governor-General. If full advantage is to be taken of the potential for the Governor-General to reflect the identity and collective experience of the nation, then women's access to the position must be improved.

The most effective way of guaranteeing this is to mandate that the position alternate between men and women.[128] This process would ensure

May 17, 2013, http://www.aec.gov.au/Elections/referendums/1999_Referendum_Reports_Statistics/Key_Results.htm.

[127] Kim Rubenstein, "Gendered Issues for a Move to a Republic" (Submission to the Senate Legal and Constitutional Committee Inquiry into the Australian Republic, March 31, 2004), 2.

[128] Ibid., 4.

equality; it would also convey through constitutional mandate the importance of equal opportunity at the highest levels. A level of precedent
can be found in the current manner in which High Court appointments
are made, which favours an unofficial quota system to balance state
representation.[129] The foremost argument against this proposition is that
gender should not be preferred over merit.

The first erroneous assumption underlying this claim is that at any
one time there will only ever be one 'best person' for the job. Rather,
there is a pool of equally qualified and capable candidates. Secondly,
detractors argue this is an unnecessary exercise of affirmative action.
This assumes that the current process is an unbiased meritocracy, when
it could be argued that we currently have systemic affirmative action
in favour of men. This system is arguably far more insidious than one
that openly proclaims the importance of equality. Finally, it is suggested
that making women's appointments mandatory will devalue them. No
evidence suggests that men have felt their triumphs were devalued because
they benefitted from a system that blindly worked in their favour.[130]
Moreover, this system will highlight that there is not just one Quentin
Bryce[131] capable of being a superb Governor-General, but a diverse pool
of women candidates.

CONCLUSION

There is cause for considerable optimism for the future of gender equality as a constitutional principle in Australia. High Court judgments have
steadfastly acknowledged since the 1990s that representative democracy
is essential to Australia's constitutional system. The character of that
democracy has become more apparent, and the need for linkage between
electors and elected, the non-static nature of the system and the ongoing
nature of representation have been emphasised. It is clear that, according to its own internal standards of what is required for a representative
democracy, Australia is falling short. The situation in regards to federalism is far more nuanced. However, it is apparent that this is a system that
has enormous potential for women, despite the geographical problems

---

[129] Ibid., 5.   [130] Ibid., 6.

[131] Quentin Bryce was appointed as the first woman governor general on September 5,
1998, and is the twenty-fifth governor general of Australia. For further information, *see*
Web site of the Governor-General of the Commonwealth of Australia, accessed May
17, 2013, http://www.gg.gov.au.

that have stymied it in the past. A number of mechanisms have been offered in this paper for the promotion of gender equality. Not all of them will eventuate, however, it is important to think of new ways to constitutionally reach gender equality by seriously debating proposals of this kind in the public arena as well as the academy. Without such innovation, we will remain a society governed by men, and that will always be "a society half governed."[132]

---

[132] This term is borrowed from a petition presented to a select committee of the New Zealand Parliament calling for equality and parity of gender representation by Jocelyn Fish, Georgina Kirby and Marilyn Waring (cited in Cass and Rubenstein, "Re/presentations of Women," *supra* n. 1, 48).

Islamic Feminism(s): Promoting Gender Egalitarianism and Challenging Constitutional Constraints

Asma Afsaruddin

Islamic feminism (or, more properly, feminisms because they can be inflected differently in different parts of the world) is a phenomenon that is gaining ground in a number of Muslim-majority societies today. One of the many noteworthy consequences of the growth and spread of this phenomenon is that it is increasingly empowering Muslim women to challenge constitutional and legal restraints that are often placed on their rights in many of these societies.

This study will focus on what is meant by the term *Islamic feminism(s)* and its deployment by particularly educated and activist Muslim women to challenge legally mandated social inequalities in their societies. As most constitutions in Muslim-majority societies claim to incorporate religious values, particularly in the sections on personal and family law, Muslim feminists have focused their attention on challenging predominantly masculinist interpretations of such religious values. As will become evident in our discussion, feminist arguments based on scriptural hermeneutics are making inroads into heavily patriarchal societies and appear to have great potential for challenging constitutionally prescribed gender inequalities.

Secular Western observers[1] might well wonder why Muslim women are choosing to work toward legal equality by resorting to religious arguments rather than modern secular discourses on human rights. In contemporary Western societies, the idea that religion is generally discriminatory toward women and therefore gender equality can only be achieved through the secularization of society is pervasive. Although this perspective speaks to the historical experiences of Westerners in general, vis-à-vis their own religious institutions, such a perception does not

---

[1] I am deliberately distinguishing secular Westerners from religious ones, because the latter often show an affinity for religiously tinged feminisms and show considerable

resonate with most Muslims. There are four principal reasons for this: (a) Islam never developed a highly centralized and authoritarian institution like the medieval Catholic church that alone claimed to speak for God and allowed for a single interpretation of canon law; (b) instead, multiple and equally valid interpretations of the religious law are possible within Islam and in fact became enshrined in formal schools of law (*madhahib*), which enjoyed equal validity; (c) traditionally Muslim religious scholars often assumed oppositional roles vis-à-vis the state, so that they were perceived as advocates for the rights of the common people and religion was understood to be liberatory, not repressive toward humans; and finally (d) secular feminism, when it has been attempted in Muslim countries, such as Turkey and pre-revolutionary Iran in the twentieth century, has been a top-down, statist enterprise, which notably failed to include women in the legislative reform process and to effect real, substantive changes in the patriarchal family. It should be noted that secularism in general has been discredited in much of the Islamic world on account of the authoritarian regimes and political injustices it has spawned after the period of Western colonization.

The specific historical experiences of Muslims and the more diffuse nature of religious authority within Islam thus make it possible, even imperative, to annex religion to the project of creating gender-egalitarian societies. Furthermore, since religious authority in Islam is epistemic – that is, based on the possession of knowledge rather than on any process of ordination – women who are trained in religious sciences can carve out a legitimate space for themselves in the ongoing project of social reform

empathy for Islamic feminism. In fact, there are useful comparisons to be made between Christian and Islamic feminism, for example, which point to their shared methodologies and religiously based arguments against gender inequalities; *see, e.g.,* Elizabeth Bucar, *Creative Conformity: The Feminist Politics of US Catholic and Iranian Shi'i Women* (Washington, DC: Georgetown University Press, 2011). Broader comparisons on a global scale are delineated by Arvind Sharma and Katherine K. Young (ed.) in *Feminism and World Religions* (New York: State University of New York, 1998).

It is also important to remember here that women's emancipation movements in the West frequently made appeals to sacred texts to validate their positions and to gain popular acceptance in their early history, even as they bucked conventional religion. Thus the eighteenth-century British feminist Mary Wollstonecraft, for example, in her publication *A Vindication of the Rights of Woman,* cites from the Bible to make the case for gender equality, while at the same time challenging orthodox understandings of the same; cf. Barbara Taylor, *Mary Wollstonecraft and the Feminist Imagination* (Cambridge, England: Cambridge University Press, 2003), 95–144. A collective historical amnesia in the West has obscured the religious slant to early Western feminisms, recovery of which helps us better understand the various forms of Islamic feminism today.

and exercise a considerable measure of religious authority. They may even command respect and deference from some of their male counterparts, as we will see in the case of the two activists, Zainah Anwar and Musdah Mulia, described later. For all these historical reasons, Islamic feminism is clearly becoming the preferred vehicle for social change, especially in regard to women's rights, in a number of Muslim-majority societies today.

UNDERSTANDING ISLAMIC FEMINISM(S)

Before we proceed further, Islamic feminism needs to be broadly defined for the purposes of this article, in full recognition of the fact that there is not necessarily a uniform understanding and application of this concept. However, there is a general consensus that it is above all a reference to feminist discourses and practices based on a dynamic and critical engagement with the foundational sources of Islam centered on the key issue of gender egalitarianism. Islamic feminism, which derives its understanding and mandate from primarily the Qur'an, seeks rights and justice for women (and for men) in all aspects of their lives.[2]

The Qur'an-centric approach of contemporary Muslim feminists is in fact the most distinctive aspect of their methodology and activism. Starting primarily in the twentieth century, Muslim women campaigning in their societies for equal rights and gender equality with men have made Qur'anic hermeneutics the linchpin of their variegated discourses and activism. This is of course a highly sophisticated and learned endeavor. As a consequence, Islamic feminist movements, both in the past and in the contemporary period, have been/are typically led by well-educated women, who often have a deep grounding in religious scholarship and sometimes legal training in the secular sense as well. This development parallels the rise of feminist movements in the West, which were initially led by upper middle-class educated women who had both the intellectual and economic resources to challenge the status quo. The expectation in both cases have been that by bringing about fundamental legal and social reform, the benefits will be shared by all women and particularly by less-privileged women who are the most affected by gender

---

[2] *See, e.g.*, Margot Badran, "Toward Islamic Feminisms: A Look at the Middle East," in *Hermeneutics and Honor: Negotiating Female "Public" Space in Islamic/ate Societies*, ed. Asma Afsaruddin (Cambridge, MA: Harvard University, 1999), 159–88; Margot Badran, *Feminism in Islam: Secular and Religious Convergences* (Oxford: Oneworld Publications, 2009), 323–38.

discrimination as far as educational and job opportunities are concerned. Islamic feminism's appeal to commonly shared religious values and ideals (while undercutting cultural, gendered perspectives) means that, ideologically and emotionally speaking, it has the greater chance of effecting grassroots change. Secular feminism, in contrast, has been the prerogative of a minority of urban, elite women who are often out of touch with the overwhelmingly religious women (and men) found in all strata of Muslim-majority societies.[3]

Women's growing presence in the field of religious scholarship today is not without historical precedent because religious scholarship in the Islamic milieu has never been restricted to men alone. The Islamic intellectual and educational landscape through the centuries is dotted liberally with the names of distinguished women scholars who were active specially in the transmission of *hadith* (the sayings of the Prophet Muhammad) and in educating men and women in the religious sciences in general, starting from the first century of Islam (seventh century of the Common Era).[4] Pointing to this rich history of women's academic activity and even religious leadership in the premodern period, Muslim feminists argue that it testifies to the fundamental valorization of women's intellectual abilities within historical Islam and that this receptivity toward women's participation in the production and dissemination of knowledge is mandated by Islam's core values. The progressive attrition that has occurred over time in women's legal and social rights is a result of a privileged masculinist interpretation of particularly the Qur'an in the context of patriarchal societies and a greater emphasis laid on extra-Qur'anic literature (hadith and exegeses in particular) rather than the Qur'anic text itself.[5] These

---

[3] For further discussion of the grassroots potential of Islamic feminism, *see* Isobel Coleman, *Paradise Beneath Her Feet: How Women are Transforming the Middle East* (New York: Random House, 2013), esp. 32 ff.

[4] *See* Muhammad Zubayr Siddiqui, *Hadith Literature: Its Origin, Development and Special Features*, ed. Abdal Hakim Murad (Cambridge, UK: The Islamic Texts Society, 1993), 117–23; Asma Afsaruddin, "Education, Piety, and Religious Leadership in the Late Middle Ages: Reinstating Women in the Master Narrative," in *Knowledge and Education in Classical Islam*, ed. Sebastian Guenther (Leiden: E.J. Brill, 2014), forthcoming; Asma Afsaruddin, "Literature, Scholarship and Piety: Negotiating Gender and Authority in the Medieval Muslim World," *Religion and Literature* 42 (2010): 111–31.

[5] *E.g.*, Fatima Mernissi, *The Veil and the Male Elite: A Feminist Interpretation of Women's Rights in Islam* (New York: Basic, 1991); Barbara Stowasser, *Women in the Qur'an, Traditions, and Interpretation* (Oxford: Oxford University Press, 1993), esp. 25–38; Nimat Hafez Barazangi, *Woman's Identity and the Qur'an: A New Reading* (Gainesville: University Press of Florida, 2004); Ziba Mir-Hosseini, "Stretching the Limits: A Feminist Reading of the Sharia in Post-Khomeini Iran," in *Feminism and*

feminists declare that this fundamental egalitarian thrust in Islam can therefore be most effectively and most persuasively recuperated from the Qur'an itself. One of the most prominent advocates of this position has been Asma Barlas, who in a much acclaimed book, has described the transformative potential of a new Qur'anic hermeneutics that seeks to undo the patriarchal past by questioning traditional understandings of key Qur'anic verses related to gender and women's roles in society.

> Even though a Qur'ānic hermeneutics cannot by itself put an end to patri-archal, authoritarian, and undemocratic regimes and practices, it nonethe-less remains crucial for various reasons. First, hermeneutic and existential questions are ineluctably *connected* [emphasis in text]. As the concept of sexual/textual oppression suggests, there is a relationship between what we read texts to be saying and how we think about and treat real women. This insight, though associated with feminists because of their work on reading and representation, is at the core of revelation albeit in the form of the reverse premise: that there is a relationship between reading (sacred texts) and liberation.... Accordingly, if we wish to ensure Muslim women their rights, we not only need to contest readings of the Qur'ān that justify the abuse and degradation of women, we also need to establish the legitimacy of liberatory readings. Even if such readings do not succeed in effecting a radical change in Muslim societies. It is safe to say that no meaningful change can occur in these societies that does not derive its legitimacy from the Qur'ān's teachings, a lesson secular Muslims everywhere are having to learn to their own detriment.[6]

This perspective constitutes the basis of new gender-egalitarian readings of Islam's holiest text in which both women and men are increasingly taking part. Barlas' work already builds on the pioneering work of a number of her predecessors who have similarly called for rereadings of the Qur'an, particularly by women interpreters who seek to unearth a gender-egalitarian and woman-friendly world view embedded in its multivalent text. Among them is Amina Wadud who in an earlier work focused on the language of the Qur'an at a microlevel to determine if there was a scriptural preference for the masculine encoded at the textual level or whether such a preference was discerned through a hermeneutic proclivity evinced by male commentators. She comments,

---

Islam: Legal and Literary Perspectives, ed. Mai Yamani (New York: New York University Press, 1996), 285–319.

[6] Asma Barlas, *"Believing Women" in Islam: Unreading Patriarchal Interpretations of the Qur'an* (Austin, TX: University of Texas Press, 2004), 3.

If the way we view the text has been predominantly articulated on the basis of male experiences and through the male psyche, then visions that respond to the male-center of being would have been considered in greatest detail, over and above any differences, inherent or contrived, in the female-center of experience. The extent to which women are seen as distinct from men, therefore, implies the necessity for a female-centered consideration of the Qur'an as the only means by which that distinctiveness will be justly considered in the formulas of basic Islamic identity.[7]

Essentially, Muslim feminists are arguing therefore that the feminist perspective has been sorely lacking in the reading of scripture and has engendered (no pun intended) skewed and ultimately unjust interpretations of it on a number of critical issues. Not surprisingly then, Islamic feminism has become a site of deep contestation as well as providing a common ground for Muslim reformists from a variety of backgrounds who stress the rereading of foundational Islamic texts. As one might suspect, traditional understandings of gender roles that are purportedly grounded in sacred texts are not easily displaced. Convincing conservative segments of Muslim populations that alternate and new readings of scripture conducing to gender egalitarianism are valid and legitimate remains the strongest challenge facing Muslim feminists.

HISTORY OF ISLAMIC FEMINISM(S)

In the twenty-first century, Islamic feminism has truly become a global phenomenon that is not restricted to any geographical region. This represents a dramatic evolution from its origins in roughly the middle to the late nineteenth century when an identifiable feminist vocabulary and consciousness in the modern Islamic milieu began to emerge primarily in the Arab world. An increased awareness among women and questioning of gendered social roles are apparent in books and articles produced by middle- and upper-class women in this era. In the 1890s, Egypt was an important pioneering site of feminism in the Muslim world, where what would later be recognized as a "feminist consciousness" arose in the context of encounters with modernity and with British colonial occupation.[8] From there it would eventually spread to other parts of North Africa

---

[7] Amina Wadud, *Qur'an and Woman: Rereading the Sacred Text from a Woman's Perspective* (New York: Oxford University Press, 1999), xv.

[8] Margot Badran, *Feminists, Islam, and Nation: Gender and the Making of Modern Egypt* (Princeton: Princeton University Press, 1994).

and the Arabic-speaking world and subsequently influence religious and feminist discourses throughout the Islamic world.[9]

In the first half of the twentieth century, women's public organized movements began to arise. There were active movements in Egypt between the 1920s and mid-1950s, in Lebanon, Syria, and Iraq in the 1930s and 1940s, and in Sudan in the 1950s. In the 1950s and 1960s, states started to coopt independent feminist movements, repressing but not totally eliminating women's independent, public feminist voices. The third period from the 1970s to the present witnessed a resurgence of feminist expression in some countries such as Egypt, Lebanon, Syria, and Iraq. It is during the last quarter of the twentieth century when the term Islamic feminism began to gain greater currency and acceptance.

From the 1980s onward, the rise of right-wing Islamist movements, however, began to affect the scope of women's activism in some cases, as we saw, for example, in Iran and in Afghanistan under the Taliban. On the other hand, Islamic revivalism has also made possible a greater support for Islamic feminism as practiced by Islamist women and men who claim that Islamic principles themselves provide the motivation and platform for effecting changes in women's lives and legitimizing their access to the public political and social sphere. We see this occurring among Palestinian women, for example, and in Egypt, especially in the urban areas, as well as other parts of the Middle East and the Islamic world, such as in Iran, Turkey, Saudi Arabia, Malaysia, Indonesia, Pakistan, and elsewhere.[10] A specifically Islamic feminist vocabulary has become part of a larger global language about Islamic reform and progress since the late twentieth century. Both modernist Muslim women and men use this common reformist idiom and arguments to wean Islamic thought and practice from what is regarded as repressive customs and beliefs that have been granted legitimacy in the name of religion.

---

[9] *E.g.*, Sirin Tekeli, "The Emergence of the Feminist Movement in Turkey," in *The New Women's Movements: Feminism and Political Power in Europe and the USA*, ed. Drude Dahlerup (London: Sage, 1986); Mai Yamani, "Some Observations on Women in Saudi Arabia," in *Feminism and Islam: Legal and Literary Perspectives*, ed. Mai Yamani (New York: New York University Press, 1996); Zakia Salime, *Between Feminism and Islam: Human Rights and Sharia Law in Morocco* (Minneapolis: University of Minnesota Press, 2011); and many others.

[10] The literature on this spreading phenomenon is extensive and burgeoning. *See, e.g.*, Saba Mahmood, *The Politics of Piety: The Islamic Revival and the Feminist Subject* (Princeton: Princeton University Press, 2005); Miriam Cooke, *Women Claim Islam: Creating Islamic Feminism through Literature* (New York: Routledge, 2001), 83–106; and many others.

FEMINISM IN RELATION TO MODERNISM

"Modernist" or "reformist" Muslims (these adjectives are often used interchangeably) is a reference to observant Muslims who, starting roughly in the eighteenth century, began to emphasize the inherent adaptability of Islamic principles and thought to modernity. Modernists will typically argue that certain freshly interpreted Islamic principles may be found to be congruent with modern liberal principles of democratic government, civil society, gender equality, and so forth, without necessarily being identical to their formulations in the Western context. Like the Islamists, they too would like to usher in social change, but their means of effecting change is essentially hermeneutic – that is, interpretive – and educational, rather than political or militant in the case of radical Islamists. Accordingly, they stress the rereading of religious texts, primarily the Qur'an and hadith, as a legitimate exercise in *ijtihad* (independent reasoning) to arrive at interpretations appropriate to their historical circumstances without jettisoning the classical heritage and to foster a sense of a continuous critical and dynamic process of engagement with this heritage through education.[11] Despite their respect for tradition in general, modernists tend to be critical of traditionalists who are perceived as unthinkingly following precedent and stymieing the efforts of Muslims to adapt to the modern world in an ethical and critical manner. Modernists or reformists are also called "liberals" and "moderates" by some.[12]

Unlike radical Islamists, modernists tend to emphasize the application of the intent and overall "objectives" (Ar. *maqasid*) of the religious law more than its literal injunctions, especially when the literal understanding of a specific ruling in a particular circumstance would result in unusual hardship and/or violation of an inviolable, broader moral imperative. Thus, many of them argue, because the *Shari'a* must uphold certain ethical values such as justice and mercy at all times, specific legal injunctions may never violate these fundamental objectives in any given historical

---

[11] For an excellent, comprehensive introduction to the development of Islamic modernism, *see* Fazlur Rahman *Islam&Modernity: Transformation of an Intellectual Tradition* (Chicago: University of Chicago Press, 1982); *see also Modernist Islam 1840–1940: A Sourcebook*, ed. Charles Kurzman (Oxford: Oxford University Press, 2002), 3–27.

[12] For very clearly defined differences between liberals and non-liberals within the contemporary Islamic milieu, *see* Khaled Abou El Fadl, *The Great Theft: Wrestling Islam from the Extremists* (New York: HarperCollings, 2005), esp. 113–288. For the most part, we refer to this group of Muslims as modernist.

and social circumstance.[13] Those injunctions that appear to do so need to be reexamined and reinterpreted.[14] They also place more emphasis on the identification of the underlying cause (Ar. *'illa*) of specific legal precepts than on their literal, textual meaning.[15]

Modernists further believe that because the *Shari'a* is essentially flexible and invariably just, it has enough checks and balances built into it to prevent miscarriage of justice. Punitive sanctions that appear on the surface to be harsh are usually difficult to implement since the conditions for proving the commission of the crime for which these sanctions exist are practically impossible to fulfill. Modernists thus hold that such punishments are essentially deterrent in nature and have been carried out infrequently in Muslim societies throughout history.[16] The law as interpreted in the premodern period, say the modernists, should not be understood nor applied in a literal manner in modern societies.[17]

Modernists argue against the assumed all-pervasive reach of the Shari'a as maintained by the Islamists and against the notion that the Shari'a comes with ready-made answers to every imaginable circumstance. They tend to affirm that the reach of the religious law extends to many aspects of human existence while not directly addressing others. Outside of worship (*'ibadat*) the Shari'a offers broad guidelines rather than detailed precepts for proper conduct in various spheres of social and other forms of interaction (*mu'amalat*).[18] The religious law certainly does not, and cannot, have a specific injunction in advance for every possible human situation or contingency. The Qur'an, the principle source of the religious law, "is not a lawbook but is primarily a moral code from which a legal

---

[13] *See further* Abdulaziz Sachedina, *The Islamic Roots of Democratic Pluralism* (Oxford: Oxford University Press, 2007), esp. 109–12. For a comprehensive discussion of justice in Islamic thought, *see* Majid Khadduri, *The Islamic Conception of Justice* (Baltimore, MD: Johns Hopkins University Press, 1984).

[14] Khaled Abou el Fadl, *The Place of Tolerance in Islam* (Boston: Beacon Press, 2002), 11–23.

[15] For an excellent discussion of this legal principle and its rootedness in historical practice, *see* Wael Hallaq, *History of Islamic Legal Theories* (Cambridge, UK: Cambridge University Press, 1997), 83–95.

[16] Muhammad Sa'id al-'Ashmawi, "*Shari'a*: the Codification of Islamic Law" in *Liberal Islam: A Sourcebook*, ed. Charles Kurzman (Oxford: Oxford University Press, 1998), 52–54.

[17] Muhammad Shahrour, *al-Kitab wa-'l-Qur'an: qira'a mu'asira [The Book and the Qur'an: a Contemporary Reading]* (Damascus: al-Ahali li al-taba'a wa al-nashr wa al-tawzi', 1990), 454–64.

[18] Tariq Ramadan, *Western Muslims and the Future of Islam* (Oxford: Oxford University Press, 2005), 31–61.

system may be derived."[19] This derived legal system is the result of human reasoning and effort that allows specific legal precepts to be extrapolated from the Qur'anic moral code, as well as from the *sunna*.

The science or the study of law (that is, jurisprudence) that leads to the derivation of legal rulings is called *fiqh* in Arabic. In its basic meaning, *fiqh* broadly refers to human understanding and rational discernment. Islamists and modernists are essentially in agreement that the Shari'a must always be respected, but they tend to talk past one another when the former mistake fiqh for Shari'a and/or use the terms interchangeably. Jurisprudence (fiqh) is a human intellectual activity and, therefore, fallible and changeable. Specific legal interpretations resulting from the deliberations of jurists were crafted in response to specific historical and social contingencies. Changed circumstances, the modernists insist (and I should add, so did a number of premodern jurists), necessitate changed interpretations in conformity with the objectives (*maqasid*) of the law. Modernists see a fundamental, grave problem arising from the equation of jurisprudence with the religious law itself – that is, of fiqh with Shari'a by hard-line Islamists (and often by traditionalists as well).

Thus in opposition to hard-line Islamists, modernists typically emphasize the malleability of the Shari'a, which allows the faithful to relate to it in creative interpretive ways in different circumstances. The broad parameters of the religious law, they maintain, leave ample room for negotiation and accommodation of its fundamental moral objectives as well as for considerations of the common good (*maslaha*) through recourse to independent reasoning (*ijtihad*). Like *maqasid* (objectives), *maslaha* is another key term associated with modernist discourses on the relevance of the Shari'a in the contemporary period that harks back to the Shafi'i jurist and theologian Abu Hamid Muhammad al-Ghazali's (d. 1111) exposition of this legal principle.[20] This principle would be further elaborated on by the jurist Abu Ishaq al-Shatibi (d. 1388), whose rational juristic thought has enjoyed a revival among modernists.[21]

Within the hierarchical ordering of the sources of law, modernists tend to emphasize the supremacy of the Qur'an over the sunna. Thus Rashid

---

[19] Fazlur Rahman, *Major Themes of the Qur'an* (Minneapolis, MN: Bibliotheca Islamica, 1980), 47.

[20] *See* Wael Hallaq, "Logic, Formal Arguments and Formalization of Arguments in Sunni Jurisprudence," *Arabica* 37 (1990): 317–18.

[21] For a detailed study of al-Shatibi, *see* Khalid Masud, *Islamic Legal Philosophy: A Study of Abu Ishaq al-Shatibi's Life and Thought* (Islamabad, Pakistan: Islamic Research Institute, 1977).

Rida, the well-known Egyptian reformer of the twentieth century, maintained that the Qur'an is the main source (*asl*) of religion and that rules
derived from the sunna, if not directly bearing on religious matters, need
not be followed. He was of course following in the footsteps of his mentor, Muhammad 'Abduh, the famous nineteenth century scholar who
sought to reform Egyptian society along modernist lines. The 'Abduh-
Rida school of thought has enjoyed a resurgence among contemporary
Muslim modernists.[22] Their rational, critical, and thoughtful approach
to the religious and historical sources resonate among today's leading
Muslim modernist thinkers, and particularly among today's Muslim
feminists.

Today's feminists in fact continue the modernist project of emphasizing human equality and dignity regardless of gender as religiously
mandated features of a properly formed, ethical Islamic society. Rashid
Rida after all had written a very influential work titled *The Liberation
of Women*,[23] which argued for women's emancipation on the basis of
religious texts. Modernist women of the early twentieth century typically
tended to focus on women's issues and continued the impetus created by
Rida to press for greater rights for women as something intrinsic to Islam.

ISLAMIC FEMINISM(S) AND CONSTITUTIONAL CHALLENGES

In the rest of this chapter, I concentrate on two women scholar activists
who are among the leading participants in the worldwide phenomenon
of Islamic feminism and who are deploying critical rereadings of the
Qur'an and Shari'a to challenge aspects of their national constitutions
and legal cultures that are discriminatory toward women. They have
borrowed heavily from modernist Qur'anic hermeneutics and exercise
their right to *ijtihad* (legal reasoning) to retrieve a woman-friendly and
gender-egalitarian thrust within the variegated Islamic tradition. The first
activist is Zainah Anwar, a Muslim feminist in Malaysia, who ran an
organization known as Sisters in Islam for about two decades. The second is an Indonesian academic and lawyer Siti Musdah Mulia who has
dedicated her life to promoting legal and social reform in her native

---

[22] *See further* Asma Afsaruddin, *The First Muslims: History and Memory* (Oxford:
Oneworld Publications, 2008), 168–82.

[23] Translated into English as *The Liberation of Women and the New Woman*, tr. Samiha
Sidhom Peterson (Cairo: American University of Cairo Press, 2000).

country on the basis of foundational Islamic principles that promote gender egalitarianism. Their lives and trajectory of reformist activities are highly illuminating of an important and growing trend of seeking legal reform within Muslim-majority societies, especially concerning gender issues on the basis of religiously crafted arguments. In the conclusion, we will have occasion to briefly dwell on the long-term effects of such trends.

Zainah Anwar and the Sisters in Islam

Zainah Anwar was born to a prominent family in Johor Bahru in Malaysia. As a young girl, she aspired to be a journalist and eventually joined the then Mara Institute of Technology (now Universiti Teknologi Mara) in Shah Alam in 1972 to study journalism. She became known as a rather hard-nosed journalist at the well-known Malaysian newspaper the *New Straits Times*. In 1978, Anwar left for Boston University where she completed her masters degree in 1978 and then studied international law and diplomacy at the Fletcher School of Diplomacy at Tufts University until 1986, when she returned to Malaysia. Between 1986 and 1991, she joined the Institute of Strategic and International Studies think tank in London and then became the chief program officer in the Political Affairs Division of the Commonwealth Secretariat. Her international experience helped her build an extensive network of colleagues worldwide, which has proven to be useful during her gender activism.

Sisters in Islam was founded in 1988, when a group of women lawyers, activists, academics, and journalists, including Zainah Anwar, launched a movement to investigate the problems encountered by Muslim women in Shari'a courts in Malaysia. A primary objective of the Sisters in Islam movement was to challenge laws and policies that claim to be founded on Islamic legal principles but that clearly discriminated against women. Its members have sponsored public debates and instituted education programs that tackle controversial topics such as equal rights for women, dress and modesty, right to hold public office including judgeships, and right to guardianship, among others. They have also expanded to deal with larger issues of democracy, human rights, and constitutionalism. Not surprisingly, Sisters in Islam provoked criticism from conservative religious scholars (*'ulama*) in Malaysia because the women leaders were not traditionally trained scholars. A number of religious organizations in Malaysia have publicly criticized the Sisters in Islam for their lack of proper scholarly credentials, and some attempts were made to ban it.

However, some of the more liberal religious clergy have responded positively to overtures from Sisters in Islam and participated in seminars with them.[24]

The sociopolitical background in which the Sisters in Islam arose needs to be addressed here in brief. In the late 1970s, Islamist groups began to gain ground in Malaysia as a consequence of a number of events and upheavals following the end of the British colonial occupation in 1946. These events included race riots between indigenous and non-indigenous Malays in the 1960s, rapid modernization and industrialization, and nationalist economic and social policies that disenfranchised poor Malaysian Muslims, all of which served as catalysts for Malaysia's Islamic revival in the late 1970s. Gradual governmental changes implementing pro-Islamic policies were propagated by the Dakwah students' movement in the early 1980s. Since the rising influence of the Islamists, women's rights have been under attack in a judicial system that began to strip women of certain rights and enabled men to justify spousal abuse and polygamous marriages.

In response to the adoption of such discriminatory laws, women's rights organizations began to publicly address issues of gender equality, forming in 1985 the Joint Action Group. When Zainah Anwar became an active member of the group, she discovered that the general discourse on women's rights blamed Islam for Malaysia's gender rights inequality. Whereas many women's rights groups believed that Islam had created the problem, Anwar argued that it was the patriarchal interpretation of Islam that caused injustices against women, and that a broader conversation about a progressive interpretation and role of Islam in daily life must be initiated.[25]

In an article that Zainah Anwar coauthored with another scholar, she identified some key challenges to legal reform in Muslim-majority societies that women's activist groups need to tackle and proactively engage with to undermine them. The following challenges were identified by Anwar:

---

[24] *See generally*, Shelia Nair, "Challenging the Mullahs: Islam, Politics and Women's Activism, Interview with Zainah Anwar," *International Feminist Journal of Politics* 9 (2007): 240–48; Amy L. Freedman, "Civil Society, Moderate Islam, and Politics in Indonesia and Malaysia," *Journal of Civil Society* 5 (2009): 107–27; Carol Anne Douglas, "Malaysian Sisters in Islam Oppose Fundamentalism," *Off Our Backs* 28 (1998): 10.

[25] "Sisters in Islam: Protecting Women's Rights in Malaysia," last accessed December 7, 2012, http://www.tavaana.org/viewcasestudy.jsp?pageId+2071502000341264062 66439&lang=.

1. The popular but inaccurate belief in many mainstream Muslim societies that Muslim family law is God's law and is, therefore, infallible and unchangeable, which renders any effort at reform as un-Islamic and contrary to the well-being of Muslims.
2. The general belief that men and women do not have equal rights in Islam, so that demands for equal rights to divorce, guardianship, and inheritance, for example, are portrayed as going against the Shari'a.
3. A widespread perception that only Muslim religious scholars or jurists have the authority to speak and comment on legal and theological matters. Since jurists are not at the forefront of reform, civil society groups and lay intellectuals assume leadership in reform movements, but their credentials and authority to engage with Islam publicly are questioned and undermined. Thus, women's groups in Muslim societies face resistance when they advocate for reform in the absence of support from the government or those who have traditional religious authority.
4. A fear of speaking out on religious matters publicly, especially when taking issue with more common "orthodox" views regarding the family and women's roles. Taking controversial positions on these matters exposes oneself to the risk of being labeled "anti-Islamic" and questioning the word of God by hardliners. In more extreme cases, progressive scholars who have the knowledge and credibility to speak out on such matters opt to remain silent so as not to jeopardize their jobs and livelihoods, invoking community hostility, and/or facing threats to their safety.
5. And finally, the challenge that is created in many countries by the tension between constitutional guarantees of equality and nondiscrimination and constitutional provisions that recognize religious and customary laws that discriminate against women in the name of religion and recognition of cultural diversity.[26]

Anwar set up the Sisters in Islam to address these concerns and offer leadership and guidance to women who were increasingly questioning the patriarchal interpretations offered by traditional religious clerics. Another problem was posed by extremist ideologues who are not trained as religious scholars but nevertheless felt free to circulate their often misogynist

---

[26] Zainah Anwar and Jana S. Rumminger, "Justice and Equality in Muslim Family Laws: Challenges, Possibilities, and Strategies for Reform," *Washington and Lee Law Review* 64 (2007): 1529–49, last accessed December 7, 2012, http://law.wlu.edu/deptimages/ Law%20Review/64-4Anwar&Rumminger.pdf.

interpretations cloaked in Islamicizing rhetoric. To counter this trend, Sisters in Islam strove to educate women in particular about their scripturally mandated rights within Islam and promoted rereadings of religious texts in view of two foundational principles or objectives of the religious law (*maqasid al-Shariʿa*): equality and justice. They have distributed pamphlets among the Malaysian public containing reinterpretations of key Islamic texts emphasizing equality and justice irrespective of gender. Several of their publications address a number of critical and controversial issues in considerable depth and include subjects such as Islam and family planning, Islam and women's reproductive rights, and the rights of Muslim women within marriage, among others. They also run legal clinics and programs to raise public awareness of general legal and more specifically gender issues and carry out research in legislative reform. In one interview granted by Anwar, she stressed her belief that over time an understanding of Islam and Islamic laws that recognize equality and justice would gain ground in Malaysia and elsewhere. To quote her:

> The reason I became involved in this movement was just outrage, really, over injustices perpetrated in the name of God. For me, leaving Islam or ignoring Islam is not an issue at all. I think for all of us who were there from the start [of Sisters in Islam], we were concerned with why Islam was being used to justify domestic violence, oppression and discrimination.[27]

Anwar is also aware of the importance of building coalitions and active partnerships with other civic and advocacy groups to create a broad public constituency in favor of legal reform. A strategic campaign must be waged to raise public awareness of the need for such reform. The dangers of not building such strategic alliances are obvious: the greater likelihood of strong resistance from groups who are not part of the public conversation and of failure because of the absence of grassroots support. Such a failed case occurred in Indonesia when a revised and egalitarian family law program was introduced by the Indonesian Ministry of Religious Affairs for vote but was defeated by hostile members of Parliament, traditional religious scholars, and hard-line Islamists (see p. 309). Officials at the ministry acknowledged later that they had not engaged in building necessary alliances among these critical groups and had not laid the groundwork for popular support for the draft legislation. In contrast, successful examples were provided by women's movements in Morocco and

---

[27] Interview with Zainah Anwar, last accessed December 3, 2012, http://www.tavaana .org/nu_upload/Zainah_Anwar_En.pdf.

Turkey, which campaigned for legal reform in these countries and focused on public educational campaigns, which effectively countered the opposition they encountered from traditionalists and hard-line Islamists.[28]

After surveying these comparable legislative initiatives in other countries, Sisters in Islam undertook a multipronged strategy to lobby for substantial reform of family law in Malaysia. The organization first drafted a model family law bill invoking Islamic principles of equality and justice that could serve as the basis of negotiation with religious and governmental authorities. The specifically Islamic arguments crafted in support of enhanced rights for women and gender egalitarianism contributed to a greater receptivity on the part of the public toward these legal reforms. By 1988, the Joint Action Group was calling for a Domestic Violence Act that would criminalize spousal abuse in Malaysia. The Domestic Violence Act, which was not passed by the Parliament until 1994, could not have become law without Sisters in Islam. It was the only Islamic group within the Joint Action group, which included three other women's rights organizations: the Women's Aid Organization, the women's wing of the Malaysian Trade Organization, and the Association of Women Lawyers. These groups lobbied together among the general population and presented a united front, which contributed to their eventual success.[29]

Sisters in Islam has recently broadened their efforts beyond Malaysian society with the establishment of a new organization by Zainah Anwar called *Musawah*, which is an Arabic word meaning "equality." As the name indicates, this group's main agenda is to work to ensure that Muslim women are treated equally within the families and communities of Muslim-majority societies. The project was initiated with a global meeting in February 2009 that brought together over 250 Muslim scholars and feminist activists from nearly 50 countries. Musawah provides its global activists with a resource kit that offers arguments and advocacy positions for those fighting to increase women's family rights. Musawah focuses on "knowledge-building," which according to their Web site, has the following three elements:

1. Commissioning background research on the role of *qiwamah* and *wilayah* within historical and present-day Muslim legal traditions and research on socioeconomic realities.
2. Conducting participatory research to collect women's and men's life stories in relation to *qiwamah* and *wilayah*.

---

[28] Anwar and Rumminger, "Justice and Equality," *supra* n. 25, 1547.
[29] Ibid., 1547–48.

3. Opening spaces for scholars and activists to discuss and forge new understandings of *qiwamah* and *wilayah*.[30]

According to traditional interpretation, the terms *qiwamah* and *wilayah* of Qur'anic provenance refer to men's authority over women and have been typically understood by male jurists to mandate women's subjugation and obedience to their husbands. Specific legal privileges emanating from classical juridical interpretations of these concepts are thereby conferred on the husband: the right to terminate the marriage contract at will, to marry more than one woman at a time, to restrict the wife's movements, and others. As stated in their mission statement, the members of Musawah "seek to apply feminist and rights-based lenses in understanding and searching for equality and justice within Muslim legal traditions. Such lenses help…uncover women's voices that were for so long silenced in the production of religious knowledge, so that their concerns and interests can be reflected."[31] Ultimately, as a knowledge-building initiative, Musawah's long-term objective is to create a women's rights and human rights-based discourse within an Islamic matrix that will effect enduring legal and social change in Muslim-majority societies.

Siti Musdah Mulia and the Counter Legal Draft in Indonesia

In Indonesia, Anwar's counterpart is Siti Musdah Mulia, an academic and a women's rights advocate who is nationally and internationally recognized for her work. Mulia was born on March 3, 1958, in Bone, South Sulawesi, and raised in a devout Muslim family. She graduated from Alauddin State Islamic University in Makassar, Indonesia in 1982, before moving to Jakarta's Syarif Hidayatullah State Islamic University (UIN), where she was introduced to the ideas of the reformist Muslim scholar Harun Nasution. In 1997, she became the first woman to obtain a doctorate degree in the field of Islamic political thought from the State Islamic University. In 1999, she became the first woman to be appointed as a research professor by the Indonesian Institute of Sciences. For twenty years, Mulia was actively involved in Fatayat NU, an organization for

---

[30] "Musawah: For Equality in the Muslim Family," last accessed December 7, 2012, http://www.musawah.org/sites/default/files/Qiwamah%20Initiative%20Overview%20EN%2026.9.11.pdf.

[31] Ibid.

young women who are members of Nahdatul Ulama, the country's largest Muslim organization.[32]

In 2004, Mulia and a team of eleven experts completed a bold and innovative project with the objective to revise Indonesia's *Kompilasi Hukum Islam*, the country's Islamic legal code. Mulia was appointed the chair of the committee in the Ministry of Religious Affairs in Indonesia that was charged with creating what has been called the Counter Legal Draft of the Islamic Legal Code. The committee consisted of legal experts and religious studies teachers and focused primarily on reforming family law and legal provisions pertaining to women's rights. Mulia's own perspective on the rationale for legal reform of this nature is contained in her following statement:

> What is needed now is to apply to society and disseminate Islamic teachings that advocate emancipation, without causing anxiety among men that their dominance might be threatened or that these new applications will lead to moral decadence in the society. The concrete solution we offer is to embark on theologically grounded deconstruction of the Islamic teachings, especially of those that pertain to the relationship between men and women.[33]

The recommendations of the Counter Legal Draft included a ban on polygamy and forced marriages, equal rights for husbands and wives, and raising the legal age of marriage for girls from 16 to 19 years old, among others. Such measures would help curtail and prevent domestic violence and child abuse. Mulia also strongly argued in favor of contraception and reproductive rights, pointing out that premodern Muslim jurists allowed birth control and first trimester abortion for women.[34] She proposed that the measures recommended by the Counter Legal Draft be submitted for

[32] For Mulia's biography, *see, e.g.,* M. Azis Tunny, *The Jakarta Post*, August 13, 2010; Manneke Budiman, "Treading the Path of the Shari'a: Indonesian Feminism at the Crossroads of Western Modernity and Islamism," *Journal of Indonesian Social Sciences and Humanities* 2 (2008): 85–93. For a general exposition of the modernist and liberal struggle for equality and justice in Indonesia, *see* Syafi'i Anwar, "The Clash of Religio-Political Thought: The Contest between Radical Conservative Islam and Progressive-Liberal Islam in Post-Soeharto Indonesia," in *The Future of Secularism*, ed. T.N. Srinivasan (Oxford: Oxford University Press, 2007), 186–256. For the Fatayat NU specifically, *see* Monika Arnez, "Empowering Women Through Islam: Fatayat NU between Tradition and Change," *Journal of Islamic Studies* 21(1) (2009).
[33] Cited by Pieternella van Doorn-Harder in *Women Shaping Islam: Reading the Qur'an in Indonesia* (Urbana and Chicago: University of Illinois Press, 2006), 261.
[34] *See* Basim Musallam, *Sex and Society in Islam: Birth Control before the Nineteenth Century* (Cambridge, UK: Cambridge University Press, 1983).

ratification by the Indonesian Parliament. Despite the sponsorship of the draft by Indonesia's Minister of Religious Affairs, sharp disagreements and violent protests over the changes recommended by the Counter Legal Draft led to its cancellation. As the chair of the committee and instigator of a number of these controversial changes, Mulia faced a barrage of criticism from conservative groups and even death threats from radical Islamist groups.

The Counter Legal Draft is remarkable for its emphasis on the Qur'an and its proper interpretation to challenge classical jurisprudential rulings on women's rights within marriage and family law in general and their appropriate roles in society. Despite the fact that it did not become the law of the land in Indonesia (although one suspects many of the draft's provisions could be revived in the future and, with successful coalition building, could be ratified, replicating the Malaysian experience), it is heuristically useful for us to focus on Mulia's scriptural and legal hermeneutics as an example of constitutional reform processes and methodologies in a number of Muslim-majority societies.[35]

Mulia's point of departure is Article 2 of the Indonesian Islamic Code of Law, which states that "[m]arriage according to Islamic law is a binding contract [that] complies with the command of God, and performing it is an act of devotion." In contrast, the Counter Legal Draft defines marriage as "a binding contract between a man and a woman, with full awareness, in order to establish a family based on the willingness and agreement of both parties."[36] The first definition draws its inspiration from classical jurisprudence, which emphasized marriage as a communal obligation rather than a personal one and that mandated the legal subordination of wives to their husbands, particularly on the issue of sexual rights.[37] Although this view is regarded as Islamic, Mulia contrasts this classical legal perspective to the Qur'anic description of marriage as one between equals and the ontological equality between men and women. Thus, she cites Qur'an 7:189, which refers to the creation of male and female from a single soul (*nafs wahida*), without any indication of male priority in

---

[35] Mulia offers us an in-depth critique of traditional legal hermeneutics in a detailed article published online titled "Toward Just Marital Law: Empowering Indonesian Women," last accessed December 1, 2012, http://www.oasiscenter.eu/files/Muliah_Eng.pdf, 1–71.

[36] Ibid., 33.

[37] This classical view may be found in Abdurrahman al-Jaza'iri, *al-Fiqh 'ala al-madhahib al-arba'a [Jurisprudence according to the Four Legal Schools]* (Beirut: Dar al-Fikr, n.d.), 4:4.

the divine creation of human beings. Mulia comments that the Qur'an employs the term

> *nafsin wahidah* to make a point that marriage is essentially a reunification between man and woman in the practical level, following the initial unification as human. (An)other verse (al-Rum, 30:21) stresses the essential unification, min anfusikun, or unification on the idealistic level with practical level (marriage) that is peaceful and full of affection. Peace and affection will not exist when a party negates and subordinates the other (spouse). There should not be any domination in marriage, as it will lead to ignorance of the spouse's rights and existence. Removing domination in husband and wife relation will create civil, well-mannered, equal and full of affection relationship (*mawaddah wa rahmah*).[38]

Accordingly, marriage is described in the Counter Legal Draft as a union that individuals enter into of one's own free volition and represents a voluntary social transaction or contract between the bride and the groom who are legally equal. This sets up another contrast to the traditional marriage contract that was typically concluded between the groom and the bride's father/guardian, instead of between the bride and the groom. The emphasis on marriage as a social contract between two equal parties eliminates the legal subordination of the wife to her husband.[39]

In regard to the requirement for a guardian to marry off the bride as mentioned in Article 19[40] of the Islamic Code of Law, the Counter Legal Draft requires a guardian in a marriage ceremony only when the bride is under 21 years old. Mulia points out that the classical jurist Abu Hanifa had similarly maintained this position in the ninth century CE, and therefore there is a legal precedent that can be appealed to (even though the official *madhhab*/legal school followed by Indonesians is the Shafi'i one). Citing a number of Qur'anic verses and hadiths that confirm women's equality with men, the Counter Legal Draft also states that an adult male or female may act as the guardian of a female minor, in contrast to the Islamic Code of Law, which recognizes only a male guardian.[41]

---

[38] Mulia, "Toward Just Marital Law," *supra* n. 34, 36.

[39] Ibid., 37.

[40] This article states that "Guardian in a wedding ceremony is required to marry off the bride," ibid., 37.

[41] The Islamic Code of Law's position is generally modeled on premodern Shafi'i works of jurisprudence, as described by Mohammad Rifa'i in *The Complete Islamic Jurisprudence Studies* (Semarang, Malaysia: Karya Toha Putra, 1978), esp. 453–512.

Similarly, Article 79 of the Code of Law states that the husband is the head of the family and the wife is the homemaker, although the rights and position of a wife are regarded as balanced and equal to those of the husband. As Mulia remarks, these two components of Article 79 are actually inconsistent with one another because the first part unambiguously states that the husband is the head of the family. As an egalitarian countermeasure, Article 49 of the Counter Legal Draft maintains that the position, rights, and obligations of the husband and wife are equal within the family or society and that both are equally vested with the rights and obligation to establish a good family based on love, mercy, and mutual benefit.[42]

Based on this basic principle of equal rights within marriage, Article 51 of the Counter Legal Draft described the mutual obligations of husband and wife as follows: (1) to love each other, to give respect, honor, and protection to one another, and to accept each other's differences; (2) to support each other and to meet the needs of the family according to their abilities; (3) to manage the household based on the agreement between husband and wife; (4) to give opportunity to one another to improve their potentials; (5) to look after, to take care of, and to educate the children.

Furthermore, the husband is most decidedly not the "head of family," a phrase that implies power and authority and that allows a husband to impose his will on his wife. This perception, argues Mulia, contradicts a foundational moral and ethical principle within Islam as stipulated in Qur'an 2:187, which describes the equal and mutually beneficial position between husband and wife (*hunna libasun lakum wa antum libasun lahunna*, meaning that a husband and wife are equally the source of comfort and protection to one another). Positioning husband as head of the family negates social reality and only accommodates one type of family, which consists of father (husband), mother (wife), and children. In reality, there are various forms of families and/or household: single mothers with children, orphans with the oldest daughter in charge, and so on. Many women are in charge as the head of family but are not recognized by law. In the condition of wars and natural disasters, such as the tsunami in Aceh, or when the husband works abroad, women are forced to act as the head of the family. These situations, as well as a number of international and national conventions – for example, the Universal Declaration of Human Rights, the Convention on the Elimination of all forms of Discrimination against Women (CEDAW), the Human Rights Convention

[42] Mulia, "Toward Just Marital Law," *supra* n. 34, 37–40.

in Kairo – can serve as legal references to buttress the more egalitarian position of husband and wife.[43]

It should be noted that even though the Counter Legal Draft has not been ratified as of yet, Mulia remains undeterred in her human-rights advocacy work related to faith and gender in particular. Like many Muslim reformers today, including Zainah Anwar, Mulia emphasizes the *maqasid* of the Shari'a, the overall objectives of the religious law, in the light of which jurists must derive legal rulings from the sacred texts of Islam that promote the common good. Mulia's legal interpre-tive work with the Counter Legal Draft was based on a perspective that included six essential points: pluralism (*ta'addudiyya*), nationality (*muwatana*), upholding human rights (*iqamat al-huquq al-insaniyya*), democracy (*dimuqratiyya*), public benefits (*maslaha*), and gender equal-ity (*al-musawa al-jinsiyya*).[44] One of the rights she is fighting for, in addition to gender issues, is the state's guarantee of freedom of religion. Musdah believes that pluralism in Indonesia's multi-ethnic and multi-religious society is a *sine qua non* and that the state should not regulate matters of religion and beliefs. Since 2007 she has been the chairperson of the Indonesian Conference on Religion for Peace, a non-governmental organization (NGO) that actively promotes interfaith dialogues, plural-ism, and democracy for peace. She remains active as an academic, speaker, and social reformer, and we have by no means heard the last from her.

CONCLUSION

It has been suggested that Islamic feminism has the potential to be more radical than secular feminism, because the former calls for comprehensive equal rights in the public sphere as well as the private sphere.[45] In fact, Muslim feminists tend to dissolve the distinctions between the two spheres and argue for full equality within the home and outside. Typically secular feminists in Muslim-majority contexts have called for equal rights in the public sphere but have settled for complementarity in the domestic realm, so that the husband continued to be recognized as head of the household and men and women played different and complementary roles within it. Muslim feminists, such as Heba Rauf in Egypt, argue

---

[43] Ibid., 51–53.

[44] Theresa W. Devasahayam, *Singapore Women's Charter: Roles, Responsibilities, and Rights in Marriage* (Singapore: Institute of Southeast Asian Studies, 2011), 8–9.

[45] Badran, *Feminism in Islam, supra* n. 2, 250.

instead that the Qur'an mandates full gender equality in all spheres of life and reject complementarity as a feature of patriarchal societies that is not consonant with the Qur'anic vision. Rauf has argued that the global Islamic community (*umma*), unlike the secular nation-state (*watan*), is a holistic space that does not recognize an artificial public-private divide and that recognizes men and women as equal citizens with equal rights, whether in domestic or public space.[46]

In many of its incarnations in different Muslim-majority societies (as well as in the West), Islamic feminism pushes the envelope with regard to claiming religious expertise on a par with that of men and sharing religious and political authority with their male counterparts. In accordance with their vision of total gender equality in all aspects of life, Muslim feminists are challenging, in particular, the conventional notion of male authority over females in marriage and the family and demanding that men live up to the egalitarian standards espoused by Islam, as mandated in the Qur'an and practiced by the Prophet Muhammad. Muslim feminists are seeking to arm themselves with traditional religious learning and mastery of seminal texts within Islam and thus acquiring the essential intellectual accoutrements with which to challenge the male-dominated preserve of Qur'anic exegesis and legal interpretations in particular.

Our two case studies exemplify the potential inherent in the agendas of Islamic feminism to bring about comprehensive legal reform particularly concerning women's rights and gendered roles in Muslim-majority societies (and Muslim-minority societies in the West and elsewhere). Both Zainah Anwar and Sitti Musda Mulia exemplify the dogged determination of modernist women reformers who seek to translate into reality what they see as the overwhelmingly egalitarian and uncompromisingly just society envisioned in the Qur'an. Although they have not yet achieved the kind of large-scale constitutional reforms they have been seeking, their arguments have entered the mainstream and are increasingly engaged in the public sphere. Islamic feminist arguments provide a powerful antidote to fundamentalist perspectives that present cultural, often tribal, and patriarchal values as synonymous with Islamic ones. Islamic feminist platforms also sometimes bring religious and secular feminists together,

---

[46] Ibid., 332. The creation of a public-private dichotomy is highly problematic; it is the result of seventeenth- and eighteenth-century Western liberal assumption that the private domain did not require protection from arbitrary and absolute political authority as did the public, a viewpoint that has been severely criticized by Western feminists themselves; *see* Joan W. Scott, *Gender and the Politics of History* (New York: Columbia University Press, 1999).

as has happened in Turkey on the issue of women's right to wear the headscarf in public. Both stripes of feminists have argued that this is a matter of personal choice and the state's prohibition against wearing it infringes on the individual's right to freedom of religious expression.[47] Islamic feminism based as it is on Qur'anic premises also has the potential to bring more male religious scholars into its fold, as we saw occurring already in both Anwar's and Mulia's cases. Such male scholars often exercise great influence on society and will prove to be important allies for feminist women who cannot effect deep-seated reform on their own.[48]

As Muslim women become increasingly better educated and continue to enter the professions in large numbers, their perspectives and concerns will become progressively more influential and percolate down to the grass roots, as it has already begun to do. Women's movements that continue to seek to bring these perspectives and concerns into the mainstream of their societies and that strive to effect constitutional reform within Islamic paradigms will become increasingly acceptable. That time is perhaps not anytime very soon – Mulia's predicament serves as a cautionary tale here even as Anwar's success story is a bracing counterexample. However, Islamic feminist-legal trends appear to have become irreversible and chart new hopeful terrain for not only Muslim women and men but also for others from different backgrounds who are increasingly coexisting with them.

---

[47] Nilufer Gole, *The Forbidden Modern: Civilization and Veiling* (Ann Arbor: University of Michigan Press, 1996).

[48] For similar assessments, *see* Ziba Mir-Hosseini, "Muslim Women's Quest for Equality: Between Islamic Law and Feminism," *Critical Inquiry* 32 (2006): 629–45. Mir-Hosseini memorably remarks, "A movement to sever patriarchy from Islamic ideals and sacred texts and to give voice to an ethical and egalitarian vision of Islam can and does empower Muslim women from all walks of life to make dignified choices. This, in the end, is what Islamic feminism is about." Ibid., 645.

India, Nepal, and Pakistan: A Unique South Asian Constitutional Discourse on Sexual Orientation and Gender Identity

Sean Dickson and Steve Sanders

INTRODUCTION

The global movement for lesbian, gay, bisexual, and transgender rights has achieved remarkable success over the past three decades, particularly in constitutional courts and human rights tribunals. In this chapter we focus on recent decisions from constitutional courts in India, Nepal, and Pakistan, and how these decisions have advanced the rights and equality of minority groups that are defined by sexual orientation and/or gender identity (SOGI).

These South Asian decisions add to a growing body of global jurisprudence that has advanced SOGI rights and equality. However, they do not represent a triumph of Western-style gay/lesbian advocacy, which has increasingly emphasized narratives of similarity between homosexuals and heterosexuals. Rather, these constitutional decisions have mandated respect for diversity and difference, and they have been driven as much or more by the negotiation of gender variation than of sexual identity. In particular, we highlight the role that has been played in each country by *hijras*, a transgender population whose members are physiologically male and have sex with men, but who adopt a feminine gender identity. Hijras, who are increasingly recognized as embodying a distinctive third gender, have occupied a unique space in South Asian history and culture since ancient times. It is especially noteworthy, then, that they have played such a visible and important role in contemporary South Asian constitutional discourse of SOGI minority liberation.

In this chapter, we use the term SOGI rather than LGBT (Lesbian, Gay, Bisexual, and Transgender) to highlight not only the different constructions of sexual behavior and gender in South Asia but also to offer a more inclusive term that accounts for indeterminacy and intentional lack of identity. The process of naming, identification, and coming out are Western concepts that impede a nuanced understanding of South Asian sexual minority jurisprudence. Perhaps more importantly, Western sexual minority labels can also damage the lives and efforts of non-Western sexual minorities, as anti-gay sentiments are often simply reframed anti-Western sentiments. Using the term SOGI instead of LGBT allows us not only to heighten the difference in the process of liberation in South Asia but also to intentionally understand it on its own terms.

Indeed, we believe the South Asian experience also confounds the doctrinal legal categories that have become familiar to Western scholars of sexuality and gender identity, a theme we explore further in our conclusions at the end of this chapter. The major constitutional decisions we discuss are all concerned prominently with nondiscrimination and non-persecution at the hands of the government. But, especially in India and Nepal, the decisions also include prominent themes of autonomy and constitutional protection for the individual's ability to construct and act on personal identity without harassment or interference from the state.

We should note as well that some of the events reported in this chapter are relatively recent and have not previously been documented or discussed in Western academic writing. For example, while others have noted the role of third-gender persons in the *Naz Foundation* decision in India,[1] discussion of the past successes of *aravanis*[2] in receiving legal recognition in the Indian state of Tamil Nadu has been limited. The recency of the events we describe in Pakistan also means that these court decisions have not been debated or examined by Western scholars. Due to lack of access to court records from these countries and the recency of events, much of our information is based on media reports and cannot be confirmed with original documents. However, we have endeavored to discuss only events that have been covered by prominent South Asian media outlets and confirmed by other media sources. Particularly in Pakistan, where the Supreme Court has been quite active in this area, new developments may have occurred while this chapter was in press. Nonetheless, we hope that our analysis encourages further scholarly examination of these important developments.

---

[1] *See* Siddharth Narrain, "Crystallising Queer Politics: The *Naz Foundation* Case and Its Implications for India's Transgender Communities," *NUJS Law Review* 2 (2009): 455; Sonia K. Katyal, "The Dissident Citizen," *UCLA Law Review* 57 (2009): 1415.

[2] The preferred local term for hijras in Tamil Nadu.

CONTEXTUALIZING THE SOUTH ASIAN CONSTITUTIONAL DISCOURSE

The right to be free from discrimination on the basis of sexual orientation or gender identity has emerged as a prominent theme in the global human rights discourse. The Yogyakarta Principles, propagated in 2006 by a group that included human rights activists, judges, academics, NGO officials, and a former UN High Commissioner for Human Rights, call on the international community to recognize that "[h]uman beings of all sexual orientations and gender identities are entitled to the full enjoyment of all human rights," and that "[e]ach person's self-defined sexual orientation and gender identity is integral to their personality and is one of the most basic aspects of self-determination, dignity and freedom."[3]

The most familiar Western judicial decisions in this arena, starting with the European Court of Human Rights case of *Dudgeon v. the United Kingdom*,[4] have dealt specifically with laws that criminalized same-sex sexual conduct. Where such sodomy laws have been eradicated in the West, the next wave of political and legal activism has focused on recognition for same-sex relationships. The U.S. Supreme Court struck down American sodomy laws in 2003, when no U.S. state yet authorized same-sex marriage; ten years later, marriage equality had come to thirteen of the fifty states, and the Supreme Court struck down a law banning recognition by the federal government of same-sex marriages. In Ireland, legislation approved in 2010 gave certain legal rights and obligations to same-sex couples twelve years after the European Court of Human Rights declared that country's sodomy laws to be in violation of the European Convention on Human Rights. Same-sex marriage has been legal in South Africa since 2006, eight years after the constitutional court struck down that country's laws prohibiting consensual sex between men.

Much of the global gay rights discourse speaks with an American accent. One commentator has described "gay pride" as "America's global gay export,"[5] and another has observed that "[g]ay culture . . . like

---

[3] The Yogyakarta Principles Web site, accessed May 19, 2013, http://www.yogyakarta principles.org/principles_en.htm.

[4] 45 Eur. Ct. H.R. (ser. A) (1981).

[5] Sonia Katyal, "Exporting Identity," *Yale Journal of Law & Feminism* 14 (2009): 97, 98 (quoting Frank Browning, *A Queer Geography* (New York: Farrar, Straus and Giroux, 1998), 24).

Coca-Cola, Madonna, and Calvin Klein underwear, has become a potent American export."[6] (Indeed, when Nepal, one of the countries we examine in this chapter, hosted South Asia's first Lesbian, Gay, Bisexual, Transgender, and Intersex Sports Festival in 2012, the guest of honor was the openly gay American Olympic diving champion Greg Louganis.[7])

In the United States, since the time when marriage rights became the defining issue for gay/lesbian equality in the late 1990s, political and legal arguments for gay/lesbian rights have focused on similarities between homosexual persons and dominant cultural narratives. Gays and lesbians, it is said, want the same things out of life and relationships that heterosexuals do, and prejudices against them should be discarded in the same way as discriminations against racial minorities and women. As the American group Freedom to Marry says on its Web site,

> Marriage matters to gay people in similar ways that it matters to everyone. Gay and lesbian couples want to get married to make a lifetime commitment to the person they love and to protect their families.... Gay and lesbian couples may seem different from straight couples, but we share similar values – like the importance of family and helping out our neighbors; worries – like making ends meet or the possibility of losing a job; and hopes and dreams – like finding that special someone to grow old with, and standing in front of friends and family to make a lifetime commitment.[8]

Compared to the advancements in rights and equality for gays and lesbians, progress has been slower and more recent for transgender individuals, who seek protections based on gender identity rather than sexual orientation. In the United States and Europe, transgender activists have united in the past decade with established gay/lesbian advocacy groups to pursue their goals under the common banner of an LGBT quest for civil rights, civic equality, and human dignity. At the risk of oversimplifying the matter, advancements in gay and lesbian rights – as reflected in social attitudes, legislative victories, and constitutional doctrine – have tended to be seen as "door openers" for similar advancements in transgender rights. Protections for gender identity in local laws and corporate

---

[6] Neville Hoad, "Between the White Man's Burden and the White Man's Disease," *Gay & Lesbian Quarterly* 5 (1999): 559, 563.

[7] "American Olympian Greg Louganis supports LGBTI rights in Nepal," October 10, 2012, http://nepal.usembassy.gov//pr-10-10-2012.html.

[8] "Marriage 101: Frequently Asked Questions," accessed May 19, 2013, http://www.freedomtomarry.org/pages/marriage-101#faq1.

employment policies, while growing, still lag behind protections for sexual orientation. As same-sex couples were celebrating legal unions in various jurisdictions around the world in 2011, including the United States, Mexico, the Netherlands, and Spain, transgender rights advocates considered it a major advancement that the European Parliament had called on the World Health Organization to stop classifying gender dysphoria as a "mental and behavioural disorder."[9]

Kenji Yoshino and Michael Kavey have observed that "[i]n the context of sexual orientation, constitutional arguments often assume a categorical, 'always/everywhere' tenor that exposes them to contestation on comparative grounds."[10] Moreover, the "global gay rights" model has been criticized for a "presumed equation between identity and conduct" and a "fail[ure] to recognize and incorporate different social meanings for same-sex sexual practices."[11] Against this backdrop, we submit that recent constitutional decisions in India, Nepal, and Pakistan provide a unique South Asian foil for critical inquiry into the nature of dominant Western rights-based discourses surrounding sexuality and gender identity.

As in the West, various identity groups within the broader South Asian SOGI rights community have proffered competing visions of equality and competing strategies for advocacy. And, as in the West, these divisions often have highlighted differences grounded in class and gender. But what is unique about the experience of India, Nepal, and Pakistan has been the remarkable success of transgender (more properly understood in cultural context as third-gender) groups in attaining recognition of their goals, relative to the success of groups advocating for gay, lesbian, or other same-sex loving constituencies. In these three countries, a mix of legislative, executive, and judicial actions have recognized the long-standing presence of third-gender communities.[12] Moreover, the recognition of transgender

---

[9] "European Parliament: World Health Organization Must Stop Treating Transgender People as Mentally Ill," September 29, 2011, http://www.lgbt-ep.eu/press-releases/who-must-stop-treating-transgender-people-as-mentally-ill/.

[10] Kenji Yoshino and Michael Kavey, "Immodest Claims and Modest Contributions: Sexual Orientation in Comparative Constitutional Law," in *The Oxford Handbook of Comparative Constitutional Law*, ed. Michael Rosenfeld and Andras Sajo (New York: Oxford University Press, 2012), 1080.

[11] Katyal, "Exporting Identity," *supra* n. 5, 123.

[12] Bangladesh is also reported to have begun to recognize the rights of third-gender hijras. However, conflicting news reports paint a convoluted picture of what rights have been recognized and by which authorities. As such, a discussion of Bangladesh is omitted from this analysis. For more information, *see, e.g.*, Anbarasan Ethirajan, "Bangladesh rally to support transgenders," *BBC News South Asia*, October 21, 2011, http://www.bbc.co.uk/news/world-south-asia-15398437.

rights has preceded judicial recognition of rights for other same-sex loving groups.

Indeed, in the discussion that follows, we suggest that the South Asian experience has been somewhat the opposite of the American and European experience: in India and Nepal (although not in Pakistan, as we shall see) transgender rights have served as the door opener to gay and lesbian rights. Or perhaps it is more accurate to say that the constitutional discourse in India and Nepal around questions of sexuality and gender identity has not been defined and limited by the "global gay rights" model, but instead has recognized that the phenomena of sexuality and gender identity are naturally interrelated (an insight that feminist and queer theory have long emphasized). For example, in these countries, hijras are biological males who have sex with men (MSM), but they also occupy a distinctive, centuries-old cultural space in which their defining characteristic is their unique third gender; other subgroups of men who have sex with men identify with indigenous sexualities rather than a homogenized Westernized model of what it means to be gay. In both India and Nepal, when constitutional courts have recently condemned government laws and practices that persecuted and discriminated against MSM, the practical effect of these decisions has been to extend legal rights and equality to all SOGI minorities, regardless of their particular sexual or gender identities or practices.

Thus, the path of SOGI rights in South Asia forms a counterpoint to the current Western model of legal and social advocacy for LGBT rights, which promotes narratives of similarity and assimilation over those of diversity or the forthright embrace of sexual difference and gender variation. The South Asian experience demonstrates how norms for the treatment of sexual orientation and gender identity have been negotiated and implemented in ways that arise from indigenous or culturally specific practices of sex and gender and local understandings of constitutional equality and dignity.

INDIA

Of all the constitutional jurisprudence we discuss in this chapter, the landmark decision of India's Delhi High Court invalidating Section 377 of the Indian Penal Code, a colonial-era provision outlawing sodomy, has received the most notice and commentary, likely owing to India's growing global profile and influence. The decision was the culmination of years of work by SOGI activists, but it occurred against the backdrop of considerable success hijras had already experienced in their quest for recognition and protection against discrimination, particularly in the Indian state of Tamil Nadu.

The 2009 decision in *Naz Foundation v. Government of NCT of Delhi*[13] provided an expansive view of SOGI rights, invoking the concept of constitutional morality to forbid government interference with private, self-regarding actions, even when such actions might run contrary to social mores. To fully appreciate the constitutional implications of *Naz Foundation*, it is important to understand the events that led to the decision, particularly how the advocacy of (and rivalries between) a broad spectrum of groups – some reflecting Western notions of gay rights, others reflecting traditional Indian sexualities – contributed to a broad constitutional ruling that expanded rights and liberty for all SOGI minorities.

Paving the Way to Naz Foundation: *SOGI Rights Activism in India*

India has the longest history of organized SOGI mobilization in South Asia. For more than two decades, a diverse set of advocacy organizations representing persons of third-gender, gay, lesbian, and indigenous same-sex loving identities have advanced a social and legal dialogue around SOGI rights, sometimes working together and sometimes competing. It is difficult for outsiders to fully understand all the various histories and fault lines among these groups, but the available accounts suggest that many of the divisions have been driven by differing conceptions of class, gender, and social acceptability among SOGI groups.

To be sure, contemporary India has well-defined groups that identify with Western conceptions of gay and lesbian rights and identity; often these groups have been funded by Western organizations in conjunction with LGBT rights movements or HIV/AIDS programs.[14] Individuals who

---

[13] Naz Found. v. Gov't of NCT of Delhi, W.P.(C) No. 7455/2001 (Delhi H.C. July 2, 2009) [hereinafter "*Naz Found.*"].

[14] The relationship between gay men and lesbian women in India is deeply complicated, in large part because the movements have evolved differently across cities, regions, and in connection with broader issues of HIV/AIDS, feminism, and sexual identity politics. For a more in-depth analysis of this relationship, particularly regarding the debate about decriminalization of sodomy, *see* Naisargi Dave, *Queer Activism in India: A Story in the Anthropology of Ethics* (Durham, NC: Duke University Press, 2012). Dave provides a rich discussion of how gay men's access to funding through grants targeting HIV/AIDS shaped the evolution of other SOGI minority groups in India as well as a broader commentary on the effects of increasing NGO-ization on indigenous sexual minority

self-identify as gay or lesbian tend to be English speaking, better educated, of a higher social class, and urban. Subgroups defined by indigenous conceptions of gender and sexuality, however, form vibrant and much larger communities. For example, *kothis* are typically non-English-speaking men who exhibit feminine characteristics and identify as preferring a receptive role in sexual intercourse. *Panthis* are men perceived as more masculine and who typically penetrate kothis, although panthi is a term used mostly by kothis to identify these men; panthis do not organize themselves as a distinct sexual minority and are unlikely to identify as gay. Both kothis and panthis are often married to women. Alok Gupta, through his own experiences as an openly gay man in India, suggests four distinct subgroups of the queer male community: kothis; working-class, non-kothi-identified gay and bisexual men (panthis); middle- and upper-class gay- and bisexual-identified men; and hijras.[15] Within India, advocacy groups representing kothis, gay- and bisexual-identified men, and hijras are well-established, whereas advocacy on behalf of panthis falls to organizations that claim a broader mission of safeguarding the health and welfare of men who have sex with men (so called MSM). The term MSM, adopted by the HIV/AIDS and health communities, is often used to avoid labeling men with an identity construct with which they might not identify, but it obscures the variation among the distinct subgroups that fall within this classification.

Although not within the Western canon of sexualities, hijras are the predominant third-gender or transgender community in India. Historically referred to as *eunuchs*, hijras occupy a long-standing social and cultural role. They are "phenotypic men who wear female clothing and, ideally, renounce sexual desire and practice by undergoing a sacrificial emasculation – that is, an excision of the penis and testicles – dedicated to the goddess Bedhraj Mata."[16] In this sense, hijras are distinct from the Western concept of transgenderism, as they do not adopt the gender attributes of their non-birth sex; instead, hijras occupy a unique gender space with distinctive behaviors not traditionally associated with either

identities. For an additional perspective on how HIV/AIDS funding has shaped SOGI identities in India, *see* Aniruddha Dutta, "An Epistemology of Collusion: Hijras, Kothis and the Historical (Dis)continuity of Gender/Sexual Identities in Eastern India," *Gender & History* 24 (2012): 825.

[15] Alok Gupta, "Englishpur ki *Kothi*," in *Because I Have a Voice: Queer Politics in India*, ed. Arvind Narrain and Gautam Bhan (New Delhi: Yoda Press, 2005), 119.

[16] Gayatri Reddy, *With Respect to Sex: Negotiating Hijra Identity in South India* (Chicago: University of Chicago Press, 2010), 17.

males or females. Although the terms are often used loosely or interchangeably, hijras are best understood as occupying a third gender rather
than identifying as transgender.[17] Hijras have come to represent the historic sexual difference of India, and they have been the subject of scholarly
and journalistic accounts seeking to chronicle their unique role in Indian
and South Asian society.[18]

Within India, hijras are not welcomed or particularly respected by
the population at large, but they are accepted for their traditional social
roles of performing dances at weddings, births, and other ceremonial
functions. At the same time, increased Westernization has reduced the
demand for many of these historical performances, and thus many hijras
engage in sex work (hence, their typical inclusion among MSM groups)
and alms seeking as a source of income.[19] Even though they are often
the objects of social disdain, hijras' long-standing place in Indian society
seems to explain the success of their constitutional and legislative claims
for equal rights.

As measured both over time and as a matter of degree, hijras have
been more successful than other sexual minorities in convincing Indian
legislative bodies and courts to recognize their rights. At least in theory,
hijras became eligible for government pensions and ration cards, as well
as voting rights, as far back as 1936,[20] although the real articulation of
their rights did not begin until the 1990s. In 1994, hijras were allowed
to register to vote as either male or female – a progressive step from their
previous ability to register only as male, although not a true recognition

[17] Contemporary conceptions of "genderqueer" or "agender"/"gender-neutral" are also
not appropriately descriptive of hijras, as these conceptions reject the construct of
gender and recognize individual performativity of a wide variety of gender-associated
behaviors. Hijras occupy a more defined gender space, with recognized expectations of
behavior distinct from male or female. *See generally*, Reddy, *With Respect to Sex*, *supra*
n. 16.

[18] A 2007 BBC documentary is a prominent example. "The Hijras of India," last updated February 22, 2007, http://news.bbc.co.uk/2/hi/programmes/documentary_archive
/6386171.stm. For a more detailed analysis of the historical Western orientalist interest in hijras and a review of contemporary scholarly ethnographies, *see* Dutta, "An
Epistemology of Collusion," *supra* n. 14.

[19] See Reddy, *With Respect to Sex*, *supra* n. 16, 78–84.

[20] Anna Livia and Kira Hall, *Queerly Phrased: Language, Gender, and Sexuality* (New
York: Oxford University Press, 1997), 431. Although the authors provide a citation for
this claim, it is a non-English source that cannot be authenticated. Other publications
provide the same citation, and there appears to be no independent verification for the
claim.

of their distinct gender identity.[21] Since then, hijras have become increasingly engaged in electoral politics. In 1999, Shabnam Mausi was elected to the provincial legislature of Madhya Pradesh and has remained active in politics.[22] The same year also saw Kamala Jaan elected to a mayorship in Madyha Pradesh (although Jaan was stripped of the position in 2003 on grounds that Jaan was a male in a position reserved for females).[23] In 2000, Asha Devi was elected as the mayor of a city in Uttar Pradesh, although a court later stripped her of this position on the reasoning that the mayorship was reserved for females and Devi was a male.[24]

[21] Reddy, *With Respect to Sex, supra* n. 16, 223. Reddy also notes that hijras were granted the right to run for political office in 1977.

[22] "Shabnam Mausi wants to join Cong," *Indian Express*, June 19, 2007, http://www .indianexpress.com/news/shabnam-mausi-wants-to-join-cong/34082/0.

[23] Sadiq Ali & others v. Kamala Jaan, Election Petitions No. 12/2000, 13/2000, 18/2000 & 21/2000 (First Additional District Court, Katni) (Unreported); *see also* Suchandana Gupta, "Eunuch's election as mayor annulled," *Times of India*, December 11, 2011, http://articles.timesofindia.indiatimes.com/2011-12-11/bhopal/30505026_1_eunuch-kamla-jaan-mayor; "HC upholds invalidation of Eunuch's Election," *Economic Times*, February 4, 2033, http://articles.economictimes.indiatimes.com/2003-02-04/news/2754 8390_1_election-petition-women-candidates-eunuch. A link to a fee-based version of court order is available at http://www.lawyerservices.in/Kamala-Alias-Kamala-Jaan-Alias-Hijrah-Versus-Sadiq-Ali-2003-02-03.

Siddharth Narrain provides an excellent account of the events of the trial:

"The Katni Sessions Judge Virender Singh, while deciding this, addressed the question: Were hijras male or female? The judge quoted from the Shatpath Brahman, the Mahabharata, the Manusmriti and the Kamasutra; in historical sources – from the courts of Akbar, Alauddin Khilji, to say that there was a category of persons who were neither male nor female (napunsaks). The judge (Justice Singh) said that all the medical and historical evidence before him showed that hijras could be of two categories–male or female but to ascertain this, there had to be a medical examination (which the respondent had refused to undertake). But, after all this, the judge came back to the simplistic reasoning that the dictionary meaning of female is 'one who can produce' a child and therefore hijras cannot be females. Justice Singh came to the conclusion that hijras are castrated males, and therefore Kamala Jaan was not female. This decision was upheld by the Madhya Pradesh High Court despite a direction from the Election Commission (hereinafter E.C.) in September 1994 that hijras can be registered in the electoral roles either as male or female depending on their statement at the time of enrolment. This direction was issued by the E.C. after Shabnam Mausi, a hijra candidate from the Sohagpur Assembly constituency in Madhya Pradesh, wrote to the Chief Election Commissioner enquiring as to which category hijras were classified under."

Narrain, "Crystallising Queer Politics," *supra* n. 1, 460.

[24] "Court unseats Eunuch Mayor of Gorakhpur," *Rediff*, May 13, 2003, http://www .rediff.com/news/2003/may/13up.htm.

The state of Tamil Nadu (where hijras are known locally as *arava-nis*) has historically been the most progressive toward hijra rights. In 2003, the state government ordered that a committee be formed to study sexual exploitation and other issues affecting hijras.[25] The local hijra community subsequently filed a petition in the Chennai High Court requesting ration cards (ration cards then only available to women). A 2004 decision allowed hijras to register as either males or females on their ration cards, although this did not meet the community's demand to be recognized as a distinct third gender.[26] Although it characterized hijras as having a "disorder" and requiring treatment, a 2006 state government order prohibited schools and colleges from denying hijras admission, established vocational and skills training for hijras, provided counseling for hijras and their families, established a grievance procedure for hijras unable to obtain ration cards or identification documents, and ordered a panel to consider legalizing sexual reassignment surgery.[27] (This order was cited by the Delhi High Court in the *Naz Foundation* decision.) The Tamil Nadu government continued its support of hijras by forming and funding the *Aravani* Welfare Board in 2008,[28] which includes hijra representatives, and by establishing guaranteed seats for hijras in state universities.[29] A 2009 state report also details that 219 transgenders had received family ration cards, although it recognized that a separate method for obtaining ration cards had not been established for them.[30]

While Tamil Nadu was leading the way in establishing rights and services for hijras, similar developments began to emerge elsewhere across

[25] Government of Tamil Nadu, Social Welfare and Nutritious Meal Programme Department, G.O. (Ms) No.201, October 23, 2003, http://www.tn.gov.in/gorders/social/sw-e-201-2003.htm.

[26] Padma Govindan and Aniruddhan Vasudevan, "The Razor's Edge of Oppositionality: Exploring the Politics of Rights-Based Activism by Transgender Women in Tamil Nadu" (Law and Social Sciences in South Asia Conference, 2009, http://www.lassnet.org/2009/readings/govindan-vasudevan2008razors-edge.pdf), 4–5.

[27] Government of Tamil Nadu, Social Welfare and Nutritious Meal (SW8) Department, G.O. (Ms) No.199, December 21, 2006, http://www.tn.gov.in/gosdb/gorders/social/sw_e_199_2006.htm.

[28] "TN constitutes welfare board for transgenders," *Indian Express*, April 10, 2008, http://www.indianexpress.com/news/tn-constitutes-welfare-board-for-transgenders/295359. For a discussion of the founding of the board and the politics involved, *see* Govindan and Vasudevan, "The Razor's Edge of Oppositionality."

[29] Government of Tamil Nadu, Higher Education (G1) Department, G.O.(1D) No.75, May 10, 2008, http://www.tn.gov.in/gosdb/gorders/hedu/hedu_e_75_2008_D.pdf.

[30] Government of Tamil Nadu, Food and Consumer Protection Department, Policy Not for the Year 2008–2009, Demand No. 13, http://www.tn.gov.in/policynotes/archives/policy2008-09/pdf/food.pdf, 6.

India. In 2004, hijra Sonia Ajmeri ran unsuccessfully for the national parliament, attracting substantial media attention.[31] In 2005, the national government officially recognized a third gender on government identity documents when it allowed hijras to select "E" (for eunuch) on passport forms.[32] After the 2006 self-immolation of a hijra who had been brutally tortured and raped by police for three weeks, the High Court of Madras recognized the transgender identity of the deceased and awarded the family 500,000 rupees (approximately USD$10,000).[33] This decision, also cited in *Naz Foundation*, was the first to explicitly recognize police mistreatment of hijras. In 2009, the Indian electoral commission approved a third-gender category – "O", for Other – on voter registration forms.[34]

The first challenge to Section 377, which would eventually be struck down in *Naz Foundation*, was filed in 1994 by the organization AIDS Bhedbhav Virodi Andolan (ABVA), a nonprofit founded by a gay man but mostly made up of progressive heterosexual activists focusing on HIV/AIDS issues.[35] The case[36] was filed largely because of concerns about increasing HIV infection among prison inmates who were frequently engaging in homosexual sex. Although there was apparent public support for the repeal of Section 377 because of its public health consequences, the petition was lost in the administrative shuffle of the courts and was neither decided nor disposed of.[37]

Although the ABVA petition failed for technical reasons, it was likely also doomed by the meager interest among SOGI rights groups in pursuing a strategy for legal rights. Anthropologist Naisargi Dave characterizes

---

[31] Peter Foster, "Six-ft Sonia aims to be MP with a difference," *Telegraph*, April 20, 2004, http://www.telegraph.co.uk/news/worldnews/asia/india/1459792/Six-ft-Sonia-aims-to-be-MP-with-a-difference.html.

[32] Jennifer Rellis, "'Please Write "E" in this Box': Toward Self-Identification and Recognition of a Third Gender: Approaches in the United States and India," *Michigan Journal of Gender & Law* 14 (2007): 223, 233.

[33] Jayalakshmi v. Tamil Nadu et al. W.A.No. 1130 of 2006 and WP.No.24160 of 2006, http://judis.nic.in/judis_chennai/qrydisp.aspx?filename=10866.

[34] Harmeet Shah Singh, "India's third gender gets own identity in voter rolls," *CNN*, November 12, 2009, http://www.cnn.com/2009/WORLD/asiapcf/11/12/india.gender.voting/index.html; "India's eunuchs recognised as 'others'," *Telegraph*, November 13, 2009, http://www.telegraph.co.uk/expat/expatnews/6560733/Indias-eunuchs-recognised-as-others.html.

[35] Dave, *Queer Activism in India*, supra n. 14, 172. We are heavily indebted to Dave's account of the relationships between various SOGI rights organizations in India regarding the Section 377 cases, collected through her extensive anthropological fieldwork.

[36] ABVA v. Union of India and Others, Civil Writ Petition No. 1784 (1994).

[37] Dave, *Queer Activism in India*, supra n. 14, 174.

the period 1994 to 2001, between the ABVA petition and the filing of the Naz petition, as demonstrating rapid growth in SOGI organizations, but

> law reform was not central to any group's agenda. Lesbian groups...
> sought to...gain support from women's organizations and to estab-
> lish...an infrastructure for domestic crisis intervention. Predominantly
> men's groups...prospered through the funding, international attention,
> and legal non-interference necessitated by the HIV/AIDS crisis....To les-
> bian collectives, the state seemed politically out of reach; to the organiza-
> tions serving gay men, kothis, and MSM, HIV provided a reason to feel
> beyond the punitive practices of the state.[38]

During this period, SOGI subgroups' activities were often incongruous, and relationships between groups were often fraught, if not antagonistic. Dave documents the gender hierarchy[39] that persisted between MSM-oriented groups and lesbian organizations in India even as leading groups of each constituency worked together to provide services.[40]

The divisions ran even deeper between MSM groups and hijras. Gay and lesbian communities intentionally distanced themselves from hijras, even though hijras were much more visible and accepted, if not embraced, as a social group. Although hijras constructed and performed their gender identity publicly, homosexuality was seen as a private matter.[41] Accord-ing to Dave, "gay respectability" was "intimately tied with gender nor-mativity" and thus required "a distancing between the concept of gay-ness...and various forms of transgender."[42] The rejection of hijras out of a classist notion of respectability was evident in the refusal of South Indian queer activists to allow hijras to attend a press conference because they were "too flamboyant" and were "camera hogs." A representative of the Naz Foundation was quoted as saying that hijras had to become "more ethical" and "less flamboyant" if they wanted to be embraced by organizations that were advocating on behalf of gay men.[43] One MSM

---

[38] Ibid., 175.   [39] Ibid., 40.

[40] Ibid., 78–79, 85–86.

[41] Hijras are frequently reported to expose their genitals, particularly if castrated, as a form of insulting an individual in public and extorting money. The relative frequency of this practice is difficult to catalog, as it seems to be over-reported by Westerners scandalized by such behavior.

[42] Dave, *Queer Activism in India*, *supra* n. 14, 221 n. 42.

[43] Ibid., Here, "ethical" presumably means abandoning sex work.

group demanded that its hijra employees stop engaging in sex work and adopt a more conventional dress code.[44]

At the same time, many hijras – as well as kothis, the men who exhibit feminine characteristics and identify as preferring a receptive role in sexual intercourse – also spurned traditional MSM- or gay-focused organizations, demanding instead to be seen as separate, insular sexual minority groups.[45] Kothis, in particular, viewed self-identified "gay" men as urban elites who did not share the traditional kothi embrace of femininity.[46] In organizing support groups for various MSM communities, the Naz Foundation developed one group for kothis and *hijras*, another for higher-class, English-speaking gay men, and a third group for non-English-speaking, lower-class men who did not identify as kothi or hijra.[47]

In summary, in the years leading up to India's major court decision that decriminalized sodomy and underscored the constitutional dignity of all SOGI minorities, it was hijras – a group whose identity is defined by gender variation rather than conventional categories of sexual orientation – who were the most successful in having their rights recognized by the government and their presence acknowledged by the broader society. Hijras were able to convince the population at large to elect them to office and to obtain welfare benefits and acknowledgement of their identity on official documents from Indian state and national governments. They also were prominent members of the coalition that challenged Section 377, and the continuing discrimination and stigma they faced would be acknowledged by the court as a serious problem of constitutional dimensions.

The Naz Foundation *Decision*

Although it was not the first Asian decision to recognize SOGI rights, *Naz Foundation* is the most important decision in Asian SOGI jurisprudence because of Indian courts' reputation for well-developed constitutional interpretation. *Naz Foundation* decriminalized sodomy and recognized the fundamental rights of SOGI persons to engage in consensual adult relationships of their choosing, free of government interference. It

---

[44] Ibid., 222–23, n. 54. Dave notes, however, that most progressive queer groups rejected this behavior.

[45] Gupta, "Englishpur ki *Kothi*," *supra* n. 15, 127.

[46] Ibid., 128.   [47] Ibid., 129.

recognized that Section 377 was a relic of the British colonial period and noted that since the 1861 adoption of the Indian Penal Code, judicial interpretation of the provision had shifted from prohibiting non-procreative sex to criminalizing "sexual perversity."[48] Several conservative organizations appealed the decision to the Supreme Court of India, which sometimes takes years to consider and decide a case. The government did not appeal.[49]

Four parties submitted arguments in the case: the petitioner Naz Foundation India, which portrayed itself as "working in the field of HIV/AIDS intervention and prevention;"[50] two government respondents with contradictory positions on the litigation, the Ministry of Home Affairs and the Ministry of Health and Family Welfare; and Voices Against 377, a coalition of twelve organizations supporting repeal of Section 377 and working with Naz Foundation.[51]

The Naz Foundation's arguments focused on the adverse impact of Section 377 on HIV prevention efforts, noting that while recent prosecutions under the law have been limited to child sexual assault,[52] the law continued to stigmatize homosexual activity and force it underground, thus increasing participants' vulnerability to HIV infection.[53] Naz Foundation's constitutional arguments alleged a violation of the rights to privacy and dignity inherent in the Indian Constitution's Article 21 right to life and liberty,[54] Article 14 right to equality,[55] and Article 15 prohibition on discrimination based on sex, which Naz argued includes sexual orientation.[56] Throughout these arguments, Naz urged a right of SOGI individuals to engage in private homosexual conduct, focusing on sexual activity rather than group identity.[57]

The group Voices Against 377 represented a broad constituency of lesbians, gays, bisexuals, transgenders, hijras, and kothis. Voices argued that Section 377 "has created an association of criminality towards people with same sex desires. It . . . fosters a climate of fundamental rights violations of the gay community, to the extent of bolstering their extreme

---

[48] *Naz Found.*, *supra* n. 13, ¶¶ 3–4.

[49] The Delhi High Court issued the *Naz* decision; high court decisions on constitutional issues have national precedential value. The Supreme Court was apparently displeased with the government's decision not to take a position, calling it "a new phenomenon" for the state to remain neutral in such a case. See http://www.legalindia .in/supreme-court-assails-states-neutrality-on-gay-sex.

[50] *Naz Found.*, *supra* n. 13, ¶ 6.

[51] Ibid., ¶ 19.

[52] Ibid., ¶ 7.

[53] Ibid., ¶ 8.

[54] Ibid., ¶ 8.

[55] Ibid., ¶ 9.

[56] Ibid., ¶ 9.

[57] *See* ibid., ¶ 10.

social ostracism."[58] Voices presented examples of hijras raped by gangs and subsequently tortured by police. It documented the Tamil Nadu case of a hijra who committed suicide after police rape, harassment, and torture; a magistrate who had extended Section 377 to prohibit a romantic relationship between two lesbian adult women; testimony by a gay man who had been raped by police;[59] and police harassment of HIV outreach workers.[60] Taken together, these arguments emphasized the rights of SOGI individuals to be free from harassment or stigmatization based on their status, rather than a right to engage in private sexual content.

The two government respondents presented contradictory arguments.[61] The Ministry of Home Affairs argued that social disapproval of homosexuals justified criminalizing their private conduct.[62] It observed that India had not yet adopted the public toleration of homosexuality found in other countries and argued that public morality could serve as a compelling state interest in keeping Section 377 on the books.[63] On the other hand, the Ministry of Health and Family Welfare focused on the difficulty that Section 377 caused in effectively reaching MSM for HIV prevention activities due to the men's fear of police harassment and prosecution.[64]

The varied arguments presented against Section 377 reflected divergent priorities that can be at least partly explained by differences in social class. Naz Foundation had a strong relationship with privileged, English-speaking gay men and the international LGBT movement, and its constituency has greater access to private spaces and is less susceptible to police harassment. Thus, its arguments tended to focus more on a right to engage in sexual conduct than on freedom from discrimination.[65] The groups represented by Voices, on the other hand, tended to be smaller and to represent more marginalized sexual communities. Their legal arguments emphasized an end to discrimination and the right of SOGI minorities to live openly without harassment.

---

[58] Ibid., ¶ 20.
[60] Ibid., ¶ 21.
[62] Ibid., ¶ 12.
[64] Ibid., ¶ 18.

[59] Ibid., ¶ 22.
[61] Ibid., ¶ 11.
[63] *See* ibid., ¶¶ 13, 14, 24.

[65] This is an admittedly overly broad description of Naz Foundation's programming and members. Although the tensions between Naz Foundation's gay membership and hijras have provoked conflict, Naz has consistently provided services for hijras and other lower-class and income SOGI individuals. However, the organization maintains a reputation as affiliated with the upper-class international LGBT movement, and Naz's English-language and urban origins continue to differentiate the group from other grassroots movements.

The Delhi High Court issued its decision on July 2, 2009, to considerable international fanfare. The court held that Section 377 violated SOGI individuals' rights to dignity and autonomy, as well as a broader constitutional right of privacy, and it said that public morality was not a sufficiently compelling state interest to justify abridging these rights. Although a detailed discussion of the court's constitutional analysis is beyond the scope of this chapter, several points are important to understanding how the *Naz* court reasoned its way toward expanding rights and liberty for all SOGI minorities in India.

First, the court affirmed a right to privacy in both its decisional and spatial varieties. Nodding to decisional privacy, the court said the Constitution protected "autonomy of the private will and a person's freedom of choice and of action,"[66] as well as "the right to be left alone."[67] In this passage, the court says that privacy deals with "persons and not places."[68] However, in a later passage the court seems to refer to spatial privacy by finding that "Section 377 IPC grossly violates [homosexuals'] right to privacy and liberty . . . insofar as it criminalises consensual sexual acts between adults in private."[69] The difference is important, because the protection of sexual acts within private spaces is more readily available to upper-class individuals in India – as one commentator has observed, the "difficulty with privacy is that not everyone can afford it."[70] Those most at risk of persecution under Section 377 were lower-class men who frequented parks and other public spaces for sexual activity, and a purely spacial privacy framework would fail to recognize the source of their vulnerability to harassment.

Second, having found that Section 377 impinged on fundamental rights, the court assessed whether the infringement was justified by a compelling state interest.[71] It was not. Citing the U.S. Supreme Court's decision in *Lawrence v. Texas*, which found that criminal sodomy laws "further[] no legitimate state interest which can justify [their] intrusion into the personal and private life of the individual,"[72] the *Naz Foundation* court similarly held that "enforcement of public morality does not amount to a 'compelling state interest' to justify invasion of the zone

---

[66] *Naz Found., supra* n. 13, ¶ 26.   [67] Ibid., ¶ 38.
[68] Ibid., ¶ 39.   [69] Ibid., ¶ 52.
[70] Sumit Baudh, "Sodomy in India: Sex Crime or Human Right?" *IDS Bulletin* 37(5) (2009): 61.
[71] Ibid., ¶ 37.
[72] Lawrence v. Texas, 539 U.S. 558, 578 (2003).

of privacy of adult homosexuals engaged in consensual sex in private without intending to cause harm to each other or others."[73]

Third and perhaps most significantly, *Naz Foundation* did more than invalidate a provision of the criminal code. It also declared an expansive view of SOGI rights under a framework of constitutional morality. As a doctrinal matter, it did so by interpreting textual constitutional references to sex as including sexual orientation.[74] As a rhetorical matter, the decision provided a clarion call for principles of Indian constitutionalism, underscoring the "role of the judiciary" in "protecting the counter majoritarian safeguards enumerated in the Constitution."[75] The court described at length the Constitution's role in mediating social difference and advancing the core principles of Indian democracy:

> [T]he Indian Constitution is first and foremost a social document. The majority of its provisions are either directly aimed at furthering the goals of the social revolution or attempt to foster this revolution by establishing the conditions necessary for its achievement. . . . The Constitution of India recognises, protects and celebrates diversity. To stigmatise or to criminalise homosexuals only on account of their sexual orientation would be against the constitutional morality.[76]

* * *

> If there is one constitutional tenet that can be said to be underlying theme of the Indian Constitution, it is that of 'inclusiveness'. This Court believes that Indian Constitution reflects this value deeply ingrained in Indian society, nurtured over several generations. The inclusiveness that Indian society traditionally displayed, literally in every aspect of life, is manifest in recognising a role in society for everyone. Those perceived by the majority as "deviants" or "different" are not on that score excluded or ostracised.[77]

Naz Foundation is in step with progressive global sexuality jurisprudence, and the casual reader could be forgiven for assuming that the decision arose out of a litigation strategy driven by a Western-style narrative of gay/lesbian rights – that it is simply the Indian counterpart to the U.S. Supreme Court's *Lawrence* decision a few years earlier, which struck down American sodomy laws. The court describes Section 377 as

---

[73] *Naz Found., supra* n. 13, ¶ 75.
[74] Ibid., ¶ 104.
[76] Ibid., ¶ 80.
[75] Ibid., ¶ 120.
[77] Ibid., ¶ 130.

violating rights of the "gay community," thus seeming to rhetori-
cally marginalize indigenous sexualities and non-male genders.[78] When
describing violence against hijras, the court repeatedly refers to the victims
with masculine pronouns – he, him, his – thus implicitly rejecting a transgender identity, much less a third-gender category.[79] These processes of
naming are consistent with Western sexuality jurisprudence, particularly
when contrasted with the hijra-focused government practices in Tamil
Nadu (which, it must be noted, the court cited with approval).[80] The
court's construction of SOGI identities often seems grounded in Western typologies. For example, although the court expressly recognizes the
distinct communities of hijras and kothis who helped impel the litigation
and who were represented by the petitioners, as well as the discrimination
and violence some hijras faced at the hands of police and others, the court
frequently uses the label "LGBT" to describe the persons whose rights
were affected by Section 377, thus lumping hijras and kothis into a Western category that does not accurately describe their sexual identities.[81]
In short, as a piece of legal rhetoric, *Naz Foundation* often seems more
like a model of Western, rather than grassroots Indian, sexuality jurisprudence.

In other places, however (at 105 pages, *Naz Foundation* is a very long
and often discursive opinion), the court demonstrates a more sophisticated understanding of gender and sexuality that eschews Western categories. It observes that "the sense of gender and sexual orientation of the
person are so embedded in the individual that the individual carries this
aspect of his or her identity wherever he or she goes. A person cannot
leave behind his sense of gender or sexual orientation at home."[82] The
court also warns against the dangers of categorizing and labeling individuals within a democratic society. Harkening back to the memory of the
Criminal Tribes Act of 1871, a British colonial law that registered and
de facto criminalized certain tribes and communities, the court condemns

---

[78] Ibid., ¶ 20. The court also frequently uses the terms *MSM* and *homosexuals*.

[79] Ibid., ¶ 22.

[80] The court cites to the liberal practices in Tamil Nadu, where government orders addressing hijras use the term *aravani* in lieu of gendered pronouns. *Naz Found., supra* n. 13,
¶ 51. Other Indian cases addressing hijras have also used masculine pronouns to describe
victims, reflecting a set of broader cisgendered practices within the legal community.
See, e.g., Jayalakshmi v. Tamil Nadu et al. W.A.No. 1130 of 2006 and WP.No. 24160
of 2006, http://judis.nic.in/judis_chennai/qrydisp.aspx?filename=10866.

[81] *Naz Found., supra* n. 13, ¶19. However, the court does note that the affidavit submitted
on behalf of Voices uses the term LGBT to refer to all represented members.

[82] Ibid., ¶ 47.

"criminalisation by virtue of... identity" and acknowledges that hijras remain stigmatized because of their historic treatment under the act.[83]

Moreover, the court explicitly recognizes the construction of homosexuality as a colonial import and notes that India has historically been accepting of sexual difference, citing with approval comments to that effect by the solicitor general of India in an appearance before the United Nations Human Rights Council.[84] The court also cites anti-sodomy law decisions from numerous non-Western nations, notably Nepal, Hong Kong, and Fiji, reflecting a distinctly non-Western approach to sexuality jurisprudence.[85] As noted by one Indian commentator, these "decisions are particularly important because they remind the cynic that gay rights aren't some luxurious Western construct."[86]

In summary, categorizing *Naz Foundation* as simply a Western-style gay/lesbian rights case would fail to understand the decision in its social and cultural context. Doing so would fail to account for the victories and struggles that preceded the case, the diverse constituencies included under the heading of "men who have sex with men," and the way in which hijras – India's most visible SOGI minority group – had begun winning greater rights and acceptance even before the nation's constitutional court stepped into the fray. And it would fail to appreciate that, whereas *Lawrence* overtly invokes assimilationist themes and what Katherine Franke has archly criticized as "domesticated liberty,"[87] the *Naz Foundation* court justifies its decision by reaffirming the Indian Constitution's commitment to values of diversity and anti-subordination.

NEPAL

Although SOGI activism in Nepal is more nascent than in India, Nepal's constitutional court is responsible for the most far-reaching and progressive SOGI rights decision in South Asia. The country's current constitutional impasse – Nepal has been operating under an interim constitution and has long passed the deadline for developing a permanent replacement – may yet limit the decision's efficacy. Nevertheless, Nepal's

---

[83] Ibid., ¶ 50.
[84] Ibid., ¶ 84. [85] Ibid., ¶ 58.
[86] Vikram Raghavan, "Navigating the Noteworthy and Nebulous in *Naz Foundation*," *NUJS Law Review* 2 (2009): 397.
[87] Katherine Franke, "The Domesticated Liberty of *Lawrence v. Texas*," *Columbia Law Review* 104 (2004): 1399.

recognition of SOGI rights remains relevant for understanding the unique cultural understandings and discourses that have culminated in constitutional protection for sexual minority rights in South Asia.

The Supreme Court of Nepal's 2007 decision in *Pant v. Nepal*[88] had somewhat unusual origins in that Nepal had no anti-sodomy or other anti-SOGI statutes that were being challenged.[89] Rather, the case was brought as Public Interest Litigation spurred by allegations of general discriminatory treatment by the state. The challenge was led by Sunil Pant, a gay and SOGI rights activist in Nepal and founder of the Blue Diamond Society (BDS), an advocacy group for gender and sexual minorities.[90] The *Pant* opinion's language is prosaic and at times convoluted, but its legal conclusions are clear and unmistakable. The decision creates a third legal category of gender, declares that all sexual minorities deserve full protection of their human rights, and orders substantial government action to enforce the court's holdings. The court relies on Article 13 of the Nepali Constitution (an equality guarantee) as well as Article 9(3) (a nondiscrimination mandate that includes sexual orientation),[91] but it also cites

---

[88] Pant v. Nepal, Writ No. 917 of the Year 2064 BS (2007 AD), *translated* in *National Judicial Academy Law Journal* (Nepal), 2008, at 262 [hereinafter "*Pant*"].

[89] The court notes that there is a law criminalizing same-sex marriage on the grounds of unnatural coition, but the case did not specifically challenge this law directly. *Pant, supra* n. 88, 276. Unlike India and Pakistan, Nepal was never subjected to colonial rule by Britain and therefore was never forced to adopt a version of the colonial penal code and its anti-sodomy provisions.

[90] Blue Diamond Society Web site, accessed May 19, 2013, http://www.bds.org.np.

[91] The court constructs the provision to include sexual orientation by reference to the ICCPR, although the reasoning employed is rather blunt:

> "Taking note of Art 26 of the ICCPR, in the constitutions of several countries, the term 'sex' has been used instead of 'men' and 'women'. This is for the purpose of eliminating possible discrimination on the ground of sexual orientation. No citizen is allowed to be discriminated on the ground of sexual orientation. South Africa may be said to be the first country which has incorporated the provision of non-discrimination on the ground of sexual orientation in the 'Bill of Rights' of its Constitution. Under the provision of right to equality, the Sub Article (3) of Article 9 of the Constitution which was adopted on 8 May 1996, amended on 11 October 1996 and came into effect from 7 February 1997 reads as follows:

> "**Article 9** (3): The state may not unfairly discriminate directly or indirectly against any one on one or more grounds including race, gender, sex, pregnancy, marital status, ethnic or social origin, colour, sexual orientation, age, disability, religion, conscience, belief, culture, language and birth.

> "Thus, it is clearly mentioned in this Constitution that no person can be discriminated on the ground of sexual orientation."

Pant, supra n. 88, 278–79.

a wide variety of other authorities including international court decisions, the International Covenant on Civil and Political Rights (ICCPR), Alfred Kinsey's classic studies of sexuality, the Yogyakarta Principles, and Wikipedia.

The court began by identifying two substantive questions: "What is the basis of identification of homosexual or third gender people? Whether it happens because of the mental perversion of an individual or such characteristic appears naturally." "Whether or not the state has made discriminatory treatment to the citizens whose sexual orientation is homosexual and gender identity is third gender."[92]

Throughout the opinion, the court speaks to both gender identity and sexual orientation, but the framework of its inquiry is predominantly gender based. The court declares that "[a]ll human beings including the child, the aged, women, men, disabled, incapacitated, third genders etc. are Nepali citizens.... The third genders among the population are also part of the Nepalese population as a whole."[93] It further observes that "[t]he issues raised in the writ petition such as gender identity, gender discrimination and obstacles faced due to it as well as the issue of gender recognition etc. are matters concerning social justice and social interest."[94]

After canvassing international SOGI rights decisions and finding that neither third-gender identity nor same-sex sexual orientation are mental perversions, the court assesses changing social norms:

> [I]t seems to us that the traditional norms and values in regards to the sex, sexuality, sexual orientation and gender identity are changing gradually. *It is also seen that the concept specifying that the gender identity should be determined according to the physical condition and psychological feelings of a person is being established gradually. The concept that homosexuals and third gender people are not mentally ill but leading normal life style, is in the process of entrenchment.*[95]

Later, the court recognizes gender as a self-defined category and not a biological construct, repeatedly referring to gender "self-feeling."[96] It observes that "[i]t has now been accepted that the gender identity of an individual is determined not only by the physical sex but also by her/his behavior, character and perception."[97] While not attempting to assess the prevalence of SOGI minorities in Nepal, the court observes that "[i]f one

[92] Ibid., 266.
[93] Ibid., 268.
[94] Ibid., 270.
[95] Ibid., 274 (emphasis in original).
[96] Ibid., 280–81.
[97] Ibid., 285.

looks at the situation prevailing in our neighboring country, India, one will find thousands of *Hijras* and *Kothis* there. To be a homosexual or a third gender is not a disease in itself."[98]

Finally, the court concludes that formal legal recognitions for gender-variant individuals and the protection of fundamental constitutional rights of all "LGBTI" persons[99] are necessary, and it calls for affirmative measures by the government to foster and protect these rights.[100] For example, the court calls for the new constitution to include formal protections for gender identity and sexual orientation in addition to sex, using the South African Constitution as a benchmark.[101] The court also holds that adults have an "inherent right" to consensual relationships and calls on the government to form a committee to study and implement the legalization of same-sex marriage. The petitioner, Sunil Pant, was appointed by the court as a member of the committee.[102]

The prominent role of gender-based language and reasoning in the court's opinion, even when it is also articulating rights based on sexual orientation, may be due in large part to how these questions were framed by the Blue Diamond Society, which brought the litigation. A 2005 report by BDS prefaced its description of the categories of gender and sexual minorities in Nepal by stating:

> Nepal's sexual and gender minorities include a number of different groups and types of people involving differing physical features, sexual orientations, identities, and choices. Many of these people may take on, or have, more than one of these 'identities' or some of these characteristics involving both issues of sexuality and gender. These may change over time. The definitions are quite complicated and in some cases overlap.[103]

This understanding of gender and sexual orientation as interconnected reflects the persistence of non-normative gender identities in South Asia. The BDS report recognizes not only the same kothis and hijras as India, but also *metis* and *strains*, kothi-like identities that privilege the feminine aspects of the male-identified person, as well as *tas*, who are similar to

---

[98] Ibid., 276.

[99] The court uses the term LGBTI – lesbian, gay, bisexual, transgender, and intersex – presumably based on the terminology in briefs submitted by the Blue Diamond Society.

[100] *Pant, supra* n. 88, 284–85.

[101] Ibid., 285.   [102] Ibid., 286.

[103] Sunil Pant, "Blue Diamond Society, Social Exclusion of Sexual and Gender Minorities: Final Report," October 2005, http://www.asylumlaw.org/docs/sexualminorities/NepalBDSreport05.pdf, 7.

Indian panthis.[104] Although there is little historical scholarship on the presence of hijras in Nepal, BDS describes them as the "most visible gender minority in South Asia," lending support for the assumption that they play a similarly visible social role in Nepal as in India.[105]

Since the decision in *Pant*, Nepal has moved swiftly to implement the court's ruling, although there have been missteps along the way. In 2008, Sunil Pant was elected to the national legislature.[106] Later that year, the Supreme Court ordered the government to implement the recommendations of the commission on same-sex marriage provided for in the *Pant* decision.[107] From this point on, Nepal began to embrace its SOGI-friendly reputation, encouraging same-sex couples to marry in Nepal[108] and even attracting an Indian prince to announce that he will marry there.[109]

In 2011, the government officially counted third-gender persons in the census.[110] The same year, government officials announced plans to build the first South Asian center to harbor victims of violence motivated by sexual orientation or gender identity,[111] although this announcement was followed by attempts from several government ministries and parliamentarians to criminalize sodomy and define marriage as between a man and a woman.[112] In 2012 the Nepali Home Ministry allowed third-gender individuals to register as "Other" on citizenship documents.[113] The inaugural

---

[104] Ibid., 7.   [105] Ibid., 8.

[106] "Sunil Babu Pant," Blue Diamond Society Web site, accessed May 19, 2013, http://www.bds.org.np/sunil_pant.html.

[107] Achal Narayanan, "Nepal's Supreme Court OKs same-sex marriage," *Religion News Service*, November 21, 2008, http://www.pewforum.org/Religion-News/Nepals-Supreme-Court-OKs-same-sex-marriage.aspx.

[108] One campaign focused on encouraging couples to marry on Mt. Everest. Dean Nelson, "Nepal 'to stage gay weddings on Everest,'" *Telegraph*, January 19, 2010, http://www.telegraph.co.uk/news/worldnews/asia/nepal/7027736/Nepal-to-stage-gay-weddings-on-Everest.html.

[109] "Prince's marriage stokes gay issue," *India Today*, November 1, 2009, http://indiatoday.intoday.in/story/Prince's+marriage+stokes+gay+issue/1/68792.html.

[110] Manesh Shrestha, "Nepal census recognizes 'third gender,'" *CNN*, May 31, 2011, http://articles.cnn.com/2011-05-31/world/nepal.census.gender_1_gender-identity-citizenship-first-openly-gay-lawmaker?_s=PM:WORLD.

[111] "Nepal to offer shelter to South Asia's battered gays," *Times of India*, June 22, 2011, http://articles.timesofindia.indiatimes.com/2011-06-22/south-asia/29689088_1_sunil-babu-pant-blue-diamond-society-gay-rights-organisation.

[112] "New law threatens to crush Nepal's gays," *Times of India*, June 9, 2011, http://articles.timesofindia.indiatimes.com/2011-06-09/south-asia/29638154_1_sunil-babu-pant-gay-rights-gay-bar.

[113] Utpal Parashar, "Nepal 3rd Asian nation to recognise sexual minorities," *Hindustantimes*, May 24, 2012, http://www.hindustantimes.com/world-news/Nepal/Nepal-3rd-Asian-nation-to-recognise-sexual-minorities/Article1-860479.aspx.

South Asia LGBTI Sport Festival was held in Nepal in 2012.[114] And continuing its progressive sexuality jurisprudence, the Nepali Supreme Court in November 2012 allowed a lesbian-identified woman to live with her female partner over the objections of her family and former husband, who together had institutionalized her for falling victim to the hypnotism of her female partner.[115]

In summary, Nepal's rapid recognition of SOGI minority rights emanated from the court's embrace of an interconnected gender and sexuality framework. Although the history of hijras in Nepal is not well documented, the use of a third-gender framework in developing constitutional protections for SOGI minorities parallels India's recognition of the visible social position occupied by third-gender persons. Indeed, the Nepali Court's recognition of both self-defined gender identity and sexual orientation as immutable traits seems to belie any socially reinforced background understanding of gender difference. Unlike Western approaches that rely on narratives of similarity between sexual minorities and heterosexuals, Nepal, led by its Supreme Court, has embraced constitutional protections for individuals who are part of the fabric of Nepali society yet different enough to require special legal recognition and protection.[116]

PAKISTAN

Of all the developments in SOGI rights within South Asia, Pakistan's experience most challenges the Western model of progressive rights realization, reinforcing the uniqueness of South Asian experience. The Pakistani Supreme Court has recognized the rights of hijras[117] under the Pakistani Constitution and aggressively moved to require the national

---

[114] "Nepal hosts South Asia's first gay sports tournament," *BBC News Asia*, October 12, 2012, http://www.bbc.co.uk/news/world-asia-19929010. The London committee for the 2018 Gay Games bid recognized this achievement in a letter to BDS. Alex Davis, Letter to Sunil Babu Pant, November 8, 2012, http://www.bds.org.np/images/Letter-from-Alex.jpg.

[115] Ananta Raj Luitel, "SC allows live-in lesbian relationship," *Himalayan Times*, November 5, 2012, http://www.thehimalayantimes.com/fullNews.php?headline=SC+allows+live-in+lesbian+relationship&NewsID=353395.

[116] The explicit counting of third-gender persons in the national census is a strong example of this accommodation.

[117] Pakistani press and court opinions frequently use the term *eunuchs* or *unix* to refer to third-gender persons or. This practice stems from the title used for castrated hijras who historically served as court attendants. However, because the hijra community in Pakistan is closely related to its Indian counterpart, third-gender persons in Pakistan often refer to themselves as hijras; because many third-gender persons do not engage in cast-

government to affirmatively protect hijras and increase their access to employment and land inheritance. The lawyer who has led the charge for hijra rights, Muhammad Aslam Khaki, is an Islamist legal scholar who is also famous for challenging Pakistan's restrictions on alcohol and conjugal visits for prisoners as being inconsistent with the Qur'an.[118] Unlike India or Nepal, however, increased recognition of hijra rights has not led to similar gains for other SOGI minorities. Indeed, while Pakistan seems to be in the vanguard of advancing third-gender rights, its society and legal institutions remain notably hostile toward homosexuality as such. Sodomy is still criminalized, and gay/lesbian groups operate in the shadows.[119]

The recent and rapid recognition of hijra rights in Pakistan began when Khaki filed a case in 2009 alleging that hijras were suffering significant discrimination, stigma, and harassment at the hands of state actors.[120] The Supreme Court immediately ordered provincial governments to issue reports on the status of hijras within their provinces. Two months later, the court held that hijras had been "neglected" on the basis of "gender disorder in their bodies" but were "entitled to enjoy all rights granted to them by the Constitution."[121] The court singled out inheritance and voting as rights that hijras could not be denied on the basis of their

---

ration, we use the term hijra rather than eunuch to describe third-gender persons in Pakistan.

[118] Khaki challenged the punishments for drinking alcohol and the prohibition on conjugal visits as being harsher than that required by the Qur'an. Declan Walsh, "Harassed, intimidated, abused: but now Pakistan's hijra transgender minority finds its voice," *Guardian*, January 29, 2010, http://www.guardian.co.uk/world/2010/jan/29/hijra-pakistan-transgender-rights.

[119] Meghan Davidson Ladly, "Gay Pakistanis, Still in Shadows, Seek Acceptance," *New York Times*, November 3, 2012, http://www.nytimes.com/2012/11/04/world/asia/gays-in-pakistan-move-cautiously-to-gain-acceptance.html.

[120] Dr. Mohammad Aslam Khaki & another Vs. S.S.P. (Operations) Rawalpindi and others, Const.P.43/2009, Supreme Court of Pakistan, filed on September 7, 2009. A companion case, Dr. Mohammad Aslam Khaki & another Vs. S.S.P. (Operations) Rawalpindi and others, Human Rights Const.P.63/2009, Supreme Court of Pakistan, was filed on February 6, 2009. However, the case appears to have been dropped or consolidated with the September case, and the Pakistani Supreme Court maintains no record of this earlier case in its online case status database. In this case, the court appears to have ordered that all hijras be registered by the government as a method of better integrating them into society. This registration system is referred to in subsequent court opinions requiring local governments to work with the national government to ensure that all hijras are included in electoral databases. *See* Basim Usmani, "Pakistan to register 'third sex' hijras," *Guardian*, July 18, 2009, http://www.guardian.co.uk/commentisfree/2009/jul/18/pakistan-transgender-hijra-third-sex.

[121] Dr. Mohammad Aslam Khaki & another Vs. S.S.P. (Operations) Rawalpindi and others, Const.P.43/2009, Supreme Court of Pakistan, order dated 11–20–2009.

gender identity. Further noting that qualified hijras were subjected to hiring discrimination, the court required provinces to implement laws rectifying discriminatory practices.[122]

One month later, the court issued a wide-ranging order recognizing hijra rights. The court observed that family members were illegally withholding inheritances from hijras, stating that "this order shall be treated as judgment in [hijras'] favour for the purpose of getting right of inheritance etc. from . . . their predecessors."[123] Building on its previous orders, the court required the government to issue national identity cards with a third gender for hijras, though it allowed the registration authority to conduct medical hormone tests as part of the identification process. The court then required the provincial electoral authorities to work with the national government to ensure that hijras were added to the electoral rolls. Similarly, the court ordered provincial authorities to ensure hijras were able to enroll in educational facilities and were appropriately accommodated, consistent with constitutional rights to education, and it also permitted the reservation of seats for hijras in technical and vocational institutes.[124] The court required that policies be developed to stop police harassment of hijras. Fully embracing hijras' role in society, the court lauded the efforts of one provincial government to provide jobs for hijras during a polio vaccination program and recommended that local governments follow the policy of an Indian state that hired hijras to act as tax collectors.[125]

In 2011, the national election authorities allowed hijras to self-identify and register as third-gender persons for national identity cards without any medical demonstration of their gender difference, apparently

---

[122] Ibid.

[123] Dr. Mohammad Aslam Khaki & another Vs. S.S.P. (Operations) Rawalpindi and others, Const.P.43/2009, Supreme Court of Pakistan, order dated 12–23–2009.

[124] Ibid.

[125] These schemes typically involve hijras dancing and performing outside of the house of taxpayers in default as a form of public shaming. Interviews with hijras indicate that they enjoy the work, as it is consistent with their traditionally recognized skill in shaming individuals into giving them alms, typically by exposing their genitals. See http://www.siasat.com/english/news/hijras-should-be-loan-recoverers ("Almas Bobby, the president of a hijra association welcomed the suggestion and said they were prepared to shame such people by clapping and dancing outside their homes. 'We will go to their homes and sing, dance and clap outside their doors and ask them to return what they have looted from the country. We will *gherao* their homes and ask them to return the loans or wear bangles and join us,' Bobby said."). *Gherao* is a Hindi word that means encirclement and refers to a typical Indian form of protest in which a group surrounds a person or building until their demands are met.

in response to a Supreme Court order.[126] This development led to the independent candidacy in provincial assembly elections of the leader of a hijra organization, Shahana Abbas.[127] Subsequent hijra protests led to the cancellation of fees for hijras to register to vote.[128] The court continued by requiring the Punjab government to provide documentation of the inheritance transfers it reported hijras had received and commended the Sindh provincial government for allocating land for the construction of a hijra colony.[129]

The year 2012, however, saw the greatest advancements in hijra rights in Pakistan. The court required affirmative action for hijras in government hiring, meaning a hijra with a tenth-grade education would be considered equivalent to a non-hijra with a bachelor's degree.[130] After three years of interim orders and requiring provinces to implement policies recognizing and enforcing hijra rights, the court finally decided the 2009 case filed by Khaki by holding that hijras were entitled to all constitutional rights.[131] In particular, the court required provinces to appoint a focal person in every district to monitor the security of the local hijra community and ordered all federal and provincial health and education officials to work with local hijra representatives to ensure that free health care and education were available to all hijras.[132] The court also referenced its earlier requirement to register hijras for elections, noting the number

[126] Qaiser Zulfiqar, "Enfranchising the fringe: SC orders registering eunuchs for 2013 polls," *Express Tribune*, November 15, 2011, http://tribune.com.pk/story/292018/enfranchising-the-fringe-sc-orders-registering-eunuchs-for-2013-polls/ ("'[Registration] centres across the country are already serving eunuchs for registration, which is carried out without any medical proof on their given particulars and details at the time of registration,' said the [government] spokesman in the statement. He added that as per the Supreme Court's instructions, third genders can have male transgender, female transgender or 'Khunsa-e-mushkil' written on their ID card as per their own will.").

[127] Owais Jafri, "President of transgender association to contest elections," *Express Tribune*, December 26, 2011, http://tribune.com.pk/story/312257/president-of-transgender-association-to-contest-elections/.

[128] "Dream come true: Transgender community celebrates CNICs, voter registration," *Express Tribune*, January 25, 2012, http://tribune.com.pk/story/326911/dream-come-true-transgender-community-celebrates-cnics-voter-registration/.

[129] Ibid.

[130] Michele Langevine Leiby, "For transgender Pakistanis, newfound rights," *Washington Post*, February 10, 2012, http://www.washingtonpost.com/world/for-transgender-pakistanis-newfound-rights/2012/02/04/gIQAMojG4Q_story.html.

[131] Qamar Zaman, "Ensuring equality: Transgenders equal citizens of Pakistan, rules SC," *Express Tribune*, September 26, 2012, http://tribune.com.pk/story/442516/ensuring-equality-transgenders-equal-citizens-of-pakistan-rules-sc/.

[132] Ibid.

of hijras (31) registered in a decision on an unrelated election case.[133] Pakistan's hijra jurisprudence goes well beyond that of its South Asian peers in imposing so many specific affirmative obligations on government officials.

From the Western frame of reference for SOGI rights jurisprudence, it might be easy to assume that all this progress for hijras in Pakistan has been the result of evolving, more favorable social views toward hijras that recognize their similarity to dominant social groups. Such changes in public attitudes, after all, have been crucial to the advancement of lesbian and gay rights in the West, a trajectory that is now beginning to benefit transgender individuals as well. Yet the fact is hijras are still viewed by most Pakistanis as aberrant and disfavored. A 2010 poll found that only 14 percent of Pakistanis would be friends with a hijra who wanted to be friends with them.[134] Notwithstanding such attitudes, 55 percent of Pakistanis believed that quotas should be set to reserve educational and employment positions for hijras.[135] Thus, as with India and Nepal, the Pakistani experience challenges conventional Western thinking that courts will most readily extend constitutional rights and recognition to minorities that emphasize their similarity to, and desire to assimilate with, dominant social groups.

CONCLUDING THOUGHTS

Sonia Katyal has observed that "the presumed equation between sexual conduct, sexual orientation, and sexual identity, so prevalent in Western legal thought, tends to swiftly unravel when viewed in a cross-cultural framework."[136] The South Asian experience with SOGI rights and equality bears out this observation. In India, historic familiarity with hijras, as well as the government's earlier extension of rights to them as a distinct group suffering discrimination, seemed to lay the foundation for the extension of rights to self-identified gays and lesbians. In Nepal, the court

---

[133] Khan & others v. Electoral Commission of Pakistan & others, Const. Petitions 31 of 2011, 45 of 2007, 111 & 123 of 2012, Supreme Court of Pakistan, December 5, 2012, http://www.supremecourt.gov.pk/web/user_files/File/Const.P.310f2011etc.pdf.

[134] Gallup & Gilani, "Cyberletter: Gilani Weekly Poll" Week #24 (2010), http://www.gallup.com.pk/News/Gilani%20Poll%20Cyberletter%20June%202010.pdf, 8. The poll found that 60 percent would not want to be friends with a hijra, whereas 24 percent were unsure.

[135] Ibid.

[136] Katyal, "Exporting Identity," *supra* n. 5, 99.

supplemented its own very young and limited jurisprudence by look-ing to international judicial decisions and human rights statements. In Pakistan, a country that remains hostile toward homosexuality as such, the Supreme Court has been solicitous of a visible, familiar third-gender group whose members sometimes engage in homosexual prostitution to survive. (According to an account in a Zurich newspaper, a Pakistani hijra "said that a policeman threatened her once with arrest for immoral behavior, and she told him simply, 'My behind belongs to me, not the Pakistani state.'") India, Nepal, and Pakistan all have applied constitu-tional principles to mediate difference between the mainstream and their countries' SOGI minorities. But they have done so by their own cultural and constitutional lights.

As we explained at the beginning of this chapter, recent South Asian SOGI jurisprudence, with its emphasis on nondiscrimination, has tended to highlight narratives of difference and tolerance rather than similarity and assimilation. This approach is in contrast to Western rights jurispru-dence, which emphasizes "an identity-based approach to equality that inevitably leads to the exclusion of some and the homogenization of others."[137] A criticism of such narratives of similarity is that they make it more difficult for non-normative sexual identities and practices to chal-lenge traditional heterosexual hegemony. The creation of a distinct sexual minority for the purpose of advancing rights may simultaneously cre-ate a target for further oppression.[138] As Elaine Craig has argued, "An equality movement that fails to disrupt these hetero-normative standards perpetuates a model of justice that remains exclusionary for many sexual minorities."[139]

It is especially noteworthy, we think, that the South Asian model of SOGI rights jurisprudence tends to avoid this problem because, as we have attempted to document in this chapter, its emphasis on nondiscrimination has been closely linked to a recognition of the diversity and non-binary nature of gender and sexuality. For example, the Indian court in *Naz* recognized how naming a group creates a target for oppression, citing

---

[137] Elaine Craig, "I Do Kiss and Tell: The Subversive Potential of Non-Normative Sexual Expression from within Cultural Paradigms," *Dalhousie Law Journal* 27 (2004): 403, 405.

[138] Ibid., 414 (citing Nancy Fraser, "From Redistribution to Recognition? Dilemmas of Justice in a 'Postsocialist' Age," in *Justice Interruptus: Critical Reflections on the "Post-socialist" Condition*, ed. Nancy Fraser (New York: Routledge, 1997), 11).

[139] Ibid., 412.

the colonial construction of homosexuality and its perversion of histor-ical Indian tolerance.[140] The Nepali court expressly refused to require an identity-based category as the marker for SOGI rights, privileging individual "self-feeling" over categorical labels and relying on the con-cept of citizenship as the basis for the abolition of state discrimination.[141] *Naz Foundation* and *Pant* are somewhat difficult to categorize doctri-nally, because they both contain themes of nondiscrimination, equality, privacy, and individual liberty and autonomy. However, it is the theme of nondiscrimination that comes through most clearly, and the same can be said of the Pakistani hijra jurisprudence.

Of course, mandates of nondiscrimination and tolerance are not enough to disrupt heteronormative hegemony, because they still tend to treat sexual subalterns as "a 'perversion' to be tolerated within the framework of liberal democracy...tolerance is deployed to deal with the excess that formal equality has failed to accommodate."[142] By using strategies that accept difference without creating formal group structures that can advocate for power and challenge heteronormative hegemony, courts and advocates do not effectively undermine oppression. The dif-ference of sexual minorities remains a negative attribute that the majority is required to accept as part of a contemporary liberal society.

Moreover, although third-gender persons have been the vanguard of SOGI minority rights in South Asia, the historic presence of hijras does not challenge traditional male dominance, because hijras are understood to be a categorical other. Martha Nussbaum's powerful argument that opposition to male homosexuality arises from a fear of contamination and being defiled by male body fluids[143] has no import in the hijra context: cisgendered, heterosexual males will not be penetrated or inseminated by hijras because these behaviors are not manifest in the long-standing gender category hijras inhabit. Hijras are not men who have been tainted by effeminacy and thus present a threat to other males; rather, they are a unique gender with clearly defined roles that do not challenge the existing patriarchy. The Pakistani example is crucial: only 14 percent of Pakistanis would be friends with a hijra who wanted to be friends with them, but 55

---

[140] *See supra* note 83 and accompanying text.

[141] *See supra* note 96 and accompanying text.

[142] Ratna Kapur, "Out of the Colonial Closet, but Still Thinking Inside the Box: Regulating Perversion and the Role of Tolerance in Deradicalising the Rights Claims of Sexual Subalterns," *NUJS Law Review* 2 (2009): 381, 384.

[143] Martha C. Nussbaum, *From Disgust to Humanity: Sexual Orientation and Constitutional Law* (New York: Oxford University Press, 2010), 19.

percent believe educational and employment positions should be reserved for hijras.[144] Were there a fear that hijras would contaminate men in power, opposition similar to that previously seen toward homosexuality in the West would be expected. The gender-based approach to South Asian SOGI jurisprudence, then, has the perhaps ironic effect of insulating patriarchy from challenge and contestation.

In the end, of course, jurists sitting on constitutional courts cannot change long-standing cultural and social attitudes with the stroke of a pen, and there is no disputing that the decisions from India, Nepal, and Pakistan are fascinating decisions that rightfully occupy a prominent place in the broader global movement for SOGI rights. Debates over the effects of these decisions surely will continue as SOGI minorities embrace the new South Asian jurisprudence, increase their visibility, and continue to work for their goals within local cultural and political contexts that have become part of broader transnational conversations.

Note on Supreme Court of India decision in Naz Foundation

As this book was going to press, the Supreme Court of India issued a decision in the appeal by several conservative groups to the Delhi High Court's Naz Foundation decision. In a decision that surprised most observers, the Supreme Court reinstated Section 377 and chastised the Delhi High Court for relying too heavily on foreign precedent respecting SOGI rights. Koushal v. Naz Found., Civil Appeal No.10972/2013 (Sup. Ct. Dec. 11, 2013), available at http://judis.nic.in/supremecourt/imgs1.aspx?filename=41070. The court reasoned that SOGI individuals are a minority in India and that the legislative will of the majority should control. Because the Delhi High Court read down the law rather than declaring it unconstitutional, the Supreme Court held that the Delhi High Court cannot read the law out of effect while still finding it constitutional. At press time, it was too soon to evaluate what effect the decision will have on the future of SOGI rights in India, but we believe that the political and social forces that have expanded SOGI rights will persist and grow.

---

[144] *See supra* note 134.

Index